W9-BGA-351

THE KEILLOR READER

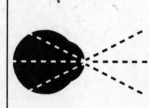

THE KEILLOR READER

GARRISON KEILLOR

THORNDIKE PRESS
A part of Gale, Cengage Learning

GALE
CENGAGE Learning·

Farmington Hills, Mich • San Francisco • New York • Waterville, Maine
Meriden, Conn • Mason, Ohio • Chicago

GALE
CENGAGE Learning®

LIBRARY OF CONGRESS CATALOGING-IN-PUBLICATION DATA

Keillor, Garrison.
  [Works. Selections]
  The Keillor reader / by Garrison Keillor. — Large print edition.
    pages cm—(Thorndike press large print core)
    ISBN 978-1-4104-7043-0 (hardcover) — ISBN 1-4104-7043-1 (hardcover) 1.
Large type books. I. Title.
PS3561.E3755A6 2014b
813'.54—dc23   2014011417

Published in 2014 by arrangement with Viking, a member of Penguin (USA), LLC, a Penguin Random House Company

Printed in the United States of America
1 2 3 4 5 6 7 18 17 16 15 14

*To my editors, Roger Angell,
Kathryn Court, Charles McGrath,
William Whitworth, Corby Kummer,
Molly Stern, Beena Kamlani, and
all the copy editors and fact-checkers*

CONTENTS

9

This is a letter that changed my life and rescued me from despair, and beyond that, it's a classic Roger Angell letter to an author — the faint embarrassment that they rejected a story and maybe they were wrong ("I don't know"), the booming praise of the story they accepted ("just about perfect in every way"), the modest suggestion ("If it's all right with you") of a few minor changes, and the hope that this is only the beginning. I sat down on the front step of our rented house at 222 30th Avenue North and thought, "Now my life is not entirely wasted." Roger was a generous letter writer, and I think of him sitting at a typewriter and banging out long, elegant, encouraging letters to far-flung authors. It gave you a big charge to get one.

EDITORIAL OFFICES
OXFORD 5-1414

May 26, 1970
Mr. Garrison Keillor
222 30th Avenue North
St. Cloud, Minnesota 56301

Dear Mr. Keillor:
  There is so much life and imagination and energy and humor in the various sections of your "Child's Life of Richard Nixon" that I am somewhat embarrassed to tell you that we are only purchasing the shortest of these tales, that "Local Family Keeps Son Happy." It's quite an "only" at that — a really funny and surprising piece, just about perfect in every way. It is

11

also <u>short</u>, which is almost a miracle these days.

If it's all right with you, we wish to make some very minor editorial changes in the story. These are mostly matters of paragraphing and style, and nothing for you to worry about. You will see a full set of proofs before the story appears, and you will be encouraged to complain if you think we have damaged the story in any way. I can't tell you just when the thing will appear, because we are under an enormous and customary backlog of unpublished stuff, but short and funny pieces seem to float to the top of the pile. I can't tell you exactly what our payment will be, either, but I'll try to get that check to you within a couple of weeks. Meantime, our congratulations and thanks for this contribution.

There was much to admire in all the other pieces here, but the Nixon satire becomes a little too broad and easy at times. I don't know, though: maybe it isn't possible to get at Nixon except broadly. There is also the problem of surpassing Nixon's own perpetual self-parody. Anyway, we seriously considered taking several of these, but various groupings of the stories seemed to make a confused whole. I especially admired THE CONCERNED INDIVIDUAL and THREE YEARS IN THE WOODS.

I hope this is only the beginning of a long list of contributions from you that we will want to publish. Please let me know whether we have your permission to go ahead with those small editorial changes that I mentioned.

Yours sincerely,

Roger Angell

RA:kb

A Sunday afternoon in July 1933, my mother, eighteen, perched on the bench in her father's backyard on Longfellow Avenue in Minneapolis, looks at the camera held by her younger sister Elsie as my father, twenty, writes his name on an entry form for a contest (Name A Lake Home) that he did not win. But they got each other, and also six children, including me.

INTRODUCTION

I come from the prairie, I've been to New
York,
A tall lonesome fellow and slightly historic,
But I am a rider, I ride every day
On a big Underwood cross the wide open
page.
I ride in the sun and the snow and the rain,
I've ridden with Thurber, Benchley, Mark
Twain.
They mostly wrote better than I and I mean
it
But I am still living and that is convenient.

When I was twenty and something of a
romantic, I thought about dying young and
becoming immortal like Buddy Holly or
James Dean or Janis Joplin and people leaving bouquets on my grave and grieving for
my enormous complicated talent lost to the
world. But I didn't have a complicated talent, nor was it enormous. Some people

17

thought I did because I wrote poems and was shy, didn't make eye contact, kept to myself. (Nowadays they'd say "high-functioning end of the autism spectrum," but back then oddity was interpreted in a kindlier fashion.) Anyway, death didn't occur. I never needed to charter a plane in a snowstorm as Buddy did, and a car like James Dean's Porsche 550 Spyder was way beyond my means, and heroin was not readily available in Anoka, Minnesota, so onward I went. An angelic being assigned to read through the mounds of unsolicited stories in a backroom at *The New Yorker* plucked out one of mine, and the magazine printed a string of them, and that led to a fact piece about Nashville, which inspired a radio show called *A Prairie Home Companion,* and then I was forty, which is too old to die young, so I headed down the long dirt road of longevity, and thus arrived at seventy, when I took time to sit down and put this collection together.

I was the third of six children of John and Grace, a young Sanctified Brethren couple in Anoka, Minnesota, on the Mississippi, a farm boy and a city girl who fell in love and married secretly in an air of scandal. There was a Model T involved, a moonlit pasture, a startling realization, a justice of the peace. I was born in Anoka in 1942, in a house on Ferry Street, and grew up along the river in Brooklyn Park township, north of Minneapolis, where we moved in 1947 into a house Dad built on an acre lot with room for a big garden. All around us were vegetable farms, fields of potatoes, peas, sweet corn. My friends and I rode our bikes with cardboard strips clipped to the rear fender brace to whap against the spokes to make a motor sound, racing on dirt roads to an abandoned grass airstrip with rusting carcasses of Piper Cubs to sit in and reenact the war, fighting off the deadly Messerschmidts and Jap Zeroes. My brother and sister and I attended Benson School, a handsome three-room country school, where I had Estelle Shaver and Fern Moehlenbrock for teachers. In first grade, I was slow to read, and Miss Shaver kept me after school to read aloud to her, which she made me believe was not for my sake, but for hers, to keep her company as she graded papers. She made disability feel like talent. She said to Bill the janitor, "Listen to him, doesn't he have a lovely voice." In time, I turned into a bookworm and a good speller. And around the time I was eleven, I began to be a writer. That was the summer Grandpa

Denham died and I was allowed to attend the funeral and look at his body. My only previous encounter with death was the Egyptian mummy in the Minneapolis Public Library. Grandpa's body, the preacher talking about death and how it may be imminent and so those who are unsaved should come to the Lord and do it *now, don't wait until later* — my aunts weeping, the solemn faces of the men, the motorcade to Lakewood Cemetery, the lunch afterward at the Gospel Hall — it was all very grand. And then in August Mother made my dad take me with him to New York City. A family friend was an Army captain stationed in Germany and wanted his brand-new Pontiac shipped over. Dad had agreed to drive it to Brooklyn to be loaded aboard a freighter. He had been stationed in the city during the war, sorting mail for the Army in the Main Post Office with its famous inscription about snow and rain and heat and gloom of night, and he had wartime friends he wanted to see. I think Mother made him take me along because she felt that the father of six children should not go waltzing off to Manhattan scot-free. The friends he wanted to see were two sisters, Nancy and Betty, both of them married now, but still.

It was the trip of all trips — the two-lane

highways through Indiana and Ohio, the country inn in Pennsylvania with the high poster bed, Valley Forge, the whine of traffic in the Lincoln Tunnel, the towers of Manhattan silvery in the afternoon sun, streets jammed with pushcart peddlers shouting in strange languages. We stayed with Don and Betty in their Brooklyn apartment, one bedroom, a kitchen alcove, a small living room with a round clawfoot dining table where we sat down for supper. They reminisced about the war years and I almost fell asleep — it was a hot night in Brooklyn — and hours later, when they went to bed, it was too hot to sleep, so Dad and I took a walk to a candy store and bought cream sodas and perched on the curb and drank them. Across the street was a park where hundreds of people lay sleeping on blankets spread out on the grass, families, little kids nestled against their mothers, and on the benches around the perimeter men sat smoking and talking in the dark. We walked back to Dad's friends' apartment and he spread a mattress on the fire escape and we slept there, five stories in the air, headlights passing below us, the elevated train rumbling by, a block away. I lay on the mattress and thought, *A person could fall asleep and fall to his death. Some criminal could come creeping up the fire escape and knife Dad and throttle me. The Russians could drop the A-bomb.* Nonetheless, I went to sleep.

I came back to Benson School as the only boy in the sixth grade ever to have laid eyes on New York City. Enormous status. A kind of nobility. A girl asked me if it was true that trains ran underground and went fast and I said yes, it was true and I had ridden them. It was the first time I had amazing firsthand experience to offer an audience. I wrote a report and read it aloud to the class and they soaked it all up: Coney Island, the Empire State Building, Ebbets Field, subways, Jones Beach, the Staten Island Ferry, Times Square, all the wonders of the world. There is nothing like good material. You only had to say *New York* and there was an awestruck silence. You went, you saw, and now you tell the others. And that was my start as a writer, age eleven, some yellow No. 2 pencils and Big Red Indian Chief tablets. Later I was presented with Uncle Louie's Underwood manual typewriter with a faint *f* and a misshapen *O.* You had to poke the keys hard to make an impression. I set it on a maple desk in my bedroom, which looked out onto a cornfield across the road, and I wrote stories about lonesome loners who kept their distance from

22

the mindless crowd and observed them with contempt tinged with envy. My parents did not encourage this. The Brethren did not favor fiction or poetry, nor did they care much for history aside from what was in Scripture.

That fall I flunked the eye test and got wire-rim glasses, and one fine day, playing softball, I was out in right field, the sissy position where there was plenty of leisure time, and I dropped an easy pop fly — took a few steps back and settled under it and it came in chest-high and caromed off the heels of my hands and the other team hooted and whooped and my teammates wouldn't look at me. I was humiliated. I got permission to spend recess periods in the school library. I got absorbed in history books. I sought out my uncles and asked about the War and the Depression. Instead of scrapping for the respect of peers, I basked in the company of old people. Why had Grandpa Denham come over from Glasgow in 1911? Why did Grandpa Keillor come down from New Brunswick in 1880? The old uncles were grateful for a boy's interest. They lavished stories about Anoka back when the North Coast Limited stopped there, when quarter horses raced at the fairgrounds and the Wild Man from

Borneo was exhibited in a tent and bit the head off a live chicken. And the terrible tornado of 1938 that blew Florence Hunt and her baby girl into a tree. It was so much easier to sit and listen to them than to hold my own on the playground. My peers thought I was strange. I didn't mind. I was a writer and writers only compete against themselves.

I tried to go out for football in eighth grade but failed the physical due to a clicky mitral valve and was disappointed but only briefly. A couple days later I walked into the office of the Anoka *Herald,* a down-at-the-heels weekly around the corner from the junior high, and asked the editor, Warren Feist, if I could write sports for him, an act of reckless bravery by a fearful young man, and Mr. Feist smiled and said, "Sure." So I got to sit in the press box at football games, high above Goodrich Field, and look reporterly as I took extensive notes, listening to the play-by-play of the KANO announcers next to me. Back at the office — thirteen years old, I had an *office* — Whitey and Russ sat at the keyboards of their monster Linotype machines, wheels turning, arms pumping, a little flame in back keeping the melted lead hot. Line by line, they clattered away, pulling the lever that poured the hot lead into the mold to make a slug, the slug slapped into the galley, which was set into the chase, which lay on the turtle. Russ and Whitey were pasty-faced with purple noses and they reeked of drink, but they were kind to me and I was honored to be there. Mr. Feist edited my stories gently, removing paragraphs of crowd description, drawing out the action on the field. The *Herald* was printed on Wednesday afternoon and I made a point to be there to watch. Whitey stood on a platform over the flatbed press and, though drunk, he could riffle a giant sheet of paper loose from the stack and flip it up and onto the flatbed, where the roller rolled over it with a *whump* and a *shwoosh* and the folder cut and trimmed and folded it, and a copy of the *Herald* slid down the chute with the sports page and my byline with my story about the Anoka Tornadoes ready to be read by dozens, if not hundreds, of subscribers, men and women in kitchens all over Anoka eager for my account of the game. A person never gets over this, the pleasure of seeing his own words in print. Unless there's a tipo. Never.

My parents were dismayed at my newspapering. My mother said that writers were a bunch of drunks, meaning F. Scott Fitzgerald, whose old neighborhood in St. Paul she had once lived near and she had heard the story of him walking into church drunk on Christmas Eve. She shook her head at that. Sinclair Lewis, Hemingway, Faulkner, O'Neill, Tennessee Williams, and Dylan Thomas, all boozers. People went to Thomas's readings to see if he could remain upright and not drop a cigarette down his pants and set himself on fire. She had read about that somewhere.

The only writing that mattered was Holy Scripture; everything else was vanity and horsefeathers — fiction, poetry, even history was suspect. When they cut loose from the Church of England in the early nineteenth century, men were being hanged for stealing spoons, aboriginal people were enslaved, the poor were starved into submission, and the Established Church sanctified it all. The Brethren stepped away from history, politics, power, the very idea of hierarchy. Rich, famous, accomplished, brilliant — those words meant very little to them — we are all naked and impoverished before the Lord — so I grew up sitting through Bible study with postal clerks and farmers, an auto mechanic, a seed salesman, engineers, railroadmen, carpenters, my tribe, feeding on the Word, leaning on the promises. The

Bible is not bad as literature, but as revelation, taken literally, it is a wild ride. I was a devout young man but when I turned twenty, I abandoned the Brethren. I thought that probably they were right, that it was sinful to want to be a writer, but I would do it anyway. It was all I really wanted. I took a last stab at self-sacrifice and wrote a letter to a Trappist monastery near Dubuque, asking for admission, and they wrote back politely suggesting that I give the matter further thought. A good Christian was supposed to sacrifice his desires to the Lord. But if I couldn't be a Trappist and lead a life of prayer and poverty in a black robe in Iowa, then nuts to that, I'd just go ahead and be a writer.

I went off to be an English major at the University of Minnesota, where John Berryman, James Wright, and Allen Tate taught. My parents were not pleased, but I paid my own way so they had no leverage. I owned the Underwood, a *Webster's Third Unabridged,* a funeral suit, blue jeans, white shirts, one tan corduroy jacket, Red Wing work boots, and a broad-brimmed hat. I had acquired a nicotine habit and was learning to tolerate coffee because *that's what writers do.* Back then, a cup of coffee was two bits, a pack of smokes thirty-five cents, and a drink was a dollar. I supported myself by washing dishes and parking cars, both educational experiences. You work the morning shift in the heat and steam of the scullery and you feel clean and contented the rest of the day, even in August. You stand on a gravel parking lot on the high bluff of the Mississippi, the wintry blast sweeping down the valley, and you direct a stream of cars to their correct spots in straight lines, tolerating no dissent or diversion, stomping out individual preference wherever it occurs, and you discover the authoritarian within. Good to know one's own capacity.

Mr. Tate was sixty-eight when I took his poetry seminar. A slim, elegant man with a Southern patrician accent — a pal of Robert Penn Warren and Hart Crane — he chain-smoked in class, so we did, too. The whole English Department reeked of tobacco smoke and was proudly alcoholic — anyone who wasn't was considered an interloper, possibly a Mormon. James Wright chain-smoked through his lectures on Dickens and Whitman, which he delivered through a haze of hangover. He always looked pale and haggard. His line "Suddenly I realize that if I stepped out of my body, I would break into blossom" was written by a man with smoke coming out of his mouth.

My hero, Saul Bellow (*The Adventures of Augie March*), had recently taught at the U and I heard about him from his pal, my advisor, Joe Kwiat, a big, hearty guy with a great bark of a voice. Snowy-haired Robert Frost came and filled Northrup Auditorium, 4,700 seats, and recited his greatest hits by heart to the awestruck crowd. Afterward I stood by the back door and watched him emerge and shuffle down the walk and climb into his limousine. Nobody asked for his autograph, it was enough to observe him up close. (He looked extremely old.) Our great alcoholic genius was John Berryman, a man of such towering intellect that I was afraid to be in the same room with him — one caustic glance and I would've gone up in flames. He wore a big beard that made him look like he was eating a sweater. He gave a reading of his *Dream Songs,* slumped against the lectern, speech slurred, a man on the verge of collapse. His greatness and his affliction seemed intertwined, an artist engaging with powerful dark forces in public, pain had driven him to alcohol and to poetry, and he could no more give up one than he could stifle the other. I thought, *If this is what it takes to be a great American writer, then I am on the wrong street. I am not screwed up enough.* Berryman's dad blew his brains out with a shotgun when the poet was twelve. My dad only worked hard and expected me to.

So I accepted that I could not be a true artist and that my future lay in the field of amusement. For the campus literary magazine, *The Ivory Tower,* I wrote stuff that owed a lot to Benchley and Thurber, A. J. Liebling and E. B. White. My journalism teacher, Bob Lindsay, encouraged this. He was a Marine Corps captain, a veteran of two wars — his bald head showed a remarkable dent as if a mortar shell had bounced off it — and he was a no-nonsense teacher. In his class, one spelling mistake on a writing assignment, no matter how elegant, earned you an F. We were horrified to hear this. But we learned to copyread, a skill that sticks with you for life. Mr. Lindsay's office was on the first floor of Murphy Hall, and when I walked down that hall, I slowed down, and if his door was open and he didn't have a visitor, I stuck my head in. He was brusque, not given to flattery, and when he said I should try to catch on at *The New Yorker,* I believed him. And then, unbeknownst to me, he sent the magazine some of my writing and a letter attesting to

30

sent off two or three stories a month and if they bought one, we were on Easy Street. It was a luxurious life for a writer, not so good for the writer's wife and infant child, isolated among clannish country people suspicious of strangers. Sweden might have been better, or Bulgaria. I wrote in an upstairs bedroom on my Underwood typewriter on a slab of 3/4-inch plywood set on two filing cabinets, my back to a window looking out on the farmyard, the barn, the cattle milling in the feedlot, the silo, the granary, the pig barn, the woods beyond. I found that I could sit and look at a piece of writing for hours at a time and not get twitchy, a skill I had picked up in Brethren Bible study, and I was a good rewriter. Day after peaceful day, visitors on weekends, the occasional big check and encouraging letter from West 43rd Street. A sculptor named Joe O'Connell befriended me, and a St. Cloud couple, Fred and Romy Petters, and that was all the social life I needed, but Mary slipped into depression; she spent whole days hardly speaking. Her mother, Marjorie, urged me to move back to the city for Mary's sake, and I took a job at Minnesota Public Radio, the 6–9 a.m. shift, played records and created a cheery on-air persona, the Old Scout, who rallied listeners to rise and shine and face the day with a smile. It was a good and useful persona. I even started to believe in it myself. I was in an awkward marriage, I was absurdly self-conscious and timid and eager to please and arrogant, all at the same time, but I was lucky. On that early morning shift, I invented a town where the women are strong, the men are good-looking, and the children are all above average. Businesses in that town advertised on my show — Jack's Auto Repair, Bob's Bank, Bunsen Motors, Bertha's Kitty Boutique, the Chatterbox Café, the Sidetrack Tap, Skoglund's Five & Dime, the Mercantile — and I talked about the women, men, and children, and that town, Lake Wobegon, became my magnum opus, unintentionally. I just sort of slid into it, like you'd go for a walk in the woods and fall into a crevasse and wind up in a cave full of rubies and emeralds. I labored in obscurity for the first few years, and then Will Jones, the entertainment columnist of *The Minneapolis Tribune,* wrote a big warm embrace of a story and that was the beginning of many good things. Will was from Ohio and admired James Thurber, and thought Lake Wobegon was Thurberesque, and his kind words in print were intoxicating.

In 1974, after writing a fact piece for the

magazine about the Grand Ole Opry, I started up *A Prairie Home Companion* on Saturday evenings, a live variety show with room for a long monologue by me ("It has been a quiet week in Lake Wobegon. . . ."), and found steady colleagues who did the hard work, starting with my boss, Bill Kling, and the producer, Margaret Moos, Lynne Cruise, Tom Keith, Bill Hinkley, and Judy Larson, and down to the present day, Sam Hudson, Kate Gustafson, Debra Beck, Kay Gornick, Richard Dworsky, Tim Russell, Sue Scott, and Fred Newman, not to mention tech guys, good stagehands, researchers, and our truckdriver Russ Ringsak, and so we sail the ocean blue in pursuit of truth and beauty, sober men and true, attentive to our duty.

Life is good when you finally grow up. You find work you enjoy, buy a car that starts on cold mornings, look for love, sing along with the radio, beget children who nestle on your lap and put their little arms around your neck and kiss you. You put away sarcasm. You mow your lawn, read history, learn to cook a few things well, seek out good shoes, converse with strangers on the bus. You find a hairstyle that suits you. Your taste changes: time goes by and contemporary art strikes you as ditzy and shallow whereas you are moved by Hopper and Rockwell and Nordic painters of snowscapes. Young Sarah Singer-Songwriter only makes you wonder if she is getting enough fresh air and exercise, whereas a Chopin étude carries visions of women in lamplight, the forbidden kiss, the whisper of silk, the nobility of kind gestures. You cross the line into your forties, the mortgage years, and the fifties, when you stand weeping at graduations and weddings, and then in the blink of an eye you land in your sixties and now you're on Easy Street. You become eminent and learn to har-rumph. And then seventy. A golden age. You are wise beyond knowing, you have embraced moderation and humility, your work is triumphant, you pee like a Palomino pony, and your imagination is more vivid than ever before. One can't wait to turn eighty and ninety.

Having once anticipated dying young, I now look back on those times when I might have and did not. The time I dashed out onto a busy freeway to retrieve a heavy mattress I'd foolishly tied with twine to the roof of the car and at 65 m.p.h. physics kicked in and it blew off. While I was dragging it off the road a truck bore down on me as if I were a raccoon and blew its air horn. I heard the Doppler effect up close and the whoosh of the draft made my pant legs go *whupwhupwhupwhup* and blew my hair back.

One summer my brother Philip and I canoed into a deep cavern in Devil's Island on Lake Superior, attracted by the dancing reflections on the low cavern ceiling. We steered into a narrow passage, ducking under rocks, and he took pictures of the formations, and after a while we paddled out, a few minutes before the wake of an ore boat a mile away came crashing into the cavern, three-foot waves that would have smashed us into the rocky ceiling like eggs in a blender. Our mangled remains would've floated out and been found by fishermen days or weeks later — TWO TWIN CITIES MEN PERISH IN BOATING MISHAP — but instead we sat in the canoe and watched the waves whopping into the cavern and said nothing, there being nothing to say. He raised his Leica and snapped a picture of the crashing waves and dropped it into the lake and it got smaller and smaller as it plummeted to the bottom.

Philip died a few years ago in Madison, Wisconsin, skating on a pond near his house. He who had survived the close call in the cave on Lake Superior fell and struck the back of his head on the ice and suffered serious brain injury and died. He was an engineer, a methodical man, a problem-solver, and I imagine that even as he fell, he was analyzing his mistake — he should've sat down on the ice and landed on his butt rather than his head. He tried too hard to remain upright; he should've collapsed. His family tried to keep his funeral as light as possible. There were three funny speeches and a rollicking gospel finish, and then we stood around the hole singing hymns as the gravedigger bent down, exposing a big slice of butt crack, and lowered Philip's body into the ground, and then went to supper.

After we buried my brother, he became a steady, flickering presence in my life, even more so than when he was alive. He was a teacher, a patient man who strove to accept people and see the goodness in them and not scorch them with ridicule, and now I try to be more like him and less like myself.

When you're in your seventies, people die all around you, at a steady rate. A high school classmate collapsed at our fiftieth reunion while I was at the microphone nattering about olden times; he died two days later. A man died in the audience at *A Prairie Home Companion* in Seattle; he was old and ill but wanted to come to the show, and during intermission he simply leaned against his wife and expired. Tom Keith, who was on the radio with me for four decades, came to a post-show party at my house, felt fine, and two days later fell down dead from an aneurysm — the man who played Mr. Big, the jowly incomprehensible man, and did the sounds of a golf swing, a man falling off a bridge into piranha-infested waters, a 350 h.p. snowmobile driven by an orangutang over a cliff and onto the ice of Lake Superior. He was a prince.

The living wander away, we don't hear from them for months, years — but the dead move in with us to stay. They exhort us to greater faithfulness, forgive us our inertia, comfort us in our agitation. My first mother-in-law, Marjorie O'Bleness, is smiling from the doorway, holding a Winston and a Rob Roy, tuned in to the conversation. My grandmother Dora is kneading bread on the counter, whistling a tuneless tune under her breath. Aunt Eleanor speaks in a soft twang a sentence that begins, "Well, you know —" and it's something I never knew, it never occurred to me to know it. My father sits waiting for us to get in the car and head for Idaho to visit some people there. My father-in-law, Ray, is about to launch into a long and very detailed story about the cars that he has owned and how

41

well they ran.

I think often of John Updike, who lovingly re-created the backyards and clotheslines of the 1940s small town and described a snowstorm as "an immense whispering" and wrote beautifully of his father bidding him goodbye on a train platform and astonishing him by planting a kiss on his cheek. I last saw John on the New York subway, riding from 155th Street down to 72nd, a white-haired gent of seventy-five grinning like a schoolkid. At 110th a gang of seminarians boarded and crowded around him, chattering, not recognizing him, and he sat soaking it up, delighted, surrounded by material.

The film director Robert Altman is a hero of mine — shooting a movie in St. Paul though he was eighty-one and in the throes of cancer and barely mobile. He loved his work and so put his mortality on a shelf. If you have flown a B-24 bomber, that screaming unheated boxcar of a plane, on fifty missions in the South Pacific at the age of twenty as Bob had, there is not much left to be afraid of. I remember him sitting in a canvas chair at 4 a.m. on the corner of Seventh and St. Peter in St. Paul, on a Sunday in July, directing a scene in which Kevin Kline gets up from a stool in Mickey's

Diner and walks out the door and scratches a match on the doorframe and lights a smoke and walks across a rain-soaked street. Bob was pushing to beat the sunrise but he loved studying that walk and lighting it, angling it, instructing the man with the hose, the man in the cherry picker with the spotlight, all the while offering running commentary to his audience of grips and extras. He was a happy man.

I am grateful for the work — more now than ever, the pleasure of scratching away on paper. I sit in my office and look up at a photograph over the fireplace of the old schoolhouse where Grandma taught a hundred and some years ago and I'm sure she hoped I'd go into a more distinguished line of work than this, but I must say in defense of comedy that it does give good value. There are plenty of discouraging facts around — e.g., half of all people are below average — and jokes relieve some of the misery. A man walked into his house with a handful of dog turds and said, "Honey, look what I almost stepped in!" (That's a joke, but I know people like that.) Solomon said, "Whoever increases knowledge increases sorrow." That's a joke, too. And "The rivers run into the sea and yet the sea is not full." That's a joke. And also "Vanity of vanities, all is vanity." And how about this one? "The race is not to the swift nor the battle to the strong nor riches to men of understanding, but time and chance happeneth to them all." That's the essence of comedy in less than 25 words. You're fast, you trip and fall down; you're strong and you poke your sword in your left foot; you're smart and you go broke. Solomon said, "The thing that has been is the thing that shall be; and the thing that is done is that which shall be done: there is nothing new under the sun." That is true and I know it, but I look forward to tomorrow morning and rising up, making coffee, watching the sun rise as it keeps doing day in and day out, and resuming the race, boats against the current and so forth. It's all been done before and it needs doing again.

I tried doing the News from Lake Wobegon sitting on a bench but my natural inclination is to pace. And sitting felt stagy. And people asked me if I was not feeling well. Pacing stimulates the mental processes. You walk in the darkness, spotlight in your eyes, along the lip of the stage, glancing down into the first row to avoid stepping off the edge and into their laps, and if your mind goes blank, you think of something better.

I.
THE NEWS FROM LAKE WOBEGON

In 1970, I moved to Stearns County with my
wife and little boy to live in a rented farmhouse
south of Freeport, an area of nose-to-the-
grindstone German Catholics, so we could
live cheaply — I was supporting us by writing
fiction for *The New Yorker* — and we found a
big brick house on the Hoppe farm in Oak
township that rented for $80 a month. With
the house came a half acre we could plant in
vegetables. It was a fine snug house, four
rooms down, four rooms up, a mansion by
our standards. A room for Mary's piano and a
room for my Underwood typewriter and a
small back room for the baby and two guest
rooms for our writer friends from the city who
liked to come and soak up the quiet and drink
beer at night and lie on the lawn and look up
at the stars. To the north of the house was a
dense grove of spruce and oak where we got
our firewood, and beyond this windbreak was
a couple hundred acres of corn. Cows stood

in a nearby meadow and studied us. The Sauk River was nearby, to canoe on, and Lake Watab to swim in. It was a land of well-tended hog and dairy farms on rolling land punctuated by tidy little towns, each one with a ballpark, two or three taverns, and an imposing Catholic church, and a cemetery behind it where people named Schrupps, Wendelschafer, Frauendienst, Schoppenhorst, and Stuedemann lay shoulder to shoulder. There were no Johnsons or Smiths to speak of.

For three years, I sat in my room and wrote short fiction and shipped it to New York. After a shipment, after a week or so, I'd watch for the mailman every day with more and more interest. He came around 1:30. I'd walk out the driveway to the mailbox and look for an envelope from *The New Yorker* — a large gray envelope meant rejection, a small creamy one meant acceptance. Acceptance meant another three months' grace. Eventually I ran out of grace and we moved to the Cities and I went back to my radio job and a couple years later started *A Prairie Home Companion* and the Lake Wobegon saga. When I invented Lake Wobegon, I stuck it in central Minnesota for the simple reason that I knew a little bit about it and also because my public radio listeners tended to be genteel folk who knew the scenic parts of Minnesota — the North

Shore, the Boundary Waters, the Mississippi Valley — and knew nothing at all about Stearns County. This gave me a free hand to make things up. I put Lake Wobegon (pop. 942) on the western shore of the lake, for the beautiful sunrises. I said it took its name from an Ojibway word that means "the place where we waited all day for you in the rain," and its slogan was *"Sumus quod sumus"* (We are who we are), and to the German Catholics I added, for dramatic interest, an equal number of Norwegian Lutherans. These don't exist in Stearns County but I bused them in. The Norwegians, ever status-conscious, vote Republican and the Germans vote Democratic to set themselves apart from the Norwegians. The Catholics worship at Our Lady of Perpetual Responsibility and the Lutherans at Lake Wobegon Lutheran church, home of the 1978 National Lutheran Ushering Champions, the Herdsmen. On Sunday morning, everyone is in church, contemplating their sinful unworthiness, the Catholics contemplating the unworthiness of the Lutherans, the Lutherans the unworthiness of the Catholics, and then everyone goes home to a heavy dinner.

If anyone asked why the town appeared on no maps, I explained that, when the state map was drawn after the Civil War, teams of surveyors worked their way in from the four outer corners and, arriving at the center, found they had surveyed more of Minnesota than there was room for between Wisconsin and the Dakotas, and so the corners had to be overlapped in the middle, and Lake Wobegon wound up on the bottom flap. (In fact, the geographic center of the state is north of there, in Crow Wing County, but never mind.)

Anyway, "Gateway to Central Minnesota" is the town slogan. And through the gateway over the years came a procession of characters. The three boys who drive to Iowa one February morning when they hear of Buddy Holly's plane crash and their discovery of his blue guitar in the snowy field. The stolid Father Emil, who said, in regard to abortion, "If you didn't want to go to Chicago, why did you get on the train?" and the town handyman Carl Krebsbach who repairs the repairs of the amateurs, and Bruno the fishing dog, and the irascible Art of Art's Baits and Night O'Rest motel, its premises studded with warning signs ("Don't clean fish here. Use your brains. This means you!!!"), and Dorothy of the Chatterbox Café and her softball-size caramel rolls ("Coffee 25¢, All Morning 85¢, All Day $1.25, Ask About Our Weekly Rates"), and Wally of the Sidetrack Tap, where old men sit and gradually come to love their fellow men by self-medication. It was Wally's pontoon boat,

50

the *Agnes D,* on which the twenty-two Lutheran pastors crowded for a twilight cruise and weenie roast. When the grill capsized and the *Agnes D* pitched to starboard, they were plunged into five feet of water and stood quietly, heads uplifted, and waited for help to arrive. It's a town where the Lutherans all drive Fords bought from Clarence at Bunsen Motors and the Catholics all drive Chevys from Florian at Krebsbach Chevrolet. Florian is the guy who once forgot his wife at a truckstop. Her name is Myrtle.

The stories always start with the line "It's been a quiet week in Lake Wobegon" and then a glimpse of the weather. It's a fall day, geese flying south across a high blue sky, the air sweet and smoky, the woods in gorgeous colors not seen in Crayola boxes, or it's winter, snowflakes falling like little jewels from heaven, and you awake to a world of radiant grandeur, trees glittering, the beauty of grays, the bare limbs of trees penciled in against the sky, or it's spring, the tomatoes are sprouting in little trays of dirt on the kitchen counter, the tulips and crocuses, the yellow goldfinches arriving from Mexico, or it's summer, the gardens are booming along, the corn knee-high, and a mountain range of black thunderclouds is piling up in the western sky. And then you go on to talk about Norwegian bachelor farmers sit-

51

ting on the bench in front of Ralph's Pretty Good Grocery or the Chatterbox, where large phlegmatic people sit at the counter talking in their singsong accent. So how you been then? Oh, you know, not so bad, how's yourself, you keeping busy then? Oh yeah, no rest for the wicked. You been fishing at all? I was meaning to but I got too busy. How about yourself? Nope. The wife's got me busy around the house, you know. Yeah, I know how that goes. — And so forth. And you slip into your story, and take it around the turns and bring it to a point of rest, and say, "And that's the news from Lake Wobegon," and that's all there is to it.

1.
BUS CHILDREN

I was a bus child, living in the country, and on schoolday mornings, fall, winter, spring, walked up our road to the highway and stood waiting for the bus to take us up to Anoka to school. My stop was the last for this bus and so all of the seats were full and I had to find one with smaller people in it so I could squeeze them in and get a few inches to sit on. Town kids walked to school and were able to stay after school for sports or to edit the school paper or rehearse for the play. They seemed hardly aware of us bus kids and ran the school and were homecoming royalty and we bided our time and looked forward to college. Whenever I drive in the country early enough to see kids waiting for a bus along the road, I feel affection for our tribe.

Out on the prairie so wide
The school buses wending their way
From the towns they travel

53

For miles on the gravel
An hour before it is day.
And the winter wind blows
Cross the corn stubble rows
Where the dirt has turned the snow gray.

And the children walk down to the road
From the farmhouses' warm kitchen glow,
Stand waiting and yearning
To see the bus turning
And the sweep of the headlights' glow.
And they climb up inside
And away they all ride
Past the farms and the fields full of snow.

And they think about math as they go
And the chemistry of atmosphere
And unequal equations
And French conjugations
And the sonnets of William Shakespeare
And then up the drive
At the school they arrive
On the darkest day of the year.

And in due course they will fly
Away, young women and men
With mixed emotions
Cross mountains and oceans
And become what we could not have been.
We will tenderly kiss them

Goodbye and miss them
And never will see them again.

2.
Growing Up with the Flambeaus

I invented John Tollefson, the hero of *Wobegon Boy,* during a time of domestic happiness on West End Avenue & 90th Street. A roomy apartment on the fifteenth floor with a kitchen that looked out at the Hudson River and the barges and scows and now and then a sail. We whomped up big dinners in a dining room with a wall of books where we sat with friends, including the two who lived across the hall, and it was very easy and charming. So I wrote a novel about a charming Midwesterner in love with a New Englander on the Upper West Side, in homage to the good life in New York.

I am a cheerful man, even in the dark, and it's all thanks to a good Lutheran mother. When I was a boy, if I came around looking glum and mopey, she said, "What's the matter? Did the dog pee on your cinnamon toast?" and the thought of our old black mutt raising his hind leg in the *pas de dog* and peeing on toast made me giggle. I was a beanpole boy, and my hair was the color of wet straw. I loved to read adventure books and ride my bike and shoot baskets in the driveway and tell jokes. My dad was a little edgy, expecting the worst, saving glass jars and paper clips, cranking down the thermostat to keep our family out of the poorhouse. On cold winter days, he felt that if you couldn't see your breath, the heat was turned up too high. He walked around turning off lights and announcing that he was not John D. Rockefeller. But Mother was well composed, a true Lutheran, and taught me to Cheer up, Make yourself useful, Mind your manners, and, above all, Don't feel sorry for yourself. In Minnesota, you learn to avoid self-pity as if it were poison ivy in the woods. Winter is not a personal experience; everyone else is as cold as you are; so don't complain about it too much. Even if your cinnamon toast gets peed on. It could be worse.

Being Lutheran, Mother believed that self-pity is a deadly sin and so is nostalgia, and she had no time for either. She had sat at the bedside of her beloved sister, Dotty, dying of scarlet fever in the summer of 1934; she held Dotty's hand as the sky turned dark from their father's fields blowing away in the drought, she bathed Dotty, wiped her, told her stories, changed the sheets, and out of that nightmare summer she emerged stronger, confident that life would be wondrous, or at the very least bearable.

My great-grandfather landed in Lake Wobegon in the center of Minnesota, from Voss, Norway, escaping from the Great Herring Famine of 1875. Lake Wobegon was a rough town then. All on one block, for five dollars, you could get a tattoo, a glass of gin, and a social disease, and have enough left over to ante up for a poker game, but Lutherans civilized it. They were hard workers, indifferent to carnal pleasures. Their vice was baseball. They were mad for it.

It was a good place to grow up in, Lake Wobegon. Kids migrated around town as free as birds and did their stuff, put on coronations and executions in the deserted train depot, fought the Indian wars, made ice forts and lobbed grenades at each other, dammed up the spring melt in the gutters, swam at the beach, raced bikes in the alley. You were free, but you knew how to behave. You didn't smart off to your elders, and if a lady you didn't know came by and told you to blow your nose, you blew it. Your parents sent you off to school with lunch money and told you to be polite and do what the teacher said, and if there was a problem at school, it was your fault and not the school's. Your parents were large and slow afoot and they did not read books about parenting, and when they gathered with other adults, at Lutheran church suppers or family get-togethers, they didn't talk about schools or about prevailing theories of child development. They did not weave their lives around yours. They had their own lives, which were mysterious to you.

I remember the day I graduated from tricycle to shiny new two-wheeler, a big day. I wobbled down Green Street and made a U-turn and waved to Mother on the front porch, and she wasn't there. She had tired of watching me and gone in. I was shocked at her lack of interest. I went racing around the corner onto McKinley Street, riding *very* fast so I would have big tales to tell her, and I raced down the hill past the Catholic church and the old black mutt ran out to greet me and I swerved and skidded on loose gravel and tumbled off the bike onto the pavement and skinned myself and lay on the tar, weeping, hoping for someone to come pick me up, but nobody came. The dog barked at me to get up. I limped three blocks home with skin scraped off my forearm and knee, my eyes brimming with tears, and when I came into the kitchen, Mother looked down at me and said, "It's only a scrape. Go wash it off. You're okay."

And when I had washed, she sat me down with a toasted cheese sandwich and told me the story of Wotan and Frigga. "Wotan, or Odin, was the father of the gods, and his wife, Frigga, was the earth goddess who brought summer, and the god of war, Thor, was the winter god, and the god of peace was Frey. So from Odin we get Wednesday, from Thor, Thursday, from Frey, Friday — Sunday and Monday, of course, refer to the sun and moon — which leaves Saturday and Tuesday. Wotan and Frigga had a boy named Sidney, and Thor had a daughter named Toots, and they fell in love and one day Sidney went to find Toots and steal her away, but Thor sent a big wind and Sidney rode his bicycle too fast and fell and skinned his knee, and that's why Saturday is a day off, so we can think about it and remember not to ride our bikes so fast." She gave me a fresh, soft peanut butter cookie. She wiped the last remaining tears from my cheek. She said, "Go outside and play. You're all right."

In Lake Wobegon, you learned about being All Right. Life is complicated, so think small. You can't live life in raging torrents, you have to take it one day at a time, and if you need drama, read Dickens. My dad said, "You can't plant corn and date women at the same time. It doesn't work." One thing at a time. The lust for world domination does not make for the good life. It's the life of the raccoon, a swashbuckling animal who goes screaming into battle one spring night, races around, wins a mate, carries on a heroic raccoon career, only to be driven from the creekbed the next spring by a young stud who leaves teethmarks in your butt and takes away your girlfriend, and you lie wounded and weeping in the ditch. Later that night, you crawl out of the sumac and hurl yourself into the path of oncoming headlights. Your gruesome carcass lies on the hot asphalt to be picked at by crows. Nobody misses you much. Your babies grow up and do the same thing. Nothing is learned. This is a life for bank robbers. It is not a life for the sensible people of Lake Wobegon.

When I was ten, I got absorbed in the Flambeau Family novels in the Lake Wobegon library and devoured them all in one summer, one by one, sequestered in my bedroom (*The Flambeaus and the Case of the Floating Barolo,* and the *Flippant Bellhop,* and the *Flying Bonbons,* and the *Floral Bou-*

quet, the *Flagrant Bagel,* the *Flamboyant Baritone,* the *Broadway Flop,* the *Flustered Beagle,* and, finally, *The Flambeaus' Final Bow*). The Flambeaus were: Tony, a boy of Manhattan, and his socialite parents, Emile and Eileen. Tony is a junior at Trinity School on West Eighty-ninth, All-City in tennis, an honor student, adored by his wise-cracking girlfriend, Valerie. Tony and his mother, an actress still beautiful at forty-one, and his father, the famed crime-solving microbiologist, live happily together in their art-filled duplex apartment on the twentieth floor of the San Remo, overlooking Central Park, and deal with the nefarious, heinous deeds of the criminal element as they lead their elegant lives, attending the opera and ballet and sampling the culinary delights of little-known restaurants and enjoying the nightly vodka gimlet with the neighbors from across the hall, Ira and Elena, a crime-busting attorney and his ballerina wife.

For a Lutheran boy whose dad ran the grain elevator in a small town where nobody had ever seen a ballet or knew a gimlet from a grommet, the Flambeaus were a revelation. They were my secret family. Nobody else took out the Flambeau books, especially after I reshelved them under Foreign Language.

Sometimes, descending the steps of Lake Wobegon High School, I would raise my hand as I came to the curb and imagine a taxi screeching to a stop and a bald cabbie with a cigar clenched between his teeth saying, "Where to, mac?" "The San Remo and step on it." "Right-o."

I set the Flambeaus aside as I got older, but in the back of my mind, I reserved New York for later consideration. I minded my manners and learned to be useful and didn't feel sorry for myself, and in my heart, even through my stringent college years and the summers spent washing pots and pans in the scullery of a hotel or guiding YMCA canoe trips in the North Woods, I imagined myself possessing an eastern elegance and was confident that someday I would land in Manhattan and be accepted by my imaginary people.

3.
MY COUSIN KATE

The kids in my family were good kids, earnest, dutiful, eager to please, ever fearful of God's watchful eye, and of course we knew bad kids but they came from bad homes where poor housekeeping and greasy food and poor sleep habits and the influence of a bad parent made it difficult for the kids to be anything but bad. Along the West River Road where I grew up, there were two such families and we all knew who they were (their lawns were bad, too) and didn't want to be like them. The first kid from a good family who chose badness was my cousin Kate, who rebeled rather dramatically in her teen years and then got even wilder in her maturity. I admired her for that. She was my Huck Finn, frank, fearless, true to herself, and she never looked back or cared what people thought about her. I cared a lot about what they thought about me and so I was devious, but Kate was brazen and after high school she tore off to strange cities to have adventures with drugs and sex and communal living that she still hasn't told me about. She's a sweet old lady now, avid about books and movies, and what's odd about her is that, despite her adventurous life in far-flung places, her voice is so much like her mother's, my dear aunt, who spent many a night weeping for her wayward daughter and sometimes got in her car at two or three in the morning and drove around town looking for the sinner, hoping to rescue her from the clutches of her fly-by-night friends. And now when Kate speaks, she speaks in the twang of her mother. I am perpetually amazed.

Saturday night, June 1956, now the sun going down at 7:50 p.m. and the sprinkler swishing in the front yard of our big green house on Green Street, big drops whapping the begonias and lilacs in front of the screened porch where Daddy and I lie, reading, a beautiful lawn, new-mown, extending to our borders with the Stenstroms and Andersons. The dog under the porch scootches down, pressing his groin into the cool dirt. A ball of orange behind the Stenstroms' house, orange shining in the windows, as if the Mr. and Mrs. had spontaneously combusted. The shadow of their elm reaches to our porch, a wavery branch flickers across my right arm in gray shade. I wish Kate would come by. She said she would but it doesn't look like she will. I wrote her a poem:

Kate, Kate,
She's so great
I would wait eight hours straight
To attend a fete
For Kate.

I lie on the white wicker swing, *Foxx's Book of Martyrs* before me, reading about the pesky papists piling huge jagged rocks on the faithful French Huguenots, crushing them, while listening to the Minneapolis Millers on the radio lose to Toledo thanks to atrocious umpiring that killed a rally in the third inning. Eruptions of laughter from the *Jackie Gleason Show* at the Andersons' to the east of us, the Great One glaring at Audrey Meadows. *One of these days, Alice — pow! Right in the kisser!* At the Stenstroms' Perry Como sings about the tables down at Morey's, at the place where Louie dwells. We are Sanctified Brethren and do not own a television because it does not glorify Christ. I know about these shows only from timely visits to the home of my so-called best friend, Leonard Larson. Accordingly, tucked inside my *Book of Martyrs* is a magazine called *High School Orgies,* lent to me by Leonard, opened to an ad for a cologne made from "love chemicals" that will turn any girl to putty in your hands. You dab some behind your ears and hold her in your arms and suddenly all resistance is gone, she is whispering for you to do whatever you like. Plus a book of sure-fire pick-up lines with a bonus chapter, "Techniques of Effective Kissing."

On the radio a male quartet sings, "From the land of sky-blue waters, Hamms, the beer refreshing." From one mail order house in the back pages of *Orgies,* you can purchase magic tricks, a correspondence course in jiu-jitsu, novelty underwear, and powerful binoculars that can see through clothing. A cartoon man aims his binocs at a high-stepping baby doll and his eyes bug out and his jaw drops and sweat flies off his brow. The cologne makes girls "eager to respond to your every wish, as if in a hypnotic trance," which sounds like a good deal, but what if someone like Miss Lewis came under your spell? You'd have a scrawny horse-faced old lady teacher in your arms. Maybe a guy should settle for the binoculars. And learn jiu-jitsu in case somebody tries to steal them.

"Where does the word *Saturday* come from?" I ask.

Daddy grunts. He thinks it comes from the Roman god Saturn.

"But it's not Saturnay. It's SaTURDay."

Not important to Daddy.

I spring the next question. "Do you think it's right for Christians to use the names of pagan gods for the days of the week?"

He grunts. I have caught him in an inconsistency of faith.

As Sanctified Brethren, we are the Chosen Remnant of Saints Gathered to the Lord's Name and Faithful to His Word, the True Church in Apostate Times, the Faithful Bride Awaiting the Lord's Imminent Triumphant Return, holding fast to the Principle of Separation from the Things of the World. Should we not testify to our faith by changing Saturday to Saintsday? How about Spiritday?

Daddy ignores this suggestion. He is good at shutting out things he prefers not to address. Above his head hangs a glass bead contraption that dingles in the breeze. It glitters like a kaleidoscope. The dingling drives him nuts, like a phone that nobody answers, but it can't be thrown out because it belonged to Grandpa, Mother's dad, and Grandpa is dead. This wicker porch furniture was his before he went to be with the Lord. He sat in this swing in his house on Taft Street and read from Deuteronomy and Leviticus and all about sacrificing calves and what was an abomination unto the Lord and how many cubits long the Temple should be, which made more sense to Grandpa, a practical man, than the Beatitudes ("Blessed are the meek" — what is *that* supposed to mean?). He was reading from God's Word and got up to go take a leak and he slipped on a loose rug and fell and broke a hip. What got into the hired girl's head that she went and waxed that hall floor? Better she should have put cyanide in his prune juice or blown his brains out with a rifle. Poor Grandpa was hauled to the Good Shepherd Home, where he lay weeping and gnashing his teeth for two years until God finally called him home; meanwhile we had been enjoying his furniture, knowing he'd never need it again.

Her hand brushed against the bulge of his maleness and suddenly his body seemed to rise as if on an ocean wave. His passion was too powerful to resist. "Oh Jack," she moaned. He leaned forward so she could better sniff his secret cologne and she began to tear at his shirt buttons. He had viewed her often through his binoculars and well knew the delights that would soon be his.

And suddenly, on the radio, Bob Motley is in a white froth yelling, "Goodbye mama, that train is leaving the station! Whoooooooooooooooeeee!" his trademark home-run cry, and Daddy perks up his ears but it isn't a homer, it's a long fly out for Miller slugger Clint Hartung: "That ball was on its way out of here, folks! And the wind got hold of it and it's a heart-breaking out to right field for a great ballplayer and just a wonderful guy! What a shame! And now Wayne Terwilliger comes to the plate." The crowd goes back to sleep.

The faithful Huguenots, our Protestant ancestors, are dying under the rock piles dumped on them by papists, and with their dying breaths the Huguenots pray for God to forgive their tormenters, a truly wonderful touch. A papist sneers at a lovely Huguenot girl as she raises her hands to heaven, as a load of rocks is piled on her. *Expertly, Jack's tongue probed her hot mouth, she loved it, the little vixen!* And now out tromps the older sister from the kitchen all hot and bothered and I must quickly switch *Orgies* from the *Book of Martyrs* to an encyclopedia as she cries out, "Why does he get to lie around and read books while everybody else

70

has to do the work around here? He's supposed to dry the dishes and he just waltzes
away and the pots and pans are sitting there
in the dish rack!"

I explain to her the principle of evapora-
tion whereby the air absorbs moisture, and
objects such as pots and pans become dry
in a short period of time with no help from
human beings.

"Why do you have to be so stupid?"

I am only being reasonable, I explain.

She leans over Daddy and touches his
shoulder, to bring him back to the point.
"Why do I have to do my chores and his,
too? It isn't fair!" You'd think she had spent
ten years on a chain gang.

The encyclopedia I stuck *Orgies* into is
from Grandpa's sixteen-volume set, of
which each grandchild received a volume.
My volume includes Pax Romana, peacocks,
the peanut, "The Pearl Fishers" by Bizet,
explorer Robert Peary, the Peloponnesian
Wars, the Pend d'Oreille Indians, penicillin,
Pennsylvania, the pentatonic scale, the
periodic table, the perpetual calendar,
perspective, photography (illustrated), the
Pimpernel (Scarlet) — Wayne Terwilliger
fouls off a Toledo fastball — a full page of
Scottish plaids by clan, the planets, the vari-

71

ous genuses of plants, the poets laureate of Britain, poisons and their antidotes, poker hands, polo, Catholic popes, presidents of the United States from Washington to Harry Truman, the prevention of forest fires, a history of printing — how could a person not love such a book? And right in the middle, surrounded by Scottish plaids, Jack is doing a push-up over Laura. *"Please, Jack, don't stop!" she murmured, as a wave of pleasure hit her like an express train.* They were teachers at the high school and suddenly it was spring, they opened the windows, and now look at them.

Wayne Terwilliger fouls off another pitch. "It's a waiting game," says Bob Motley. "Wayne's looking for the inside fastball."

Daddy says he wishes I would be kinder to my sister and do my share of the chores. The sister has him wrapped around her little finger. She works him like a marionette. She stands behind him, touching his shoulder, and he tells me to go dry the pots and pans. Even though I have today mowed the entire lawn. "I will," I say. "In a minute."

"Why can't you do what you're told to do?" she hisses at me.

"Don't make a federal case out of everything." Wayne fouls off another pitch. Still looking for the inside fastball. I tell her that

72

a person can't poke along washing the dishes and complaining about everything under the sun and expect me to stand and twiddle my thumbs and wait for her. And steady Wayne Terwilliger takes a called third strike ("Un-believable! Un-believable, folks! That pitch to Twig was *in the dirt,* ladies and gentlemen! How can a man be expected to hit a pitch like that? In the dirt! And the fans here are letting home-plate umpire Larry Cahoon know they're upset about that call!") and the Millers are set down, scoreless, and there's a commercial for Rainbow Motor Oil and then the Burma-Shave Boys ("You can put on suntan lotion, where the ocean meets the sand. / Find he-man perfection and a complexion well-tanned. / You can dream of sweet amore on your surfboard on the wave, / But listen, pal, you'll get your gal if you use Burma Shave").

"Go dry the pots and pans," says Daddy. "How many times do I have to tell you?"

"As soon as I move the sprinkler, I will go and put away the pots and pans, which are undoubtedly dry already."

"So move it, then," he says.

"I'll go check and see if it's ready to be moved." I set the encyclopedia down on the porch swing and put a pillow over it.

The sprinkler is placed at the exact point where it douses a quadrant of front yard from the birch tree to the sidewalk, allowing a little overlap. I check the grassroots. Wet but not soaked.

"Not ready to be moved yet," I say.

I step to the door and stand, one ear cocked to the game, the sprinkler whirring, the circle of drops flung glittering out into the gathering night. Faint in the distance a tractor chugs. *They lay side by side on the classroom floor, their love juices spent.* I am going to hell. This is becoming increasingly clear. As Aunt Flo says, you don't get to be a Christian by sitting in church any more than sleeping in a garage makes you a car. What sort of Christian can open up *High School Orgies* to the picture of resplendent breasts with pointy nipples and feel that happy twitching in his shorts?

I am going to spend eternity in hellfire for what is twitching in my mind right now.

"Boy, you never know how kids are going to turn out, do you," says Grandpa, looking out the window of heaven, wearing his best wool suit and starched white shirt with the armbands, his hair perfectly combed. "I used to think that kid might become a preacher. Now I don't see how he's going to stay out of prison."

74

"Yes," says Jesus, "you never know about these things."

He and Grandpa are drinking cups of coffee and eating gingersnaps. Grandpa says, "When are you planning to return to earth?"

"Soon as I finish this coffee," says Jesus. "Pretty good, isn't it."

"Never tasted better in my life," says Grandpa.

Back when he was on earth, Grandpa used to drop in on Saturday and cry out, "Who wants to go for a ride?" And for years I said "Me!" and went with him, and then one year I said, "I can't. I have homework. I'm sorry." Three lies in five seconds. I hated riding around and listening to Grandpa reminisce about who used to live in that house. Once I liked it okay and then I didn't anymore. I wonder if Grandpa still thinks about how we treated him.

"Why don't you just go and dry those pots and pans?" says Daddy. "It'll take you five minutes."

"The pots and pans are probably dry by now," I inform the sister. "All that needs to be done is to put them away in the cupboard and I'll come in and do that in a moment. Soon as I'm done reading about the Huguenots."

"It's not pronounced *hug-you-nots,*" she says. "For your information, it's hue-ge-nots. Hue-ge-nots," and she leans down and quick as a snake she snatches the naked couple out of the encyclopedia.

Give it back. Please.

She grins at me all boney and wolfish, and her muzzle twitches at the smell of blood. She backs away, clutching *High School Orgies.*

"Please give me back that magazine," I say firmly.

She gazes at it. "What is this?" — her eyes widen in mock horror, she flips through a few pages. "Oh my goodness." She looks to Daddy but he has spotted a pair of houseflies and is stalking them into the corner, a swatter in hand. Daddy is a sworn enemy of flies. Flies walk around in fecal matter and if you don't kill them you may as well be eating your dinner off the barn floor with the hogs.

"You really need to go see a psychiatrist," she says.

"I don't know what you're talking about."

"Talking about this." She waves the magazine at me, wrinkling the cover. "Touch not the unclean thing," says the sister, who is getting a bad Scripture-quoting habit. "Whatsoever things are pure, whatsoever things are holy, let your mind be fixed on these things." I could club her.

"I have no idea what you're talking about." She wants me to beg for mercy but remorse is an endless highway where she's concerned, I know her, so I must take the 100 percent denial route. I never saw those pictures of that naked couple and their hot love juices. I know nothing about this magazine. I have no idea where the sister found it. I had no idea she was interested in such things. Frankly, I'm shocked.

"You know this would break Mother's heart. She would cry her eyes out if she knew," she says.

"If she knew what?"

"You know what," says the sister. "You know." She tosses her head and reminds me that the dishes are waiting to be dried and wheels toward the kitchen, *High School Orgies* in hand.

I will swear up and down I never laid eyes on it, I will lie my face off until I am tied in knots — *I never saw that magazine in my life, Mother. I demand a polygraph test! Call in the FBI. Boston Blackie. Sam Spade. Get me City Desk! We'll get to the bottom of this! Find out who is infiltrating our household with this despicable literature!*

■ ■ ■ ■

I was a very good boy right up until the age of eleven. Everybody said so. I stayed out of people's way and didn't ask too many questions. I sat up straight at meals and when visiting other people's homes, I said Thank you for the lemonade and Please may I use your bathroom? I never picked my nose except behind closed doors and when grown-ups spoke I was attentive. I was often pointed out to other children as an example. "Why can't you behave like Gary? Look at him, he doesn't wriggle around like a trapped squirrel during Prayer Meeting, he sits up straight and listens and Gets Something Out of It." And then one day in 1953 I said out loud, "Oh, to hell with it," in connection with a sack of garbage Daddy told me to take to the garbage can. I was standing on one side of the screen door and he on the other. I was wearing khaki trousers and an old Boy Scout shirt of the older brother's. I was surprised to hear these words myself. They just sprang out, like a sneeze, "Oh, to hell with it." And a great darkness fell over the earth.

Daddy was speechless with apoplexy. He thought I had said "Go to hell" to him.

I was sent out to sit in the car. It was a hot day, the sun beat down. I sat in the backseat, the window rolled down, pretending I was on a train to Chicago. Kate came by. I told her what I had said and she grinned. "You're up shit creek now," she said.

And then Daddy came out and drove me to the farm. He talked about how hard he worked as a boy and how Grandma brooked no back talk and if you didn't toe the mark it was the leather strap for you, but of course Grandma never was like that to me at all. He said, "You go spend a few days on the farm and maybe it'll make you think twice about what you say."

Aunt Eva was tickled pink to take possession of me. Daddy told her I'd said a swearword, and after he left, she cut me a slice of chocolate cake three inches thick with a glob of whipped cream on top. She said that everybody thinks swearwords sometimes and there isn't much difference between thinking them and saying them, according to the Gospel. When she was young, she said, she used to go to the barn and say every bad word she knew, and that way she got it out of her system.

I asked if I was going to hell and she said, Don't be ridiculous. And then she did something that nobody in our family did, ever, she told me she loved me, and she threw her big arms around me and I took a deep breath of her and she squeezed and said, I wish you lived with me, Precious.

I was so happy. It was a blazing hot summer afternoon. Grandma was taking a nap. Eva said we'd go swimming later in the river. We sat in the shade on the back steps. I asked, "What would you do if you had a million dollars?" I would take a trip around the world, I said. This thought didn't seem to interest her. She picked up a bucket, and we headed out past the machine shed to the garden drenched in sunshine, picked a dozen ears of sweet corn, two cucumbers. Bees busied themselves among the vines, the pea vines and melons and pumpkins and squash, the whole jungly spread of vinous stuff, dipping under the broad fuzzy leaves. Eva picked a few tomatoes. I picked one and wiped it off and bit into it and sucked up the warm juice.

Daddy came and took me back to town.

— How's Eva and Grandma?

— Fine.

— Did you think about how you need to control what you say?

—Yes, I did.

— And what did you decide?

— I'm not going to swear.

— I hope you mean it.

— I do.

In my head I thought, *I've got to get out of here, damn it.*

Cousin Kate was the only one I could say it to and she said, "You're damn right you do."

Kate is older than I, and even then she dwelt on a plane of sophistication extremely rare for Lake Wobegon, Minnesota. She was a devotee of *The New Yorker* and shared copies with me and pointed out the best things and explained the cartoons. She wore her dark hair short with bangs in homage to the great Audrey Hepburn and she acted in school plays, but usually as the mother, or the maid, dusting the drawing room as the curtain came up. She didn't care, she loved to perform. She liked to say things to make people's jaws drop, and then be nonchalant about it, *What's the big deal?* and walk away, cool. She told a girl from Youth for Christ that she thought it was okay if people had sex, so long as they loved each other. The other girl burst into tears and said she would pray for Kate, but it was all a big show. If you dared her to show her underpants, she would. If Miss Falconer needed someone to sing a solo at the Christmas choir concert, Kate's arm was high in the air, her hand fluttering.

Kate knew sophisticated songs. She read Tolstoy and Dostoevsky. She smoked. When she was in the mood, she spoke in a Hepburn glissando, cool and thrilling — she'd say, "Darling, what a day I have had, I am in an absolute *state,* the things I put up with, don't ask me about it" — not a Lake Wobegon way of talking, and she'd reach into her coat pocket and pull out her Herbert Tareytons and plant a cigarette between her lips and say, "Darling, I have been *dying* for this since noon," and light it and let the smoke trickle out her mouth and draw it up her nose. Once Kate and I ran into Aunt Flo downtown and Kate quickly hid her cigarette behind her back and said, Hi Aunt Flo, and when Flo passed, Kate smiled at me and exhaled smoke, cool as could be. She learned to smoke at Bible camp, from some unsaved kids the Brethren tried to convert, and she also learned how to swear and dance the shimmy.

That spring in 1956, her poem "soliloquy" was rejected by Miss Lewis for the *Literary Leaf* —

death is easy like taking a bath
with an electric fan and waving hello to god
you could die like walking in front of a bus
or jumping into the big blue air
or doing almost anything
you could die by living in minnesota
god is love but
he doesn't necessarily drop everything and
   go save everybody
does he

Miss Lewis told Kate she was a sick person. She sent the poem home to Aunt Ruth and Uncle Sugar, and it scared them silly. How could Kate talk about putting an electric fan in the bath? And why wasn't "god" capitalized?

Kate announced that she planned to attend Athena College in Melisma, Iowa, where, on May Day every year, the students run naked as jaybirds across the Quad and through the fountain and into the Arboretum (PROF DOFFS DUDS AT MAY DAY DO was the headline in the *Minneapolis Star*). Uncle Sugar said he would rather eat a can of Dutch cleanser than have her attend a school like Athena. But Kate just laughed. "Darling," she said to me, "I don't intend to spend my life baking cookies and waxing the kitchen floor. I am not a scrubwoman. I am an artist, my darling. Artists are put here to paint big strokes of color in a dull gray world — and if some people prefer the dull gray world, too bad for them. Don't be a bump on a log. Wake up and die right."

A few days after the "soliloquy" scandal, Kate waltzed into school in a blue angora sweater unbuttoned three buttons from the top, a dramatic touch. She seemed even more coltish and *Oh Darling*ish than usual, flying around the halls, crying out *Woo-hoo* and blowing kisses and striking a Come Hither pose and hugging people. It was the day of the spring talent show. The whole student body packed into the auditorium, and the lights dimmed, and the spotlight focused on the microphone in front of the blue-and-gold L.W.H.S. curtain. A girls' sextet sang "Green Cathedral" and a boy in a red-striped suit lip-synched to a Spike Jones song and a sweaty girl in a pink formal played "Deep Purple" at the piano in a studious way. Leonard Larson recited "Stopping by Woods on a Snowy Evening." Painful. The sextet returned and sang "To Know Him Is to Love Him." Kate hated them because they wouldn't let her join, even though she sang better than any of them. They rejected her because she wasn't cute enough. They sang a third song about wanting to be loved by you, boop-boop-a-doop, in which Cathy Tollerud did a stutter-step rag doll dance that showed flashes of white panties, and boys around me whooped and whistled, and right after that came Kate, determined to show them up. She danced to the Doo Dads' recording of "Dance Me" —

Baby, baby, I'm your man.
Kiss me, squeeze me, hold my hand.
Kiss me sweet and kiss me strong.
And dance me, dance me, all night long.

As she danced, she pulled her sweater down so you could see her bare shoulders. Then she turned her back and showed off more of her shoulders. She didn't seem to be wearing anything underneath. She stood with her hands on the sweater as if she might take the whole thing off and boys whistled and yelled, "Do it! Do it! Do it!" and she smiled and flounced off to whoops and yells, and came back for a deep bow that revealed a little more. After the show, Daryl Magendanz saw her in the hall and grabbed for her bra strap and didn't find one and threw back his big flat head and hollered, "She ain't wearin no UN-der-wear!"

Kate was sent to the school nurse, Mrs. Dahlberg, for inspection. Kate told Mrs. Dahlberg to sit on it and spin. The nurse threw her up against the wall and tried to stick her hand up Kate's sweater when Kate squirmed loose and raced out the door and down the hall past the English classrooms and came pedaling for dear life around the corner by Home Economics as I was opening the door to the boys' can.

I had gotten out of Miss Lewis's class to go to the library and do research on the Globe Theatre.

Kate yelped at me and slid into the can ahead of me and we hustled into the far stall and latched the door and I sat on the throne and she sat on my lap with her legs braced against the door.

"What are we doing?" I said. She put one hand on the toilet paper roll and lay back against me, her legs slightly bent, her brown shoes on the green door, and then she said, "You better pull down your pants so it looks like you're taking a dump." She hoisted herself up an inch and I slid my trousers and underpants down, and she sat on my naked lap. She told me what happened in the nurse's office. I put my arms around her. I could feel her rib cage, breathing, her back against me. I put my face in her hair.

She was a little heavy but it didn't matter.

A door slammed open and the nurse yelled, "Who's in here?" I jumped and felt my innards quake and there were two little splashes in the toilet. Kate bent over and almost burst out laughing. She clapped both hands over her mouth.

"I said, Who's in here?"

"Me," I said. Kate snorted.

"Somebody in there with you?"

"No."

"Did a girl come in here?"

"No, of course not, Mrs. Dahlberg."

"Come out here and let's have a look at you."

Kate shook from the effort of not laughing out loud. She scootched up and I slid out from under and opened the stall door and looked out and there was Mrs. Dahlberg breathing fire. Her hair had come loose and she was grinding her teeth. "Step out of there, young man," she said. She was so ticked off she didn't even recognize me as Kate's cousin.

I stepped out, pants around my ankles, shirttails out, my hands over my pecker, and she looked at me with pure loathing. "What do you think you're doing out of class? You came in here to smoke, didn't you."

"I had to go to the toilet."

She snorted. "Let's see your hall pass."

I dug the pass out of my pants pocket. She shook her head. "If I don't see you in the library in five minutes, young man, there better be a good reason why." She wheeled around and out the door and lit out down the hall.

The door slammed and Kate almost split a gut. "Good I had you take your pants down. Boy, she scared the poop right out of you." She hoisted herself up and I slid under her, on the throne. I asked her what we should do now.

She said, "Sit tight, darling, and wait for the coast to clear."

I sat, half naked, with my arms around her middle, and closed my legs. She said, "You know, they just might kick me out of school for hitting Mrs. Dahlberg." She chuckled. "Oh well. If they kick me out, I'll run away from home. I'll hide out in the woods and I'll steal for a living."

"I'll visit you in the woods," I said.

She said, "That's very thoughtful of you, sweet pea."

We did not hear the boy come in and pee in the urinal trough but he heard us and I guess he peeked through the crack between the stall door and the post and saw us in there and since he was a good boy he reported us to Mr. Halvorson, who came storming in a few minutes later, while I was imagining living with Kate in a shack in the woods and talking late into the night and writing stories for *The New Yorker.* She had just said she had to go home and put on a bra and I said, "You don't have a bra on?" and she took my hands and put them up her sweater, and that was when he burst in with a triumphant shout and escorted us to his office and sat us down on hard oak chairs for almost an hour and gave us a somber talk about how we must accept the consequences of our deeds whether we intended those consequences or not — I had no idea what he meant — but he was so embarrassed by what had happened in the boys' can that he could not bring himself to say what it was, except he used the word *unnatural* several times, and then he gave us a mournful look and let us go. It was a gentle spring day. Two cats lay on the sidewalk, soaking up the sun, meadowlarks sang in a vacant lot. The steeple of the Lutheran church rose up before us. Inside a soprano was singing. *Abide with me, fast falls the eventide.* Then we saw the hearse parked in back.

"A funeral, darling, and it's not ours. What

could be better?" We went down the hill and headed toward the trees by the swimming beach. She sat down and leaned against a pair of birch trees. I sat next to her.

"This is what I call a good day," she said. "You ever worry that you might turn out to have a boring life? I do. I worry about it all the time."

I said I was worried I'd wind up going to hell.

"Either there is one or there isn't, and if there is, either you're going or you're not, and God knows which it is, so there's not much to be done about it, is there?"

The sister returns to the porch, having stashed the magazine for blackmail. Toledo is at bat in the bottom of the seventh, their shortstop, Denny Davies, who poked the triple in the second, now knocks out a single — he has three for three. "I think Gary has something to tell you," she announces.

Daddy looks at me. "Go dry the dishes."

"I will in a minute."

I will not surrender. I never saw *High School Orgies* in my life and have no idea where she found it. I will go to the kitchen *when I choose to* and dry the pots and pans *when I choose to and not a moment before.* She leans down and whispers, "I'd be very careful if I were you, because you're not going to get away with this. I could have that filthy magazine in Mother's hands in two minutes!"

And just then, out comes Mother, my old ally and defender, iced tea in hand, in her green linen pants and white sailor blouse, barefoot, her bushy blond hair tied back, and settles down in the white wicker chair with *The Minneapolis Star.* "What a lovely evening," she says.

"He won't dry the pots and pans," says Miss Misery. "And there's one more thing —"

Mother looks up. "They're dry. I put them away in the cupboard."

The sister seethes. She steams, she fumes, she foams at the mouth. She informs Daddy that the pots and pans had to be rewashed because flies had walked all over them for the past half hour due to my disobedience. They are in the dish rack now and await my dish towel.

He looks over at me on the porch swing, a pillow behind my head, glancing through the *Collier's,* reading about peanuts, a leguminous plant (*Arachis hypogaea*), bearing underground nutlike pods.

"Go do what you said you were going to do before I completely lose my patience."

I walk down the front steps. Frames of porch light stretch over the beautiful grass, and drops of water fly into the light. Thousands of drops enjoying a split-second life as individuals before mingling in the ooze. The grass is drenched, the ground soused. I pick up the green hose and crimp it to shut off the spray and drag the hose around to the side of the house, and in the shadows the Stenstroms' cat, who knows my accuracy with water, slinks for cover in the lilacs.

I set the sprinkler so it waters a sphere of backyard from the cellar steps to the tomato plants to the clotheslines, and I come in the back door into the kitchen, where the sister sits smirking at the table. I tell her she really ought to do something about her personality. And also her appearance. And she hisses at me, "Fornicator!" and stomps upstairs, and I dry the three pans and one pot she has rewashed, the ones that flies purportedly trod on, and as I put them into the cupboard I sneeze and a string of snot lands in the pot and I open the cupboard under the sink to get the detergent and there is *High School Orgies* hidden in a dish basin. *Yes! Thank you, Lord!* I slip it under my shirt, and return to the porch and plop back into my nest on the swing and sit, pretending to read about peanuts.

4.
JUNE

What I know about doing a monologue is to forget about structure and what you learned reading the short stories of Flannery O'Connor and just go fast and keep changing the subject. And if you skid off course, don't slow down: go in the direction of the skid. "June" is a pretty typical monologue that starts with a tender summer cabin scene, visits Pastor Liz and a worried father, throws in an adoption story, a high school reunion, tent caterpillars, high school graduation, and manages to quote Kierkegaard, all while the monologuist takes personal pleasure in naming a few real people he has known: the in-laws from his first marriage whose summer cabin he used to frequent and Lieutenant Henry Hill, a smart, disciplined, dearly loved graduate of Anoka High School, whose life was taken in Vietnam, a black kid in a white school who never acknowledged racism. Old Anokans wrote me to say that when they heard his name in the

News from Lake Wobegon, they got choked up. There he was, along with my dead in-laws, on the porch at Cross Lake, and tent caterpillars, all impromptu in a pool of light on an outdoor stage in the Berkshires, where the young Bernstein conducted the Boston Symphony, families sprawled on blankets in the grass, and Richard Dworsky at the piano waited to play a Chopin étude after the line about the strong women, good-looking men, and smart children. Dear God, what a lovely way to earn a living.

It's been a quiet week in Lake Wobegon. Low 70s, dry, sun shining, nice breeze. Put people in a good mood. The peonies are in bloom, the lake water is warm enough to swim in, the water lilies are opening up. We went up to clean out the lake cabin and get it ready for summer. You drive up through the trees and stop and clear the fallen branches off the road and unlock the back door. You can smell the dead mice, so you open the windows and you throw the little bodies out in the brush. Thank goodness nobody broke in, no screens are torn. You crawl under the cabin and throw the switch on the fuse box and the pump works and the water comes out and you let it run until it doesn't smell like rotten eggs. Then you clean out the fridge and plug it in and put the groceries in and you climb up and clean the leaves out of the gutters. You dust and vacuum with the old Electrolux and mop the kitchen and wash the windows, and get out the clean sheets and make the beds, and open the chimney flue and make sure there are no nests, and get some firewood in and you cook supper, sloppy joes, an old family tradition, and the smell of it in the old enamel pan on the fire brings tears to your eyes for the dead. Hilmer and Helen and Gene and Marge and Ed and Jen and Florence and LeRoy — this was their sacred haven, their resting place, where they sat on that front porch drinking their Manhattans and gin and tonics and brandy and sodas and laughing and laughing, playing gin rummy or 500, and this is how you want to remember them. They'd gone through the Depression and the Dirty Thirties and the dust storms and the war and after all of that, to sit on a screened porch and feel the breeze off the lake and eat sloppy joes and have a beer and be among familiar faces was pure pleasure.

The summer cabin is like a family history center. The old wicker furniture from Grandpa's house. The old dishes you grew up with as a child, now entombed here. Your childhood books. Uncle Gene's outboard motor. Say what you will about his drinking, he maintained this motor very well and it comes to life every Memorial Day and the smell of exhaust brings back the memory of Gene. Why didn't you bury him here instead of in the cemetery? The Larsons did — they cremated their parents and their ashes are in two urns on the porch.

Pastor Liz went down to the Minneapolis Synod conference on the eighteenth because she wanted to be there for the election of a woman bishop, Rev. Ann Svennungsen, the first in Minnesota. And then she came back and gave a sermon about how we should do our righteous deeds in secret and not be a show-off. And she does. She visits the old and infirm and if they want her to feed their cats or make them some chicken soup or find them a cleaning lady, she does that, calls up Clint Bunsen, a volunteer, who's good at plumbing, and he comes out and replaces the float in the toilet tank. She gives hand massages, dries tears, takes temperatures, listens to people complain about their children, makes tea. All that training in theology but you don't go visit Mrs. Oberg and talk about the problem of free will and could an omnipotent God create us with the freedom to reject Him, you open a can of peaches and you feed them to her, she who had a stroke a month ago and not of her own free will and not necessarily God's either, it just happened. It is exhausting to go around and absorb the sorrows of the world and sometimes Pastor Liz comes home and weeps and if there's a knock at the door, she can't answer it, her eyes are all red and swollen. What helps is if she puts on a record and dances to it — "My Girl," "You're Gonna Lose That Girl." She had the music turned up loud and she didn't hear his footsteps. Clint Bunsen coming in to see if she needed her float replaced. "Hey, getting ready for the talent show, I see," he said. She had started to change out of her clerical garb and she had taken off her skirt and hadn't put her jeans on.

He knows about the sorrows of the world, though. He's a father. His daughter Tiffany is in Atlanta, unemployed, has a yearlong lease on a wreck of an apartment, thanks to a boyfriend with a temper. Walls with fist holes in them. Clint's son, Chad, is getting rich in California designing video games in which demented people walk into fast-food restaurants and gun people down. And Kira, his youngest, is in Fargo running a French restaurant called Fargo Monet. It's not doing well. She hasn't been paid in three months. Twenty-two years old and she's beautiful and broke. Her real joy is training dogs. Works late at the restaurant, gets up early and trains big Labs to walk like ballerinas. It's for her that Clint carries a cell phone in his pocket, in case she needs him to tell her what to do. Which she hasn't yet. Twenty times a day he'd like to press 1 on speed dial but he knows she'd be irked. "What?" she'd say. "I'm busy. What?"

Liz went to put her jeans on and Clint replaced the float in the toilet and he opened the window and cardinals were singing in the maple trees. The phone rang and it went to the answering machine and he heard an old woman's voice ask for the pastor to come, she needed to take Bernie to the hospital and could the pastor come and see to her cats. Clint opened her refrigerator door and there was a ham. It looked good. It was quiet back there in the bedroom where Pastor Liz was. She was waiting for him to leave. She was embarrassed. She didn't want to see him. He wanted to ask her if he could have a slice of that ham. He called down the hallway, "Are you okay, Pastor?" "No," she said. What to say? "Anything I can help with?" "No." "Okay. Bye." "Bye." The ham looked so good, but he didn't want to be a thief. Bad enough to be a voyeur. His cell phone vibrated in his pocket. It was Kira calling from Fargo. He dashed out of the parsonage and closed the door and opened the phone. "Yeah," he said. "What you up to?" "Not much." "You okay?" "Yeah, I'm fine."

Father Wilmer was sitting in the Chatterbox Café, brooding over his chili and grilled cheese. He is a good man of charity and devoted to the gospel, kind, forbearing, gentle, and he has just discovered that he is Swedish. He was born in Chicago and adopted at birth by a family in Milwaukee named Mueller whose brother was a Franciscan priest, and Wilmer admired him and followed in his footsteps, and a month ago he got a letter from Child Services in Chicago that his birth mother would like to be in touch, and he went down to see her. Her name was Inga. She had been a waitress and she had taken up with a cook named John Johnson. One night of passion and then he left town and she had the baby put up for adoption and was ostracized by her family and she played piano in a saloon. One night she went to a Baptist revival meeting and was moved by the message and stood up and was possessed of the Spirit

100

and told her story of sin and disgrace and told it so beautifully and so passionately that a rich woman took her in and Inga cared for her until the woman died and she had left everything to Inga, a big house and a car and a warehouse downtown and stocks and bonds and Inga started playing piano in church. She played very lively and syncopated just like in the saloon except she played hymns about Jesus, but they made you want to dance, and people loved it. And now she was eighty-four and she wanted to find her lost boy. She said, "I prayed for you every day and I can see my prayers were answered." He was not wearing his clerical collar when he met Inga. She said, "Are you a churchgoing man?" He said yes, he was. "I hope you ain't Catholic," she said. "It would kill me if you were." "I'm a Christian," he said. "Well, that's a relief to hear." She died in February and last week he got an envelope: a slip of paper said, *Be not conformed to this world: but be ye transformed by the renewing of your mind. . . .* And a check for $18,000. There was only one stipulation, that he attend church regularly. Well, he does that, of course. He's thinking he'll take a vacation this summer and go to Ireland. Spend the money before anyone can ask him to donate it.

■ ■ ■ ■

Class of 1962 held their fiftieth reunion and
stood under a big tent out in the park by
the lake and reflected on how much they
liked each other, people who had once been
beset with angst and envy and wild ir-
rational ambitions and now here they were,
older and sort of satisfied. They stood in
honor of their classmate Henry Hill, who
died in Vietnam, a first lieutenant. Janet
Oberg, who was in the class play with him
— she played Juliet; Henry, Romeo — stood
and recited:

> Give me my Romeo; and, when I shall die,
> Take him and cut him out in little stars,
> And he will make the face of heaven so
>   fine
> That all the world will be in love with night
> And pay no worship to the garish sun.

That's what high school does for you:
gives you some art and music and history
so that even if you spend your life raising
kids and writing computer programs, still
there was a time when you argued about
the First Amendment and talked about the
Civil War and read *Romeo and Juliet*.

The high school choir came to the reunion. Arrived at 10 p.m. in their black gowns and stood outside the tent and hummed the Alma Mater and looked at all these old people in their sixties standing weeping. Unbelievable.

Hail to thee, our Alma Mater,
Would that we might dwell
Longer in thy hallowed hallways,
But we bid farewell.
Through life's dangerous lonely passages
Long the coasts of grief and fear,
In our hearts we'll e'er remember
How you loved and taught us here.

Corinne Tollerud is back from St. Olaf after her freshman year and she is all torn up over Kierkegaard — a seeker after truth, living without income, piles of dirty clothes on the bedroom floor. *Life can only be understood backwards; but it must be lived forwards.* Kierkegaard said that. So she told her mother, "What is the point, really, of vacuuming? There has always been dirt, always will be. Dirt is organic. There is nothing new under the sun. People say to me, 'A young woman like yourself should be out seeing the world, not living at home,' but what do those words mean, *young* and *woman*? Those don't define me. They limit

103

me. Life is a race with no finish line and no prize. You could skip the race and stay home and just let God pick the winners. It's all the same. Yes, it would cause anxiety but anxiety is the dizziness of freedom. Why do we live the way we do?"

Meanwhile the smell of burning charcoal is in the air, and hamburgers, and though we longtime residents may think about the meaning of life, we also think about the tent caterpillars who are out in great numbers, droves of them, eating the leaves of trees, so you don't feel bad as you walk along crushing them underfoot, but nobody is going barefoot, and at night you lie in bed and you can hear them pooping on your roof. You come down to breakfast and a tent caterpillar crawls out of the butter dish. You look down at your chair and there are two of them there. Your wife sits down. A tent caterpillar is crawling up her nightgown toward her bare shoulder as she drinks her tea and reads about Afghanistan. The caterpillar is heading for an Afghanistan of its own — it ventures out onto bare skin and she whoops and her tea goes up in the air and she smacks it hard and runs into the toilet to wipe it off her and comes back and looks you in the eye and she knows, she *knows* — women know — that you saw it and said nothing. You wanted to see it.

There are pesticides, of course, but the one that deals with the tent caterpillar is alleged to have side effects for humans — it causes sleepiness. And that's something we don't need. The presence of caterpillars stimulates alertness. A skunk paraded through town on Tuesday, walked up from the lakeshore past Ralph's Pretty Good Grocery and the Mercantile and across the street past Skoglund's Five & Dime and the Sidetrack Tap and the Feed & Seed and everyone in town watched him walk across the ballfield and into the cornfield and Mr. Berge turned from the window in the Chatterbox Café and took a forkful of his salad and got a fuzzy feeling in his mouth and he coughed it up and spat and spat and everyone in the café was laughing so hard they were weeping. Darlene had twisted some pieces of yarn together and that's what he felt on his palate — she did it to pay him back for the time he put the mouse in her apron pocket and got her excited and she went to the ladies' room and while she was there he switched her hot fudge sundae and substituted a liquid laxative for the hot fudge.

The caterpillars are out for survival.

Survival is victory. We have it easy. We lie in our beds at night and hear what sounds like rain on the roof and it's caterpillar poop falling through the trees. A thin layer of it on the ground. Pastor Liz serves communion and something in the dish of wafers is moving. She flicks it away and her acolyte Brian says, "Hang on," which he's never said during communion, and he removes a caterpillar from her chasuble. "Thank you," she says. "And also yourself."

The graduating seniors pay no attention to caterpillars. They are thinking about summer and the great beyond — their favorite part of town is the road out. Mr. Halvorson is hoping to repress any and all attempts to disrupt the commencement with some prank or other. Last year twelve of the seniors, eight boys and two girls, dropped their robes in the procession going out and walked along naked, a memorable moment. Flashes of cameras. People screaming. Students clapping. The seniors will undoubtedly be planning this at their big bonfire tonight out at the Hansens' farm. The Hansens will be home, but they don't plan to stay up all night, nor do the constables Gary and LeRoy. In the hours between 2 and 6 a.m. there is great freedom in Lake Wobegon. You could, if you wanted, go in the back doors and sit in the living rooms and go through books, look in closets, check out the fridge. There are sound sleepers in this town — you could go up the stairs and stare at them in their sleep, and if you did you might see a tent caterpillar walking up a neck and through hair and up a cheek and around to the open mouth, snorting and groaning, and up to the left nostril, and he puts his head in and feels around with his antennae and the sleeper crinkles up his nose and the caterpillar humps off to the side just as the sneeze comes out. An explosion.

On Wednesday the high school kids gathered out on the parking lot and watched Venus cross over the sun. They wore paper eye protectors, and as usual when grown-ups are involved, the thrill of the moment was oversold. Kids were expecting some sort of galactic explosion and instead there was a tiny speck of shadow that some of them saw and others thought they saw and others weren't sure. It made you wonder what else has been oversold. The joy of seeing Paris, France. The joy of seeing someone's underpants. Maybe marriage is like this. You stand around with paper over your eyes and then it's over and she says, Did you see it? And you say, I think so, I don't know.

Corinne saw Pastor Liz on the street and she ran over and she said, "I never understood the Christian faith until last month. Kierkegaard said that people pretend not to understand the faith because they know if they did understand it, it would obligate them to follow it and they don't want to do that. It means: Have nothing. Want nothing. Give everything away. Live without effort. Love people you don't like. It's not complicated." I was right there, I saw a caterpillar crawling up her shoulder. I didn't take it off her. I didn't feel I had the right.

5.
GOSPEL BIRDS

On a Saturday morning before a show, I sit down and write out the News from Lake Wobegon monologue, about three pages single-spaced. A sensible person would do it on Monday, but old habits die hard and I seem to require a high level of adrenaline to get the job done. On Monday the show appears very far away, on Saturday morning I am looking over the precipice. Sometimes I print out the three pages, sometimes not. If I print them out, I will glance at them before going out on stage. You don't want the monologue to sound like you're reading it, so you don't read it — you want it to sound like a man thinking aloud, so you stand in the spotlight and try to think of what you wrote down, unconsciously editing the three pages approximately in half, rearranging things, and, if your mind goes blank, you grab the first thought you can think of and hang on. It's exciting.

Ernie and Irma Lundeen and their Performing Gospel Birds came to LW Lutheran last week. Attendance had been poor at Wednesday night prayer meeting and Bible reading, so the elders had gone to a Christian talent agency which also offered them Brother Flem Hospers, the world's tallest evangelist, and the Singing Whipples, who play among the six of them thirty-seven musical instruments, and Rev. Duke Peterson, former runner-up for Mr. Minnesota and champion weight lifter whose use of bodybuilding drugs reduced him to the level of a wild animal and almost led to his death — he was dead for six and a half minutes and saw visions of the other side, but then he was revived and entered the ministry. On Wednesday night, it was Ernie and Irma and the Performing Gospel Birds who walked into the sanctuary, a full house, each of them covered with birds — doves, canaries, parakeets, a couple of parrots, a crow — there must've been forty birds perched on them, and all the birds were singing at the tops of their voices. It was awesome. So beautiful. Then Ernie bowed his head to pray and the birds were quiet. Not a peep. And it was a long prayer. He prayed that those who had come to mock and scoff would have their hearts opened to the message. That shut them up in back, in the scoffers' seats.

The birds did some tricks: some did acrobatics and walked a tightrope blindfolded, and the parrots talked — Scripture verses — and the canaries picked out a couple of hymns on a xylophone, which was nice. Ernie told the story of Noah; meanwhile Irma got the birds dressed as elephants and lions and llamas and horses and other animals walking two by two into the ark, and then from the back of the sanctuary — and who knows how it got back there — a dove swooped over their heads and circled the room three times. It descended on the ark, and the ark opened and all the birds rose from it in a cloud. It was good. They did the Nativity, and the parable of the Prodigal Son, and the Last Supper, and you were sort of afraid they'd do the Crucifixion, but they skipped that, and did the Rapture instead, which was like Noah's Ark but with different lighting. Then the birds took up the collection. They flew around and took the dollar bills out of your fingers on the fly and brought them forward — pretty exciting — and someone held up a fifty-cent piece, and a parakeet took that and lost altitude suddenly but somehow made it back to port.

It was about a forty-five-minute program, and everything in it was absolutely memorable. Ernie and Irma talked about when they were children, which was sad — they were poor and they were lonely, and birds were so lovely and graceful and free. Ernie said he sat and watched birds for hours, and then one day a bird landed on his shoulder and he felt it was the Holy Spirit blessing him in some mysterious way he could not understand but could only accept. For God's eye is on the sparrow; God knows if a sparrow falls, so we know that God is watching over us. And then four parakeets picked out that hymn on tiny silver bells: "I sing because I'm happy. I sing because I'm free. For his eye is on the sparrow. And I know he watches me." It was lovely. Two-part harmony.

And then Ernie said, "And now, to close our program, I'd like you to feel that same thrill I felt when the bird landed on my shoulder. I'd like every head bowed and every eye closed as all of us contemplate God's great love in our lives, and when the bird comes to you and lands on your shoulder, if you feel that special blessing in your heart, I'd ask you to stand at your seat. You don't need to come forward. Just stand where you are. And now, the Blessing of the Birds."

The Lutherans of Lake Wobegon are a very cautious bunch and it lent a certain excitement to meditation to close your eyes knowing that a bird was about to land on you and wondering which one. Minutes passed in silence as people got down to the business of meditation and thoughts of divine providence came to mind — ways in which their lives had been supported and upheld by powerful love outside themselves; powerful evil resisted despite the desire to follow it; acts of love and kindness they had felt called to despite embarrassment; and more than that, a presence of grace in the world that is almost beyond our comprehension. Then they heard a rush of wings as if angels were in the room, and one by one felt a light weight on their shoulders as if someone tapped them, and one by one stood, eyes closed, and felt not only touched by this but filled somehow. They were stunned, especially the ones who had come to be amused and make fun of the performance. Something had happened; they weren't sure what, but something. Everyone agreed that it had been a mysterious experience.

■ ■ ■ ■

For everyone except Ernie and Irma. They'd worked this show for twenty-seven years and seen the Blessing of the Birds too many times to be moved by it. Their take was almost $300 including CD and postcard sales, and that was good for a Wednesday night. Irma wants to retire. The preaching bothers her and all the Jesus stuff; she's Unitarian. Unfortunately, people of her persuasion don't go for a performing bird troupe. So they're forced to work among evangelicals. And there they are in the front seat of their van as they drive out of town, heading for Aitkin, and the last we see of them is Ernie grasping the wheel, big and impassive, staring straight ahead, and Irma leaning toward him, telling him something. Something long and involved. And a dove on her shoulder.

6.

Pontoon Boat

I went out on the lecture circuit when I was going through an expensive divorce and loved it immediately — a bare stage, a microphone on a stand, a stool, a glass of water — and stayed on the circuit even after the bills were paid. It was beautiful. You go out for a week or two, one-nighters, performance at night, up at dawn to catch a plane to a hub city and another plane to the next town, a fresh motel room, a nap, a light lunch, and then off to the stage. I had once told a story on the radio about a boatload of Lutheran pastors that tipped over on Lake Wobegon and I worked this up — added an old aunt and a hot-air balloon and a boy on a parasail towed by a powerboat — and it became a nearly perfect ninety-minute performance piece that I trotted around about a hundred times. I had the whole thing by heart and it worked like a precision instrument, the laughs came right on time and they built toward big boffo laughs at the end and I could see men and women wheezing and leaning up against each other, weakened by merriment. The problem with a piece as good as that is: nothing you do afterward seems good enough. You go out on the road with your new piece, which is about aging, and your old fans come up afterward and say, "We saw you a couple years ago the time you told the story about the pontoon boat. My gosh, we laughed all the way home." I worked up the piece into a full-blown novel, which got a good, thoughtful review in *The New York Times.* It is an honor to be read carefully, an honor one does not always deserve, and of course you can understand if the reviewer cannot resist the temptation to torpedo you — it's the witty put-downs that are quoted and remembered, the tributes are mostly forgotten — but the reviewer of *Pontoon* said that Lake Wobegon stories were neither nostalgic nor gentle but contained sadness and dread, and to be taken seriously by another writer made me happy for days afterward.

My aunt Evelyn was an insomniac, so when they say she died in her sleep, you have to wonder about that. At any rate, she died in her little stucco house in Lake Wobegon, in her own bed, under a blue knit coverlet, reading a book about Utah, where she was planning to travel soon. She was eighty-two. She had gone out that evening with her buddies Gladys and Margaret to the Moonlite Bay supper club, where she enjoyed the deep-fried walleye and a slab of banana cream pie, along with a mai tai and a Pinot Grigio. Three old Lutheran ladies, sitting at a table by the window and laughing themselves silly over the chicken salad Margaret's nephew brought to the Fourth of July picnic, which had been sitting in the rear window of his car for a few hours, and the waves of propulsive vomiting it caused. Men mostly. Big men so sick they couldn't hide; they had to stand and empty their stomachs right there in plain view of their children. The ladies chortled over that and then they took up Gladys's husband, Leon, who had discovered Viagra and now, after a ten-year layoff, was up for sex. Viagra gave him a hard-on like a ball-peen hammer. "Or in his case, like a Phillips screwdriver," said Gladys and they all cackled. Scheduling was an issue. He preferred mornings.

"The other day I had bread in the oven and I told him I had to go check it — I was baking for the Bible school bake sale — he said, 'Don't go! Don't go! I'm coming!' Then he kept at it for another five minutes — I said, 'Jesus, if you can't come just say so.' He got all mad then, said it was hard being married to someone who didn't care for sex and who kept poking holes in his confidence."

"Who's poking holes?" cried Margaret and they all three gasped and wheezed — *O God — O God I am going to die — don't make me laugh like that, I swear I'm going to wet my pants.* The busboy heard all this and was quite surprised. A good boy from a nice home. And then Evelyn said, "Tell him if he needs to hump something, you'll thaw out a chicken." And Margaret laughed so hard a whole noseful of something shot out. The busboy retreated to the scullery. The ladies wiped their eyes. *Oh I swear I am never having dinner with you two again, you are a bad influence. A bad influence.*

And they drove back to town in Margaret's car and Evelyn got out at her house on McKinley Street and leaned on the car and said, "See you Wednesday." There was a full moon and she stood and admired it and headed for the house. She stopped and pointed to her moon shadow on the walk and danced a couple steps as if to elude it and that was the last anyone saw of her. She was wearing a denim wraparound skirt and a white blouse embroidered with roses and a silky red vest and sandals, and she danced in the moonlight and went indoors to lie down and die.

Uncle Jack had died nineteen years before, leaving behind a basement and garage full of his accumulations, which had taken her months to disperse, and she didn't want to burden Barbara with the same grim chore. Barbara lived three blocks away, up the street from Our Lady of Perpetual Responsibility, alone since Lloyd drifted away to the Cities and Kyle went to college. "When I die," Evelyn told her, "I want you to be able to sweep out the place, take the sheets off the bed and the clothes out of the closet, clean out the medicine chest, and hang out a For Sale sign. Two hours and you'll be rid of me. I'm a pilgrim. I travel light."

Barbara found Evelyn's body, lying in bed, faceup, green eyes staring vacantly at the ceiling, long tan arms at her sides, red lacquered nails, blue blanket up to her waist. Barbara is what you might call tightly wound, not the person you'd choose for the job of finding dead people. She shrieked, clutched at her mother's hand, shrank back from the bed, knocked a lamp off the bedside table, yelped, and ran out of the room and into the kitchen, where she tried to collect herself. She breathed deeply, once, twice, again, again, and told herself to be calm. Nobody had murdered Mother. Then she looked around for a drink.

In recent years Barbara had developed a crème de cacao problem. She liked to pour it on her breakfast cereal; it put her in a gentler place. She climbed up on the step stool to look in Mother's cupboards for liquor, and found a bottle of Kahlúa, unopened. She got out a jelly glass, filled it up to the third fish and drank it down, and went back in the bedroom. She opened the top drawer of the night stand and riffled through the clippings and postcards and aspirin packets and a poem on an index card — one of Mother's poems. . . .

Life is not land we own.
O no, it is only lent.
In the end we are left alone
When the last light is spent.
So live that you may say,
Lord, I have no regret.
Thank you for these sunny days
And for the last sunset.

Not a great poem, if you ask me, thought Barbara. *Sorry, Mother.*

Under it was an envelope labeled AR-RANGEMENTS. She opened it. The letter

120

was typed on thin blue paper with PAR AVION printed below and a French flag.

Dear Barbara,

   In the event of my death I want you to make arrangements as follows: I wish my body to be laid out in the green beaded rhinestone dress that was a gift from my dear friend Raoul the week we spent in Branson, Missouri. —

Barbara stared at the name. Raoul. Who he? Mother had never mentioned a Raoul. There were none in town. A boyfriend. Mother had a boyfriend. Good God.

— I would like someone to be sure to let Andy Williams know that "the lady in the green beaded dress" died and that his kiss on the cheek was one of the true high points of my life. I wish to be cremated. I do not wish to be embalmed and stuck in the ground to rot. I wish my ashes to be placed in the green bowling ball that Raoul also gave me, which somebody can hollow out (I'm told), and then seal it up, and I would like the ball to be dropped into Lake Wobegon off Rocky Point where Jack and I used to fish for crappies back years ago when we were getting along. I do not wish any eulogy or public prayers said for me, none at all, thank you, and the only music I want is Andy Williams singing "Moon River," which was "our song," mine and Raoul's, and I'm sorry to have kept all this a secret from you. I am so sorry that you never met him. He is an old dear friend who I reunited with about twelve years ago. We loved each other and we had some high old times. I realize that these are unusual wishes but you are a strong girl and I know you will respect them. I love you, dear. I always did and I do now, more than ever. Please forgive me.

Love,
Mother

Barbara pulled the sheet up over Mother's face as she had seen people do in movies. She dialed Kyle's number at his apartment in Minneapolis. He picked up on the third ring. He sounded distracted. Kyle was a sophomore at the University, studying engineering, and he studied all the time.

"It's Mother, honey. I'm awfully sorry but I have bad news. Grandma died."

"Omigod." He let out a breath. "When did she die?"

"She died in her sleep. Last night. It must have been sudden. She was reading a book and she just died. I know it's a shock. Me too. I just walked in and there she was. She must've had a heart attack."

Barbara said that Grandma was not afraid of death, she looked it straight in the eye, and don't you think she had such a good life because she knew life was short and that pushed her to do more than most people her age would dream of.

"When's the funeral?" Kyle asked.

"Well, that's what I called you about." And she read him Mother's letter. Word for word.

"That is so awesome," he said. "Wow. A bowling ball!! You mean, like a real bowling ball?"

"I found it in her closet. It's green. Like green marble. Expensive. It looks Italian."

"And no eulogy, no prayers. Boy. She had a whole other life, didn't she."

"I am just a little worried about this Raoul. What if he shows up?"

"Of course he'll show up. We'll invite him. He was her boyfriend. He loved her." Kyle sounded a little giddy. "God, Grandma! I always thought she had something else going on!"

"You think we should? Really? I don't know what to do," said Barbara.

"We're going to do it just exactly the way she wanted it," he said. "I'm going to do it myself." He was all excited now, bouncing around and yipping about his parasail — the one he had built from a kit — he was going to *fly* that bowling ball out over Lake Wobegon and drop it in from a great height.

Kyle's friend Duane Dober had an 18-foot speedboat with a 75-horsepower outboard. Duane wore pop-bottle glasses and lived in dread that a ray of sun might catch a lens and burn a hole into his brain and leave him a helpless cripple who makes ashtrays from beer cans, so he wore long-billed caps and stayed out of the sun as much as possible but he loved to race around in his boat with the prow up in the air and smoke dope and listen to the Steel Heads. When Kyle called and said, "I need you to tow my parasail so I can deposit my grandma's ashes in the lake," Duane said, "Hey. Count me in."

The man from Waite Park Cremation Service arrived, shortly after noon. Barbara had polished off the Kahlúa. The phone rang and it was someone asking if she was satisfied with her current long-distance provider. "We're thrilled," she said. "Couldn't be happier." She didn't call Aunt Flo to tell her

Mother was dead. In fact she locked the doors and pulled the shades for fear Flo'd barge in and take over. She was a great one for grabbing hold of something you were doing and saying, "Here, let me do that," and wresting it out of your hands — "That's not how you do that" — a rake, a screwdriver, a mixer: the woman would not let you so much as *whip cream with a Mixmaster* even though you were sixty years old and had raised a child, nonetheless *you were not to be trusted.*

The man from the crematorium arrived in a plain old black delivery van, no name on the side. He was young, but of course everybody was nowadays. His name was Walt. He held a folded plastic bag under one arm.

"Where is your mother?" She pointed to the bedroom door. He had a fold-up gurney, a skinny thing the size of an ironing board. The phone rang just as he emerged from the bedroom with Evelyn zipped up in a plastic bag and wheeled her out the back door. The shock of seeing this — the house suddenly empty — she picked up the phone and it was Flo saying, "What is going on? What is that truck doing in the alley? Speak up!" and Barbara sobbed, "My mommy's dead."

Flo pulled up in front two minutes later, her hair in curlers, as the truck pulled away in back. She'd been at the Bon Marche Beauty Salon, having it blued. She was hopping mad. She took one look at Barbara and said, "You're a souse, that's what you are! You need to get a grip on yourself. Where is Evelyn?" She went into the bedroom and found Walt's business card and came charging out and glared at Barbara and shook her fist. "Sending your mother to be burned up like she was garbage. Why didn't you just chop her up with an axe and throw her in the incinerator? You ought to be shot." And Flo called up the crematorium and left a long message on the machine, to get the hell back with her sister Evelyn's body unless he wanted to be in court that evening. "Driving around preying on the grief-stricken who happen to be intoxicated, too —"

Barbara pulled out her mother's letter and handed it to Flo. Flo read it and looked up, aghast.

"You should have burned this. If you had an ounce of common sense, you would've put a match to it and buried it in the garden. This is just outrageous. I ought to wring your neck." And then Flo put her old wrinkled face in her hands and sobbed.

"What has this family come to? We'll never be able to hold our heads up in this town again. A bowling ball! People will think we are fools, no better than the Magendanzes. I wish I had dropped dead rather than know this. Why couldn't God have taken me first?"

She looked up at Barbara, her old eyes full of tears. "Who is this Raoul?"

Out on the sidewalk three little girls were playing jump rope, two twirling and one in the middle jumping, and the two were chanting:

Little Joe ate some snow
He got a part in a movie show
Had a claw
On his paw
Ha ha ha he was Dracula.
Blood was dripping
Down his chin
How many crypts does he live in?
One, two, three, four, five . . .

Two hours after Barbara found Evelyn dead in bed, Debbie Detmer drove into town in a blue Ford van and pulled into her parents' driveway and started unloading her bags, expensive ones, blue leather. She had come to town to get married on Saturday to

Mr. Brent Greenwood, thirty-nine, of Sea Crest, California. The Detmers lived three blocks from Evelyn's little bungalow but they hadn't heard about her death yet. They had been out of the social whirl ever since January when Mr. Detmer slipped and banged his head. He was toweling off after his shower while watching the *Today* show on the tiny TV Betty gave him for Christmas and he stepped into his underpants and caught his big toe on the elastic band. He hopped a few times, reluctant to give up on it, and fell and concussed himself against the side of the tub, and it had made him forgetful. He started calling his wife "Mother" instead of Betty.

Debbie was lithe and lean, her hair red and spiky. She had flown in from California, where she had lived since dropping out of Concordia College. Fifteen years earlier, she had taken a philosophy course on Kierkegaard, who fired up her jets and convinced her that she was a pilgrim, and she headed for San Francisco. She first worked in a topless bar, a good Lutheran girl serving drinks to old men who ogled her spheres of existence. A month later, she hitchhiked north to Bolinas and a Christian ashram, clothing optional — Scripture said, "Think not what ye shall wear" — and she got into meridians. And then she became a veterinary aromatherapist at All Creatures Wellness Center, treating puppy dogs and kitty cats with eucalyptus and peppermint and chamomile, and earned buckets of money and met Brent. He was the only heterosexual male in her yoga class — or at least willing to give it a shot — and the wedding was all set for Saturday. The same day that Kyle and Barbara planned to fly Evelyn's ashes in a bowling ball over Lake Wobegon and drop it into the water.

Debbie went all out for her wedding. She rented Wally's pontoon boat, the *Agnes D,* and made a big banner, CELEBRATION OF COMMITMENT, to hang on it. She laid in crates of giant shrimp shish kebabs and wheels of imported cheese and fifty pounds of French pâté with peppercorn crust and cases of French champagne. She talked the Sons of Knute into lending her two of their giant duck decoys, 18-foot fiberglass numbers in which the hunter lay on his back inside the duck and pedaled the drive shaft that turned the propeller as he looked out through a periscope in the duck's neck, scanning the skies for incoming ducks, and when they came in for a landing, the hunter sprang up and threw open a trapdoor in the tail of the duck and blasted away from there.

129

The Ingqvist twins would pedal the ducks, following the pontoon boat, and strew flower blossoms out the ducks' tails. And after the vows were said aboard the *Agnes D,* Debbie's ex-boyfriend Craig would descend in his hot-air balloon and pick up Brent and Debbie and take them away — free! Drifting with the wind! Craig was her classmate who'd persuaded her to take the philosophy course and now he taught geometry in St. Paul and flew hot-air balloons.

It was going to be a beautiful wedding and then on Wednesday it all collapsed. Brent arrived in a bad mood, having dropped his cell phone in the urinal at the airport. He had left his favorite dark glasses on the plane and then the liquor store in St. Cloud didn't have his brand of gin, Bombay, and as the limo drove him along Main Street, past the Mercantile and the Sidetrack Tap and the Chatterbox and Ralph's Pretty Good Grocery, he felt like a door was slamming shut and he was going to start living the wrong life. When he heard about Craig the ex and the hot-air balloon, he told Debbie, "That's it. This is not me. Let's not take this any further." She called him an asshole and ordered him out of town.

"Whatever," he said.

So the wedding was off.

Debbie left her parents with the champagne, the pâté, the cheese, the giant shish kebabs, and headed back to California. The Detmers, after a night of confusion and dismay, called up Pastor Ingqvist and donated the whole kit and caboodle to the Lutheran church, which — to him — felt like God working in mysterious ways His wonders to perform. Lake Wobegon Lutheran was responsible for entertaining a group of twenty-four Lutheran pastors from Denmark on Saturday and he had just remembered it on Tuesday night, that he'd need to put together some sort of elegant lunch for Saturday, and here was the solution to his problem, dropped in his lap.

The Danes were on a two-week tour of the United States, having been sent over by the Danish church because they had signed a profession of doubt as to the divinity of Jesus — so they had been packed off on a junket to America for a cooling-off period.

Barbara had got wind of the Detmer nuptial cancellation but she knew nothing about the arrival of twenty-four Danes. She had located Raoul in Minneapolis and he was on his way, and then she had a sudden thought that maybe they should postpone the memorial until after dark. "We could just row her out at midnight and drop her over the gunwales," she said to Kyle. "Why do we need to do it from a great height?"

He shook his head. He'd gone to a lot of trouble: Why back out now? Grandma had a flair for drama, she went in for shooting off rockets at midnight on Christmas Eve. You sang "Deck the Halls" and lit the fuses and a trail of sparks whooshed into the winter sky. Birthdays were big, large packages with bows and ribbons, stripey hats, horns blatting, and "Happy Birthday" *and* "For He's a Jolly Good Fellow" *and* the Minnesota Rouser, everybody marching around the table banging on pans and then the birthday boy and Grandma hooked little fingers and farted for good luck. Grandma was no wilting lily.

"The ladies in the Bon Marche are going to feast on this," said Barbara. "They'll be cackling for a week."

"So let 'em cackle. Who cares?" he said.

Aunt Flo called to ask what time the service would begin. "It's not a service," said Barbara. "Mother didn't want one, remember? Anyway, we hope to get going around eleven." And then she said, "We'd love to see you and Al there." Poor Flo was a changed woman. The news of Evelyn's

132

secret romance with Raoul had humbled her. The bossy quarrelsome Flo who relished a good sharp retort, the Flo who could bring you to tears — that battle-axe Flo had been replaced by a sweet Flo who dropped by on Friday with a basket of peanut-butter cookies. She handed it to Barbara, who said, "Come in." "I can't," said Flo, and then she did. And once she got inside, she melted into tears. She sat on the couch and bawled and Barbara held her in her arms and after ten minutes, Flo got up and said, "Thank you," and left.

Raoul arrived in town around 9 a.m. Dorothy saw the maroon Pontiac pull up in front of the Chatterbox and the old man in mirror shades climb out. He wore yellow plaid pants and lizard-green shoes and a sportcoat that looked as if it had been made from the skins of a thousand rainbow trout. It had a liquid glitter to it that caught the eye. Below it was a Hawaiian shirt, tails out. Pink hibiscus. Certainly festive. He took off the mirror shades and put on blue-tinted glasses. He was smoking a small cigar and carried a boom box that was quietly playing, an opera tenor singing love songs in Italian.

The bus carrying the Danish clergy rolled

up in front of the Chatterbox Café at eleven a.m. and the door opened and up stepped a sandy-haired man in T-shirt and jeans. The T-shirt said "Lutherans: It could be worse."

"I'm David Ingqvist," he said. He climbed aboard the bus and said something to them in Danish that made them all laugh.

And then a parade of people came marching around the corner, led by a gaunt man in a Viking helmet with horns and wearing a cape and a silken sash with blue fringe, followed by a woman in a blue robe carrying a green bowling ball, a man in a sparkly sportcoat, a young man in red swim briefs and flip-flops carrying an enormous red parasail, a young woman playing Dvořák's "Going Home" on the trombone, and an old coot waving a couple of sparklers. Plus a gaggle of others, most of them elderly, including an old lady in a purple pantsuit, wearing a jet-black wig and scratching her butt. They crossed Main Street and disappeared behind a brick building with manikins in the window.

The Danes came trooping off the bus, all twenty-four, and Pastor Ingqvist led them across the street and down the lake bank to the pontoon boat, the *Agnes D,* with a sign hanging from the rail, *Celebration of Commitment.* Two dozen bottles of Moët champagne sat in three big washtubs full of chipped ice, and smoke rose from the barbecue in the stern, where giant shrimp shish kebabs were grilling. Wheels of cheese and tubs of pâté and a basket of baguettes sat on a white cloth on a table along the port side.

"Lunch aboard ship!" he cried. *"Frokost paa skibben."* Their eyes brightened. They moved slowly down the dock toward the boat.

"I am attending a memorial service for an old parishioner at noon," he said, "so help yourselves, enjoy the champagne, take it easy, and I'll be back and we'll go for a cruise."

The boat, he noted as the Danes trooped aboard, was riding rather low in the water, but there was no time to worry about that.

The Evelyn memorial troupe had gathered at the other end of the lake. The bowling ball was cradled in Barbara's left arm, a chain attached to it. Raoul had the boom box in hand, and Aunt Flo and Uncle Al stood by, silent, dabbing at their eyes, Flo in dark glasses for possibly the first time in her entire life. Enormous wraparound goggles that made her look extra-terrestrial. They stood together in tall grass at the edge of the rocky beach and looked across Lower Lake Wobegon toward Duane in his silver runabout, the motor idling, emitting blue smoke, his pop-bottle glasses shadowed by the great brim of his yachtman's cap. Kyle adjusted the trapeze of the great parasail, which Mr. Hoppe, in his Viking outfit, and Wally of the Sidetrack were holding gingerly by the tips of the wing. Kyle had set the waterskis in the water. He wore a fluorescent green Velcro belt around which he would wind the chain that was fastened to the setscrew he had drilled into the bowling ball. He explained that he was making last-minute adjustments to guard against a sudden nosedive.

"Darling," said Barbara, "Grandma would be horrified if you hurt yourself doing this, you know that. She didn't specify that she be *flown,* honey." He looked rather fragile in his red swim briefs, her pale slender dappled son with the light down on his arms and legs shining in the sun, sliding the aluminum trapeze assembly a few inches aft on the bracing struts. "Shouldn't you be wearing a life jacket?"

"I'll be harnessed in. Don't worry about it."

A quarter-mile away, the Danes were on

their third glass of champagne, which was lovely with the Camembert and the Raclette and the lovely pâté. Half of them stood on the *Agnes D* and the others on the dock, studying the little town spread out on the slope, the high brick bell tower of the Catholic church, the lesser wood steeple of the Lutheran, the blue and brown and green roofs of houses. "Why is there so little color in America?" cried one. "Is there a fear of color?" "A fear of art and culture, if you ask me," said another.

And then a mangy yellowish Labrador came walking along the shore. The dog stank to high heaven. You could almost see stink waves rising from his scraggly bur-infested fur. He was carrying a dead fish in his mouth and it appeared to have been dead for a long time. The head hung by a thread and then fell off as the dog strolled down to the dock and headed for the Danes.

The dog was deaf and practically blind. He had a lot on his mind, having been to the town dump and foraged there and found nothing, an old mattress, some rope, gunny-sacks of junk from the garages of dead farmers. He had picked through it all and found nothing worthwhile. He was hungry. His name was Bruno and he was eighteen years old and a legend in the town. As a pup, he had caught a two-pound walleye while wading in the shallows and he had wrestled it to shore and hauled it to Inga, his owner. He carried the fish by its tail, four blocks to Inga's front porch, set it down, and barked. She made a big fuss over him. His picture was in the paper. She cooked the fish for him and let him sleep on the couch. This imprinted him with his mission in life, to catch big fish. He had been wading in the shallows ever since and had not matched his early success. The only fish he brought home were ones who lay on the beach or floated on the water. Inga turned against him, and so did everyone else in town. "Get the hell out of here, Bruno!" people yelled whenever they saw him. He was rejected on every hand, like an old drunk, on account of his rank odor of rot and mildew and algae, but he persisted. Half his teeth were gone, his eyes were rheumy, his ears leaked pus, but the dog kept fishing, and now he made his way toward these interesting men who smelled fresh to him, who had never rejected him, hoping to find a pat on the head, a scratch on the belly.

The Danes smelled him right away and turned and stiffened. One of them shouted at the dog in Danish, which didn't impress him. One of them waved a giant shish kebab at the dog but that only piqued his interest. As he approached the boat, the Danes on the dock, cornered, decided to go aboard, all of them, in a big rush, and to cast off the lines and start up the motor.

The boat almost sank under their weight. Water glittered on the deck and a few pastors cried out a warning and then one succeeded in starting the motor and revved it up and away went the *Agnes D,* its deck awash but making slow progress. The Danes crowded in tight in the middle, so as not to push the bow any lower or to bump into the barbecue in the stern, the red coals glowing under the giant shrimp shish kebabs. It looked like twenty-four men walking on water, carrying an awning and towing a barbecue.

At the lower end of the lake, Kyle had attached the bowling ball to himself, wrapping the chain around the green Velcro belt, and Duane had thrown the towrope out of the stern of the runabout and the show was about to start. For a moment, Barbara considered making a speech — *Mother was a free-thinker, it's as simple as that. There is no God, we are free agents, each one of us, and if you want to go around with a big knapsack of guilt on your back like a person in a cartoon, okay, but I choose to be free, just as my mother, in a lucid moment, wanted you to know that she is free.* But she did not.

"Okay, Grandma," said Kyle, "let's get the show on the road."

He waded gingerly into the water, on the sharp rocks, harnessed to the trapeze, the great parasail above him, and he staggered a couple times, pushing the skis ahead of him with his feet and then his knees until he was in water up to his thighs. He sat down and slipped his feet, first the left, then the right, into the foot holsters. Then Duane gunned the motor and the towrope went taut and Kyle rose up on the water and skied over the waves, his knees bent, the towbar lashed to the trapeze. The little crowd watched the slender figure in the red swim briefs go skimming across the water. As the boat made its turn, Kyle appeared to adjust the trapeze, the towbar clamped to it, as the bowling ball swung between his knees, and Barbara pulled out her camera. Raoul had a videocam out. "Here he comes!" said Raoul. But something was wrong — Kyle wasn't lifting off the water. Mr. Hoppe waved his arm in a circle to tell Duane to pick up speed. "He must've adjusted the trapeze wrong," said Barbara.

Then the speedboat swerved, and they saw

why — two giant fiberglass ducks were racing across the water, strewing pink flower petals from their butts. There were people inside, pedaling, propelling them crookedly, slewing around.

The speedboat was racing due north when it swerved again. The *Agnes D* had just come into view from behind the point, its deck crowded with men in pale blue and green and violet shirts and pants, a trail of black smoke rising from the barbecue. The men on deck were singing lustily what sounded like a hymn to alcohol, their arms linked, the boat riding extremely low in the water — but that troubled them not at all, they were brothers united by champagne. Loping along the shore, plunging through bushes and tall weeds, came Bruno the fishing dog, stink waves rising, a dead fish in his mouth. The *Agnes D*'s prow was a couple inches above water and the engine was almost submerged. It gave off a sucking and sobbing sound. Duane cut sharply to the left to avoid the pontoon boat and at that moment Kyle lost his balance, the bowling ball between his legs swung to the right and he fell, still harnessed to the trapeze — Barbara cried out, *"Jesus Christ"* — the skis flew off him and he disappeared under the parasail, which came skimming over the waves with him in the harness, dragged at high speed underwater. They could see his pale body racing submerged through the water — "Stop! Stop!" Barbara cried — and then they saw his red swimsuit and the Velcro belt and the green bowling ball, all three, torn from his body by the sheer force of the water — and then the parasail lifted into the air, carrying Kyle aloft. He hung from the trapeze, entangled in the towrope, stark naked, his legs pedaling, fifty feet in the air, and that blind idiot Duane at the controls cranked the speedboat directly in front of the pontoon boat, whose drunken crew stopped singing now and clutched the rails as the *Agnes D* pitched violently left to right in the speedboat's wake. The Danes would've hung on except for the barbecue tipping over — hundreds of red-hot coals came skittering across the deck like a manifestation from the book of Revelation and over the rails the pastors dove. Twenty-four manly forms belly-flopped in the water — only five feet deep, thankfully — as the boat righted itself and plowed ahead toward the shore. Duane steered around the ducks, who had split up, and, still planing at high speed, he roared past the mourners and the naked young man flew by, arms spread, harness around his waist, high in the air, a big pink bird.

It appeared to Barbara that something about flying had excited her son — yes indeed that was most certainly true. Yes, that was certainly true — Flo and Al were waving and shouting at Duane to stop, meanwhile Raoul in his distress had pressed the PLAY button and Andy Williams sang "Moon River, wider than a mile, I'm crossing you in style someday" as the naked young man flew in the clear blue sky and the parasail banked and now a hot-air balloon came drifting at low altitude over the tree line.

"Oh dear God," said Barbara.

It was blue and green, silver and gold, a magnificent silken bag from which hung a golden wicker basket and the kerosene burner on a frame above it, a man in a white naval outfit and officer's cap, his hand on the rope that pulled the switch that fired the burner, scanning the water below for the wedding couple he was to scoop up and carry away, descending, descending. The naked Kyle spotted the balloon as Duane made the turn and the parasail appeared to be on a collision course with the balloon — Kyle let out a high-pitched yelp, but Duane was busy steering around the pastors floundering in the water and the giant ducks paddling in circles and the crewless pontoon boat.

Suddenly, there came a monstrous roar and a mighty flame burst from the burner of the balloon, the pilot attempting to ascend, but alas he overshot with the throttle and the flame ignited the bag, burned a hole through the top of it, and the rigging caught on fire, all in a few seconds, as the naked young man flew on, towed by the crazed Duane, and the ropes parted. The basket and burner and pilot dropped into the water with a great *kershroommm* — big pieces of burning silk drifted in the air like fiery sails and the naked boy heading straight toward them threw his weight to the left and the parasail banked and missed the flaming silk by inches — a little burst of dark cloud appeared where he emptied his bowels — and flew on.

The two giant ducks came aground nearby. The Danes came straggling out of the water — one of them, stepping on a chain, fetched up the bowling ball and brought it to shore, where Raoul took it in his arms, weeping, Andy Williams still singing about the river and the huckleberry friends — and finally Duane saw his friend, naked, flying helpless, and he made a beeline for shore. He promptly caught the edge of

144

the sandbar and ran aground, shearing the pin, and the towrope snapped, and the naked man glided overhead on his parasail. He glided over the mourners, a great shadow passing on the ground, and cleared the spruce trees behind them, and set down in the field beyond, where Mr. Hansen had his raspberry bushes. He yelped twice and then was silent.

Al turned to go to the rescue, but Barbara put a hand on his arm and said, "Let him be. Kyle likes to do things himself." She looked out at the lake strewn with wreckage and dotted with survivors and thought that it was the most exciting day she had spent in years. She was exhilarated. Most memorial services she'd ever attended were quiet sodden affairs and Mother's was nothing but gangbusters. Pastor Ingqvist was hauling these foreign men out of the water slopping and dripping and muttering things in their singsong guttural tongue and Duane waded to shore pulling his speedboat behind him saying that he wished people would watch where they were going for Chrissake and the Ingqvist twins climbed out of the giant duck decoys and explained that Debbie paid them $25 apiece to do it and what were they supposed to do with these ducks now? And the man in the white sailor suit towed his basket and burner up on the rocks and said that whoever had planned this wedding had done a pretty lousy job of it and he regretted ever having agreed to be in it. It would be the last favor he would ever do for anybody, that was for sure.

The chaos was marvelous, Barbara thought.

"Are you all right?" It was Pastor Ingqvist, his hand on her elbow.

"Never been better in my life," said Barbara.

7.
WHAT HAVE WE LEARNED SO FAR?

When I attained my maturity, people started addressing me as Sir, and when I spoke, they got all hushed as if it were the invocation, which was deeply gratifying and also slightly unnerving. A person ought to know a few things by this stage of life. My life is a series of bad moves, interrupted by occasional bursts of good luck, and I am not so much wiser for it, but the things I've learned are more impressive if I put them in a list and number them.

1. There isn't a lot you can do but you ought to do that much and if you do you'll likely find there is more you can do and you should try to do that too. When all is said and done, there is more to be done and that goes without saying.
2. Acts have consequences and we are responsible for them even if we

didn't intend them. Be kind and exercise caution. Step on a crack and break your mother's back. Who knew it could happen? Anyway, it's your fault so quit your job and take care of the old lady and don't complain.

3. Don't stick beans up your nose. Life is too short for that and it's getting shorter every day. On the other hand, don't buy cheap shoes.

4. Be hospitable to strangers. You have been a stranger yourself and you will be again. Extend yourself. On the other hand, your home is your home, it isn't the bus station. Scripture says to give all you have to the poor, but if you did, then you would be poor and they'd have to give it back, and so on and so on. But anybody can afford to give 10%.

5. Your brain thinks it is smarter than you and when you go down a road you cannot resist and it turns out badly, your brain mocks you, heaps abuse on you, says "You should have listened to me." No. Good judgment is born from experience, especially experience that results from poor judgment. Only a fool

tries to outsmart himself.

6. It's good to dream, but the urge to perform is not in itself an indication of talent.

7. You can't live life all at once so take it one day at a time. The lust for domination does not make for a good life. The urge to be No. 1 leads to an echo chamber in a house of mirrors. Charisma is an illusion, and brilliance depends on who's writing the test. Find work to do that gives you pleasure and be prepared to be very lucky.

8. Put a big dish by the door, next to an electric outlet, and when you come home, put your car keys, your billfold, your extra glasses in the dish and plug your mobile phone into the outlet to recharge. In the time you'll save not looking for them in the morning, you'll be able to write *War and Peace*. Or the *Mass in B minor*.

9. Don't discuss a personal relationship with the other person. And don't refer to it as a relationship. Either it's a friendship or it's a romance or you're married or you're in business together or you're

related or you're neighbors. Intimacy is a mystery so don't treat it like an investment.

10. The rules for mothering and fathering are: keep your voice down; no sudden moves; don't crowd the child. Keep all thoughts of disaster to yourself. Find out how to enjoy being with your child and do that as often as possible even if it almost kills you.

11. Don't think ill of crazy people, you may be one of them. The same is true of Democrats.

12. No matter how much you want to keep your secret secret, you know that eventually people will find out so you should start now to think up a good story. The secret may be shameful but if you can make it interesting you'll be less an object of pity and scorn and that is good.

13. Take care of your friends, because there will come a time when you're not much fun to be with and there is no reason to like you except out of long-standing habit.

14. Do unto those who don't like you as you would have them do unto you but you know they won't. Do

this before they can do the shameless devious dirty deeds to you that they would do if given the chance. Shame them with goodness. Kill them with kindness. Cut their throats with courtesy.

15. Flattery is the reverse side of malicious gossip and this coin is very quickly flipped. Beware.

16. Be cheerful. It could be worse. Someday it will be. Be glad that it isn't yet.

17. Don't beat up on yourself. Endless contrition is a pain. Make your apology, repair the damage, hold your head up, and march on.

18. There is a lot of human nature in everybody, so if you're an idealist, don't go into politics or teaching. Try copyediting or library science. Cartography. Flower gardening.

19. People have made perfectly rational decisions that turned out to be dumber than dirt. There doesn't seem to be any way around this.

20. After the age of eighteen, if you want a big birthday party, you need to make it yourself. At twenty-one, you should start forgiving your parents for how you were raised.

When your first child comes along, you will know why.

21. Tall people cannot count on short people to look out for things they might bump their heads on. They have to take care of that themselves.

22. Never marry someone who lacks a good sense of humor. She will need it. It is a challenge to live intimately with your best-informed critic. Look before you leap.

23. Most tragedy is misunderstood comedy. God is a great humorist working with a rather glum audience. Lighten up. Whatever you must do, do it gladly. As you get older, you'll learn how to fake this.

24. Your friends are very fond of you but there are limits. Sadness is tedious. When discussing your troubles, be concise. Five minutes and then change the subject.

25. The way to get something done is to do it. The way to stop doing something is to not do it anymore. Not drinking is easy so long as you don't drink. If you can't make yourself do what you tell yourself to do, it's all over.

26. The best cure for a disastrous day

is to go to bed early and wake up fresh in the morning and start over. In fact, I am going to do exactly that right now. Good night.

8.
CHICKENS

My family really did slaughter chickens as described here, which, believe me, was highly unusual in Brooklyn Park Township in the early fifties. The neighborhood was getting built up, the cornfields divided into acre and half-acre lots, lovely lawns planted, patios, and here, in the midst of suburbanization, stood my father, axe in one hand, a chicken in the other. He had bought about two dozen birds from a farmer, transported them in gunnysacks in the back of a station wagon, kept them overnight in the garage, and in the morning he and Mother and I proceeded to kill them in the yard and clean and butcher them, wrap them in brown paper, and take them to a locker plant — where you could rent space in a walk-in freezer — and keep them for eating. My father had his own ideas about saving money and that was one of them. He'd grown up on a farm and slaughter to him was as ordinary as shoveling snow. The neighbors,

I'm sure, looked on it as savagery, and my mother was sensitive to their opinion, even unspoken. So that part of the story is truthful, and also my family's sensitivity to anesthesia: it makes us hallucinate. And who can say where hallucination may lead? And it is also the truth that my ancient mother was highly amused by this story about her and made a point of asking for a copy so she could hear it again.

Today is my mother's ninetieth birthday, and she called this morning to make sure I'm coming up for supper. Two years after Dad died, she misses him but doesn't talk about it, at least not to me. We talked about chickens instead. She wants filet mignon for supper and would I pick up some on my way? She hated it when we butchered chickens — she had the miserable job of plucking them and cleaning them. I was the chicken chaser and Dad chopped their heads off. Dad was a farm boy but Mother and I grew up in town and were more sensitive about killing. We were the last family in town to slaughter chickens, everyone else bought theirs at Ralph's Pretty Good Grocery, big white cold oblong things in plastic bags, but Dad said that store-bought chicken never tasted right to him. So we

155

butchered, in our backyard, a chopping block by the garage, two big pots of water boiling in the kitchen, the axe blade sharp, and me with a clothes hanger to hook them by the ankles. Small neighborhood children gathered to watch, much as people used to gather for public executions before Minnesota got civilized. The chickens had been herded into the garage the night before, to settle them down, and I could hear them grumbling in there. When I opened the side door of the garage, a volunteer chicken flew up in my face and escaped but I grabbed its companion and there was the first victim. I handed it to Dad and turned away and heard the *whack* and went for the next one. All the chickens had to die, so it wasn't like I had the power of clemency, but they seemed to think I did. They milled away from me where I stood in their midst, hook in hand, and I snagged one and she cried out, "Oh no, gosh no, please no, don't do this," and I carried her to my dad and turned my back, not wanting to watch as this creature, who had been alive in my hands just a moment before, now — *whack* — was gone from the face of the earth. Dad handed the corpse to Mother, who had filled a big boiler on the back step with steaming hot water, and she dipped the body in and ripped the feathers off and laid the naked corpse on newspaper to be cut open and gutted.

The crowd in the garage got smaller and smaller, six and five and four, and Dad dispatched them one by one, holding the legs in one hand, flopping it down on the block, the axe in the right hand already on the backswing and *whack* and the head drops like a cut flower and the blood trickles out in the dirt. We were down to the last chicken, and Dad said, "You do the next one." Okay, I said. I caught the chicken, the last witness to the massacre. Dad said, "Want me to hold it for you?" I shook my head. My mother said, "You be careful, now." Imagine going to bat against your first chicken, you cut your own foot off and walk funny the rest of your life, a stiff walk, like a chicken's.

I got a grip on the chicken's legs and swung it up on the block and hauled off with the axe and swung hard and missed by two inches. I had to pry the axe out of the wood and now I was mad. I swung again and missed and again and down it came dead center *whack* and at the same time I let go and the chicken took off running. It had no head. It dashed across the yard and out in the street and was gone — I never saw a chicken move so fast. I guess without the extra weight they can really go.

My dad explained afterward that when I missed the first time and planted the blade in the block, the blade got hot. So when I cut the chicken's head off, the blade cauterized the wound and stopped the flow of blood, and you had a running chicken in pretty good shape except with no brain.

We ran after it down the street and around the corner and spotted it racing through the flower bed and bouncing off a fence. Ran past a dog, who looked up and decided not to get involved. My dad and I were falling behind. The chicken was fast, heading downtown. We heard the squeal of brakes — two cars stopped and the headless chicken flapped across Main Street and up behind the Chatterbox Café toward Our Lady church, losing momentum, and Mrs. Mueller, loading up her garbage can, was able to grab it. "This your chicken?" she said. "What happened to it?" She didn't believe us when we told her. She thought we were carrying out a perverse experiment. Whenever she saw me after that, she shook her head and muttered something in German. And then a chicken with a head walked by. It was Chicken No. 1, the escapee, and we chased her, and she managed to fly up into a tree, a major achievement for a chicken. She was all tuckered out from the exertion and I climbed up and got her and she came without a struggle. Dad killed her. It was quite a morning.

It was around this time, or soon after, when he found a story I'd written in which I had invented a new dad for myself named Al who was a writer of adventure stories. It hurt his feelings — Dad's feelings, that is — and he didn't speak to me for weeks. He wanted me to do something useful in the world, like slaughter chickens or fix cars. "Aren't you curious to see how an engine works?" he said. No, I wasn't. I was curious about places I could go in a car, but not the car itself. He asked me once, "Whatever is going to become of you?"

It was a lovely birthday supper, just me and Mom. She had a glass of white wine, which was pretty bold of her. Had my siblings been there, she probably wouldn't have ordered wine, but dining with her prodigal son, she allowed herself a little slack. And for the first time in her life, she broiled her filet mignon medium rare instead of well done.

I asked her if she remembered the time I went to the hospital to sit with her while

she went under the anesthetic for the operation to inject camel cartilage in her knee so
she could go to the gun range again and
shoot clay pigeons. People in my family
don't react well to painkillers. She did not
remember that, though she remembered
how well the knee worked after that. And of
course she remembered trapshooting. It was
an emotional release for her. She had six
children and no hired help and did the
washing and cleaning and cooking, and at
the end of a long day, she'd take the shotgun
and a bag of tomatoes out behind the barn.
She'd toss them one by one, left-handed,
high in the air, and blow them to bloody
shreds, a couple dozen tomatoes in rapid
succession, and she came back feeling much
better.

"You told me all sorts of secrets when you
were going under," I said.

"Oh, I doubt that very much. I don't know
any secrets. Do I?"

"You talked about how you used to go out
to Annabel's farm near Cottage Grove with
Elsie and Genevieve and Flora and danced
to a Victrola and stayed up late talking and
made a vow that none of you would ever
marry and break up the gang and to defend
yourselves against men you learned how to
shoot. A hobo named Helge Gobel lived in

160

Annabel's barn and he had a rifle and showed you how and he fell in love with all four of you and he drove you four out to California in Annabel's Model A with a rumble seat and got to Santa Monica at midnight and walked across the beach and a woman in a green spangly suit came out of the water and it was Marion Davies the movie star and she knew Helge and invited you to stay at her beach cottage — and the next day you found out that Helge's younger brother Claus was Clark Gable. You went to his house for a party and Howard Hughes flirted with you and Helge socked him in the jaw and the next morning Mr. Gable put the four of you on the *Super Chief* to Chicago and the *Empire Builder* to Minneapolis."

"That is quite a story," she said. "I am thinking about the banana cream pie. Trying to decide between that and the blueberry pie with ice cream." She ordered the banana cream, which turned out not to be fresh, rather mushy and tasteless, a disappointment, but Mother is not one to complain. She would've eaten the whole lump of mush, but I insisted she order the blueberry. "And let this go to waste?" she said. "Yes," I said. So she did. It was a first for Mother. The blueberry was everything the banana

161

cream was not.

"Life is short," I said. "Get pleasure while you can."

"It is not short. Look at me."

"So did you go to California and meet Clark Gable?"

She took a deep breath. "If Elsie or Florence were around, I'd ask them. They remembered everything."

"So how does it feel to be ninety?"

She grimaced. Ridiculous question. "I wish I could get back to where I used to be. I would give anything to be eighty again."

She looked around the room, the big windows looking out on the lake at twilight, the candles on the long table at the end of the room and the eight people sitting around it. "I don't know who anybody is anymore."

"The Frauendiensts, the Schoppenhorsts, the Schmidts, and the Zieglers. You don't know them because they're Catholic."

She was getting sleepy, I could tell. "Does the name Frayne Anderson mean anything to you?"

"What should it mean?"

"When you were going under the anesthetic, you told me you dated him before you knew Dad. I asked you about him because I saw a picture from 1935 or so at Minnehaha Park of you with flowers in your hair and dancing with a man with a mustache who was not Dad and you were laughing. You told me it was Frayne Anderson and he played the ukulele and you and he used to sing, *Roses love sunshine, violets love dew, angels in heaven know I love you.* You used to go trapshooting with him and you said you might've married him except he didn't believe in the Resurrection. He was a theosophist and believed in the immortality of the soul and reincarnation, but not the Resurrection. So you broke up with him and Dad came along and you married him."

"Well, isn't that something. Frayne who?"

"Anderson. He was in the theosophists and he told you how the Gnostics of the third century believed that Jesus had commanded us all to be fishermen in a gospel called the Codex Angularis, written down by an apostle named Sandy, who liked to sleep on the beach. He was one of the original twelve, but they later revised it and took him out and put Judas Iscariot in because it made a better story. And Sandy said that nowhere had Jesus commanded anybody to work hard day after day. Jesus had said, Don't worry about what you shall eat or what you shall wear. Don't worry about money. Jesus didn't get up and go to

163

work in the morning. He did some teaching and preaching and healing and a lot of hiking, and he was a fisherman. But the men who put the New Testament together threw out a lot of what Jesus said, such as 'Blessed are they who fish for they shall have more time.' And 'Answer not when thy wives shall rebuke you, neither make reply. Keep silent. And again, I say, keep silent.' You told me all of that."

Mother said nothing. I don't think she even heard me. She was now half-asleep. I paid the check and Carolyn the waitress and I got her into the car and I drove her home and as we came up the driveway, she said, "I can't marry you, Frayne." I said, "That's okay. I understand." I helped her to the door and opened it. "Thank you for the evening, Frayne," she said. "Don't come in. I'll be fine." And I guess she was. I called her in the morning and she remembered the steak and the glass of wine. "Don't tell anybody about the wine," she said. "I hope I didn't get out of hand." Not at all, I said. Not at all.

9.

THE DEATH OF BYRON

My father died in March 2001 when I was in Dublin doing a show. He was eighty-eight. My sister Linda called regularly to tell me how he was doing and then he took a steep turn and she called to say he was close to the end and then somebody spoke to her from across the room and she said, "He's going. . . . I'll call you later." And he was gone. I sat in the hotel room and thought of him back in his late thirties, building our house, the whine of his power saw as he cut the two-by-fours and then the six-whap beat of his hammer as he nailed them up to make the studs and rafters. Once a month Dad sat me down on a saw-horse in the garage and cut my hair with scissors and a hand-clipper and tried to make small talk with me but I wasn't in the mood. I had gotten the notion that a home haircut meant we were poor. It was a gift of attention, to hold your son's head still and patiently trim a thick growth of hair, and now that he was dead I could appreciate this — the kid with the bedsheet wrapped around him, the man plying unfamiliar tools with great care to give the boy a respectable appearance, unwilling to spend money on personal vanity. This little wisp of memory of his hands on my head made me weep for my father in a Dublin hotel room. I repaid him for the haircuts by presenting him with his last grandchild, my daughter, four years before he died. She visited him toward the end when he lay in bed, and he wriggled his left big toe under the blanket and when she grabbed at it he moved his foot away and made her laugh. This game of hide-and-seek went on and on. All of his other pleasures were gone, but this one was as good as ever.

In *Wobegon Boy,* John is feeling weary and slow in New York when his father dies back in Lake Wobegon. John flies home to a town he had fled eagerly years before and is startled at how comfortable he feels there now. The small talk, the reticence, the food, the smell of home — he is slightly alarmed at how he, a rebellious son, fits in so well.

John's father died early on a Tuesday morning in mid-January. He was seventy-three. He collapsed on the basement stairs bringing a bag of frozen peas up from the freezer.

166

John was in New York, asleep, in bed with a young woman named Kyle, the daughter of his friend Ben. She sat up. His brother Bill was on the phone, telling him about the peas, and then Mother came on. "He said he wanted spaghetti for lunch and I said, Well, go down and get me a package of frozen peas, and he said, How about some hamburger, and I said, I got that in the fridge, so he went down and on his way up he sat down on the steps and died. I was on the phone with my sister and when I opened the door to the stairs, he lay there, he was just gone." She said he had seen a doctor in January — less than a month ago — and everything was fine.

"Well, listen. I'm going to jump in a cab and go out to LaGuardia and I'll be there by early afternoon. Okay?"

His first thought was that it was a sensible death: to die while still in good health, at home — not sink into geezerhood and shakiness and dementia. Just sit down and give up the ghost.

Bill had spoken to Ronnie in Dallas and Diana in Tucson and everybody would be flying to Minnesota that evening. "It's snowing like crazy," said Bill. The funeral would be on Saturday at the Lutheran church.

"I'm on my way," John said. "My dad

died," he said to Kyle and then noticed that she'd slept in the nude. Odd he hadn't noticed that before. "I've got to go back to Minnesota."

"Really?" She reached over and patted his hair and smoothed it down. "I'm sorry we didn't finish making love. We had such a nice start."

He headed for the bathroom and turned toward his living room lined with bookcases, the window looking out on Columbus Avenue. He walked into the kitchen and opened the refrigerator.

"This is so weird," she said. "I never was with someone when somebody close to them died. Were you close?"

"No," he said. "When you leave, could you slip the key back under the door? The cleaning lady comes Friday, so don't worry about the mess."

"When will you come back, do you think? I mean, just ballpark."

"I honestly don't know."

"I'd like to see you again."

He murmured something agreeable about that and she said, "Minnesota is in the Midwest, right?" He nodded. "Are you from, like, a city out there?"

"Small town."

"Oh. You don't seem like you're from a

small town."

"I am."

He went into the bathroom and closed the door behind him and peed. A small town courtesy. She knocked on the door. "Would you like to take a shower together?"

"I'm in a hurry, sorry," he said. Making out in a hot shower with a soapy girl twenty-five years younger than yourself on the morning your dad died: it didn't seem right. Not at all.

He packed his dark brown pinstripe suit and a white shirt and caught a cab to La-Guardia. The woman at the ticket counter gave him a look of pity, as if he wore a name tag that said: Dead Man's Son. The plane was packed. He curled up in a window seat, stuffed two pillows between the seat and the window, pulled the thin blanket over himself, and awoke as the plane taxied through gusts of blowing snow to the lighted windows of the Minneapolis–St. Paul terminal. A little line of drool trickled from the corner of his mouth. The woman in the seat ahead turned and gave him a look of disgust, and John guessed that he had been snoring.

He rented a black Pontiac and headed north on the Interstate, traffic creeping along at twenty-five miles an hour. The road felt frictionless, as if he were at the wheel of a destroyer on the North Atlantic and the shapes in the mist off to starboard weren't farmhouses but cargo ships in the convoy, and the windshield wiper was a sonar antenna tracking German U-boats. At any moment the whole thing could blow up, but a man's got to do his duty, and either you go forward or you go hide somewhere, and, yes, I believe we're going to win this war.

When he was a kid and the family drove home at night from visiting relatives in the Cities, John always stood behind the front seat, his chin next to his father's head, watching the parade of approaching headlights, their beams filling up the car with a big whoosh of light. Smelling his dad's hair oil, his aftershave, trying to get the feel of what it was like to be a man driving a car, John would have been happy to go all night. His dad steered with his left hand low on the wheel, thumb and finger on the spoke, and he never sped or tried to ace out other cars. He drove with his right arm across the seat back, and John watched, imagining driving, how the wheel felt, how it would be to be alone in your own car. Just you.

It was two in the afternoon when he reached Lake Wobegon, snow drifting in the streets, the house a dim shape in the storm, all the lights on, Mother in a gray housedress waiting at the back door. "How were the roads?" she asked. "Not that bad," he said. He kissed her on the cheek and she put her arms around him and they clung tightly to each other for a moment. "It's good to have you all safe under one roof," she said.

Everybody was there in the kitchen. Ronnie and Bill and Judy. Diana stood up to give him a hug. She had put on some weight since she became a vegetarian. Tears ran down her puffy cheeks. She wore a lacy white dress and big turquoise jewelry, earrings the size of juice glasses, enough beads to fill a bread box.

"Daddy's gone," she said. "We'll never see him again in this whole world."

Ronnie sat perched on the counter, in green pants and a short-sleeved shirt. His blond hair was cut short, and it glistened with oil, and his face was nicked from shaving. "Nice to see you," he said in his squawky voice. "Been a while." His legs dangled down, new white shoes with tassels, white socks.

Bill sat at the table, looking gray and haggard, his face slack, and John shook hands with him, and hugged Judy.

"Hi, stranger," she said.

"Would you care for spaghetti?" said

Mother, already filling a bowl with a long skein of pasta. She dumped a cup of red sauce over it and added another. She set it on the table, with a paper towel for a napkin. "Well," she said, looking around at their silent faces, "here we all are."

She told them the story again, that Dad died on the next-to-top basement step on his way upstairs from having taken a box of rubber binders to the basement that Mother had told him to get rid of, binders saved from his years of running the grain elevator, thousands of binders, a lifetime supply. While in the basement, he fetched a bag of peas from the freezer in the laundry room, which he kept full of hamburger patties, fish sticks, vegetables, hash browns, as a hedge against disaster. He also kept silver dollars in a flour sack stashed behind the paint cans under the basement stairs. And then disaster struck as he climbed the stairs. As he approached the top, Mother heard him gasp. She called to him, "What's the matter?" and he said, "Nothing. I'm all right." She was making spaghetti sauce. She put a little more seasoning in it, and then opened the door to the stairs a moment later, and he was gone, slumped against the wall, the bag of frozen peas in his right hand. His eyes were open and he was dead. She sat on the stair beside him and put her arm around his shoulders and smoothed his hair and kissed his cheek. She told him she loved him and always would love him. And then she took the frozen peas from his hand and took them up to the kitchen and put them in the refrigerator, and called the rescue squad. They came five minutes later and tried to revive him and Dr. DeHaven came over and pronounced him dead and had him taken to the funeral home, run by Dad's old buddy Mr. Lindberg.

Diana said, "He was unconscious and you took the peas from him before you called the rescue squad?"

"He didn't need an ambulance, he was dead," said Mother.

"But how did you know that?"

"He wasn't breathing. I checked his pulse."

"You didn't think you should call a doctor?" said Diana. She looked around at the rest of them. John ate his spaghetti. Bill and Judy drank coffee. They ate cookies from a box that the neighbors had sent over. A string hung over the table, a three-by-five index card (PANTRY LIGHT: DO NOT YANK) taped to it.

"Dr. DeHaven? No, it never occurred to me," said Mother. He had done a cardiogram on Dad a few weeks ago and said everything looked fine, said Mother.

"He sat there dead and your first thought was to make sure the peas didn't thaw?" said Diana.

"It was silly, wasn't it," said Mother. "I don't know why I even thought of it."

And then Diana clapped her hand to her mouth. "Those weren't the same peas —"

"Yes," said Mother. "Actually, they were. Of course they were."

She had put the peas in the spaghetti, with the tomato sauce. The death peas.

"We ate the peas Daddy held in his hand as he died?" Diana whispered.

"Dad touched everything in this house," said John. "You're sitting in his chair. What's the problem?"

He took a forkful and held it to his mouth, smelled the sweet uncomplicated sauce — it reminded him of when he was in sixth grade and his mother had the school send him home every day for lunch. She fed him her spaghetti and they had grown-up conversations. She told him how much she had loved her one year at the University of Minnesota. One year was all that Grandpa Petersen could afford. "I knew I must make the most of it," she said, "and get all I could in one year," so she attended every free lecture and concert, haunted the library, soaked up her classes, wasted no time making friends because she only had the one shining year.

"I want you to do something for me," she said. She held up a brown grocery bag. "Take this over to John Lindberg at the funeral parlor. These are the clothes I want Dad to be buried in."

John squinted at the bag.

"It's his work clothes," she said. "I want him buried in the clothes that we always saw him in. He hated suits and ties."

He and Bill walked up the street to Lindberg's. The snow had stopped falling, and a few conscientious souls were already out shoveling in the dark. It was a light, dry snow, and it glittered where the porch lights shone on it, and in the dark it glowed.

"I wonder what it's like to embalm people you've known all your life. To cut their arteries and drain out the blood and clean them up," said John.

"Let's not talk about it."

"But when you take over your dad's undertaking business in the small town where you grew up, you figure you're going to know the clientele."

"He never married, did he," said Bill.

175

John said, "Some people shouldn't."

Lindberg's was in the same old big white house with the curved veranda on Cleveland Street, a driveway alongside the house running under the little portico with the double door through which generations of Wobegonians had been carried for their funerals. The old black Cadillac hearse sat, nose out, ready to take Dad to church on Saturday and then to his grave.

They knocked at the back door, and Mr. Lindberg opened it. He was tall and plump, with a wild shock of white hair and watery blue eyes. He wore an old brown wool suit and a brown plaid shirt, a tuft of white hair poking up at the neck. He led them into his tiny kitchen. Beyond was the funeral parlor. The kitchen was his office, his larder, his den, and upstairs was his bedroom. He plopped down on a white kitchen chair and Bill took the other. John leaned against the counter. Mr. Lindberg gave them a sorrowful look.

"This is a hard one for me," he said. "I knew your dad long as I can remember." He took a deep breath. "We used to raise hell when we were kids, you know. I've been putting off working on him."

Mr. Lindberg offered them coffee. John said yes, and the old man poured a mugful and said, "How about some whiskey in it to keep the flies off you." John nodded, and the old man poured a wallop of whiskey in and handed it to him. John took a sip. The smell made his nose hairs tingle.

"Oh yes," said Mr. Lindberg, "your dad was a rambunctious young man before your mother settled him down. I remember when he took the pastor's Model A apart on Halloween and reassembled it in the church basement. I imagine you boys didn't hear about that."

"He told me about tipping over privies," said John.

Mr. Lindberg chuckled. "Torben Saetre. He used to get very apprehensive whenever Byron was around. Your dad used to drive a car that when you flicked a switch under the dashboard and revved up the engine, a flame six feet long blew out the tailpipe. We'd cruise around town and just amaze people.

"I remember your dad playing a joke on a guy on the football team named Finsen who was quite taken with himself and drove a red roadster, which he parked in front of school. Everybody was duly impressed, and one day your dad snuck out and threaded a wire loop into the upholstery in the driver's seat and ran the wire out the back. A couple nights later Finsen was parked by the train depot with his girlfriend, and your dad and I crept up from behind with a battery and waited until it got very quiet in the car and then the girl said something like, No, or Don't do that, and your dad touched that wire to the battery and it sent a thousand volts through the seat and poor old Finsen flew out the door like a pigeon out of the coop, and when he stopped, he discovered he had soiled his pants. Your dad and I took off running and we spent the summer working on threshing crews in North Dakota. It was a great summer. I heard that Finsen died young. Apoplexy, I believe."

Bill handed him the paper bag and said, "Well, we won't keep you, Mr. Lindberg. We came over with Dad's clothes." Mr. Lindberg set it on the table. He leaned back and smiled and shook his head. "The last privy we tipped was out at Mr. Starr's lake home. The editor of the paper. He knew we were laying for him out in the dark and he took a lantern and a shotgun down the path to the outhouse and he yelled at us that it was loaded and he wouldn't hesitate to use it. Well, that just made it more interesting. He had to go pretty bad and he went in and sat down and we crept forward through the weeds and when we heard him doing his business we rushed up and pushed it over onto the door. The gun went off and the lantern busted and the privy caught fire and there was only one way out for Mr. Starr — out the hole he was sitting on — and he came leaking out and he tried to avoid going into the pit and he almost succeeded. He stood there moaning and it was the sorriest thing you ever saw. We never tipped a privy after that. We didn't have the heart to."

"Mr. Lindberg," said John, "I'd like to go down and see my father." His heart was pounding as he said it. He half hoped the old man would say no, but Mr. Lindberg pointed him to the door to the basement. "Right down there," he said. "I haven't started on him yet, he's just the way he arrived."

John descended the stairs, into a cold cellar with a sour chemical smell. A refrigerator hummed in the corner. Two large tubs stood against one wall, and a row of cabinets against the other, and in the middle was a table, and there, covered by an old rubber sheet, lay the body. He stood beside it for a moment, and then pulled the sheet back.

His father lay curled on his side, knees drawn up, his eyes closed, his mouth slightly open as if sucking wind, the hands clenched.

John touched a hand and it was cool. He put his hand on top of his father's head and smoothed his hair. He could not remember ever touching his father like that. Showing affection did not come easily to members of this family. The body seemed restless, straining — he stroked the head, and he put his other hand on his father's cool, dry hand. Norwegians were not a people given to kissing and hugging. Even direct eye contact could be uncomfortable. John had once seen his brother Henry stand back-to-back with their father and converse. A whole life spent maintaining distance.

The only time John ever heard his father talk about love, as such, was in describing a horse that Uncle Svend gave him when he was seventeen. The horse was named Beauty and he rode her bareback every day after chores. He hated school, he was shy, he wasn't in the clique of town kids who ran things, but he had that horse. "I loved that horse. She made you feel like the Prince of Paris," his father said.

One morning his father went into the barn and Beauty was moaning and sweating, rearing up, and he saw that the old icebox that held the oats was open. She'd worked the latch open and eaten half the oats and she was foundering on it. "A horse can't vomit," his father explained, "so the oats were fermenting in her gut and she was bloating, which cut off her circulation, and there's a place in the middle of the hoof, if it doesn't get blood, it gets so painful the horse can't walk, but you have to keep the horse walking, you can't let her lie down, because that makes it worse."

He walked her up and down all day, but then he fell asleep for a few hours and when he woke up, she was lying on the ground and he couldn't get her up. She was in agony. He called the vet and the vet was out on a call, so he had to get a gun and put her away himself. He wouldn't say more, but John could imagine him crying, putting his arms around her neck, then putting the muzzle of the gun to her beautiful forehead and thinking about how much he loved her and the gun going off and the boy, numb in shock, reaching for the shovel, digging the pit beside her, rolling her in.

John bent down and kissed his father's hand. He whispered, "Goodbye, Dad. I love you," and his eyes filled with tears. He pulled the sheet back over, and climbed the stairs, turning the light off behind him.

Bill and Mr. Lindberg sat in silence at the table.

"I'm going to take my brother down to

the Sidetrack Tap and buy him a beer," said John. "Mr. Lindberg? How about you?"

The old man shook his head. "I've got work to do," he said. "I put it off long enough."

Bill and John walked around the side of the house, past the hearse, and Bill said, "Why'd you do that?"

"I wanted to see him before he gets all made up, that's all."

"What did he look like?"

"He looked very much like our father."

They walked down Cleveland to McKinley and turned toward downtown. The Christmas lights still hung over Main Street.

The Sidetrack was dim and smoky. A twangy song played on the jukebox, a deep mournful voice, a man sorry for his misdeeds while still persisting in them. A few patrons sat staring up at the TV like a row of rock bass on the dock, the reflection playing on their faces. Wally stood, one foot up on a beer case to ease the pain in his back. Three Norwegian bachelor farmers sat in the bachelor booth, beside the door to the men's can, their grizzled old faces and ropy necks lit by a match flaring up. They had a bottle of Four Roses and a bucket of ice and three glasses and were looking up at

Mr. Berge, who stood, one hand on the door to the men's can, serenading them. His face was flushed, his eyes shone, as he sang:

The shepherd lay in the cool green grass,
His faithful dog lay by his ass,
His faithful sheep licked at his balls
Through a well-worn hole in his overalls.
A magpie sat in a nearby limb,
And spread its wings and shrieked at him.
The dog he barked, and the sheep she bit,
And the man he yelled, and the magpie
   shit.

John and Bill perched at the end of the bar near the door. Wally said, "That's why Evelyn refuses to tend bar, she got tired of the smutty jokes." He pulled two glasses of beer and filled two shot glasses with rye whiskey and reached across the bar and shook their hands. "Your dad was one of the finest individuals I ever met," he said. "I knew him since we were in the fifth grade together. It's hard to believe he's gone. I don't know what this town is going to do without him." Bill put down a five and Wally waved it away. John saw a sign above the bar: "I want to die peacefully in my sleep — like my grandfather — not screaming in terror like the passengers in his car."

"I wish the funeral were tomorrow," said Bill. "It's depressing hanging around here."

"I noticed," said John.

"Look out," said Bill. "Harley's coming over this way. Speaking of depressing."

John felt the big hand on his shoulder, and turned, and Harley sat down next to him, unshaven, wisps of gray hair poking out from under his orange cap, and he pulled out a hanky and honked. He and John's father used to duck hunt together.

"How's everything?" said John. Harley rubbed the back of his head gingerly.

"Slipped on the ice getting into my pickup the other night and banged my head. Don't know if it's a concussion or what. Slid under the truck and lay there and my sheepskin coat froze to the ice and if it hadn't been for the fact that I was able to wiggle out of the coat I'd be a dead man right now. Me and your dad together. Two funerals in one week."

Having survived this close call, Harley said, he felt Lady Luck calling to him, and drove to the Mille Lacs Indian casino, and won several hundred dollars at blackjack, when an elderly lady in an orange pantsuit and a brown wig dropped her purse and like a true gentleman he bent down to fetch it and collect the stuff that dropped out of it, and when he came up, all his chips were gone and so was the lady. The dealer said, "I thought she was your wife." Harley tore out to the parking lot and saw a white Caddie pull out, a lady at the wheel, and he chased her and made her pull over and then it turned out to be a different lady. Not the thief.

She had called the sheriff on her car phone meanwhile. It took Harley three hours to clear things up, sitting in the sheriff's office, being talked to like a teenager.

"Let me buy you a drink," said John.

Harley ordered a double bourbon on the rocks.

"Yeah," he said, "I thought that'd be my lucky day because it was on that very same day in 1957 the St. Paul Saints invited me to come to their camp in Florida and try out. They had scouted me when I pitched for the Whippets in the State Men's Tournament. The scout was a little guy named Ricky with a big cigar. I was working for the rendering plant picking up downed cattle, so baseball looked good to me, but Hazel about went nuts. She was my first wife. Scary woman. She told me that anybody could see I didn't have the stuff for pro ball, even she could see it. I rode the dog down to Florida and hitchhiked twenty-five miles to the ballpark and got suited up and went out and warmed up and a coach waved me over to the mound to throw. There was a batter at the plate and the coach said, 'Don't mind him, he's only there to give you the strike zone.' Well, they forgot to tell the batter that, and he swung and hit a line drive that bounced off my forehead, and when I came to, I was in a hospital bed. They said I owed a hundred fifteen dollars for the X-rays and whatnot. I had to shinny out of there, not a dime on me, and hitch-hike back to Minnesota, and it was raining to beat the band, and who wants to pick up a wet hitchhiker? Worst time of my life. I slept under bridges. I stole tomatoes out of people's gardens."

John put down a fiver and signaled for Wally to refill Harley's glass.

"You wouldn't mind if I had a beer too, would you?" Harley said. He took a swig of whiskey and chased it with a long swallow of beer.

"Anyway, I got home and Hazel was fit to be tied. She called me a sapsucker, said she rued the day she met me. There I was with these ferocious headaches and only whiskey seemed to relieve the pain, beer didn't do the trick. I drank and she called me names

186

and one night she came at me with a pistol and said, 'I'll bet you think I wouldn't dare,' and I said, 'I'm not thinking anything,' and she said, 'That's your problem,' and she shot me. I woke up three days later in General Hospital. They decided to leave the bullet in. I pretty much recovered except I can't remember songs. Nothing. You could play me 'Happy Birthday to You' and I wouldn't remember ever having heard it. I was a big Buddy Holly fan, and now I hear 'Peggy Sue' and I can tell it's music but it doesn't mean anything to me. Otherwise, I was normal, except for the headaches, and sometimes I'd have a seizure and they would have to hold my tongue down. Otherwise, I was okay."

John signaled to Wally, and Wally poured Harley another shot of bourbon and a glass of beer.

"Yeah, they put me on muscle relaxants for a while, until I figured out it was those pills that gave me an overwhelming urge to drive toward bright lights. I'd see headlights approach and have to pull over to the shoulder so as not to drive head-on into someone. Once I picked up a hitchhiker and asked him to drive and he did and I dozed off and when I woke up the car was on a parking ramp in St. Paul and my billfold was missing. But that's another story. Johnny, can I borrow ten dollars from you until Wednesday?"

John pulled out his billfold and gave Harley a twenty. "Thanks," Harley said. He turned to Bill and said, "It was a pleasure meeting you. I was a good friend of your dad's. He was a fine gentleman." He tossed down his drink and stood up, thanked John and Bill again, and when they departed a few minutes later, he had changed the twenty for two rolls of dimes and was engaged in cribbage with Mr. Berge at the end of the bar and seemed to be winning.

Everyone was in bed when they got home; the house was dark. Bill tiptoed up the stairs, and John picked up the kitchen phone and called his apartment. He sat on the counter and looked out the window at the backyard, lit by a streetlamp in the alley, a cone of light on the snow, the garbage cans crowned with snow. The phone rang six times in New York and then his voice said, "Hi. It's John. At the sound of the beep, leave a message, and don't forget to smile." And a beep. "Kyle?" he said. "Kyle, if you're there, pick up. Just want to say hi. It's me. John." But she was gone, evidently.

He could see her naked sitting up in bed beside him but she was gone, all gone.

10.
TRUCKSTOP

I did this story at the Seattle Opera House on a bill with the guitarist Chet Atkins, the first of many shows we did together. He was an elegant man, a better storyteller than I, a musician who never had a bad night, and I flew out to be his opening act, or thought I would be, and then he insisted on putting me on in the second half. I was going to tell jokes and he said, "No, tell a story, that's what they're going to want you to do." And this one about Florian Krebsbach was the one he suggested. Chet liked to pace backstage, noodling on a small guitar, and not be interrupted, and in the vast darkness of the opera house stage, he walked back and forth playing stream-of-consciousness guitar, and I sat on a stool and managed to remember most of "Truckstop."

It has been a quiet week in Lake Wobegon. Florian and Myrtle Krebsbach left for Minneapolis on Tuesday, a long haul for them. They're no spring chickens, and it was cold and raining, and he hates to drive anyway. His eyesight is poor and his '66 Chev only has 47,000 miles on her, just like new, and he's proud of how well he has cared for it. Myrtle had to go down for a checkup. She doesn't go to Dr. DeHaven or the doctors in Saint Cloud, because she's had checkups from them recently and they say she is just fine. So she doesn't trust them. She is pretty sure she might have cancer. She reads "Questions and Answers on Cancer" in the paper and has seen symptoms there that sound familiar, so when she found a lump on the back of her head last week and noticed blood on her toothbrush, she called a clinic in Minneapolis, made an appointment, and off they went. He put on his good carcoat and a clean Pioneer Seed Corn cap, Myrtle wore a red dress so she would be safe in Minneapolis traffic. He got on Interstate 94 in Avon and headed south at forty miles an hour, hugging the right side, her clutching her purse, peering out of her thick glasses, semis blasting past them, both of them upset and scared, her about brain tumors, him about semis. Normally she narrates a car trip, reading billboards, pointing out interesting sights, but not now. When they got beyond the range of the *Rise 'N Shine* show, just as Bea and Bob were coming to the "Swap 'N Shop" feature, a show they've heard every morning for thirty years, they felt awful, and Florian said, "If it was up to me, I'd just as soon turn around and go home."

It was the wrong thing to say, with her in the mood she was in, and she was expecting him to say it and had worked up a speech in her mind in case he did. "Well, of course. I'm sure you would rather turn around. You don't care. You don't care one tiny bit, and you never have, so I'm not surprised that you don't now. You don't care if I live or die. You'd probably just as soon I died right now. That'd make you happy, wouldn't it? You'd just clap your hands if I died. Then you'd be free of me, wouldn't you — then you'd be free to go off and do your dirty business, wouldn't you."

Florian, with his '66 Chev with 47,003 miles on it, wouldn't strike most people as a candidate for playboyhood, but it made sense to her — forty-eight years of marriage and she had finally figured him out, the rascal. She wept. She blew her nose.

He said, "I would too care if you died."

She said, "Oh yeah, how much? You tell me."

192

Florian isn't good at theoretical questions. After a couple minutes she said, "Well, I guess that answers *my* question. The answer is, you don't care a bit."

It was his idea to stop at the truckstop, he thought coffee would calm him down, and they sat and drank a couple cups apiece, and then the pie looked good so they had some, banana cream and lemon meringue, and more coffee. They sat by the window, not a word between them, watching the rain fall on the gas pumps. They stood up and went and got in the car, then he decided to use the men's room. While he was gone, she went to the ladies' room. And while she was gone, he got in behind the wheel, started up, checked the side mirror, and headed out on the freeway. Who knows how this sort of thing happens, he just didn't notice, his mind was on other things, and Florian is a man who thinks slowly so he won't have to go back and think it over again. He was still thinking about how much he'd miss her if she was gone, how awful he'd feel, how empty the house would be with him lying alone in bed at night, and all those times when you want to turn to someone and say, "You won't believe what happened to me," or "Did you read this story in the newspaper about the elk in Oregon?" or "Boy, Johnny

193

Carson is looking old, ain't he? And Ed, too," and she wouldn't be there for him to point this out to — and he turned to tell her how much he'd miss her and she wasn't there. The seat was empty. You could have knocked him over with a stick.

He took his foot off the gas and coasted to a stop. He hadn't noticed her crawl into the backseat, but he looked and she wasn't there. She hadn't jumped — he would've noticed that. (Wouldn't he?) It couldn't've been angels taking her away. He thought of the truckstop. He was a good ways from there, he knew that. He must've gone twenty miles. Then, when he made a U-turn, he noticed he wasn't on the freeway anymore. There was no median strip. He was on a Highway 14, whatever that was.

He drove a few miles and came to a town named Bolivia. He never knew there was a Bolivia, Minnesota, but there it was. Went into a Pure Oil station, an old man was reading a Donald Duck comic book. Florian asked, "How far to the Interstate?" He didn't look up from his comic. A pickup came in, the bell dinged, the old man kept reading. Florian went down the street into a café, Yaklich's Café, and asked the woman where the Interstate was. She said, "Oh, that's nowheres around here." "Well, it must be," he said, "I was just on it. I just came from there."

"Oh," she says, "that's a good ten miles from here."

"Which way?"

"East, I think."

"Which way's east?"

"What way you come in?"

"That way!"

"That way is northeast. You want to go that way and then a little southeast when you get to the Y in the road. Then keep to your left. It's about two miles the other side of that old barn with Red Man on the side. Red Man Chewing Tobacco. On your left. You'll see it."

There was a funny look about her: her eyes bulged, and her lips were purplish. Her directions weren't good either. He drove that way and never saw the barn, so he turned around and came back and looked for the barn on the right side, but no barn, so he headed back to Bolivia, but Bolivia wasn't there anymore. It was getting on toward noon.

It was four o'clock before he ever found the truckstop. He had a long time to think up something to tell Myrtle, but he still had no idea what to say. But she wasn't there anyway. The waitress said, "You mean the

195

lady in the blue coat?" Florian didn't remember what color Myrtle's coat was. He wasn't sure exactly how to describe her except as *real mad,* probably. "*Ja,* that's the lady in the blue coat," she said. "Oh, she left here hours ago. Her son come to get her."

Florian sat and had a cup of coffee and a piece of apple pie. "Can you tell me the quickest way to get to Lake Wobegon from here?" he asked. "Lake what?" she said. "I never heard of it. It can't be around here."

But it was, not too far away, and once he got off the freeway he found his way straight home, although it was dark by then. He stopped at the Sidetrack for a quick bump. He felt he owed it to himself after all he'd been through and what with what he was about to go through. "Where's the old lady?" asked Wally. "Home, waiting for me," he said.

He headed south and saw his house, and kept going. Carl's pickup was in the drive-way and he couldn't see facing the both of them. He parked on the crossroad and sat, just beyond Roger Hedlund's farm, where he could watch his house. It was dark except a light was on in the kitchen and one in the bathroom. Roger's house was lit up. What if Roger should see him and come out to investigate? Out here in the country, a parked car stands out more than a little bit, you might as well be towing a searchlight behind you. It's considered unusual for a man to sit in his car in the evening on a crossroads an eighth of a mile from his own house, just sit there. If Roger came out, Florian thought he'd explain that he was listening to the radio and it was a Lutheran show, so the old lady wouldn't let him listen to it in the house — Roger was Lutheran, he'd like that.

He ducked down as a car came slowly past, its headlights on high beam. The preacher on the radio might be Lutheran, he didn't know. The man was talking about sinners who had wandered away from the path and wound up on a steep, rocky hillside in the dark, and it seemed to Florian to fit the situation. "Broad is the road that leadeth to destruction, and narrow is the path of righteousness" — that seemed to be true, too, from what he knew of freeways. The preacher mentioned forgiveness, but Florian wasn't sure about that. He wondered what this preacher would do if *he* had forgotten his wife at a truckstop and gotten lost. A woman with a warbly voice sang, "Softly and tenderly Jesus is calling, calling for you and for me. See by the portals he's

197

waiting and watching. Calling, O sinner, come home." He could not imagine Myrtle singing such a song or taking such a position.

Come home, come home —

Ye who are weary come home.

Florian felt weary. Seventy-two is old to get yourself in such a ridiculous situation. He waited as long as he could for Carl to leave, and then the coffee inside him reached the point of no return and he started up the engine. Taking a leak in another man's field: he drew the line at that. He turned on his headlights, and right when he did he saw Carl's headlights far away light up and the beams swung around across the yard and Carl headed back toward town.

Florian coasted up his driveway with the headlights out. He still did not have a speech ready. He was afraid. He also had to pee. Outside, on the porch, he smelled supper: breaded fish fillets. He was surprised that the door was unlocked — they never have locked it but he thought she might if she thought he was coming.

He hung up his coat in the mud room and looked around the corner. She was at the stove, her back to him, stirring something in a pan. He cleared his throat. She turned. She said, "Oh thank God." She dropped the spoon on the floor and ran to him on her old legs and said, "Oh, Daddy, I was so scared. Oh, Daddy, don't ever leave me again. I'm sorry I said what I did. I didn't mean it. I didn't mean to make you so angry at me. Don't leave me again like that."

Tears came to his eyes. To be so welcome — in his own home. He was about to tell her that he hadn't left her, he'd forgotten her; then she said, "I love you, Daddy. You know that." He was going to tell her, but he didn't. It occurred to him that leaving her on account of passionate anger might be better than forgetting her because of being just plain dumb. There wasn't time to think this through clearly. He squeezed her and whispered, "I'm sorry. I was wrong. I promise you that I'll never do a dumb thing like that again."

She felt good at supper and put on the radio; she turned it up when she heard "The Saint Cloud Waltz." *Sometimes I dream of a mansion afar but there's no place so lovely as right where we are, here on a planet that's almost a star, we dance to the Saint Cloud Waltz.* That night he lay awake, incredulous. That she thought he was capable of running away, like a John Barrymore or something. Seventy-two years old, married forty-eight years, and she thought that maybe it hadn't worked out and he might fly the coop like people do in songs? Amazing woman. He got up at six o'clock, made scrambled eggs and sausage and toast, and felt like a new guy. She felt better too. The lump on her head felt like all the other lumps and there was no blood on her toothbrush. She said, "I wonder if I hadn't ought to call down there about that appointment." "Oh," he said, "I think by now they must know you're all right."

11.
FAITH

A monologue from 1985, inspired by a friend's daughter's confirmation into the Lutheran church. I remember the audience's pleasure at suddenly hearing me pop up as a character in the story. I was pleased by it, too, and put a Gary Keillor into *The Book of Guys* and *Pilgrims* and *Guy Noir and the Straight Skinny.*

It has been raining off and on most of the week, long wet nights and rain in the mornings sometimes changing to snow, cold. The sky misty. The Bloodmobile came but after the long winter our blood was too salty and they went away. Said they'd come back in June. It was Confirmation Sunday. In olden times girls would dress in bright new spring hats and white dresses and white gloves and boys would wear suits and ties. Those days are gone, never to return. If the girl has a grandma who wields some influence (a grandma with property), the girl may wear a nice dress, but the hats and gloves are gone. I miss the white gloves, which was a way of saying *This day is different from other days.* Many confirmation kids come in jeans and sneakers, which is in line with the idea that God looks on the heart, not on one's exterior, but is that a license to attend church in our underwear? It's Sunday, after all. It's not Tuesday. But the truth is that some Lutherans actually are Unitarians. Just as you have people at a basketball game who don't care about the game, they go just to be sociable.

Church went long last Sunday. I drove by at twelve thirty and the parking lot was full. And then I remembered that I was supposed to be there for the confirmation of Lois Tollerud, my goddaughter, and I slowed down but couldn't think of a good enough excuse for being two hours late and drove on.

A whole herd of deer came through town on Tuesday, ten of them, like a tour group, and Pastor Liz saw them on her morning walk, standing in the church parking lot. They lifted their heads, and stood perfectly still, ears perked up, and she stood still, thinking of things to tell them. Deer carry ticks that transmit Lyme disease, which has hit a few people in town, a couple of them disastrously. Stoicism can carry a terrible price. Pastor Liz ran into a deer once that leaped out of the ditch at dusk when she was heading back to town for confirmation. The animal was knocked across the road where it flopped around on the shoulder and expired and Liz drove to church and lit the candles in her office and led the confirmands in a review of the Nicene Creed and what it means. She didn't mention the deer. She didn't want death to trump the creed, but she couldn't help thinking about how she had dragged the carcass by its hind legs off the road and what about deer ticks? She had hugged the children. Should she tell their parents? Well, yes, of course. Eight phone calls, varying degrees of consternation, dread. Ten minutes later, Val Tollefson called to anguish about liability and then his brother-in-law the retired attorney in Minneapolis called to offer advice. Grim.

Pastor Liz had been on her way to meet Cindy Hedlund at the Sidewinder in Millet, which is open for lunch these days. Drinking and dancing don't pay the bills anymore, so they added lunch. A crisis of faith, Cindy said on the phone. She was crying. Connie the church secretary told Liz that Cindy has been looking at new cars at Krebsbach

Chev. *Whatever,* said Liz, but of course it matters to people — Lutherans drive Fords bought at Bunsen Motors, Clint and Clarence being church members — likewise Catholics drive Chevies. *Be true to your own.*

A red hatchback, a Caprice. Donnie Krebsbach sidled over and asked if she wanted to drive it. "I shouldn't even be here," she said.

"Times change. I think you need to please yourself. I mean, Ford makes a good car, it's not that, but a lot of people think they don't handle all that well. This Caprice is a real good handler." He jingled the keys. She bolted for the door — "Let me think about it." And that night over supper Roger said he'd heard that she'd been looking at Chevys. "Up to you," he said, "but Clint is an old friend."

Arlene Bunsen returned from visiting her son Duane and his attractive (childless) wife, Denise, in their lovely two-bedroom condo outside Houston which is full of DVDs and exercise equipment and things people use to fill up their lives who do not have children. Duane and Denise were out kayaking and left a key at the desk for Arlene and she plunked down her grocery bag full of rhubarb and strawberries and flour and butter — to make a rhubarb pie for them — and could not find a bowl to mix dough in, or a knife to chop rhubarb with. Their kitchen appeared never to have been used. She knocked on a neighbor's door, and it opened two inches, the length of the chain, and when Arlene asked for a knife, the door closed. She wound up mixing the dough in an ornamental Chinese bowl from the mantel and she found a knife in the box of nice silverware they'd gotten for their wedding which was in the closet, still in a plastic wrap. Arlene turned on the oven as she whomped up the dough and soon there was acrid smoke in the air and she opened the oven and it was full of melting DVDs.

Denise and Duane appeared to be subsisting on take-out. Like take-out spaghetti from a pizza place, with garlic bread and wine in a carton. For breakfast the next morning, they took Arlene to a pancake house. Denise is slender and goes to a gym four times a week. She is tan and beautiful in a modelish way and Duane is crazy about her and they travel a lot. They both work. Good jobs. Plenty of money. They've been in counseling for the entire ten years of their marriage. "Is there a problem?" Arlene said. "No," he said, "that's to catch problems before they come up."

■ ■ ■ ■

Well, there it was. A preventative lifestyle. You steer away from trouble. Children are trouble. Everyone knows this. Arlene loves Duane but couldn't imagine flying down to Houston again — what for? To watch DVDs? Not her style. Anyway, she came back in a good mood and went to the church council meeting and when someone brought up the subject of Ernie Rasmussen she volunteered to go visit him. He's been coming drunk to church and leaving un-signed checks for $100 in the collection plate and evidently Lottie has left him and gone to her sister's in Bemidji but who knows. So Arlene went right up to his house, which people refer to as the Peterson house — Pete Peterson and his family lived there for years, until they found a python living in the crawl space under the kitchen. An aluminum patch covers the hole. The snake was 16 feet long and weighed 240 pounds, and lived under there for about sixteen years, during which the Petersons lost six Chihuahuas and numerous cats. Their youngest girl, Julie, discovered the snake when she crawled into the hole to hide during Starlight Moonlight and saw pale yellow eyes in the dark, and was paralyzed with fear but luckily she had just eaten peanut butter and pythons are repelled by the smell of peanuts and she ran and told her mother. Mrs. Peterson went to look. She stuck her head in and there were the yellow eyes. Like Julie, she was paralyzed with fear but the little girl had the good sense to grab her mother by the ankles and pull her to safety. The Volunteer Fire Department was called and the firemen were about to blast the creature with a fire hose and then someone remembered that warm cheese will make a snake drowsy so Mrs. Peterson heated up some leftover macaroni and cheese and pushed it in toward the snake and sure enough the yellow eyes closed. It took six men to haul it to the truck and they drove it to the zoo in Duluth but around McGregor the snake woke up and fell off the truck and slithered away and nobody cared to give chase. The Petersons moved to Napa Valley soon after and opened an inn called Paradise Inn that caters to couples taking their first vacation without children — their kids have grown up or the parents have decided to stop worrying about them — and they go to Napa Valley to see if they still like each other and have anything to talk about. Thirty-five years of marriage and a lot of puke and snot and disease and squalor and bad companions and suspicious odors and big attitudes and eye-rolling and ingratitude and the man and woman who procreated the brood open a bottle of Pinot Noir and look at each other and try to remember what it was they were thinking of back when their flesh was united.

Arlene walked up to the Peterson house, knocked, and there was no answer, so she stepped into the kitchen, and heard sounds of groaning and sighing upstairs. "Oh God," a woman said. "Oh my God." It was a video. She yelled, "Ernie??? It's Arlene Bunsen. From church. You forgot to sign your checks." And the groaning stopped. And he hollered from the top of the stairs, "Well, leave 'em there on the table and I'll get to 'em as soon as I can." Arlene looked around at the piles of dirty dishes, clothes on the floor, garbage overflowing, flotsam, wreck-age of a misspent life. "Is Lottie here?" she yelled. She heard rustling and creaking under the floor where the python had lived.

Years ago a famous wild-game hunter named Lyle Bradley was brought in to look for snakes, a man in leather boots and a pith helmet and jodhpurs, and he spent two days and found nothing but garter snakes and black snakes and said he thought the python must've escaped from a circus sideshow and simply adapted to cold weather. He said we'd never see another one. "Of course," he said, "you never know."

Ernie came lumbering down the stairs, supporting himself against the walls. She was glad to see that he had put his pants on and zipped them up. "Do you have twenty bucks I can borrow until Tuesday?" he said. She peeled two twenties out of her billfold. "I just need a little help until I can get on my feet," he said.

His brothers, Tom and Jack, went away to college though they weren't that smart, and did well for themselves, or so you hear, and Ernie had his own septic tank business with plenty of work, but he and Lottie never got along. The house is cursed, Arlene thinks. The Petersons got divorced after they opened Paradise Inn.

She wrote up a report on Ernie for the Pastoral Care committee, saying that he'll need some support, and she wrote to Tom and Jack and asked if they could contribute $100 each per month. No word yet from them.

Cindy Hedlund's story went like this: she was awakened by Roger snoring and came downstairs, turned on the radio, found a jumble of talk shows but there was a good jazz show from Grand Rapids and she listened to it and revisited an elaborate fantasy she's had for years, in which she's in New York City, in a restaurant on the forty-seventh floor, a jazz trio is playing, she sits at a table looking downtown toward the Empire State Building in the mists, the lights of the city twinkling. In the fantasy, she's dressed in black, her fingernails bright red, and she pulls a cigarette out of her purse and two slender hands with fine black hair on the backs reach over and light her cigarette, and she looks up through the smoke and there is a very handsome man, sort of Italian. Sometimes it's a gay man, sometimes it's an old friend from high school who lives in the city, who always told her, "When you're in town, look me up." But last night, in the fantasy, she was a widow and the man asked her to dance. He danced beautifully. Jazz isn't about getting old and raising kids and earning a living, it's about youth and freedom, she told Liz. "I know," said Liz.

"I found an old classmate in a chat room online," Cindy told her. About six months ago. My first big love. Jimmy. He's a Lutheran pastor in California now, very miserable, wrong line of work, wrong wife, wrong place, his kids are strangers to him, and he wants to get together with me. He says he'd been thinking about me for years. He says he always thought of me as a kindred spirit and maybe a person only gets one of those in a lifetime and I'm his." The Sidewinder serves half-pound cheeseburgers and the fries are really good. The place is dark and smells of smoke and beer and the furniture looks like it's been thrown around. The bartender stared at Liz. A guy with blond streaks in his hair, who was a little too aware of his own prettiness. Was he pursing his lips or was he puckering in her direction? Hard to tell. She was wearing her clerical collar. Jesus. Contain yourself, wouldja? Cindy said she thought she was falling in love with Jimmy and that she wished she could find a way to meet him for a weekend in San Francisco. She was in a chat room with him last night for an hour and he said he wanted to quit the church and take a job waiting on tables in Seattle and go to acting school. "What should I do?" she said. Liz was right there. *Take responsibility for your own actions. When you meet him online, you are choosing to go deeper into the woods. If you met him in San Francisco, you'd cross the river. This is a choice, it isn't happenstance. But whatever you choose to do, it'll be better if you do it with a whole heart. The whole heart is a cheerful heart, not divided against itself. One thing at a time. One day at a time. Whatever you do, do it heartily, as unto the Lord, and not unto men.* Liz took Cindy's hand and said a prayer for gratitude. Give us gratitude, Lord. Fill our hearts with gratitude. Cindy was weeping. That was a good thing. But Pastor Jimmy is a shithead to be preying on an old friend online. The Internet is a swamp where mischievous people can cause all sorts of pain and misery. Liz paid the bill. "No, no, let me pay," said Cindy, after Liz had already put a twenty down and the smirky bartender had come over to pick it up. "How was everything?" he said. "Stupendous," said Liz.

"You from around here?" he said. She shook her head. "I've seen you before," he said. "In your dreams, sir." That shut him up.

I felt bad about missing Lois's confirmation so I dropped by their farm. Eight cars and two pickups parked in the yard. I snuck around to the front of the house. They were all gathered in the living room, Daryl and Marilyn and the kids and relatives I couldn't identify and they were just about to cut the cake. Lois has grown four inches this year and now is five feet eight and one-half inches tall, a shy girl with long brown hair she has learned to tie in an elegant bun, and creamy skin that she keeps beautiful by frequent blushing. She happened to be in a sensitive mood that day, having gotten a six-page single-spaced letter from a boy in church telling her that he thinks God has written their names together in the Book of Love. The cake was on the coffee table in front of her, white with the Scripture verse in blue frosting: "Be not conformed to this world: but be ye transformed by the renewing of your mind, that ye may prove what is that good, and acceptable, and perfect, will of God." It was a large cake. Lois didn't know how to tell everybody that she wasn't sure that she believed in God. She was pretty sure that she might've lost her faith and though she was hoping to get it back, she didn't know how. It happened Friday night when she was babysitting at the Christiansens' and that boy came over and she let him in, though she wasn't supposed to have guests, and they sat on the couch watching men in khaki uniforms beat people senseless with rifle butts, and she said, "Oh my God," and the boy took her in his arms, to console her, but then started kissing her and unbuttoned her blouse, and told her how much she meant to him. She took his hand out of her shirt and she prayed that he would go away and heard something like an echo, as if the prayer had been dropped into a deep well. And suddenly it seemed to her that the world was in the control of dark powers, working senseless evil on the innocent, and this boy was capable of evil too, a potential rapist, and that prayer went up in the air like smoke.

When Marilyn cut the confirmation cake and served it with butter-brickle ice cream, Lois thought she ought to say something about her loss of faith, but couldn't do it, she just couldn't. She excused herself and went upstairs and put on jeans and a white jacket and walked out across the cornfield toward the road and the ravine to think about her faith on this cloudy day, and, walking west over a little rise, she saw, just beyond the ravine, a white car she'd never seen before, and a strange man in a trench coat standing beside it. She walked toward him, thinking of the parable of the Good Samaritan, thinking that perhaps God was calling her to go witness to him and thereby recover her faith. He stood and pitched stones up over the trees, and as she got closer, he turned and smiled, put out his hand, and came toward her. She saw her mistake. Something glittered in his mouth. She stopped. He was a killer come looking for someone, it didn't matter to him who it was, anyone who came down the road would do. He walked toward her; she turned and fell down and said, "Oh please no, please God no."

I hadn't seen her for five years. I said, "Lois, Lois — it's me." I helped her up. *How are you? It's good to see you again.* We shuffled along the rim of the ravine, looking for the path down, and she told me about her confirmation, which I have a godfatherly interest in and also because she was named for my favorite aunt, whose favorite nephew I was. She was my youngest aunt and loved to pretend and sometimes we played a game called Strangers, pretending we didn't know each other. We'd sit and make up stories about ourselves and usually she was a missionary in Africa and I was a novelist. It was exciting for a while and then it was scary, Strangers.

Lois Tollerud asked me, "Why did you stop here?" I told her I was looking for a spot where our Boy Scout troop used to camp and where Einar Tingvold the scoutmaster got so mad at us once, he threw two dozen eggs one by one into the woods and when he ran out of eggs he reached for his

215

binoculars and threw them. We scouts searched for them for a whole afternoon, thirty years ago.

"That's not a true story, is it?" she said. "No, it's not."

I stopped there because, frankly, I'd had a lot of coffee, but I couldn't tell her that. And she had appeared before I could pee, so when she invited me to the house, I said, Sure.

We walked in. I got a fairly warm hello, and was offered coffee. "In a minute," I said. "Excuse me, may I use your toilet?" They cut me a slice of cake that said "Con but for," a little triangle out of her verse.

Be not conformed to this world: but be ye transformed. Our lovely world has the power to make us brave. I was afraid to see the Tolleruds but needed to empty my bladder. I enjoy being someone else and then it isn't enjoyable anymore and I need to be known and that's when I come home. So my mind can be renewed by what is so familiar, the old hymns, God watching the sparrows, the gates of thanksgiving.

II.
ICONIC PAJAMAS

People ask, "How do you ever think up all that stuff for a weekly radio show?" and the answer is, "Steal from your old work, and if your mind is blank, do parodies." The Supreme Court ruled in favor of satire in *Campbell v. Acuff-Rose Music, Inc.* (1994), saying that parody is "transformative" and is protected as fair use of copyrighted material. In other words, you do not have to pay for the privilege of making fun of people, a beautiful idea. Thus we swiped Edgar Allan Poe's "The Raven":

And Larry still is sitting, pleading as I do my
knitting,
Though I've said, "You must be kidding.
You're a bozo and a bore."
And still he gets this feeling and his eyes
roll toward the ceiling
And then suddenly he's kneeling, weeping,
facedown on the floor:
"C'mon, honey. Please, let me come back. I

217

implore."
And I say: "Baby. Nevermore."

Plus the Bible stories, the Beatitudes, Ginsberg's "Howl," Frost's "Stopping by Woods," *Hamlet, A Streetcar Named Desire,* and famous American sacred songs:

Don't come angel band
Hands off my prostate gland
I'm not ready to go quite yet
But if you say this is it
Bring me a carton of cigarettes
I'm sorry that I quit.

The canon of the familiar is vast and it's all available to the parodist. You can do Bob Dylan:

May you grow up to be beautiful
And very rich and slim
May God give you everything you want
Though you don't believe in Him
May you stick your finger in the pie
And always find the plum
May you stay forever dumb.

And Paul Simon —

Hello darkness, my old friend
It is nighttime once again

I've been sleeping since this morning
Because this town is very boring
I am tired
Of the tedium and silence
I want violence
I love the sound
Of sirens

Parody is a game of patience. And it's a tribute to the parodee. Only true originals can be parodied, and that eliminates 95 percent of the poets and songwriters out there. I saw a kid do a parody of me once — he was fourteen, he wore a white suit, red socks, red shoes, a big straw hat, and he spoke in a flat voice very slowly and the story he told was about vampires and werewolves. It was hilarious. Up to a point.

1.
HENRY

I discovered Thoreau in high school, as a member of the Film Operators Club, a bunch of geeks who ran the projectors for classes. I sat in a little booth in the back of the auditorium and threaded the film onto the sprockets and through the lens and onto the take-up reel and sometimes sat and watched it, *Our Town* or *Hamlet* or *Romeo and Juliet,* and once the sophomore English classes traipsed down for a movie about Thoreau's *Walden.* He was a geek, too, awkward, shambling, a loner, hiding his loneliness behind a curtain of disdain, and he and I became very close for a couple of years. Very close. When I read that he had traveled by steamboat to St. Paul and Minneapolis in 1861 and hiked around Lake Calhoun, I was absolutely thrilled.

Mr. H. D. Thoreau
c/o Mrs. John Thoreau
Concord, Mass.

Dear Henry:

I wrote to you at the pond but the letter came back marked "Not There Anymore. Skedaddled" so I am sending this
to your mother's house. I hope this finds
you enjoying good health and the society
of your Concord friends. And thank you
for allowing us to see the manuscript of
Walden; Or, Life in the Woods.

All of us here at Weiden & Longman
are great fans of your work and so there
was great excitement when the book arrived.

Let me just say that there is so much
to admire in *Walden* — the energy, the
certitude, the elegance of the writing —
that I am terribly sorry to report that we
cannot publish it as it stands.

When you told me two years ago that
you were going to the woods to write, I
assumed it would be on the order of
James Fenimore Cooper's *The Deer-
slayer* and so did my colleagues who
kept asking, as they made their way
through a long chapter about beans,
"Where are the Indians? Where is the

narrative?" The book keeps jumping around. The first twenty pages are slow going, you must admit, with all the preaching about the evils of materialism, a subject that God knows has been covered elsewhere, and then bang, suddenly you've got the axe in your hand and you're building the cabin, and that's great, and you give prices on nails and boards and all, but just when the reader might like to see a floor plan and maybe some advice about preventing dry rot, suddenly we're hearing about beans and nature and then it's woodchucks and then reincarnation, and the reader quietly closes the book and goes back to Dickens. "The mass of men lead lives of quiet desperation," okay, maybe so, but most men will never read that line because they got quietly desperate a hundred pages earlier reading about man's innate goodness. What this book needs is structure, and what I'm thinking, Henry, is that we try to make it into a calendar, on the order of *Poor Richard's Almanac*. One page per month, one aphorism per day, one of your quickies like "Time is but the stream I go a-fishing in" or "Beware of all enterprises that require new clothes" — both great.

The one about marching to your own drummer. Great stuff. Nobody writes sentences better than you do, not even Emerson — it's the paragraphs and the chapters where you run into trouble. So let's do a book of aphorisms, epigrams, adages, pithy sayings, whatever you want to call them. "There is no remedy for love but to love more." I can see us developing that into a series of greeting cards — are you familiar with those? Very popular in England. Or "If one advances confidently in the direction of his dreams, and endeavors to live the life which he has imagined, he will meet with success unexpected in common hours." Simply beautiful. I read that aloud to my colleagues and they said, "Let's have more of that and less of the transcendentalist stuff."

As you yourself say in the book, "Our life is frittered away by detail. Simplify. Simplify." That's all we're asking you to do, Henry. Simplify: make it a calendar. People get inspiration, they get a space to write in doctor appointments and birthdays, they get some etchings of trees and leaves, and along the way they start to wonder, "Where can I read more of this Thoreau? He's not bad." And then we bring out your next book, which I hope is going to be less about the universe and more about you. And about Emerson, Hawthorne, Margaret Fuller, personal anecdotes about the homely lives of the celebrated. As you yourself say, "Only that day dawns to which we are awake." In other words, if nobody buys your book, then what's the point? Think about it. Let's aim for an 1855 calendar. That would give us plenty of time to line up advertising. Would you have any objection to Winchester rifles or a company that makes woodchuck traps? Let me know. Meanwhile, I remain,

Your faithful friend,
Edw. Wheeler
Senior Editor

2.
LITTLE HOUSE ON THE DESERT

I wrote a fan letter to Laura Ingalls Wilder when I was ten years old and got back a form letter from Harper & Row saying that she appreciated hearing from me but that she was too busy to answer all the letters she got and hoped I would understand. I did not understand. My letter was longer and much better written than other children's letters and I expected Mrs. Wilder to appreciate that fact. What Harper & Row did not say was that she had died the year before, a fact I learned years later. I guess they thought that this knowledge would detract from our enjoyment of her work. I adored her work. When I heard that she had passed on, I wished that Harper & Row would ask me to write some sequels and keep the Ingalls family saga going. I would have been the best person to do that.

Many years ago, Pa and Ma and Mary and Laura and Carrie and their dog Jack left their little house on the prairie of Minnesota and packed their clothing and some furniture in the wagon and Pa hitched up the team and they headed for Arizona. Ma was pretty sick with chronic fatigue syndrome and Doc Williams thought that Tucson would do her good, the warm desert air and the yoga classes. Ma couldn't do yoga in Walnut Grove because it was considered a form of witchcraft. So off they rode through Nebraska and Colorado and when they came to Arizona, Laura said, "Pa, this land is too dry to raise corn on."

Pa chuckled. "That's right, Laura, and I'm not going to raise corn. I've got a job building patios."

When they reached Tucson, Pa found them rooms at a motel with a swimming pool. "What does it look like?" said Mary.

"It's like a castle, with turrets and a high wall and a moat," said Pa.

He winked at Laura. Mary was blind and couldn't see that the motel was a one-story cinder-block structure that resembled a shed. Pa was always pulling stuff like that.

After supper, Laura sat on the edge of Ma's bed.

"You seem better, Ma. Is your chronic fatigue all gone?"

Ma smiled. "Don't tell your pa, but I was

faking the whole thing. I'm not sick. Just sick of Walnut Grove. Tired of calico and gingham dresses. I want to live where there's fresh ground coffee and fresh arugula."

"Arugula?" said Laura.

"What do you think of this?" said Ma. She threw back the covers.

"Wow," said Laura.

Ma was wearing white silk pants and a painted silk top, big silver bracelets, turquoise earrings, and her hair was pulled back with a silver clip.

"It's time you should be in bed, Laura," said Pa. He had slipped into the room without them hearing him. "You're gorgeous, Caroline," he said softly. He pulled out his old fiddle and played "Just a song at twilight while the lights are low" and Laura sang along with the fiddle.

"Go to your room, Laura," he said.

"Yes, Pa."

She went into the next room, where Carrie and Mary lay on a rollaway, the blanket pulled up to their chins. "Is Pa coming in so we can say our prayers?" said Carrie.

"Pa is busy," said Laura.

"Doing what?"

"Guess," she said.

Laura dreaded the thought of Ma having

a baby and she, Laura, having to feed the thing and clean it and keep it amused. And worse, a baby brother who would inevitably take her place as Pa's favorite — it made her want to gag herself with a spoon. She was planning to write a book about the family — a family of five was just about perfect for a novel, with herself as the leading character — and one more child would wreck the whole thing. Laura went out in the hall and banged on Ma and Pa's door. "What about our prayers?" she hollered. They stopped messing around and pretty soon Pa came out in his night shirt, looking cross, his hair tangled up, and came in and knelt by Mary's bed and they all said their prayers. Laura added a silent prayer of her own that she would become a very very wealthy author. Pa said good-night and went back to his room. "You go stand guard at their door," Laura whispered to Jack, "and if you hear any sound from their room, bark as loud as you can."

Nevertheless, Ma gave birth to a baby boy nine months and ten minutes later. He was a fretful and troublesome baby and they named him Henry. He was an odd little boy who liked to be alone and draw pictures of monsters. Many years later, Laura wrote *Little House on the Prairie* and put Henry in it, except not fussy. Her daughter Rose edited Henry out.

"But why?" said Laura. She and Almanzo had earned buckets of money from *Little House in the Big Woods* and were living in the St. Regis Hotel in New York.

"You don't need him. He only confuses the story," said Rose.

"But he is my brother," said Laura. "He may be odd but he's part of the Ingalls family."

"If you put him in the book, then I'm out of here," said Rose. She was a stubborn little cuss. "And if I go, then I plan to tell the world how the Ingalls family really lived in Arizona and not on the prairie."

Laura wanted to shoot her on the spot. Rose could be such a pill. She considered herself superior to Laura because she had traveled in Europe and Laura had not. Granted, Laura had never been close to Henry, who had become a cowboy and was now in Nevada and involved with the gaming industry. He was impetuous and cruel but a real charmer with the ladies. Nonetheless, he was her brother and she felt it would be dishonest to cut him out of the story. But Rose was insistent and Laura needed her help in order to finish the series. And Laura thought of the hundreds of thousands of schoolkids who adored the *Little House* books and would be heartbroken if they didn't continue. She also thought how sad she would be if she and Almanzo had to leave the St. Regis and go back to live in Missouri.

"Okay, take him out," she said.

"Good," said Rose. She put her hand on Laura's arm. "It isn't a memoir, it's a work of art, and art is a creation, not a photograph. The good that the books will do far outweighs the slight dishonesty of omitting your ne'er-do-well brother."

"I suppose," said Laura, but she wasn't sure. She kept a picture of Henry in her jewelry box. He had long black hair that he kept slicked back and a thin black mustache and he wore a black shirt and white tie and a pink sportcoat with a red carnation in the lapel. He was quite a looker. Maybe, she thought, when the *Little House* books were done, she could write a book about her trip to Nevada in 1928 to visit Henry, when he introduced her to Jelly Roll Morton and Theda Bara and Douglas Fairbanks. She discovered the tango and the gin fizz and the meaning of the term "one-man band" and also "juicin' the jasper." It was quite a week.

3.
BILLY THE KID

A legendary figure of the West about whom not much is known for sure, so some people have made him into a Robin Hood and some have seen him as a punk caught in a range war and some as a cold-blooded killer. I alone see Billy as a crafty shape-shifter who made himself into a great success.

Billy the Kid
Didn't do half of what they said he did
He rustled cattle, I guess that's true,
But nobody knew who they belonged to
He killed some men, but if you knew 'em
You'd say they had it coming to 'em.

Billy the Kid went on the run
Down to Mesilla in 1881.
Sheriff Pat Garrett put on the heat
And came to the ranch of Billy's friend Pete
But it wasn't Billy who was shot by Pat,
It was someone wearing his pants and hat,

Billy the Kid was miles away
In Santa Fe with flowers in his hair
And I know 'cause I was there.

He made a fortune in fermented juices
And built a mansion in Las Cruces,
Changed his name to William Bonney,
Wrote "Way Down upon the Swanee"
And he may have been guilty to a degree
But he was always real good to me
And generous to my family.
Always sent us a Christmas turkey
From Albuquerque
And a bottle of brandy
From the Rio Grande.
They called him a killer and I guess he
    could be
But he was always good to me.
I spoke at his funeral in 1942.
He was living in Malibu,
Big house
On the beach.
I gave a nice speech.
People were impressed.
They didn't know he was
The most famous outlaw in the West,
Feared from Tucson to Reno.
They knew him as Rudy Valentino.

4.
LONESOME SHORTY

Written for *The New Yorker,* this story inspired the radio serial "Lives of the Cowboys" on *A Prairie Home Companion,* with Dusty and Lefty, Lefty's lost love, Evelyn Beebalo, and the villain Big Messer, which takes place in and around Yellow Gulch, Wyoming. It's Samuel Beckett for fourteen-year-olds. The cowboys suffer extreme loneliness, which drives them to visit town, where, in a short time, they are disgusted by society and return to the godforsaken plains, where, in due course, they suffer extreme loneliness and return to Yellow Gulch, only to be disgusted. That's how life seemed to me when I was fourteen.

The summer before last, I was headed for Billings on my horse Old Dan, driving two hundred head of the ripest-smelling longhorns you ever rode downwind of, when suddenly here comes a balled-up newspaper stuck inside some tumbleweed. I had been

without news for weeks so I leaned down
and snatched it up and read it trotting west,
though the front page was missing and all
there was was columnists and the Lifestyle
section, so bouncing along in a cloud of
manure I read an article entitled "43 Fabulous Salads to Freshen Up Your Sum-
mertime Table," which made me wonder if
my extreme lonesomeness might not be the
result of diet. Maybe I'm plumb loco, but a
cowboy doesn't get much fiber and he eats
way too much beef. You herd cattle all day,
you come to despise them, and pretty soon,
by jingo, you have gone and shot one, and
then you must eat it. Meanwhile, all those
cattle tromping around on the greens takes
away your taste for salads, just like when
you arrive at a creek and see that cattle have
tromped in the water and drunk from it and
crapped in it, it seems to turn a man toward
whiskey.

I thought to myself, Shorty, you've got to
get out of this cowboy life. I mentioned this
to my partner, old Eugene, and he squinted
at me and said, "Eeyup."

"Eugene," I said, "I've been cowboyin for
nigh onto two decades now. I know every
water hole between Kansas and the Sierra
Nevada, but consarn it, I miss the company
of my fellow man. Scenery ain't enough for

me, Eugene, nor freedom. I'm sceneried out, pardner, and freedom is vastly over-rated as an experience, if you ask me. I got to be with people. I'm a *people* cowboy, not a cow cowboy."

A few miles of purple sagebrush drifted by and a hawk circled high in the sky. "Do you hear what I'm sayin?" I inquired.

He said, "Eeyessir."

A few miles later, I said, "You ever think of just calling yourself Gene, Eugene? Gene is more of a cowboy name. Eugene is sort of a bookkeeper's name. How about I call you Gene, Gene?"

He thought this over for a few miles as we jangled along, eating dust. Then he said, "You do that and I'll lay for you and jump you and gouge your eyes out and bite off your ear."

"You'd rather be Eugene, then?"

"Eeyup."

We rode along for a ways. "Is there some topic you have a desire to talk about, Eugene?" I inquired.

"Nope."

A taciturn sidekick is like buying a ticket to see the sun set. Who needs it? You go humping along the trail, you would like some conversation, but no, Eugene could no more think up things to say than he could sing *La Traviata.*

That night, I was feeling low. The wood was wet and the campfire smoked, the beans were cold and the pork half raw, the mosquitoes descended in a cloud, and then it took hours to get the cattle bedded down, and as I was fetching a camp stool from the saddlebags, Old Dan accidentally stepped on my foot and about broke it. I hopped around on the good one and swore a blue streak, but none of it woke up Eugene. He was wrapped in his blankets, dead to the world.

To distract myself, I sat down and drew up a list of pros and cons on the back of a picture of my mother.

Reasons to Be or Not to Be a Cowboy

Freedom to be your own man. *The awful loneliness of doing so.*

Most beautiful country on God's green earth to look at. *No home, nowhere to sleep but on the cold ground.*

You get a bad back, pretty soon you're too bent over to look at scenery.

Good old Dan — what else can he do but ride the trail? *You can't live for your horse, especially not one who steps on you.*

Love to be with my pals. *Those cheating lying gin-soaked idiots? They all moved to town a long time ago.*

The West must be won for the White Man. *I done my part.*

The chance to be a True Cowboy, who stands up for what's Right and Fair. *Fine, but it's time to settle down and start building up equity. You have got nothing to show for your hard life, nothing.*

So it was an even draw, six of one, half a dozen of the other, but my foot hurt me so bad, I couldn't sleep. I dosed it with a few slugs of whiskey and only managed to give myself a sour stomach. When morning came I announced to Eugene and the other boys that I was packing it in.

I said, "The problem is I don't drink enough water and I don't eat right. That pork last night was full of fat, for example. And riding a horse, you never get the cardiovascular exercise you need. I've got to think about my health." Well, you'da thought I'da put on a dress and high heels the way they laughed and carried on. I said: "I quit. I'm a cowboy no longer. It's a rotten lonely life and I'm done with it." And I jumped on Old Dan, who luckily was right there, and I rode away.

I headed into a friendly town named Pleasant Gulch, having read in the paper that it offered a healthy climate, good soil and water, good schools and churches, a literary society, and "all the adornments of advanced civilization." *That's for me,* I thought. I became deputy to Sheriff Dibble, a full-time job with a decent pension plan, and bought a condo over the saloon. The Realtor, Lefty Slim, had a four-bedroom ranch house with great views for cheap — "Must sell, owner is wanted for murder," he said — but I had seen all I wanted of ranches, so I bought the condo. Partly furnished with a nice walnut bedroom set and dining-room table and carpet, and I could move in right away because the previous owner had been shot.

I bought sheets and towels and hung up blue dotted-swiss curtains. You miss curtains so much on the trail; there's really no way to hang them. (I know. I've tried.) And I bought myself a set of china. A cowboy gets sick of the sound of his fork scraping a tin plate, and this was the first *good* china I ever owned: four place settings with salad bowl, soup bowl, cup and saucer, dinner plate, and dessert plate, plus two platters, two serving bowls, gravy boat, teapot, and soup tureen, in the Amaryllis pattern.

The truth was, I didn't know three other people in Pleasant Gulch well enough to invite to dinner, but I felt confident I soon would because the town was perfect, its lawns and porches and street lamps so welcoming and warm compared to rocks and buttes. I hiked around town twice that first evening, just to absorb the beauty of it, and then returned home and fixed pork and beans, but they looked like cassoulet on my Amaryllis.

I had eaten exactly two bites when shots rang out and some cowboys whooped and bullets tore through my curtains and one busted two teacups, and another one hit my good serving platter and blasted it to smithereens. But when I stalked downstairs and out into the street, it was deserted except for a cowboy lying facedown in the dirt.

"What in the Sam Hill is going on around here?" I yelled.

He said he had been shot clean through the heart and was done for.

I knelt down by him and yelled, "You busted my Amaryllis china, you dink! I came in off the trail to get away from your ilk and here you are messing around in town. Well, not for long."

He asked me to take a letter to his mother in Pittsburgh.

"Your mother has no interest in hearing from you, so don't even think of it. You're nothing but a filthy savage and death is too good for you," I said. And then he died, presumably. At any rate, he didn't have any more to say.

Next day, I went back to the General Store to replace that serving platter, and they were plumb out of Amaryllis. And that night, the old couple next door banged on my door and said, "You're gargling too loud in there, Mr. Shorty, it's driving us nuts, and you twirl your rope and jingle your spurs, and your yodeling is a pain in the neck. No more *yodeladihoo* or *whoopitiyiyo,* okay?"

I told them that it was my home and I would yodel in it as I pleased.

So they called the sheriff and he said, "Sorry, Shorty, but they're right. We have a yodeling ordinance here and also one against gargling after ten p.m."

I got so dagnabbed mad, I stomped home, put my Amaryllis into saddlebags, climbed on Old Dan, and left town at sundown. I was burned up. I yelled at them, "Okay, I'll show you! You can take your damn piddling laws and ordinances and regulations and stuff 'em in your ear!" And back out on the range I went. Frankly, I'd left so many towns by then that I was used to it and didn't get nearly as mad as in the past. Leaving town is what cowboyin is all about.

You find a nice place and it's wonderful and then suddenly you can't stand it. So you drift off down the trail and get wet and miserable and lonesome till you can't bear it for another minute, so you gallop into the nearest town and are overwhelmed by the beauty of society — cheap floozies, old coots, preachers, lunatics, hoboes, school-teachers, old scouts with their sunburned faces and their voices raised in song, the jokes and gibes and yarns, the barn dances, the woman who invites you to stay the night — *people are great when you haven't seen any for a few months!*

So you find a job and an apartment, settle down, get comfortable, think, "This time it's for real" — and two minutes later you are brokenhearted, mad, miserable, and back in the saddle again. This is the basic cowboy pattern.

From Pleasant Gulch me and Old Dan headed for Dodge, with all the china, and ten miles beyond the Little Crazy River a rattler sprang at us and Dan shied away and I slid off and we busted a gravy boat! And one morning a grizzly came into camp and

I reached for something to throw at him and I tossed my teapot — it was the worst trip — and the next night, two cougars snuck in and stole my pants as I slept and it was snowing and I headed for a little town called Pit City. Rode along in my underwear, cold and soaked to the skin, and a woman waved from a porch, people smiled at me, and a nice lady cried out from a white frame house: "My brother Dusty is just your same size, mister — if you need a pair of pants, you can have one of his. And if you haven't eaten I'll rustle you up a plate of grub. And if you care to set and talk a spell, why, that'd be just hunky-dory."

The Andersons. Euphonia and Bill Anderson. Kindest people you'd ever meet.

I sat in their toasty warm kitchen by the coal stove and gabbed for three hours and told them everything about myself, personal stuff, and it was satisfying.

"Your problem is that you never found the woman you loved enough to make you want to come in off the range and settle down," said Euphonia. She introduced me to their daughter, Leonora, a beautiful redhead who worked at the Lazy Dollar Saloon — "as a bookkeeper," Euphonia emphasized.

Leonora treated me like the lover she

242

never had. She and I went for long walks out across the prairie to the ridge above the town. I sang to her, *"Mi amor, mi corazón,"* and she liked that pretty well. We got close. She did my laundry and saw the name tags on my shirts and started calling me Leonard, which nobody had done since I was a child.

"You're a gentle person, Leonard. Not like other cowboys. You like nice things. You ought to live in town," she said, lying with her head in my lap in a bower of prairie grass.

I told her, "Leonora, I have tried to live in town, because the cowboy life is a hard, wet, miserable, lonesome life, so town is wonderful, but doggone it, you go there and two days later, somebody kicks you in the shins and it's back in the saddle again. A guy can't live with people and he can't live without them. And besides, I am a cowboy and have got to be on the range." I spat on the ground to emphasize this.

"When you fixin to go?" she inquired.

"Tomorrow. Mebbe Tuesday."

"For long?"

"Six months. Mebbe longer. Depends."

"Six months is a long stretch of time to be away from a relationship," she said.

"Sometimes it is," I said. "And sometimes

243

it's just long enough."

"Well, Shorty, you just go and do whatever you're going to do, because that's what you're going to do anyway, makes no matter what I say. I know cowboys," she said.

I cried, "Well, if I don't cowboy, tell me — what would I do for a living in town?"

"You could write a western," she said.

So I started in writing a western novel with lots of hot lead flying and poetic descriptions of western scenes: "The setting sun blazed in the western sky as if a master painter had taken his brush to the clouds, creating a multihued fantasy of color reflecting brightly off the buttes and mesas." That night I showed it to Leonora. "Not what you'd call a grabber," she said.

I sat there with my face hanging out and wished she'd say, *Well, it ain't all bad, actually some is rather good, Shorty, and I loved where the dude cuts down the tree and the bear bites him in the throat,* but of course a sweetheart isn't going to tell you that, their critical ability is not what attracts them to us in the first place.

She was the prettiest woman I ever knew in my life, the sweetest, the kindest. I discovered that Amaryllis was Leonora's china pattern too. She had four place settings, as I did. Together, we'd have eight. It was tempting to consider marriage. And yet she had a way of keeping me on a short rope — she'd look at me and say, "What are you thinkin?" Nuthin, I'd say, nuthin in particular. "What is it?" she'd ask. *I don't care to talk about it,* I'd say. "Silence is a form of anger," she said. "A person can be just as aggressive with silence as they can be with a gun."

Oh for crying out loud, dear God of mercy, I cried, and jumped up and went straight to the barroom, not the Lazy Dollar but the Dirty Dog Saloon, and sat in a dim corner and had a stiff drink and then another to keep the first one company, and by and by, who should mosey in but Mr. Higley, author of numerous western songs, including "Goin Back to Colorado" and "How I Miss the Old Missouri," so I bought him a drink and me one too and said, "Tell me how it is that you love it so out here on the plains. You write poems about the beauty of the land and the goodness of the folks — what am I missing, pardner?"

He said, "I have not set foot in Colorado in forty years, nor seen the Missouri for thirty-seven. Does that answer your question, L.S.?"

We hoisted a number of drinks then, and I staggered back home about midnight and slept on the porch swing, the door being locked, and the next morning Leonora and I had a tiff. She said, "How come you go do a dumb thing like that, Leonard? Can you imagine how it makes me feel? Or do you think I don't notice that you got drunk and were walkin around this town singin and whoopin and ropin street lamps and laughin like an idiot at two in the morning? Do you think that decent people don't *talk* about this and wonder why you're not home here with me? Don't you see that it makes me look like a fool?"

I said, "If I have got to ask permission to take a drink, then let me out of it. I quit."

She said, "Don't you see there's a pattern in your life, Leonard? You're someone who avoids conflict. It's what makes you a cowboy."

"You're mad at me, ain'tcha," I said. She was mad.

"I'm not mad. Only concerned. We have a dysfunctional relationship, that's all."

"You're mad and you're always *going* to be mad," I said.

She said she had read an article in the Emporia *Gazette* that said male restlessness may result from a hormone imbalance caused by an eating disorder.

"That's the westward impulse you're talking about, Leonora! That's what brought us here!" I cried. She said it wasn't an impulse, it was an imbalance. She said, "Maybe you should get help. The schoolmarm is a therapist part-time, you know."

Okay, I said.

Twice a week for eight weeks, I lay down on Mary Ellen Henry's parlor sofa and told her everything about myself. She used cats as a medium. (She explained why, but I forget.) A cat lies on your chest and you talk to it, and she listens, e.g.:

ME: Boy, I sure feel confused, Puff. I'm so sad and mixed up I could go get drunk and jump off the roof. But with my luck I'd probably miss the ground.

HER: Puff, you tell that nice man to tell you more about when his mama left him at the train depot and went off with the dry goods salesman.

It felt dumb but I did it. Lay on the couch, cat stretched out on my chest, Mary Ellen sat in the rocker, I talked about Mama to the cat — "My mother was the saintliest woman who ever trod this earth, Puff, and my daddy was the meanest sumbitch ever drew breath" — and Mary Ellen said to the cat, "Puff, I want you to tell Lonesome Shorty that some people might say that riding the open range is a cowboy's only way of keeping that powerful mama at a distance. You tell him that, Puff, and see what he says."

"Why, Puff, I believe that is the biggest crock of horse poop I've heard yet," I replied.

"Puff," she said, "remind Shorty of how his mama ran his daddy off so she could control her boy better."

"Lies, Puff. You're lying, ya miserable cat."

And on it went. I gave it my best shot but was no good at therapy, and one morning I said, "I've decided that you've probably done as much for me as you possibly can, Puff, so this will be my last visit. Thank you."

Mary Ellen was stunned, as if I had slapped her. Her eyes welled up with tears. "How can you *do* this to me?" she cried. "Don't you realize that you're my only client? You're important to me, Shorty! How can you walk away from me like I was just your hitching rail?"

This was much too complicated for me. So I saddled up and without a word to Leonora I rode off down the trail toward the Bitterroot, feeling dumber than dirt. Couldn't bear to be alone, couldn't bear the company. Thought it might be due to a lack of fluoride. Or it could be genetic —

it's hard to tell. My daddy left home when I was two. If we had any fluoride, he took it with him.

Rode seven days through Arapaho country and was full of loneliness and misery, thinking only of Leonora, her touch and smell, until finally I began to sing *"Mi amor, mi corazón,"* and burst into tears and turned around and rode back to Pit City. A bitterly cold day, windy, snow flurries, and me without shoes — I'd forgotten them at a campsite — and I was a sorry sight, but when Euphonia saw me she said, "Welcome back, honey, and come in and let me get you a pair of Bill's shoes."

I took a shower, and the towels were soft and smelled lemony. Had split-pea soup and Leonora came home and hugged me and cried, and the next day I got a job at the stagecoach office as assistant director of customer service and group sales, and the next few days went along like a song. Euphonia made my breakfast and Leonora made my bed and I bought six new place settings of Amaryllis, and we made plans to marry.

Then the Chautauqua put on a play called *The Secret Forest of the Heart* that Leonora had a big part in, so I went and I hated it, it was the dumbest sheep-dip show you ever saw, about good women who nurture and heal and men who rob and control, and Leonora held out a magical garland of flowers and vines and herbs and celery and sang, "Know the quiet place within your heart and touch the rainbow of possibility; be alive to the gentle breeze of communication, and please stop being such a jerk." People with big wet eyes stood and clapped and a stagecoach driver named Gabby turned to me and said, "I could sure use a big hug right now." I got out of there as fast as I could.

I told Leonora, "You hate me 'cause I walked out on yer dagnabbed play and you're going to give me my walkin papers, ain'tcha?" and she said, no, she wasn't, she didn't expect me to like the play, she knew me well enough to know *that,* and I said, "Oh, there you go again, just like always, you never stop finding fault with me, so I might as well go be bad, there's no percentage in being good," and she said I was crazy. "Well, to hell with you," I said, and I got so mad, I went in and robbed the bank. Pulled my hat down low and went in with six-guns in hand and yelled, "Everybody facedown on the floor! Nice and easy, now, and nobody gets hurt."

They said, "Why are you doing this,

Shorty? You're a wonderful guy and have a good job and you're blessed with the love of a wonderful woman."

"If that's what you call blessed, then I'd like to try damned to hell for a while."

"What do you have to be mad about?" asked the lady teller.

"Doggone it, I can be mad if I want to be. If I say I'm mad, I mean I'm mad."

"You'll never get away with it," someone yelled as I rode away with $34,000 on me, and as it turned out, they were right, but I didn't know it yet.

I headed off across the sandy flats on Old Dan toward the big mesas, rode hard for a week, then lay back. I was rich, and lonesome as an old galoot. Wanted to hook up with a partner but then thought of the trouble involved and decided against it. Made up a song as I rode along, "Livin inside / I'm dissatisfied / Guess I'm qualified to ride." Rode to Big Gap. No family took me in, no woman offered me comfort, and I sought no solace in the church. I paid with cash. A man in a saloon said he knew my old partner Eugene. "He got bit by his horse and was laid up with gelding fever and had fits and hallucinations and talked a blue streak for a month before he died, mostly about economics," he told me. I was sorry I had not been there to see it.

I rode on. I tried not to think about Leonora but I missed her terribly.

I wished I knew how to patch things up but there's no way. The love between two people is fragile and one false move can break it like fine china, and when it breaks, it's broken. I rode on, but I rode slower, and after a while I felt sick. I was so lonely. I lay down in the dirt and wrapped myself in a blanket and lay shivering all night and woke up in the morning and — I was about thirty feet from the Colorado Trail! All these wagon trains were going by and now and then a pioneer or a gold prospector'd call over to me — "Howdy! How are you doing over there yonder? You headin' west, too?"

And I'd answer: "I feel like I'm coming down with something. I don't know, I got a headache and chills and I feel weak and list-less. You got a thermometer with you? Is saltpeter supposed to be good for this? You think maybe I should bleed myself?"

And they'd lope over near me and ask if I had a fever. "You're supposed to starve a fever," they said. "Just lie there and rest and don't eat anything and pretty soon you'll feel better."

And I did that, and three days later I died.

The vultures came and feasted off me and the dogs fought over my bones and some old bum came and took the $34,000 in twenty-dollar bills out of my saddlebags and stomped on my china set and pretty soon what was left of me lay bleached and white on the lone prairie, but I didn't care because I was in heaven. I assume it was heaven. It was like Brown's Hotel in Denver, a suite, with a bathtub eight feet long, and a canopied bed, and an angel to bring me my breakfast.

It's a good breakfast: fresh biscuits and butter and two strips of thick crisp bacon and two eggs soft poached and fried potatoes and all of it on a beautiful pale blue Amaryllis plate. But it does not vary from day to day, and neither does the angel, who sings beautifully but always the same song.

It is perfect here and a person should be grateful, I reckon, but I am about fed up with it and ready to move on to the other place, if only I could think of something bad enough to say that would get me sent there, and, being a cowboy, I suppose, that won't be a problem. Something will come to mind.

5.
THE BABE

Back when I was twenty-four, I pitched up at Time-Life Inc. in its forty-eight-story box headquarters on Sixth Avenue and Fiftieth Street, one more desperate job applicant, and was directed to *Sports Illustrated,* where a kindly woman named Honor Fitzpatrick looked at my writing samples and gently discouraged me. "Your talent is for fiction," she said. "The only opening I have is for a fact-checker. I don't think you'd be happy doing that." Discouraging at the time, but in retrospect one is grateful. Profoundly grateful. A job in that box might've sent me down a path that turns into a deep trench, only to awaken at age forty-eight, divorced, in a junk-ridden studio apartment on West Twenty-third where I sit night after night beating up on a clunky novel about the Midwest. Twenty years later, an editor at *S.I.* asked me to write something for them and of course I said yes — I took it as corporate capitulation — and wrote a piece of fiction.

Our Lake Wobegon teams did not do well last year, the Whippets with no pitching finishing dead last, the Leonards pitiful and helpless in the fall even with a 230-pounder to center the offensive line, and now it's basketball season again and already the boys are getting accustomed to defeat. When they ran out on the floor for the opener versus Bowlus (who won 58–21), they looked pale and cold in their blue-and-gold silks, and Buddy had the custodian turn up the heat, but it was too late. These boys looked like they were on death row, they trembled as their names were announced.

It's not defeat per se that hurts so much, we're used to that; it's the sense of doom and submission to fate that is awful. When the 230-pounder centered the ball and it stuck between his tremendous thighs and he toppled forward to be plundered by the Bisons, it was, I'm sure, with a terrible knowledge in his heart that he had this debacle coming to him and it was useless to resist. Two of the basketball players are sons of players on the fabled 1958 squad that was supposed to win the state championship and put our town on the map, but while we looked forward to that glorious weekend our team was eliminated in the first round by St. Klaus. None of us ever recovered from that disappointment. But do our children have to suffer from it too?

As Harry (Can O'Corn) Knudsen wrote: "In the game of life we're playing, people now are saying that the aim of it is friendship and trust. I wish that it were true but it seems, for me and you, that someone always loses and it's us."

Can O's inspiration came from playing eleven years for the Whippets, a humbling experience for anyone. The team is getting trounced, pummeled, whipped, and Dutch says, "Come on, guys, you're too tense out there, it's a game, go out there and have fun," and you think, *This* is *fun? If this is fun, then sic your dogs on me, let them chew me for a while, that'd be pure pleasure.* But out you trot to right field feeling heavy-hearted and not even sure you're trotting correctly so you adjust the trot and your left foot grabs your right, *you trip on your own feet,* and down you go like a sack of potatoes and the fans in the stands are doubled up gasping and choking, and you have dirt in your mouth that you'll taste for years — is this experience good for a person?

Some fans have been led to wonder if maybe our Lake Wobegon athletes are suffering from a Christian upbringing that stresses the unworthiness angle and is light

256

on the aspect of grace. How else would boys of sixteen and seventeen get the feeling that they were born to lose, if not in Bible class? And the uneasiness our boys have felt about winning — a fan can recall dozens of nights when the locals had a good first half, opened a nice lead, began to feel the opponents' pain, and sympathized and lightened up and wound up giving away their lunch. Does this come from misreading the Gospels?

Little Jimmy Wahlberg used to sit in the dugout and preach to the Whippets between innings, using the score of the ball game to quote Scripture; e.g., John 1:1: "In the beginning was the Word, and the Word was with God, and the Word was God," or Matthew 4:4: "Man shall not live by bread alone, but by every word that proceedeth out of the mouth of God." That was fine except when he was pitching. God had never granted Little Jimmy's prayer request for a good curveball, so this fine Christian boy got shelled like a peanut whenever he took the mound, and one day Ronnie Decker came back to the bench after an eternal inning in centerfield and said, "First Revelations 13:0: Keep the ball down and throw at their heads."

Ronnie is Catholic, and they have more

taste for blood, it seems. (Was there ever a *Methodist* bullfighter?) In St. Klaus, the ladies chant, "Make 'em sing and make 'em dance / Kick 'em in the nuts and step on their hands." The boys are ugly brutes with raw sores on their arms and legs and with little ball-bearing eyes, who will try to hurt you. A gang of men stands by the backstop, drinking beer and talking to the umpire, a clean-cut Lutheran boy named Fred. Fred knows that, the week before, Carlson called a third strike on a Klausie, dashed to his car, the men rocked it and let the air out of the tires but couldn't pry the hood open and disconnect the spark plugs before he started up and rode away on the rims. Fred hopes to keep the fans happy.

For a Golden Age of Lake Wobegon sports, you'd have to go back to the forties. The town ball club was the Lake Wobegon Schroeders, so named because the starting nine were brothers, sons of E. J. Schroeder. Nine big strapping boys with identical mops of black hair, big beaks, little chins, and so shy they couldn't look you in the eye, and E.J. was the manager, though the boys were such fine ballplayers, he only sat in the shade on a white kitchen chair and grumbled at them, they didn't require management.

E.J. was ticked off if a boy hit a bad pitch. He'd spit and curse and rail at him, and then R.J.'d go up and pound one out of the park (making the score 11–zip) and circle the bases and the old man'd say, "Boy, he put the old apple right down the middle, didn't he? Blind man coulda hit that one. Your gramma coulda put the wood on that one. If a guy couldn't hit that one out, there'd be something wrong with him, I'd say. Wind practically took that one out of here, didn't even need to hit it much" — and lean over and spit. When the Schroeders were winning every game, E.J. bitched about how they won.

"Why'dja throw to first for, ya dummy?"

"But it's the third out, Dad. We won the game."

"I know that. You don't have to point that out to me. Why'ntcha get the guy at third?"

"It was easier to go to first."

"Easier! *Easier??!!*"

The tenth son, Paul, had a gimpy right leg but still tried to please his dad and sat in the dugout and kept statistics (1.29, for example, and .452 and .992), but E.J. never looked at them. "That's history," he said, spitting, "I am interested in the here and now."

So his sons could never please him, and if

259

they did, he forgot about it. Once, against Freeport, his oldest boy, Edwin Jim, Jr., turned and ran to the centerfield fence for a long long long fly ball and threw his glove forty feet in the air to snag the ball and caught the ball and glove and turned toward the dugout to see if his dad had seen it, and E.J. was on his feet clapping, but when he saw the boy look to him, he immediately pretended he was swatting mosquitoes. The batter was called out, the third out. Jim ran back to the bench and stood by his dad. E.J. sat chewing in silence and fnally he said, "I saw a man in Superior, Wisconsin, do that a long time ago but he did it at night and the ball was hit a lot harder."

What made this old man so mean? Some said it happened in 1924, when he played for the town team that went to Fort Snelling for the state championship, and, in the ninth inning, in the deepening dusk on Campbell's Bluff, Lake Wobegon down by one run, bases loaded and himself the tying run on third, the Minneapolis pitcher suddenly collapsed and writhed around on the mound with his eyes bulging and face purple and vomiting and foaming and clawing and screeching, and everyone ran to help him, including E.J., and he jumped up and tagged them all out. A triple play, unas-

260

sisted. *What a rotten trick,* but there they stood, a bunch of rubes, and all the slickers howling and whooping their heads off, so he became mean, is one theory.

And he was mean. He could hit foul balls with deadly accuracy at an opponent or a fan who'd been riding him, or a member of the fan's immediate family, and once he fouled twenty-eight consecutive pitches off the home-plate umpire, for which he was thrown out of the Old Sod Shanty League.

"Go! Hence!" cried the ump.

"For foul balls?"

The umpire and the sinner were face-to-face. "Forever!" cried the ump. "Never again, so long as ball is thrown, shall thy face be seen in this park."

"Foul balls ain't against any rule that I know of!"

The umpire said, "Thou hast displeased me." And he pointed outerward and E.J. slouched away.

So he coached his boys. He never said a kind word to them, and they worked like dogs in hopes of hearing one, and thus they became great, mowing down the opposition for a hundred miles around. In 1946 they reached their peak. That was the year they disposed easily of fifteen crack teams in the Father Powers Charity Tournament, some by massacre, and at the closing ceremony, surrounded by sad little crippled children sitting dazed in the hot sun and holding pitiful flags they had made themselves, when E.J. was supposed to hand back the winner's check for $100 to Father Powers to help with the work among the poor, E.J. said, "Fat chance!" and shoved away the kindly priest's outstretched hand. That was also the year Babe Ruth came to town with the Sorbasol All-Star barnstorming team.

The Babe had retired in 1935 and was dying of cancer, but even a dying man has bills to pay, and so he took to the road for Sorbasol, and Lake Wobegon was the twenty-fourth stop on the trip, a day game on November 12. The All-Star train of two sleepers and a private car for the Babe backed up the sixteen-mile spur into Lake Wobegon, arriving at 10:00 a.m. with a blast of whistle and a burst of steam, but hundreds already were on hand to watch it arrive.

The Babe was a legend then, much like God is today. He didn't give interviews, in other words. He rode around on his train and appeared only when necessary. It was said that he drank Canadian rye whiskey, ate hot dogs, won thousands at poker, and kept beautiful women in his private car,

Excelsior, but that was only talk.

The sleepers were ordinary deluxe Pullmans; the *Excelsior* was royal green with gold-and-silver trim and crimson velvet curtains tied shut — not that anyone tried to look in; these were proud country people, not a bunch of gawkers. Men stood by the train, their backs to it, talking purposefully about various things, looking out across the lake, and when other men straggled across the field in twos and threes, stared at the train, and asked, "Is he really in there?" the firstcomers said, "Who? Oh! You mean the Babe? Oh, yes, I reckon he's here all right — this is his train, you know. I doubt that his train would go running around without the Babe in it, now, would it?" and resumed their job of standing by the train, gazing out across the lake. A proud moment for them.

At noon the Babe came out in white linen knickers. He looked lost. A tiny black man held his left arm. Babe tried to smile at the people and the look on his face made them glance away. He stumbled on a loose plank on the platform and men reached to steady him and noticed he was hot to the touch. He signed an autograph. It was illegible. A young woman was carried to him who'd been mysteriously ill for months, and he laid his big hand on her forehead and she

263

said she felt something. (Next day she was a little better. Not recovered but improved.)

However, the Babe looked shaky, like a man who ate a bushel of peaches whole and now was worried about the pits. He's drunk, some said, and a man did dump a basket of empty beer bottles off the train, and boys dove in to get one for a souvenir — but others who came close to his breath said no, he wasn't drunk, only dying. So it was that an immense crowd turned out at the Wally (Old Hard Hands) Bunsen Memorial Ballpark: twenty cents per seat, two bits to stand along the foul line, and a dollar to be behind a rope by the dugout, where the Babe would shake hands with each person in that section.

He and the All-Stars changed into their red Sorbasol uniforms in the dugout, there being no place else, and people looked away as they did it (nowadays people would look, but then they didn't), and the Babe and his teammates tossed the ball around, then sat down, and out came the Schroeders. They ran around and warmed up and you could see by their nonchalance how nervous they were. E.J. batted grounders to them and hit one grounder zinging into the visitors' dugout, missing the Babe by six inches. He was too sick to move. The All-Stars ran out and griped to the ump but the Babe sat like he didn't know where he was. The ump was scared. The Babe hobbled out to home plate for the ceremonial handshakes and photographs, and E.J. put his arm around him as the crowd stood cheering, and grinned and whispered, "We're going to kill ya, ya big mutt. First pitch goes in your ear. This is your last game. Bye, Babe." And the game got under way.

It was a good game, it's been said, though nobody remembers much about it specifically, such as the score, for example. The All-Stars were nobodies, only the Babe mattered to the crowd, and the big question was Would he play? He looked too shaky to take the field, so some said, "Suspend the rules! Why not let him just go up and bat! He can bat for the pitcher! Why not? It wouldn't hurt anything!" And nowadays they might do it, but back then you didn't pick up the bat unless you picked up your glove and played a position, and others said that maybe it wouldn't hurt anything but once you start changing the rules of the game for convenience, then what happens to our principles? Or do we change those, too?

So the game went along, a good game except that the Babe sat sprawled in the dugout, the little black man dipping cloths in a bucket of ice and laying them on the great man's head — a cool fall day but he was hot — and between innings he climbed out and waved to the fans and they stood and cheered and wondered would he come to bat.

E.J. said to Bernie, "He'll bat all right, and when he comes, remember the first pitch: hard and high and inside."

"He looks too weak to get the bat off his shoulder, Dad. He looks like a breeze would blow him over. I can't throw at Babe Ruth."

"He's not sick, he's pretending so he don't have to play like the rest of us. Look at him: big fat rich New York son of a bitch, I bet he's getting five hundred dollars just to sit there and have a pickaninny put ice on him. Boy, I'd put some ice on him you-know-where, boy, he'd get up quick then, he'd be ready to play then. He comes up, I want you to give him something to think about so he knows we're not all a bunch of dumb hicks out here happy just to have him show up. I want him to know that some of us *mean it.* You do what I say. I'm serious."

It was a good game and people enjoyed it, the day cool and bright, delicious, smelling of apples and leather and woodsmoke and horses, blazed with majestic colors as if in a country where kings and queens ride through the cornfields into the triumphant reds and oranges of the woods, and men in November playing the last game of summer, waiting for the Babe, everyone waiting for the Babe as runs scored, hours passed, the sky turned red and hazy. It was about time to quit and go home, and then he marched out, bat in hand, and three thousand people threw back their heads and yelled as loud as they could. They yelled for one solid minute and then it was still.

The Babe stood looking toward the woods until everything was silent, then stepped to the plate and waved the bat, and Bernie looked at him. It was so quiet you could hear coughing in the crowd. Way to the rear a man said, "Merle, you get your hands off her and shut up now," and hundreds turned and shushed *him.* Then Bernie wound up. He bent way down and reached way back and kicked up high and the world turned and the ball flew and the umpire said, "BALL ONE!" and the catcher turned and said, "Be quiet, this doesn't concern you," and the umpire blushed. He knew immediately that he was in the wrong. Babe Ruth was not going to walk, he would sooner strike out and would do it himself, with no help from an umpire. So the umpire turned and walked away.

The Babe turned and spat and picked up a little dirt and rubbed his hands with it (people thought, Look, that's our dirt and he's putting it on his hands, as if the Babe might bring his own) and then stood in and waved the bat and Bernie bent way down and reached way back and kicked high and the world turned and the ball flew and the Babe swung and missed; he said *huhhhnnnn* and staggered. And the next pitch. He swung and cried in pain and the big slow curve slapped into the catcher's mitt.

It was so still, they heard the Babe clear his throat, like a board sliding across dirt. They heard Bernie breathing hard through his nose.

The people were quiet, wanting to see, hear, and smell everything and remember it forever: the wet fall dirt, the pale white bat, the pink cotton candy and the gentlemen's hats, the smell of wool and the glimmer of a star in the twilight, the touch of your dad's big hand and your little hand in it. Even E.J. was quiet, chewing, watching his son. The sun had set beyond right field, darkness was settling, you had to look close to see — Bernie took three steps toward home and pointed at the high outside corner of the plate, calling his pitch, and the Babe threw back his head and laughed four laughs. (People were glad to hear he was feeling better, but it was scary to hear a man laugh at home plate; everyone knew it was bad luck.) He touched the corner with his bat. Bernie climbed back on the mound, he paused, he bent down low and reached way back and kicked real high and the world turned and the ball flew and the Babe swung and it cracked and the ball became a tiny white star in the sky. It hung there as the Babe went around the bases in his famous Babe Ruth stride, the big graceful man trotting on slim little feet, his head down until the roar of the crowd rose like an ocean wave on the prairie and he looked up as he turned at third; he smiled, lifted his cap, strode soundlessly across home plate looking like the greatest ballplayer in the history of the world. The star was still in the sky, straight out due northwest of the centerfield fence, where he hit it. The ball was never found, though they searched for it for years.

"Did you see that?" your dad says, taking your hand.

You say, "Yes, I did."

Even E.J. saw it and stood with the rest and he was changed after that, as were the others. A true hero has some power to make us a gift of a larger life. The Schroeders broke up, the boys went their own ways, and once they were out of earshot, E.J. sat in the Sidetrack Tap and bragged them up, the winners he produced and how they had shown Babe Ruth a pretty good game. He was tolerated but Babe Ruth was revered. He did something on that one day in our town that made us feel we were on the map of the universe, connected somehow to the stars, part of the mind of God. The full effect of his mighty blow diminished over time, of course, and now our teams languish, our coaches despair. Defeat comes to seem the natural course of things. Lake Wobegon dresses for a game, they put on their jockstraps, pull on the socks, get into the colors, they start to lose heart and turn pale — fear shrivels them.

Boys, this game may be your only chance to be good, he might tell them. You might screw up everything else in your life and poison the ones who love you, create misery, create such pain and devastation it will be repeated by generations of descendants. Boys, there's plenty of room for tragedy in life, so if you go bad, don't have it be said that you never did anything right. Win this game.

6.
1951

I have never moved to a warmer climate — never gave it a thought — because, after the brutal winter of 1951, every winter since has seemed mild and pleasant to me, especially with the advent of thermal underwear and heated steering wheels, which didn't exist back then. Nowadays you can plug your car into an electrical outlet to keep the radiator warm so the car starts instantly in the morning. Ice choppers are better, snow boots, emergency medical care: progress on every hand. People complain about winter and I tell them, "It could be worse," which I happen to know something about, having been around in 1951.

I was nine years old, the invisible middle child in a family of eight. We had been a family of ten but little Ralph had been carried away by coyotes and my twin sister, Gertie, had been perforated by a giant icicle. She was going to school and slammed the door in a fit of pique, and the icicle, which had been suspended from the eave and was the size of a Sidewinder missile and pointed at the end, split the child nearly in two.

This was before we moved to town. We lived way out on the county road, in a rickety frame house at the old Crandall farm, eight of us in three bedrooms, plus Aunt Cooter and Uncle Dud, who weren't related to us. Mother took them in because they had nowhere to go and we were Christians. They lived in the living room, wrapped in horse blankets, gumming their food and conversing with historical figures such as Ulysses S. Grant or Mrs. William McKinley. When they weren't complaining about their troubles, they were muttering dark prophesies: "It's a-coming! The big one! Who can withstand the power of the Lord God Almighty if He shall set His Hand against them!" Demented elderly people do not make good houseguests but peach brandy made them manageable: Dad poured half a cup for each of them at eight every night and they were out cold by nine. All in all I'd say that with them living with us, I always looked forward to school, so that was good.

■ ■ ■ ■

Unlike today, there was no accurate weather forecasting back then. America's radar was focused on defending us against Soviet attack, not on locating high-pressure fronts. All we had from day to day was a general sense of foreboding. Blinding blizzards came sweeping suddenly down from Alberta and Saskatchewan without warning. Thirty below zero was considered moderate; fifty below was cold, eighty below darned cold. At a hundred below, school was canceled and everybody stayed home. Years later it came out that the chief meteorologist at the U.S. Weather Bureau was on the take from the Chamber of Commerce and that temperatures and snowfall were "adjusted" so as not to harm "public morale," but we knew how cold it was. When you dumped boiling water out the back door, it hit the ground as ice crystals. The snow was ten feet deep — the downstairs of our house was dark from January on and we had to exit through a tunnel. You could walk on the hard-crusted drifts. Our furnace burned coal, and when we ran out, it burned tree stumps, old tires, furniture — we burned the entire twenty-four-volume C. H. McIntosh Commentary on the Ephesians one night, which was Grandpa's wedding gift to my parents but he was dead and they were still married so it wasn't a problem.

One night, engrossed in a Hardy Boys mystery, I lay by the heat register while my sisters and Mother listened to Jack Benny on the radio, jawing with Rochester and Mary, trying to save a nickel on a necktie. Mother asked me to go out and bring in the clothes hanging on the clothesline. I put on my coat and buckled up my overshoes.

"Put a scarf over your face," she said, "and remember to breathe through your nose, not your mouth." We knew that mouth breathing would lead to frosted lungs, which would lead to pneumonia and then death.

I walked out into the bitter cold and found the laundry frozen stiff as lumber on the clothesline, the world silent and frozen all around. Blue light flickered from the Wicks' Muntz TV across the road. We did not have a TV — there were Hollywood movies on TV and Hollywood was a polluter of the minds of young people — so I sometimes snuck over and stood around watching *I Love Lucy.* The Wicks were always piled in around their old TV with the rabbit ears antenna like a den full of dogs curled up, each dog in his spot. Once when their picture got snowy, I stood and held the antenna and the picture got clearer. They paid me a quarter to do this.

As I took the frozen laundry off the line, I thought about putting my tongue on one of the clothes poles, where it would freeze to the iron instantly and soon the volunteer fire department would come rolling up, sirens screaming, red lights flashing, to rescue me, the very nice boy with glasses, and Mother, weeping with her arms around me, at last would realize what a prize she had. But it was only a thought.

That night I lay in my cot in the attic and could see my breath. I always slept in my clothes, never wet the bed, never even considered it. I lay quietly, warming up my little trough, and soon after I fell asleep, Mother was thumping on the door. Five a.m., time to rise and shine. I went to the kitchen and took a bowl of Hot Ralston, which tasted like sweeping compound, and a cup of Folger's coffee, and put on parka and gloves to go help Dad start the car, which was frozen solid in the driveway. We had burned the garage for fuel the winter before.

It was a 1946 Ford coupe, a good-looking

car, and my job was to get behind the wheel
while Dad pushed. The windshield was
heavily frosted, so I put my bare hand
against it to clear a little peephole. Dad
yelled, "Ready?" and I said I was. "Pump
the gas," he yelled, and he gave a big heave
and the tires came loose from where they'd
been frozen to the ground and the car
started to roll down the slight incline of the
driveway. I clung to the wheel and strained
to see out through the peephole as the car
picked up speed, jolting and bucking over
the bumps, the shock absorbers frozen solid.
At just the exact right moment, I was to
pop the clutch and throw the car into
second gear; if I had pumped the gas pedal
just the right number of times, the momentum of the car would turn over the engine
and it would start firing, and if I hadn't
done everything right, the car would jerk to
a stop and Dad would have to call up Mr.
Wick to come over with jumper cables and
start us. Dad did not care to be beholden to
a Catholic, so there was a lot at stake. The
car was rolling fast now, and when my foot
came off the gas pedal and Dad said, "Now!
Now!" I popped her into second and the
engine roared and I stepped on the brake
while pushing in the clutch to slip the car
into neutral, and stopped at the end of the

driveway, engine idling at high speed as Dad came running up. "Shove over," he said. I slid over, and he put the car in reverse and backed her up the long driveway to where the garage had been, and we were all set to go. I don't remember that he said "Good job" or "Well done, son"; I suppose he may have, but I doubt it. Dad didn't believe in praise; he felt that it contributed to a prideful attitude.

Nor did he believe in driving his children to school in town. It was almost half a mile from the Crandall farmhouse to the county road where the schoolbus would come and Dad had strung clothesline from our porch railing to the telephone pole at the end of the driveway and on, pole by pole, up the township road to the county road. On blizzard mornings we grabbed hold of that rope and followed it through the blinding snow. You could hear other children whimpering in the whiteness and sometimes hear wild animals growling — of course we thought of little Ralph, who had been small for his age and easy prey for coyotes. When we came to the county road, the girls huddled inside a snow fort that we boys had constructed; we boys stood on the outside and peed in the snow to keep coyotes at bay until the bus came — or if the bus didn't come, then a sleigh came, pulled by a pair of black horses and driven by a man named Snead. A man with enormous eyebrows and a big mustache, he was said to have fought in the Battle of the Bulge and spent two years in an Army psychiatric ward. But he had a sleigh and a team of horses and the superintendent was deathly opposed to canceling school — "Once you start canceling school, where would you stop?" Mr. Bye liked to say — and so Mr. Snead got the job when the roads were too treacherous for motorized vehicles. We kids tumbled into the sleigh under the buffalo robes and he cracked his whip and off we went to school. It took almost two hours to get there, crossing the river over the ice, taking a detour around the woods where the coyotes dwelled, and avoiding the rocky ravine where the desperate O'Kasick gang had holed up in a sod hut after robbing the First National Bank of Anoka and shooting a teller in cold blood. I suppose Mr. Snead was trying to shield us from harsh reality by avoiding that ravine but we already knew all about the O'Kasicks and their bloody end, as we knew all about the grave-robber Ed Gein and the rampage of Charlie Starkweather, who shot his girlfriend's parents, and the merciless deeds of Dillinger and Ma Barker and Alvin (Creepy) Karpis, not to mention the James-Younger gang.

We knew that not far from the Crandall farm was the house where Confederate bushwhackers holed up in February 1865, on a foray to kidnap children for ransom to buy explosives in Canada — only it was bitterly cold and they were not properly dressed, so after they had ridden around and whooped for a while, they were happy to be taken into custody in a warm jail.

Mr. Snead drove his team past these scenes of violence and despair and we could smell the smell — so strange to a child's nose — of the raw whiskey he was nipping from a flask in his big hairy bearskin coat. Soon he was singing about the halls of Montezuma and the caissons rolling along, which moved him to depths of emotion and he wept and at the same time he lifted up a corner of the buffalo robe and yelled at us, "You kids know nothing. You think the world is peppermint candy and chocolate cake. Well, it isn't. Just ask me." One of my sisters said, "Mr. Snead —" And he said, "If any of you tells Mr. Bye that I've been hitting the bottle, I will kill you and burn your house down. Hear me? Don't think I won't. I was Jimmy O'Kasick's best friend. Him and me went way back." And then we were at school. None of us told on him. Who would we tell? Grown-ups always stood up for each other. It was them against us. Nowadays Mr. Snead would be locked up for psychological harassment and put into a treatment program, but back then he drove a sleigh and eventually was hired as a janitor when there was an opening at the grade school. Most janitors back then were shady characters with a seedy past but as long as they washed and waxed and kept the furnace lit, they were allowed to stay around. The O'Kasicks could've gotten janitor jobs if they hadn't shot that bank teller.

Winter was cruel but it was beautiful, too, the snow drifted against house and barn, ice on the bare limbs of trees, the orange winter sun low in the sky. Cold as it was, we got out our sleds and knelt on them and opened our jackets for a sail and let the wind blow us across the crusted snow. That was how I met the Jacobson family who lived south of town, eleven miles from our house as the crow flies or as the sled blows — I got going fast and it felt like such an accomplishment, steering around houses and barns by dragging one foot or the other, zooming along in ditches and across open fields, and I just plain lost track of how far I'd gone.

The Jacobsons had one daughter but they had always wanted a son and there I was, nine years old, bright as a penny, and I loved their house, which was warm and well furnished and had TV and no demented elderly persons in residence. My mother called the sheriff a few days later — the absence of a quiet, polite child is not noticed right away. He said I had turned up at the Jacobsons' and eventually she got in touch with them, by which time they and I had become rather chummy. They'd given me the nickname Buddy. I had yearned for a nickname for years and now a wonderful family had bestowed one on me. They were Methodists and very lighthearted and given to playing cards and singing around the piano and telling jokes, none of which was big in my family.

Mr. Jacobson called up Dad and invited me to stay with them for a few weeks and what with money so scarce Dad said yes and the few weeks turned into four months and by that time I had been pretty well corrupted. The Jacobsons gave me forbidden books to read, fiction and the like, and allowed me to taste red wine. They encouraged me to talk at the dinner table. They listened to my harebrained notions and didn't scorn them outright. They lent me a typewriter. I wrote stories and showed them to the Jacobsons and they said I had a lot of talent. "A ton of talent" was what they said. "Talent to burn." That was what did it.

When I returned home, I was a different person, or so I thought. It was May, the lilacs were in bloom, I was a writer. For some reason, my dad called me Harold for a few weeks and nobody seemed to notice except me, and back then a kid didn't correct his elders. So I was Harold for a while. I didn't mind.

The winter of 1951 made every winter since feel like a Sunday school picnic. Some Minnesotans head for the sunny South after Christmas, and let me tell you — they are the ones we've always wished would move away. Complainers, malcontents, people who never shoveled their sidewalks. Good riddance.

I live in St. Paul now, which is beautiful after a fresh snow, the old streetlights, the lights of houses through the trees, the walkers out, the headlights moving slowly. I have a car of my own and after I start it (instantly, no rolling) the heating pad in the front seat gets warm and so does the steering wheel. I still write stories now and then. Life is good. It could be worse, and it was in 1951, and now it isn't. That's as good as it gets.

7.
LITTLE BECKY

I wrote three stories for *The New Yorker* about a fictitious Minneapolis radio station, WLT, drawing on faint memories of the radio shows of my youth, *Good Neighbor Time* on WCCO with Bob DeHaven and Wally Olson and His Band, and a Norwegian cowboy duo, Slim Jim and the Vagabond Kid, on WMIN, and the *Sunset Valley Barn Dance* on KSTP. I felt confident enough about the material to launch into a novel, *WLT: A Radio Romance,* which was about the power of the medium to deceive, gospel singers who were drunks and adulterers, that sort of thing. I ought to know: as a kid, I got very peeved at my dad pretending to be a hick, which he often did, and then I did the very same thing in the early years of *A Prairie Home Companion.* Put on a twangy accent, and wore a big straw hat, and sang sad songs about Mother and home and Old Shep.

Friendly Neighbor with Dad Benson, the Ole Lunchtime Philosopher, came on the air at noon, and in a good many towns around the Midwest, the noon whistle was blown a couple of minutes early to give people time to get their radios warmed up. The announcer said, "WLT, seven-seventy, the Air Castle of the North, from studios at the Hotel Ogden, Minneapolis," and the WLT chimes struck twelve, the organ played "Whispering Hope," and the announcer said, "And now we take you down the road a ways to the home of Dad Benson and his wife, Mom, his daughter, Jo, and her husband, Frank, for a visit with the Friendly Neighbor, brought to you by Milton, King Seeds, the best friend your garden ever had. As we join them today, the family is sitting around the kitchen table, where Jo is fixing lunch." Wherever you were back then, everything stopped. Dad Benson ran a feed store in Elmville and he was like a real person who sat down next to you, he just talked and said the things you had always thought yourself. The show might start with Jo saying, "I don't know why I can't make this egg salad as good as what I used to," and Dad saying, "Oh, your egg salad is the best in town and you know it," and Frank saying, "Sure looks like we might get some

285

snow tonight," and then Dad would remember the big blizzard of '09 and how dangerous it was, you couldn't see two feet in front of your face, and how it taught everybody to keep a weather eye out and use the sense that God gave geese and take care of each other. Dad preached a pretty simple philosophy: the Golden Rule mostly, with plain common sense tossed in. Smile and you'll feel better. East or west, home is best. There's no summer without winter. What can't be cured must be endured. Hunger makes the beans taste better. We must work in the heat or starve in the cold. Nobody is born smart. Do your best and leave the rest.

The friends and neighbors in radioland thought of the Bensons as real people. Anytime the Benson family suffered misfortune, contributions poured in to WLT, even when Dad dropped a piece of glass fruit:

(SFX: GLASS BREAKAGE)

DAD: Oh gosh. What a butterfingers I am. And that was Aunt Molly's good one. Did I ever tell you, Jo, about the time she and I went sugarmapling and treed a skunk?

JO (chuckling): I don't believe I ever heard that yarn, Dad. Did you, Frank?

FRANK: Nope, not me.

The next day, dozens of glass apples, oranges, pears, and bananas arrived, cases of them, and from then on, Dad designed the Bensons' troubles for charitable purposes. Once, for the Ebenezer Home's annual spring rummage sale, Dad went walking down to the widow's house with a pan of Jo's fresh oatmeal cookies and tore his best suit jumping over a fence when a dog chased him, and the station received more than a hundred good suits in four days. In the fall when the Salvation Army needed warm coats, Dad would do an episode in which he forgot his coat on the train, and in a few days, the coats would be piling up in the WLT lobby by the hundreds, and Dad shipped them over to the mission. The coats were mostly size 48 and larger, because people thought of Dad as a big fellow, but as Dad said, beggars can't be choosers.

For the Home's drive to build a recreation hall, there were several financial crises — a sudden hailstorm that wiped out the corn, a stolen wallet, a dishonest stockbroker, a needed operation for the dog, Buster — and the money rolled in.

Friendly Neighbor ended at 12:30 p.m. and every day the WLT lobby was full of fans,

287

twenty or thirty, standing modestly behind a rope, quiet, smiling, hopeful, like job-seekers or orphans. Some of them held gifts, hand-knit socks or bags of vegetables. They waited, almost motionless, as the minutes ticked by, and then suddenly the elevator opened and there was Dad. They all clapped, and he ducked under the rope and walked into the midst of them. *Hi, Dad.* "Hi. How you doing?" *Fine. Real good.* "That's good." *Mighty good show today.* "Thanks." *You got a minute?* "Of course, I've always got a minute."

"How is your back doing?" a woman asked.

Dad looked puzzled. She said, "You strained it last week pushing Pops Simpson's car out of the snow."

"Oh," he said. "My *back.* Yes, it's fine. Just a strain. Thought you said my 'bag' and I was trying to think what you meant."

An old man shook Dad's hand gravely, looking deep into his eyes. "Don't you think Eunice is ever going to come back? We sure miss her."

"Oh, I'm sure she will. Nice to see you," he murmured. "But which niece is that you're asking about?"

"You think Eunice *will* come back?"

"Eunice! Well, we'll just have to wait and

see." He was signing all the pieces of paper they held out to him. He pressed the flesh and nodded and beamed and squeezed elbows and patted heads and chummed around. He signed an autograph book, posed for a snapshot.

"What about Carl?" a woman said. "Carl Farnsworth? At the Mercantile?"

"Right," said Dad. "Carl."

"He was married to Myrt. You know? She worked at the beauty parlor a while back?"

"Right, Myrt."

"But today you mentioned Carl going to Little Rock with Margaret. He didn't get a divorce, did he?"

"No, of course not. No, they've never been happier. No, that's just me being forgetful. I must've been thinking of Margaret Dono-hue at the bank."

"Donovan," said a woman in back.

"Of course. Quite a gal."

"We haven't heard her in a long time. She didn't leave town, did she?"

No, Dad said, she was fine. Everybody was fine. He worked his way through the crowd to a door marked NO ADMITTANCE, STAFF ONLY and waved and disappeared.

The show was written by Patsy Konopka, who had sung in the Radio Cowgirls on *Slim*

Jim and the Bunkhouse Gang, and she was a serious student of theosophy and positivism who had studied with a Gnostic master in Sioux Falls who could telepathically open a can of coffee. She had learned there the secret of the Oval of Life and the Four Powers (Ability, Capacity, Facility, Vitality) and the Seven Doorways of Celestial Selection. These are brief openings in the cosmos, when a great leap of spiritual knowledge is attainable. Now she was turning her attention more toward ethereology and the science of electivism with its vast lore on the determining power of radiation. Radiation was Patsy's true passion, the study of the nimbus of light around the body. The practiced eye could read it like a book.

She had told Dad Benson all about radiation one night when he had invited her to Charlie's Café Exceptionale for dinner and drinks. He asked her to read his nimbus and she told him he was a man of generous spirit, swift of intuition, starved for truth, lacking depth but seeking to improve and to penetrate the darkness. "And," she said, "you are hoping to get me to take my clothes off."

He agreed that this was true and inquired if it were possible.

She said that there is a hand of inevitability that guides these matters and it can be perceived only with time.

He said he was *not* only interested in sex, that he was interested in *her,* that sex was maybe his way of getting to know her, that he admired her as an artist, that he could get the Cowgirls their own radio show, perhaps a Saturday night spot.

"I'm so sick of yodeling, I could spit," she said. She told him she wanted to be a writer and help people understand the principles of theosophy — such as *It is always too late for grief.* Or *Patience expects joy.* Or *Fate smiles on the one it fools.*

So Dad offered her a job as a writer at forty dollars a week. She accepted with pleasure.

She created *Golden Years* (Monday–Friday, 11 a.m.), about the multimillionaires Elmer and Edna Hubbard, who, dissatisfied with the frenzied pace of life in the big city and the emptiness of material success, move to the little town of Nowthen and open a coffee shop and bestow anonymous gifts on deserving townspeople through the mail. She wrote *Love's Old Sweet Song* (Wednesdays, 8:30 p.m.), the story of Folwell Hollister, wealthy New York executive, who moves back to his hometown of Hollister Corner after doctors tell him that he has six months to live and buys the farm he had always wanted, the old Reddin place, and stocks it with prize Orpington hens and blackface Highland sheep and chops kindling and hoes the tomatoes and observes the slow graceful turning of the seasons and then falls in love with Jane Maxwell, his boyhood sweetheart and the woman he should have wed instead of chasing off east, who is married to a jerk, and to relieve the pain of "a love that cannot be," Folwell does good for others in small, anonymous ways. It was hard, week after week, to compose rhapsodies to falling leaves and snowy fields, even for a positivist like Patsy, so one week Mr. Maxwell was killed in a gold-mine explosion and Folwell swiftly married Jane, who called him Folly, and the show took a sharp turn. Jane was quite a looker, even at sixty, and Hollister Corner was a place she'd been wanting to escape since she was eleven, and so the Hollisters purchased a large home in Golden Valley, a stone's throw from Minneapolis, and she took up theosophy and they traveled to New York often.

She created *The Hills of Home* and *The Best Is Yet to Be* (Monday–Friday, 9:45 and 11:30 a.m.), further variations on the theme of weary-striver-finds-contentment-in-doing-good, and she also created *Arthur Fox, Detective* and *Another World* and *The Lazy W Gang.* The approach of a deadline inspired her. The clock ticked, and she wrote, and the big hand crept toward airtime, and the pages came faster and faster. She believed in the power of threes, based on an old theosophist concept of virtue as triangular, and always looked for threes in a story, trios of characters, trilateral story lines, beginning-middle-end, thesis-antithesis-synthesis, quest-defeat-redemption. She believed in the morning, as her father had taught her ("Some work in the morning may neatly be done that all the day after may hardly be won"), and rose early and went straight to work at her trusty Underwood. She believed that friends steal away months and families steal years, so she stayed single and she kept friends at bay.

When she took over writing *Friendly Neighbor,* Patsy made the Bensons a little more human. Jo and Frank started bickering over money — Jo sent off for some youth-giving face cream made from bee hormones and ground antlers, and Frank hit the ceiling. "Three dollars! Three dollars?" Frank was liable to drop work at any time and go out fishing for walleyes, though he always came back empty-handed — "Three hours!" cried

293

Jo. "Three hours!" — and one day Patsy had Mom Benson struck by a car while out shopping for underwear and she lay in the hospital in a coma. The coma went on and on. Katherine Doud, the actress who played Mom, was a lush and had come to the studio the day before, stewed to the gills, and the coma was to give her time to go to a sanitarium and dry out.

One day a man in a blue tuxedo strolled into Dad's feed and seed in Elmville and demanded directions to the Moonlight Bay Supper Club. He was accompanied by a little girl in a pink prom dress and a tall buxom bejeweled woman named Ginger, and you knew the moment she said, "Pleased to make yer acquaintance, I'm shur," that she and the man were not married.

The club could be reached only by back roads through the bird refuge and along the banks of the Whispering Willow River. It was a hideaway where the well-to-do cavorted with their paramours, not on the main road, so the directions were complicated. And when Dad said, "And then turn left at the farm with the red barn with the Chaska Chick Starter billboard," the man blew up — he threw his cane and his top hat on the counter next to a sack of Illini sweet-corn seeds and said, "Boy, isn't this the rotten luck! Go away for a swell weekend and you wind up stuck in a stupid little burg where people can't even give you directions out of town! Boy, that takes the cake!"

He stalked around and fumed for a few minutes; meanwhile Dad struck up a conversation with the little girl. "My name is Rebecca," she said, very sweetly. "I'm almost ten. If we get to Moonlight Bay, my dad is going to take me swimming."

Dad said, "Oh?"

"Yes! And if I'm real good, we'll go fishing, too."

"Well, if ifs and ands were pots and pans, there'd be no trade for tinkers," remarked Dad.

They chatted away and she asked him what he sold in this store and he gave her a tour. "This is our most popular tomato seed, the Milton, King Big Red Beefeater," he said. She'd never seen tomato seeds, didn't know tomatoes came from seeds. She'd never had a garden in her life, living as she did in a big suite on the thirtieth floor of the Waldorf Towers in New York, and she skipped along from bin to bin, scooping up handfuls of seeds as if they were jewels, sniffing their sweet dry seedy essence, as her father groused and grumped in the background and demanded a telephone and Ginger smoked a cigarette and whined, "You promised me a nice weekend, Bobbsie. You said we'd go swimming and dancing and we'd do a little cootchie-cootchie-coo — you didn't say nothing about hanging around in no feed store," and meanwhile Dad and Becky were getting to be fast friends. She had never ridden a bicycle or thrown a ball or had her own dog or cat, either. "No bike? Oh, you should come and visit us sometime," said Dad.

"Ohhhhhh, I wish I could," she whispered.

"And you never said word one about bringing the brat along neither," Ginger said and blew a big cloud of smoke, and her heels went *rapraprap* like a tack hammer. "Quit foolin around, Bobbsie, and let's go there and start having some fun, honey. C'mon! Puhleeze?"

Becky began to weep softly. "Oh, that's just great!" said her dad. "Bring you along and you bawl like a baby. Look at you!" He took Dad aside. "Lissen," he said, "sorry I talked so rough before, I've been under a lotta pressure. Here's a hundred bucks. Think you could look after my little girl for a few days until I get back? You and her seem to get along. Whaddaya say?"

296

There was a short, sweet pause, where you could hear Dad loathe the man, then he said, "It would be my privilege. She is as welcome here as if she were my own."

So in she came, Little Becky, played by Marjery Moore. Marjery Moore was fourteen but she played a little girl just fine. She was the daughter of Dr. W. Murray Moore, the physician who was treating Dad's hemorrhoids, a big hearty man and more of a kidder than you'd want your physician to be. His daughter took after him. She was a handful. She smoked Camels, half a pack a day, and swore like a cowboy. Her mother brought her from school at 11:30 and dropped her off at the WLT entrance and she smoked a cigarette in the elevator and another one in the studio before the broadcast. Dad told her, "Honey, those coffin nails are going to hurt your voice," but she just made a face. "It's my business if I do. You're not the boss of me, ya old dodo."

It dawned on Marjery within days of coming on *Friendly Neighbor* that she could get a big rise out of the radio folks by saying off-color things in her Little Becky voice. She could make Dad levitate an inch by tiptoeing up behind him in the hall and crying, "Look at me! I'm naked as a jaybird!"

"Honey," he said, "it's not funny. We got sponsors back here, sponsors' kids, employees' families. Don't ruin it for them."

"Well, don't have a shit fit about it."

"Honey, what you do drunk you pay for sober. Sin in haste and repent at leisure. Think about it."

"Stuff it, Pops."

Leo LaValley, the old WLT chief engineer, believed that Becky was a boy. He was certain of it. "We are paying three hundred fifty dollars a week for a so-called child to mince around like a girl, and when the story hits the papers, boys, you and I will be out on the street looking for work. If that kid's a girl, then I'm Greta Garbo. I keep seeing razor nicks on the little nipper's cheeks, don't you?" He stood in the engineer's booth, looking at the actors through the big slanted glass window, and pointed at Becky, who was lighting a cigarette as Harmon Tremaine the announcer read the commercial ("Cottage Home is chock full of vitamins and protein and all the good stuff that helps little girls like Becky grow up tall and strong, and Cottage Home is the cottage cheese with that mmmmmm-good real honest-to-goodness homemade flavor. Right, Little Becky?" LITTLE BECKY: Oh boy!"), and said, "Some hermaphrodites can pass for children until they experience the change of voice in their late thirties. They have only one gonad, like John Wilkes Booth. He had a piping soprano voice and played women's roles until he was thirty. Had no lead in his pencil. That's why he shot Lincoln. Another was Typhoid Harry, the Georgia farm boy who milked his father's cows day and night and spread the deadly disease that almost wiped out Atlanta. Another hermaphrodite." He told the other engineers to keep a close watch on Little Becky. "You can tell," he said. "You'll know."

A few days after Becky's arrival in Elmville, Dad took Patsy for lunch to Richards Treat and told her to get rid of the kid. "She talks like her shoes are too tight. She's worse than Little Buddy. In fact, she makes him sound almost reasonable." Little Buddy was the son of Dad's friend Slim Graves, who came on *Friendly Neighbor* from time to time to sing maudlin ballads about dying children. "Ditch her," said Dad. "Have her dad come back from New York and pick her up. Have her die and have Little Buddy sing at her funeral. Do anything, but get rid of the kid."

"Dad, we got five hundred letters about

that show where she arrived in town. Most popular we've ever done. Milton, King want to put her picture on their spring catalogue. They want to put out a Little Becky Scrapbook in the fall, give it away for three empty seed packets. Our contract with them comes up in two months. Little Becky is a moneymaker, Dad. And I want a raise."

Dad didn't like the premise of it. "You take a child away from her own father and what's next! You want all the kiddos to hate their dads?"

One day Marjery tripped along behind the owner of WLT, Ray Soderberg, and said, in her Little Becky voice, "How come your pants are so big in front, mister?" He beat a fast retreat to his office and closed the door and wrote Patsy a note: "Fire Marjery Moore. She's a bur in the butt. Give her malaria or something. She could die of an infected tooth like F. W. Woolworth. That would encourage listeners to go to the dentist. Children are inherently unreliable and when you make a child into the star of a show you are building on quicksand. They are easily spoiled by attention, and they quickly grow up and become unattractive."

The next day, Little Becky got terribly sick, and Dad was in something of a panic, what with Jo and Frank away on a car trip to Michigan and no money on hand for a specialist — and finally she was knocking at death's door, 105-degree fever, babbling about angels and bright heavenly emanations — "Uncle Dad, Uncle Dad, they have such beautiful faces." Marjery talked through a bath towel to get the faint voice of the dying child, and Dad said, all choked up, "Lord, I never doubted You until now, but — how can You let this child suffer? Lord, take her home or work a miracle, but please, Lord, do it soon." The switchboard was jammed with sobbing fans — more than $20,000 was raised in one week for the children's wing of Abbot Hospital. Becky's fever continued. She babbled about nimbuses and auras and wholeness and purity. A few days later, Ray relented and gave Marjery a six-month contract, and the next day Dr. Jim burst in the door with a brand-new serum flown in from the city. Buster barked for joy and Jo and Frank came back with a tidy sum inherited from a Michigan uncle they never knew they had, and Becky said, "Uncle Dad, why are you crying?" "Oh, don't mind me," he muttered. "I'm just a foolish old man, that's all. And sometimes I wish I were smarter. It seems like life is half over before we know what it is. But you close your eyes and get some sleep now."

BECKY: Why is Dr. Jim here?

JIM: Just came to make sure my girl is all right.

DAD: You rest now, honey.

BECKY: Uncle Dad?

DAD: Yes?

BECKY: Heaven is the beautifulest place I ever saw. It was all bright and starry and full of music, like a carnival except the rides were free, and Jesus was there and jillions of angels, and there was no sadness there, no crying, or nothing, just happiness, but still, I'm glad they sent me back to be with you, Uncle Dad.

DAD: I'm glad, too, little Beeper. You rest now, honey, I'll just sit here beside your bed and hold your hand.

BECKY: Oh, and there was a nice lady who said to say hello to you. Her name was Benson, too. Florence Benson.

DAD: Mom!

He rang up the Home and found out Mom had passed peacefully from this life a few minutes before. The first person to come bearing condolences was a neighbor lady, Miss Judy, who brought a pan of fresh banana bread and Becky's geography lesson (South America) and fixed a pot of coffee and told Dad that he should always feel free to count on her.

WLT got hundreds of letters, and Little Becky recovered, and Ray got an angry note from Katherine Doud (who played Mom), who hadn't been informed that her character would drop dead and told Ray that Dad had promised her that Mom would stay in the Home until she, Katherine, had quit drinking. "He is a dirty rotten liar and a cheat and maybe it's time you know that he is having an affair with Faith Snelling, Dale's wife," she wrote. Dad? In the sack with the actress who played his daughter, Jo? Ray sent Katherine some money and told her that when she got on the wagon for good she could return for one episode as Becky's New York mom, visiting Elmville to take the wretched child home. He would pay her handsomely for it. If the fans loved Little Becky before, they were even crazier

303

about her after her terrible illness. They baked pies and cakes for her by the hundreds, enough to keep the oldsters at the Ebenezer Home stuffed for weeks, and they wrote her bags and bags of mail.

"A hermaphrodite!" said Leo LaValley. "A freak of nature, but the outlook for these little fellas is not cheery. They tend to go berserk and walk into a grocery store with a shotgun and shoot the clerk for a couple rolls of quarters. That child is an undeveloped adult male tortured by his own desire for a woman and that's why the little shit is a big star. Women can hear that throb in her voice. But then that's true of most singers. A real man's man can no more sing than a dog can read books. It's pure frustration that makes for performing talent. All that la-di-da and the big grins, that's hermaphrodism talking." He leaned forward and pointed a finger into his own chest. "I," he said, "have no talent for performance whatsoever. I am quite happy to be normal."

8.
Casey at the Bat

In the Ernest Thayer original, it's a tragedy when Casey strikes out, but of course that depends on which ballpark you're in. In my version, the game is not in Mudville, it's in Dustburg, and people are overjoyed. When I wrote this, the line about the pigeons made me laugh out loud, and I *almost* laughed out loud at the line about the crowd grabbing hold of the bumpers and rocking him to and fro. A cruel poem.

It was looking rather hopeful for our
  Dustburg team that day:
We were leading Mudville four to two with
  an inning left to play.
We got Cooney on a grounder and
  Muldoon on the same,
Two down, none on, top of the ninth — we
  thought we'd won the game.
Mudville was despairing, and we grinned
  and cheered and clapped.

It looked like after all these years our losing
    string had snapped.
And we only wished that Casey, the big fat
    ugly lout,
Could be the patsy who would make the
    final, shameful out.
Oh, how we hated Casey, he was a blot
    upon the game.
Every dog in Dustburg barked at the
    mention of his name.
A bully and a braggart, a cretin and a
    swine —
If Casey came to bat, we'd stick it where
    the moon don't shine!
Two out and up came Flynn to bat, with
    Jimmy Blake on deck,
And the former was a loser and the latter
    was a wreck;
Though the game was in the bag, the
    Dustburg fans were hurt
To think that Casey would not come and
    get his just dessert.
But Flynn, he got a single, a most unlikely
    sight,
And Blake swung like a lady but he parked
    it deep to right,
And when the dust had lifted, and fickle
    fate had beckoned,
There was Flynn a-hugging third and
    Jimmy safe at second.

Then from every Dustburg throat, there
  rose a lusty cry:
"Bring up the slimy greaseball and let him
  stand and die.
Throw the mighty slider and let him hear it
  whiz
And let him hit a pop-up like the pansy that
  he is."
There was pride in Casey's visage as he
  strode onto the grass,
There was scorn in his demeanor as he
  calmly scratched his back.
Ten thousand people booed him when he
  stepped into the box,
And they made the sound of farting when
  he bent to fix his socks.
And now the fabled slider came spinning
  toward the mitt,
And Casey watched it sliding and he did
  not go for it,
And the umpire jerked his arm like he was
  hauling down the sun,
And his cry rang from the box seats to the
  bleachers:
Stee-rike One!
Ten thousand Dustburg partisans raised
  such a mighty cheer,
The pigeons in the rafters crapped and
  ruined all the beer.
"You filthy ignorant rotten bastard slimy son

of a bitch,"
We screamed at mighty Casey, and then
    came the second pitch.
It was our hero's fastball, it came across
    the plate,
And according to the radar, it was going
    ninety-eight.
And according to the umpire, it came in
    straight and true,
And the cry rang from the toilets to the
    bullpen:
Stee-rike Two!
Ten thousand Dustburg fans arose in joyful
    loud derision
To question Casey's salary, his manhood,
    and his vision.
Then while the Dustburg pitcher put the
    resin on the ball,
Ten thousand people hooted to think of
    Casey's fall.
Oh, the fury in his visage as he spat
    tobacco juice
And heard the little children screaming
    violent abuse.
He knocked the dirt from off his spikes,
    reached down and eased his pants —
"What's the matter? Did ya lose 'em?" cried
    a lady in the stands.
And then the Dustburg pitcher stood
    majestic on the hill,

And leaned in toward the plate, and then
   the crowd was still,
And he went into his windup, and he
   kicked, and let it go,
And then the air was shattered by the force
   of Casey's blow.
He swung so hard his hair fell off and he
   fell down in disgrace
And the Dustburg catcher held the ball and
   the crowd tore up the place,
With Casey prostrate in the dirt amid the
   screams and jeers
We threw wieners down at him and other
   souvenirs.
We pounded on the dugout roof as they
   helped him to the bench,
Then we ran out to the parking lot and got
   a monkey wrench
And found the Mudville bus and took the
   lug nuts off the tires,
And attached some firecrackers to the
   alternator wires.
We rubbed the doors and windows with a
   special kind of cheese
That smells like something died from an
   intestinal disease.
Old Casey took his sweet time, but we
   were glad to wait
And showered him with garbage as the
   team came out the gate.

So happy were the Dustburg fans that
  grand glorious day,
It took a dozen cops to help poor Casey
  get away,
But we grabbed hold of the bumpers and
  we rocked him to and fro
And he cursed us from inside the bus, and
  gosh, we loved it so!
Oh, sometimes in America the sun is
  shining bright,
Life is joyful sometimes, and all the world
  seems right,
But there is no joy in Dustburg, no joy so
  pure and sweet
As when the mighty Casey fell, demolished
  at our feet.

9.
MAROONED

A story about a loser trying to get back in the game, inspired by my friend's beautiful red-haired daughter, seventeen, who was sensing her peers edging ahead of her, getting good grades and cool summer jobs and hunky boyfriends, meanwhile a twerp beat her out for class president and she was horrified by a rash of pimples, so one night at supper her father tried to buck her up and tell her that life is not about racking up points, while the girl ignored him, her face in a book, as he murmured something about the virtue of self-awareness, whereupon she looked up from her book and asked, apropos of nothing at all, "Is fellatio considered a normal sexual practice?" and her poor father almost coughed up his meatballs. It was her way of declining his sympathy by firing a warning shot into the air. I was there. I was impressed.

I remember exactly when the marriage took

an odd turn. I was on the examining table with my shorts around my ankles and my tail up in the air and Dr. Miller surveying my colon through a cold steel periscope and making *hmmmm* sounds, his ballpoint pen scratching on a notepad, and at this delicate moment, he said, softly, "Do I strike you as a selfish person?"

"No . . . why?" I asked. The periscope felt like it was about six feet up me and I'm only five foot eight.

"I took a personal-inventory test in that book about getting ahead that everybody's reading — you know, the book that I heard you're related to the author of," he said. According to the test, he said, he was rather selfish.

I groaned, feeling the excavation of the Holland Tunnel within me, but of course I knew which book he meant. My dumbbell brother-in-law Dave's book, that's which one.

He told me Dave's book had meant a lot to him. "I never buy books other than science fiction," he confided, "but my partner, Jamie, gave it to me for my birthday and I opened it up and I couldn't put the rascal down. Heck of a book." Meanwhile, the periscope was way up there in my hinder, probing parts of me I had been unaware of

312

until now. "He says that what holds us back is fear, and that fear is selfish, and that getting ahead is a problem of getting outside yourself," and he gave the periscope a little nudge for emphasis. "You have to really focus on a goal outside yourself in order to succeed. My goal is to open a restaurant. Jamie's a wonderful cook. Chinese and Mexican, what do you think?"

I felt sore afterward. I went home and told Julie that a person as dim as my proctologist was exactly who Dave's book was aimed at, one ream job deserves another, and so forth. I was steamed.

She said, "You've always resented my brother, Danny, and you know why? I'll tell you why. Because your life is in Park and the key isn't even in the ignition. You're all about negativity, Danny. You stopped growing twenty-six years ago. And how would I know? Because I'm your wife, that's how I know."

Twenty-six years ago I graduated from the University of Minnesota journalism school with honors, the editor of the Minnesota *Daily,* and got a job as a professional copywriter at a Minneapolis ad agency. Dave Grebe was a clerk in his dad's stationery store, peddling birthday cards, and he and I played basketball on a Lutheran church team; that's how I met his sister Julie; she picked him up after the game because he'd lost his driver's license for drunk driving. He was twenty, big, and porky and none too bright, just like now. "I'd sure like to get the heck out of stationery, I hate the smell of it, mucilage especially, and the damn perfume, it's like someone vomited after eating fruit," Dave remarked to me once.

So I was not too surprised when, one fine day, Dave walked away from his job and shaved his head clean and moved to a commune in south Minneapolis, living with sixteen other disciples of the Serene Master Diego Tua, putting on the sandals of humility and the pale-green robe of constant renewal. "I have left your world, Danny," he told me on the phone.

Julie, who had become my wife, thought that Dave "just needed to get away for a while." I pointed out to her that the Tuans were fanatics who roamed the airport jingling bells and droning and whanging on drums, collecting money to support their master and his many wives and concubines. The Tuans believed that they possessed the immaculate secrets of the infinite universe and everyone else was vermin.

Julie thought they were Buddhists of some sort.

"They could be Buddhists or nudists or used-car salesmen who like to dress up in gowns, but whatever they are, they're working your brother like a puppet on a string."

She thought that Dave was only following his conscience and exploring life beyond stationery. Subject closed. So I did double duty for a few years — was a copywriter and kept the Grebe stationery store going — and Dave went around droning and whanging and announcing that he possessed the true light and making a holy nuisance of himself.

"We are God's roadblocks," said the Happy Master, Diego himself, "warning the people that the bridge ahead has fallen into the river of uncaring." His real name was Tim U. Apthed; he chose the name Diego, *Die-ego,* and crunched his initials into a surname, and founded a church for jerks. My agency, Curry, Cosset, Dorn, flew me to Atlanta or Boston or Chicago occasionally, and I'd come running through the Minneapolis–St. Paul terminal to catch a plane and hear the drums and bells and there were the Tuans in the middle of the concourse, holding up their signs, "YOUR LIFE IS A LIE," and chanting, "Only two

315

ways, one false, one true. Only one life, which way are you? Back! back! turn away from your lies! And God will give you a beautiful surprise!" and I had to squeeze through the crowd of shaven-headed men in sandals and robes, including my blissful idiot brother-in-law, and get on board the plane. It was like Run, Sheep, Run.

"Well, when he talks about people being so materialistic, I think he has a good point," said Julie. Who loves her kitchen, her eight-burner range, her big stainless-steel fridge with the glass door, her copper skillets, her king-size bed with Egyptian cotton sheets, et cetera, et cetera.

Then, fifteen years ago, Mr. Grebe died of a cerebral hemorrhage — clapped his hand to his forehead one morning and said, "Oh mercy. Call Ann and tell her I'll be late," and fell over dead onto the mechanical pencils. The rest of us were living in the rollerball era, but Mr. Grebe never gave up on mechanical pencils, or on carbon paper, or the mimeograph, despite the advent of photocopying. The family was devastated at the loss of this vacuous and bewildered man. They mourned for weeks, during which I was the bulwark, arranging the funeral, paying the bills, ordering stock for the store, hiring part-time help, and Dave sat in a corner weeping and chanting. They never found out who Ann was.

Dave left the Tuans and let his hair grow out and went back to work at the Wm. Grebe Stationery Shop. Every few days he'd call up and say, "I don't know how I can ever make it up to everyone for the embarrassment I have been. I was a dope and I don't deserve forgiveness. I ought to change my name and join the merchant marine and never come back."

You get tired of remorse when it becomes a broken record. Dave kept saying, "You've been so great, Danny, and I've been a big zero. I don't know why God lets me live." After a few months of it, I told him that I didn't know either but that he could take his guilt and put it where the moon don't shine. He reported this to Julie. She canceled our vacation trip to the Bahamas out of sheer spite. "I can never forgive you for saying that to my brother," she said, and she was right, she couldn't.

Meanwhile, Dave, who once had renounced material things, took over Wm. Grebe, stocked it with rollerballs and home copiers and iPads and iDoodads, and expanded into malls and branched out into discount bookselling, got rich in about three years, and became one smooth guy: bought a Hasselblad camera, Finnish furniture, a 1927 Martin guitar, four Harleys, a Peterbilt truck, an original Monet (*Girl with Light Hair*), and next thing I knew he was going around giving pep talks to basketball arenas full of shiny-faced men, and then, he wrote his book about getting ahead, *Never Buy a Bottle of Rat Poison That Comes with Gift Coupons.* It sold more copies than there are rats in New York. He turned Tuanism inside out and restated it in capitalist terms, and made low cash flow seem like a denial of God's love.

On the same day that an interview with Dave appeared on the front page of *The Wall Street Journal,* I got canned at the ad agency. Twenty-five years I had labored at Curry, Cosset, Dorn, and on Monday morning, as I sharpened my pencils, a twenty-nine-year-old yahoo with a red bow tie leaned over the wall of my work cubicle and said, "The folks at Chippy called and cut back on the campaign, Danny. I'm going to have to let you go for a while."

"Are you sure?" That's all I could think to say. A quarter-century with the company — "Are you sure?" He was sure.

I crawled home, bleeding, and Julie was glued to the TV, watching Dave talk about the irrelevance of suffering. It was a videotape, not a live appearance, but even so, she did not turn it off when she heard my tragic news. She said, "That's too bad," and then, "I'm proud of him. This is so cool, it's one of his new videotapes. He's going to put out twelve of them. He just seems to touch a chord in people, don't you think? People can't help but respond to him. It's a natural gift." She recommended that I study *Rat Poison* to give me the confidence to find a new job and wait for his next book, *How to Find Your Rear End Without Using Both Hands.*

"Your brother," I said, "is one of the world's biggest B.S.-ers."

This was when Julie decided that we needed to face up to my problems. "You are a dark cloud in my life, Danny. A small dark cloud," she said.

I don't know what she meant by that. I'm a happy guy who loves life, it's just that I have a moony face. A guy can't help it that his face won't light up. Inside, I'm like a kid with a new puppy. Though being flushed down the toilet while your brother-in-law is getting rich certainly puts a crimp in a guy's hose. Dave was hot. I was dead. For twenty-five years, I had been a happy guy who created dancing ketchup commercials, who made high-fiber bran flakes *witty,* who wrote those coffee commercials in which the husband and wife share a golden moment over a cup of java. I brought lucid emotion to capitalism, and Dave brought gibberish, and he walked off with the prize.

The next day, Julie told me that Dave thought that she and I should go away and be alone and he'd given her fifteen thousand dollars so we could charter a fifty-foot schooner for a two-week cruise off Antigua, where we could try to put the marriage back together.

"Fifteen thousand dollars would come in handy in other ways than blowing it on a vacation," I pointed out. "We could invest it. I'm unemployed, you know."

"Aren't you willing to invest in our marriage?" she said.

"We could *buy* a boat for that kind of money and sail on the Mississippi every weekend."

She said that fifteen thousand wasn't enough to pay her to get into a boat with me at the tiller.

"Remember the time we drifted powerless down the river because you put oil in the gas tank? Remember how you tried to rig up an overcoat on an oar to make a sail? Remember how we drifted toward that oncoming coal barge and stood and waved our arms and cried out in our pitiful voices?"

Ten years had not dimmed her memory of that one bad afternoon.

So off we flew to Antigua.

We flew first-class, in those wide uphol-stered seats, where everything is sparkly and fresh and lemony and candles flicker on the serving cart. A painful reminder of how cheery life can be for the very rich. People like my brother-in-law. The flight attendants wore gold-paisley sarongs slit up the side and pink-passion lipstick, they were Bar-nard graduates (cum laude) in humanities, and they set a vase of fresh roses on my table, along with the ceviche and salmon loaf and crab puffs with Mornay sauce, and they leaned over me, their perfect college-educated breasts hanging prettily in place, and they whispered, "You've got a nice butt. You ever read Kant?" They only flirted with me because I was holding a first-class ticket, they wouldn't have given me the time of day back in economy class; I wanted to say, "I'm forty-seven, I'm broke, ashamed, in pain, on the verge of divorce, and sponging off a despised relative. I've hit bottom, babes. Go away unless you want to see a has-been burst into tears."

■ ■ ■ ■

We stayed one night at Jumby Bay, dropping a bundle of Dave's dough, and headed
off by cab to the Lucky Lovers Marina, and
there, at the end of the dock, lay the *Susy Q*.
I put my arm around Julie, who was shivering despite the bright sunshine and eighty-
five degrees. She did not seem to welcome
my arm so I removed it.

"Is that a schooner or a ketch?" I said.

"It's a yawl," she replied. It was hard not
to notice the frayed rigging and rusted
hardware, the oil slick around the stern, the
sail in a big heap on deck, and what appeared to be sneaker tread marks along the
side of the hull. Evidently the boat had
capsized at one point and the crew had to
evacuate — even worse was the fact that
nobody had scrubbed the marks off. But we
had put down a deposit of fifteen hundred
bucks already, so we banished doubt from
our minds and tried to be hopeful.

"Hello! Anybody below?" I hollered. There
was a muffled *yo,* and a beautiful young
man poked up his head from the cockpit
and smiled. His golden curls framed his
Grecian godlike face, his deep tan set off by
a green T-shirt that said, "Life Is a Series of

Beginnings." He was Rusty, our captain, he said. "I was just making your bed downstairs. Come on down. Your room's up front!"

This struck me as odd, that he said *downstairs* instead of *belowdecks,* and I mentioned this to Julie as we stowed our bags in the cabin. "How can you get upset about poor word choice when our marriage is petering out and there is so little real love between us?" she asked.

The *Susy Q* cleared port and sailed west toward Sansevar Trist, and she and I sat below discussing our marriage, which I have always believed is not a good idea, certainly not for Julie and me. My experience tells me that we should shoot eight ball, sit in a hot tub, go to the zoo, rake the lawn, spread warm oil on each other's bodies, do anything but talk about our marriage, but she is a fan of those articles like "How Lousy Is Your Marriage: A 10-Minute Quiz That Could Help You Improve It," and of course the first question is, "Are you and your husband able to sit down and discuss your differences calmly and reasonably?" No! Of course not! Are you kidding? Who discusses these things without raising their voice and becoming *very emphatic*? Name one person! So she launched into a reasonable discussion of differences and how she needs *engagement* and I am basically a narcissist, and two minutes later we're hissing and slamming our fists on the table and striding to the other end of the room and saying things like "I can't *believe* this!" and "Where do you *get* this hogwash?" We simply are unable to discuss our marriage — does that make us terrible people? Our marriage is like the Electoral College: it works okay if you don't think about it.

"Truth time. Do you love me?" Julie asked as the boat rocked in the swell, Rusty thumping around on deck overhead, dragging something.

"How do you mean that?"

"I mean, is it worth it to try to stay together? Marriages have their rough passages. It's only worth it if there's love. If there isn't, why waste time trying to patch this up."

"Do you love me?"

"I asked first."

"How come I'm the one who has to say if I love you or not? Why is it always up to me?"

There was a loud crash above, like a tree falling, and Rusty let out a cry, "Oh shoot!" I poked my head up out of the hatch. "It's the steering thing," he said. The tiller had broken off and was now bobbing in our wake. I told him to lash an oar in its place and come around and retrieve the tiller, and I ducked back down into the cabin. Julie was sitting on the bunk, her back to the bulkhead, her trim brown legs drawn up.

"I better go up and help Rusty," I said.

"You can't run away, Danny," she said. "It's a simple question. Do you love me or not? What's so complicated about that?"

I flopped down on the bed. "Why can't we converse about this in a calm friendly way instead of beating ourselves up over every little thing —"

"A little thing," she said. "Our love. A little thing. Oh right. Sure. Great way to start off a vacation. Our love, a little thing."

There was a loud *cra-a-a-ack* above and a muffled splash. I stuck my head up. The sail was gone, and the mast. "I was gonna turn right and the whole thing broke and fell off," he said, shaking his head. "Boy, I never saw anything like that! Whole sail just fell off!" He shrugged and grinned, like he'd just burned the toast. "Oh well, we still got a motor." I told him to come about and retrieve the sail and mast and then head for port.

I told Julie that we had serious problems above and maybe we should postpone our talk. She said we had been postponing it for twenty years.

I was about to tell her how full of balloon juice she was, and then I heard the motor turn over, a dry raspy sound, like gravel going down a chute, and I got the impression that Rusty had neglected to gas up and that the *Susy Q* was not going anywhere. Still, it wasn't as aggravating as Miss Priss there, sitting and telling me about my marriage.

"Dave recommended a great book to me and it opened my eyes. *The Silent Chrysalis.* I read it twice. Danny, in some way my love for you is a symptom of my denial of myself, an attempt to make myself invisible."

The starter cranked over once and wheezed and coughed a deep dry cough.

Julie's eyes locked with mine. "We need to change that love from something angry and selfish to a mature *giving* love," she said. "I can't use you as an instrument of my self-hatred."

"What is that supposed to mean?" I asked.

"Dave thinks you're trapped in narcissism, like a lot of guys. You just honestly are incapable of thinking outside the box that you are in."

How does a stationery-store clerk suddenly become an expert on the human heart? I wondered, but then Rusty's face appeared in the hatch, his boyish confidence gone, a little taut around the eyes. "We may have to ditch the boat in a minute, you guys. We're coming real close to the reef, I think. The water looks sort of bubbly out there."

Julie grabbed my arm when I got up to go topside. "You're not going to just walk away from this one, Danny. You're going to face up to what's wrong, which is your selfishness. Your selfishness is a fact, Danny. Let's stop denying it. Let's deal with it."

Rusty's voice was hoarse. "Come on, folks. No time for yik-yak. Gotta go."

I poked my head up. The Great Navigator had a horrified expression on his face, and his chin was aquiver. He wore an orange life jacket. "Want me to take the helm?" I asked.

"No helm left to take, and there's big jagged rocks up ahead, folks, so if you see a cushion, better grab on to it. This is not a test."

There was a distant roar of waves that was not as distant as before.

I ducked down and told Julie we were about to abandon ship. "If you can't deal with the truth, Danny, then I can't be married to you," said Julie, softly. "I don't want a marriage based on a lie."

I was just about to tell her that she wouldn't have that problem much longer, when there was a jagged ripping tearing crunching sound from just below our feet, and the boat lurched to a dead stop. Water began boiling up from below. I grabbed Julie and hoisted her through the hatch, grabbed a carry-on bag and a couple cushions, and took Julie by the hand, and we jumped into the water. Rusty was already on shore, waving to us. It was shallow, all right; the water frothed around our hips as we crossed the jagged coral, but we managed to wade in to shore, a beautiful white sandy beach that curved around and around a very pretty island — uninhabited, we soon discovered. "Well," said Rusty, "looks like you guys may get a little more than two weeks. Nice place, too." And he glanced down at Julie. Her T-shirt was wet from the surf, and her breasts shone through. He looked at her a little longer than a hired man ought to, I thought.

We made a hut from palm fronds and the jib sail. Julie had rescued her purse and suntan oil and four books about marriage and communication, and I had dragged in our suitcase and a bottle of Campari, and Rusty had salvaged the oregano, sweet basil, rosemary, chives, coriander, cayenne pepper, paprika, orange zest, nutmeg, cinnamon, pine nuts, bay leaf, marjoram, tarragon, caraway, and saffron.

"The boat sinks and you rescue the spice rack?" I cried. "You're the captain and your boat goes down and you come ashore with the spice rack?"

Rusty looked at Julie. "Just because we're marooned on an island doesn't mean the food has to be bland and tasteless," he said.

She nodded. "It's no dumber than bringing a bottle of Campari. You don't like Campari," she said. "You only like beer." I didn't explain that Campari is useful as a bug repellant; I read that somewhere.

And an hour later, Julie had made beds out of pine boughs and Rusty had carved a salad bowl from a stump and tossed a salad in it — "Just some ferns and breadfruit and hearts of palm," he said. He had also baked a kelp casserole over an open fire. Julie thought it was the best salad in salad history. Actually, it was okay. "And this casserole!" she cried. "I have never tasted kelp that tasted like this kelp tastes. What's the secret?"

"Paprika," he said.

Julie couldn't get over it. She said, "Danny couldn't boil an egg if you held a pistol to his head. I kept offering to teach him the rudiments of cooking, but he never wanted to learn."

It was hard not to notice that she was talking about me in the past tense.

"No, Danny couldn't have made a salad like this in a million years. Are you kidding? Not him," she chortled. "No, no, no, no, no."

We sat under the palm tree as the sun went down, and Julie and Rusty talked about the American novel, how they didn't care for John Updike, who had never written strong women characters and was hung up on male menopause and had no ear for dialogue.

"No ear for dialogue?" I cried.

"No ear for dialogue," she said.

"John Updike? No ear for dialogue? Are you kidding me? Updike? That's what you said, right? Updike? His dialogue? No ear?"

"He has none," she said.

"None. Updike."

"Right."

"I can't believe this," I said. "You're sitting here under this palm tree and saying that John Updike — *the* John Updike, who wrote the Rabbit books — that he has no ear for dialogue? Tell me something. If John Updike has no ear for dialogue, then who do you think does have an ear for dialogue?"

Rusty looked at Julie. "Maya Angelou. Alice Walker. Doris Lessing," he said.

"Doris Lessing," I said.

"Yes," she said. "Doris Lessing."

"Pardon me if I should lose my kelp," I said. I stood up. "You know, I must be going deaf, but I could swear you just said Doris Lessing. Or did you say Arthur Schlesinger?" I kicked a little dirt toward Rusty.

"I said, Doris Lessing," he said.

It was the first of many discussions where I was in the minority. One morning, over a dried-seaweed breakfast, Julie said she thought there is such a thing as a "masculine matrix" and that it is basically controlling and violent. Rusty agreed. "But some of us are working to change that," he said. Julie felt that men are inherently competitive, i.e., linear, hierarchical, and women are circular, i.e., radiant. "I think you have a good point," said Rusty. Julie and Rusty started meditating together every morning, sitting on the beach facing east. "Hey, mind if I sit in?" I said cheerfully.

Julie squinted up at me. "I think you'd block the unity of the experience," she said.

Rusty nodded.

"Well, far be it from me to block anyone's unity," I said, and walked away.

That night, Julie and Rusty were cooking a bark soup and she looked up at me and said, "Rusty is such an inspiration. I'm glad this happened, this shipwreck. Out of this wreck, something wonderful is coming."

I grabbed her arm. "This numbskull who ran the boat onto the rock is an inspiration?"

Rusty confronted me later that night, after Julie went to sleep. "I've decided to take Julie away from you," he said. "You two do nothing but fight, and she's obviously attracted to me, so if she and I paired up, at least there'd be two happy people on this island. It makes more sense that way. Two out of three isn't bad. So why don't you go and sleep in the jungle someplace. This tent is for Julie and me."

I said, "Okay, you're right," and I turned and bent down and picked up my Campari bottle and then whirled and swung it straight up into his nuts and he staggered back and I threw a handful of dirt in his eyes. He bent down, blinded, and I kicked him as hard as I could in the gut, and he went *whooomph,* like a needle sliding across an LP record, and down he went, and I picked him up and threw him over the cliff and into the ocean and suddenly the water was whipped to a froth by thousands of tiny carnivorous fish and the frenzy went on for a half a minute and subsided and whatever was left of Rusty sank bubbling to the bottom.

It wasn't the Zen way but it got the job done.

Julie was distraught in the morning. She dashed around the island screaming his name. "What have you done to him, Danny?" she shrieked.

"He got high looking at the Milky Way and he fell into the water and the fish ate him," I said.

"You killed him!"

"Nothing ever dies. He is at one with the fish."

Two weeks later, when the big cruise ship saw us and anchored a half mile to leeward and sent in a launch to take us off, Julie had calmed down and was almost ready to talk to me again. I could tell. I yelled up to her where she sat on the ledge of the rocky promontory, "You know something? I think the secret of marriage is that you can't change the person you love. You have to love that person the way he or she is. Well, here I am!"

"You didn't think of that, you got that out of a book," she called back. It was the first time she'd spoken to me in two weeks.

A man in officer whites with big tufts of hair on his chest was on the launch. He said,

"You the couple who went down with the *Susy Q*? Where's the captain?"

"He drowned," I said. Julie said nothing. She still has said nothing about Rusty to me at all, and nothing about our marriage, but we have had sex more often than any time since we were twenty-four. It has been nice. I definitely think there is a vital connection between anger and an exciting sex life.

When we got back to the States, I saw a newspaper in the Newark airport with a picture of Dave on the front page glowering at the photographer and trying to stiff-arm him. He had been arrested for fondling a couple of young women in his swimming pool at his birthday party and was charged with six counts of sexual assault. I chuckled, but it was a low chuckle, and Julie didn't hear it. We were back two days and a publisher offered me $50,000 for a book about our "desert-island" experience. "Nah," I said, "nothing happened. Worst part was having to go around in a wet bathing suit." Since returning, I have done little except be a help and a support to Dave and Julie and the whole Grebe family. I have been a monster of sympathy and understanding. I have been there for them every moment in their terrible suffering. Dave sat weeping in

334

our kitchen and told us, "I've been under so much stress, and it was like it was somebody else tugging on those girls' thongs, and I was only watching." I said, "Don't feel you have to talk about it." He told me that he didn't know what he would do without me and thanked me for the strength I gave him in this awful time. "It's my pleasure," I said sincerely. I suppose he will write a book about this. I don't care. Heaving Rusty into the sea has given me an enormous sense of peace. I suppose it was a transformative experience for him, too. Death is the ultimate reality check. His death at my hands has leached away all my anger and I am devoted to Julie in a way I never could be before. She wants to return to our island and erect a stone cairn in Rusty's memory and maybe take Dave with us. I am all in favor of it. I can't wait. We never did learn Rusty's real name — the owner of the *Susy Q* had vanished — but in whatever plane of existence Rusty is experiencing now, names don't count for much, and we feel there is a universality about a cairn with no name on it. Both Julie and I do.

10.
MOTHER'S DAY

As my mother got older and older and then older still, I liked to amuse her now and then by putting her into stories, making her into a Thirties movie musical star or a champion skeet-shooter or the head of a crime syndicate. She listened faithfully to my show on the radio and hearing these tales gave her a good jolt and also inspired people she knew to call her up and say hello. "Oh, we listened to Gary's show and heard about how you jilted Scott Fitzgerald," they said. "Oh, he just makes up that stuff, you know," she said. When you embark on a career in fiction, you can't imagine the uses it will have someday, and there is one unexpected one: making your old mother laugh and shake her head.

I was going to visit my mother on Sunday and bring her a jonquil and a ballpoint pen for Mother's Day, but that's all off thanks to my brother Larry, who is awaiting trial for mail fraud. His lawyers have asked me not to discuss his case, and so I won't, except to say that he's guilty, the little stinker, and richly deserves what's coming to him, but of course you can't tell Mother that, she thinks he is the sun and the moon.

She turns ninety-four this week and still lives in her own home, drives her own car, and only recently gave up playing senior women's hockey. She was tough, let me tell you, and as she slowed down, she resorted more and more to high-sticking and tripping. As she says, "I didn't get to be ninety-four by baking cookies."

I went shopping for a Mother's Day gift at a clothing store, but, as it turned out, it was a men's store. So as long as I was there, I bought myself a few nice suits.

And anyway, Mom said, "No gifts for me until Larry gets out of the pokey." I said, "Mom, Larry was selling Powerball Bibles with the winning number hidden in Scripture. He was selling stock options to evangelicals with the promise that the Lord would come again in 2008. It didn't happen. He's going to spend ten to fifteen years making license plates." She said, "So he misread prophecy. He's not the first." I said, "Ma, he misread it to the tune of 1.6 million dollars in profit to himself that is sitting in a bank in the Bahamas."

She said, "You can't believe everything you read in the papers." I said, "Ma, he's been a liar and a cheat since he was a kid. Remember for your birthday he used to give you those little certificates that said 'Good for one hug' and 'Good for doing dishes' — Ma, you never collected on those. It was a scam." She said, "It's the thought that counts."

There were four of us, Larry, me, my other brother, who works in a small dim office and does something he can't explain, and my sister the singer-songwriter, who recently had her lower lip pierced and a large wooden disk implanted in it which she says gives her more resonance.

The other day, Mom said, "Notice anything different about me?" Which of course made me nervous. A man wants to come up with the right answer to this question. You don't want to say, "You got a haircut" if the correct answer is that her leg was amputated. I checked her out: snow-white hair, hockey jersey, jeans, high heels. I said, "Only thing different about you, Mom, is that you're looking younger than ever." And she said, "Nope. I'm carrying a concealed weapon."

My mom, packing a pistol. She said, "I

am not going to let your brother rot in jail because of a big misunderstanding." I told her to read the indictment — Larry is a creep — but she stood up for him, as she has all these years despite his dirty deeds, and then on Tuesday she got the drop on three U.S. marshals and freed Larry at gunpoint and drove him to a grass landing strip south of Minneapolis and they took off in a small jet and made it to Venezuela, and there they are today, my little mom and her son the felon. She is learning Spanish and working as a cleaning lady and he is at the beach, plotting how to get his fingers on that Bahamian treasure.

And here I am, the loyal son, the one who has looked after her all these years, the one who had made his mark in the world as a syndicated newspaper columnist. Why does she devote her life to a cheater and ignore the son who has done everything in his power to make her proud?

Frankly, I think that mothers have a masochistic streak that makes them love the bad eggs more. I wish I could be meaner to my mother, but it's too late. I wouldn't know how. I pass this on for what it's worth. Go out and steal a car, she can't do enough for you. Happy Mother's Day.

A serious author driving down Lake Street in Minneapolis with his photographer friend Tom Arndt in 1971, looking defiant, back when there was plenty of time for driving aimlessly around and when defiance was a useful defense against raging self-doubt.

III.
GUYS I HAVE KNOWN

Back around 1992 I did a tour with the singer Kate MacKenzie and the pianist Richard Dworsky, an evening of duets and stories, and also a monologue that succeeded in eliciting cheerful booing and hissing from a lot of women in the audiences wherever we went. It was a knowing sort of booing and hissing, ironic booing, and it put them in a cheery mood. They knew they were supposed to boo and they did it with relish, but very stylishly. My marriage to a staunch Danish feminist had broken up, ending a five-year period when I tried hard to be a Dane and a social democrat — and it was a relief to stop trying and to resume life as a Midwestern American guy. And a pleasure to do shows in America again and to see the Great Plains and the Rockies and the Gulf and the California coastline.

One of the stories I told was about one January night when I drove my truck deep into the woods north of Anoka to attend the annual Sons of Bernie bonfire in a grove of birches, twenty below zero, five feet of snow, and there, under the Milky Way and a nearly full moon, we ate chili out of cans and drank bourbon and sang mournful songs like "Long Black Veil" and "Old Man River" and "It Ain't Me, Babe," about thirty of us, not exactly my crowd, guys unluckier than I who had suffered cruel fathers, treacherous lovers, abject poverty, dust storms, prison, tuberculosis, car wrecks, the boll weevil, and poor career choices, not to mention bad skin, halitosis, bleeding cuticles, and lusterless hair. They looked so much older and sadder than you want people your own age to look. I was by far the soberest and handsomest one in the bunch. I decided to stay for a while and write about them so that they would not be completely forgotten, but as the night wore on, I came to see that we were truly brothers. It was an epiphany. It changed my life.

We stood close to this fire, smoke in our eyes, hot coals landing in our hair, left arm over the shoulder of the man to our left, right arm free to pass the bottle, and we sang "Hard Times Come Again No More," "Abilene," "Love in Vain," "Streets of Laredo," "I'm So Lonesome I Could Cry," and recited poems, such as "When in disgrace with fortune and men's eyes I all alone beweep my outcast state," and then someone recited, "There was an old sailor named Tex who avoided premarital sex by thinking of Jesus and terrible diseases and beating his meat belowdecks."

It was not a tasteful or reverent occasion, not something you'd want your wife or daughters to see. A man can down a quart of whiskey in subzero temperatures and still keep his feet, and when you are that drunk, you will say things that you wouldn't care to see in print, but nevertheless I would hate to come to the end of my life and think, "I never ever once got drunk in the woods on a winter night with a bunch of guys who all knew the words to 'Dead Flowers.' " And now I won't.

We sang about Old Paint and Frankie and Johnny and somebody recited the famous poem:

Whenever Richard Cory went downtown,
The women on the streetcar looked at him:
He was a gentleman from sole to crown,
Clean shaven, his aftershave Royal
    Platinum.
And he looked terrific in a suit.
And he was always pleasant when he
    talked;
He certainly made the heads turn en route
To his office as he walked.
And he was rich, a man of style and grace,

And married to a beautiful woman named
    June.
And yet none of us wished that we were in
    his place.
We knew June and she was a Gorgon.
And one calm summer night, under the
    summer moon,
Richard Cory put a bullet in his noggin.
No big surprise, not if you knew June.

We got to feeling awfully close, hooked together, the fire blazing away, the whiskey doing its work. After the poem, a guy said, "I don't want you to take this the wrong way but I'm glad there aren't any damn women here to look at us with disgust." (LAUGHTER) Another guy stepped forward and said: "I have worshipped women all my life and avoided objectifying them and when in conversation with a woman have maintained steady eye contact and not eyeballed their you-know-whats and then the other day, a woman I know told me that she felt empowered when men stared at her breasts, and I said Oh really but maintained eye contact — 'Oh yes,' she said, 'I have a fantasy that one day a man will reach down there and scoop them up like two Bosc pears and nibble on them' — Interesting, I remarked — 'A man who doesn't enjoy look-ing at my bazongas is missing a circuit in the

344

brain,' she said — and so I glanced down at her and she whacked me in the chops and she said, 'I knew you'd do that,' which makes me think that maybe women have gotten more mileage out of feminism than they should've and maybe we could stop bowing whenever one comes in the room."

A ripple of excitement passed through the circle: Guys were Speaking Out! Us! Saying things we wouldn't dare say in polite society (i.e., women).

A guy with snow-white hair stepped into the circle. "Listen, you pineapples. I am no misogynist but I got to say, women are getting impossible to please these days. I've been busting my butt for years trying to keep women happy, and they're madder at me now than before I started trying so hard. I quit playing poker and hockey and going deer hunting and took up painting watercolors, still lifes mostly, and tossing salads, and learned how to discuss feelings and concerns and not make jokes about them, and they're still angry at me. A guy can't win. Boys, let me tell you: most women down deep believe that everything that is wrong with the world is men's fault and nothing you can do will ever change that. So don't worry about it. Live your life."

"Oya!" we all yelled.

A great big bearded guy stepped into the

circle. "I sort of miss communism. When the Soviet Union fell apart it seemed like everything went slack and we gave up on manhood. Guys lost interest in guns and quit messing with cars. My son never gets under a hood. Instead he tries to understand his girlfriend and keep a close relationship. We're selling out our manhood, bit by bit, one ball at a time, trying to buy peace and quiet, and you know something? It won't work. Self-betrayal never works! I say nuts to sensitivity. Go ahead and fart. Go ahead."

So we did. All at once. The fire flamed up blazing bright. It felt good. And right.

I realized right then, standing in that circle, that for thirty years I have been nudging women and pointing out dopey men to them so that women would know that I am no bozo or redneck. And here I was arm in arm with the very sort of guys I had always made fun of. I felt shame.

And then the head man of the S.O.B., the Big Burner himself, stepped into the circle, to talk about Bernie. He had been Bernie's best friend and accountant.

"Bernie was a good guy who married a great girl, Jackie, who read Betty Friedan on their honeymoon and became a militant feminist, but that was okay by Bernie, he supported her in all that she did. They had four daughters, Susan B., Elizabeth Cady, Willa, and Betty. Bernie was a good dad and good husband, and the rest of the time he was a cement contractor. He had fourteen trucks pouring concrete. One winter when the concrete business slacked off, Bernie thought he'd maybe go ice fishing for a week with the old gang, play poker and tell some stories, have some laughs — though Jackie thought it was dumb beyond belief and gave him a hard time about it, so Bernie canceled the fishing trip — and then, on the day he had planned to leave, he ran into me on the street and told me how wonderful it would be to see the old gang again. 'I haven't gone fishing in fifteen years, but someday I hope I can get Jackie to let me go,' he said. 'Well,' he said, 'I gotta cash a check before the bank closes.' And he turned and five seconds later he was rubbed off the face of the earth by a gravel truck making a sudden left turn.

"Bernie was looking forward to being with us someday and someday we will join him in the clubhouse in the sky. He was a hard worker, a good husband and daddy, and he was a great pal, and in his memory we meet and toast him — may he rest."

We raised our glasses.

"She got the house, the concrete business, everything, all that he'd worked so hard to build up, and you know? She didn't share much of it with those daughters either. She sold the company for six million dollars to some jerks who ran it into the ground and she bought herself a penthouse in Manhattan where she holds fund-raisers for snooty big-ass liberals. That's what happened to the life and hard work of Bernie, boys. His money went to people he couldn't stand to be around and he never got to go fishing."

We all leaned forward and spat on the ground.

"Well, here we are, boys, we are all losers, we're drunk, confused, sad, and we smell like dead trout — but I loved him and I love all of you. Here's to Bernie. Let 'er rip."

And we drank a long toast and gave six long whoops, Eeeeeeee-ha!

By four a.m. there was little left to say and nobody in any condition to say it. So I went home. And ever since that night, I've tried to be more understanding of my fellow men. They are in a bind. Manhood used to be an opportunity and now it's a liability to be overcome. Plato, St. Francis, Michelangelo, Mozart, Leonardo da Vinci, Vince Lombardi, Van Gogh — you don't find guys of that caliber today, and if there are any, they are not painting the ceiling of the Sistine Chapel or composing *Don Giovanni.* They are trying to be

348

Mr. O.K. All-Rite, the man who can bake a cherry pie, go coach girls' basketball, come home, make melon balls and whip up a great soufflé, converse easily about intimate matters, participate in recreational weeping, laugh, hug, be vulnerable, then go upstairs and be passionate in a skillful way, and the next day go off and lift them bales into that barge and tote it. A hard life, all of it closely monitored by women.

Men adore women. Our mothers taught us to. Women do not adore men; women are amused by men, we are a source of chuckles. That's because women are the makers of life, and we are merely an appliance. We will never carry life within our bodies, never breast-feed. Our role in procreation is to get crazy and howl and spray our seed and then go away and not frighten the children. I have to go now. The S.O.B. meet on the night of the first full moon of the year. See you then.

1.
EARL GREY

Thirty years later, people still come up and tell me they remember "Buster the Show Dog," a radio serial I wrote in the early Eighties, with Timmy the Sad Rich Teenage Boy and Father Finian and Sheilah the Christian Jungle Girl. "Earl Grey" was meant to be another serial but then I left the country for Denmark and forgot about radio and set out to be a great novelist, so when I picked up Earl a couple years later, I made him into a novel, howbeit a very short one.

Earl Grey flew to San Francisco to speak to the Tea Congress ("A Toast to Tea") and stayed overnight at a four-star hotel and was awakened at three a.m. by some jerk singing Gershwin and looked for the phone to call the front desk and tripped in the dark and fell and broke his arm and was taken to the hospital where surgeons mistakenly removed his left lung, thinking he was a

man named Ray, a very bad outcome indeed, but not so surprising to Earl. He was
a middle child, the third of five kids, so he
was accustomed to being misunderstood.
His older brother, Vern, was prone to weeping and his older sister, Vivian, was a
pyromaniac and his two younger siblings
were bed wetters and teeth grinders and cat
torturers, so his parents had a handful of
trouble. Earl was sociable and polite and
bright as a penny and because he *required
no special attention whatsoever,* he was
ignored by his parents. Once he was toilet
trained (at age two) he was on his own. His
dad, Bob Grey, was a conservative congressman from Georgia, the minority whip, and
Earl grew up in Washington, a city of broad
streets and granite plazas, full of curiosities,
such as the Monument to Horses of the
Civil War and the Museum of Ideas and the
national headquarters of the Federated
Organization of Associations. The Greys
loved Washington and lived in dread of the
next election, afraid that they might lose
and have to leave their comfy home in
Georgetown and go back home to Macon,
Georgia, where Daddy's daddy owned a
pancake house. Daddy was a conservative
Republican and his seat should have been
safe, but he was something of a bon vivant

and loved black-tie dinners and dancing the tango and drinking espresso in a little French café over the *Post* and the *Times*. He belonged to a madrigal ensemble. He read Proust. He was a civilized man and it was hard for him to get ginned up for campaigns and do what he had to do to get reelected, ranting and raving against Washington.

"Daddy's got to say some mean things, children," said Mrs. Grey, "otherwise we'll have to live in Georgia and attend church and have clunky furniture and no art on the walls."

For the campaign, they rode around in the back of a pickup truck, dressed in Sears outfits, and Daddy spoke out for the American flag, the American family, the American family dog, and railed against the State Department for selling out our country's vital interests abroad, mopping his brow with a red bandanna, sipping from a Dixie cup. And in November, Daddy got reelected and the Greys made a final appearance at the victory rally and the next morning they took off the dumpy clothes and made a beeline back to Washington, glad to be done with the filthy business for another two years. They put on their nice clothes, and talked normally, and Daddy resumed his lovely life of grace and elegance. And young Earl resumed his life as an invisible middle child. Sometimes Daddy called him Timmy. His mother hardly knew he existed.

INTERESTING FACT: TODAY EARL GREY TRAVELS MORE THAN TWO HUNDRED THOUSAND MILES A YEAR, SEEING TO HIS FAR-FLUNG TEA BUSINESS, APPEARING AT CHARITABLE FUNCTIONS, AND WHEREVER HE GOES, PEOPLE GET HIS NAME WRONG OR MISTAKE HIM FOR SOMEONE ELSE.

In 1956, Daddy had a real stinker of an opponent, a bullet-headed, red-necked, carpet-chewing radio preacher named C. J. Buzzhardt, who accused Daddy of losing touch with the common man and being part of the Washington establishment. He crisscrossed the district in a cheap, wrinkly suit yelling, "Where's Grey, the big phony? Why's he afraid to show his face in Georgia?"

Mrs. Grey told Daddy to get down to Georgia and rip into the State Department, but Daddy had a tennis tournament to play in, and early September was when his madrigal group gave its big recital at the Folger Library, so it wasn't until October that the Greys trooped down to Georgia to do their business.

They forgot to bring Earl. He was standing by the car, about to climb in, and his mother said to him, "You be sure and mow the lawn every week, Hector, that's what we pay you for." Earl's eyes filled with tears, he turned to blow his nose, and away they went without him.

So he spent the next six weeks with the housekeeper, Anna Tin, a nice Sumatran lady who took excellent care of him. In Sumatra, a middle child is treasured as a living keystone, a bridge, a bond, a fulcrum, a vital link.

Meanwhile, down in Georgia, Mr. Buzzhardt ran circles around Daddy on the stump, campaigning on the slogan "Honor America and Send a Real Man to Washington," and he flew hundreds of flags at every appearance, outflagging Daddy by a ten-to-one margin. He spread rumors that Daddy had only one testicle, smaller than a dried lentil, and he found photos of Daddy singing in his madrigal group, wearing a foofy shirt with chin ruffles, his mouth open in a prim oval for a *falalalala.*

One hot night, in Marietta, at a debate on a flag-draped platform in the courthouse square, when Congressman Grey was waxing hot and heavy about the pinheads in the State Department and how, if elected, he'd clean them out of there and replace them with God-fearing folks with a farm background, it was not going over well with the crowd. The congressman was pretending to be stupid, but Buzzhardt was genuinely stupid and voters prefer what's genuine. And suddenly Buzzhardt jumped up and strode to the podium and hollered, "What you got in that Dixie cup theah?" And he snatched it from Daddy and sniffed it and yelled, "Tea. And not sweet tea, no suh, but oolong."

"Oolong?" the crowd murmured.

"Oolong!" yelled Gerald K. "This peckerwood is standing up here sippin at tea from a foreign country. Not American tea. Oolong!!!! Well, la-di-da. Ain't we fine?"

Everyone laughed and laughed, and Daddy was dead.

Georgia men didn't drink oolong tea, it was strictly for fruitcakes, pantywaists, college perfessers, and hermaphrodites. Buzzhardt held up the picture of Congressman Grey *falala*ing and said, "You folks intendin to vote for a poof and a priss and a pansy? I say ole oolong has been in Congress toolong!" and that was that, the election was over. Daddy was swamped by a large margin, and the family slunk back to Georgetown, heartsick and bitter.

There was Earl, dazed with pleasure, having been adored all the long summer. "What's wrong?" he asked.

"We got our butt kicked," said his mom. "And it's your fault. Why weren't you there?"

TEA FACTS: BELIEVE IT OR NOT, EARL GREY TEA IS NOW THE MOST POPULAR TEA IN GEORGIA. IT OUTRANKS BOURBON AMONG MALES BETWEEN TWENTY-FIVE AND SIXTY AND IS STEADILY GAINING ON COCA-COLA. IT IS THE FASTEST-GROWING BEVERAGE IN THE ATLANTA AREA.

The Greys did not return to Georgia. They spent a last Christmas in Washington and in January, Daddy took his remaining hundred thousand in campaign funds and they motored west to California, where Daddy would have a job at the Hoover Institution, thinking about great issues. They stopped in Minneapolis, where he delivered a speech on campaign reform at the Stassen Institute, and the following afternoon they stopped at the Lucky Spud restaurant in Platt, North Dakota, for lunch, and half an hour later they went off and left Earl there.

The Spud specialized in mashed potatoes: there were twenty-four varieties on the menu, including the Big Cheesie, White Cloud, Land O'Gravy, Tuna Whip, and the

Elvis Parsley. Earl, a slow eater, ordered a Big Cheesie *and* a White Cloud and sat and savored every bite, while Daddy paid the check and went to the car with Vance and Vince, and Mom, who had been in a sour mood for months, said, "Hurry up, Earl. I mean it," and disappeared with Vivian and Vera. Earl finished up the last four bites in a big hurry, but when he ran out the door, the car was gone.

The waitress tried to comfort him. "They'll be back in a jiffy, snuggums, just you wait and see. Here. Have some more spuds." But the family never returned. Never called, never wrote, never filed a missing-child report.

They cruised on to Palo Alto, enjoying the scenery, without a peep out of his brothers and sisters as to the empty spot in the back-seat. He had taken up so little room in their lives, being polite and quiet and consider-ate, so why should they notice his absence?

And if they had reported him missing to the police, the police would've asked, "What does the boy look like?" and the Greys would've looked at each other and said, "Now, what *did* he look like? He was me-dium height, wasn't he? Didn't he have brown hair? I seem to remember that it was brown."

TEA FACTS. EARL GREY TEA HAS BEEN
USED AS A WATERCOLOR WASH BY NUMER-
OUS PROMINENT ARTISTS TO LEND A RICH
BUT SUBTLE BROWN TONE TO THEIR WORK,
BUT EARL'S HAIR IS, AND ALWAYS HAS
BEEN, STRAWBERRY BLOND.

So Earl grew up in Platt from the age of
fifteen. He was raised by Sandy, the waitress
at the Lucky Spud, who lived with her
boyfriend, Butch, in a trailer behind the
café. It was crowded and Earl slept on the
sofa and was often awakened by Sandy and
Butch arguing. They drank quite a bit and
she'd yell, "Get your hands off me. I'm not
in the mood." And Butch'd say, "You used
to like it when I did that," and it was nothing that Earl cared to hear. He attended
Platt High and did his homework sitting at
the café counter among old guys grousing
about the government, the weather, fishing,
farming, and their wives, who sat and chain-
smoked, eyes straight ahead, saying nothing.

One day Earl saw a package of Sumatran
tea on the shelf of the Platt Piggly Wiggly
supermarket and bought it and back at the
trailer he made a pot of tea for Sandy and
himself and she was an instant convert. She
was dizzy with pleasure.

"I feel like a new woman," she said. "I

have to wonder if the reason people here are so mean isn't that they drink too much coffee. Coffee makes you want to go out and kick the dog and throw trash in the creek. Tea brings out the best in people." North Dakotans, she said, prefer their coffee bitter with a rainbow of oil slick on top. That's why they were the way they were, proud of their guns, owners of vicious dogs.

It wasn't only tealessness that cursed the prairie, Earl thought. The land was bleak and windswept, and religion offered little comfort. Christianity taught that humanity is worthless and vile but that if we agree to hate ourselves God will forgive us. Earl longed to leave; he wrote numerous letters to his dad at the Hoover Institution, which were answered by an assistant who thanked him for his interest and passed along the congressman's best wishes. Earl struggled through the Platt public school, where his love of tea made him a target for cruelty, and boys drew pictures of him wearing a dress, with snot pouring from his nose, and a petunia sticking out of his butt.

But Earl couldn't survive a day without tea. To him, tea represented civilization and kindness. He found a book in the Platt Free Lending Library, *Wild Teas of North America,* and from it learned to make dandelion tea, sassafras, rhubarb tea — each one delicious and comforting. Sandy thrived on the teas he made, became lovelier and more self-assured. "They are even better than a high colonic," she said. Her color improved. She let her hair hang loose and kicked Butch out of the trailer and made him sleep in the truck. When he begged to be allowed back, she told him to stick his head in the toilet and flush it.

Butch hung around the Spud for two days, groveling and begging, and Sandy wouldn't give him the time of day. Butch told Earl, who was washing dishes after school, "You don't get what you want in this world. Keep that in mind. People are no damn good for the most part."

Earl said, "Butch, that is a coffee philosophy. I could make you a cup of tea that would change your way of thinking. This tea could turn on the porch light in your eyes. If you drank tea, Sandy would love you to pieces." Paula, her back to them, snorted.

"Truck drivers do not drink tea," said Butch. "It does not happen. Only thing that could put a light in these eyes would be if Sandy pulled up her dress and gave me the green light. And that's not going to happen either."

TEA BULLETIN. TWENTY-SEVEN PERCENT OF ALL LONG-HAUL TRUCK DRIVERS NOW DRINK TEA, EVEN GUYS HAULING STEEL BEAMS, CARS, EVEN HOGS AND STEERS. MORE AND MORE, THEY REQUEST TEA AT TRUCK STOPS AND TELL THE WAITRESS HOW TO MAKE IT CORRECTLY. THE TEA MUST ALWAYS BE PUT IMMEDIATELY INTO THE BUBBLING, BOILING WATER. FRESH LOOSE TEA, NOT A TEABAG.

For a few years, Earl kept checking the Personals section in the Platt *Pilot*, hoping to see: *Lost: our beloved son Earl Grey, at a restaurant. Call home, honey, and we'll come and fetch you. We love you so much. Mom and Dad.*

But no such ad ever appeared, only ads from men seeking younger women: *Married Guy, 57, seeks single woman, 18–19, must be a real looker; pert and perky, and have a thing about bulky fellas who don't say too much. Send photos.*

"Your folks're sure missing a good thing, not watching you grow up, honey," Sandy told Earl six years later, when he was twenty-one. It was January and the arctic winds swept the frozen tundra and moaned in the weather stripping around the front door of the Lucky Spud and whistled in the chimney. It was cold and dark and a heavy pallor hung in the air, the aroma of burnt coffee.

And then a beautiful thought occurred to him: *I don't have to stay. I can go.* (Middle children often suffer from stationariness as a result of being crunched in the middle with siblings on either side, and many of them take years to realize that free choice is an option — that a person can, if he wishes, have a will of his own, decide things, and act.)

Earl withdrew his savings from the Platt State Bank, $420, and arranged a ride with Butch, who was hauling a load of soybeans to San Francisco.

"God bless you, Earl Grey, for making my life a lot less dingy," said Sandy, and they had a last pot of tea together. It was delicious. So calm and good.

"I had no idea my life would turn out to be so rotten," Butch told Earl as they cruised west in the big rig. "Back when she drank ten cups of java a day, she was the lovingest woman you ever met, and then she quit. If I ever meet the man who turned her on to tea, I'd knock his block off." Earl dropped off to sleep, and when he awoke, the truck was in Palo Alto, parked in front of the Hoover Institution, a Spanish-mission edifice like a California bank.

"Well, this is as far as you go, I guess. Hope you enjoy your family. See you around," said Butch, anxious to get going. Earl climbed down from the cab and a moment later the big rig pulled away and disappeared over the hill.

TEA LORE: TEA IS A PART OF FAREWELL CEREMONIES IN MANY CULTURES MORE ADVANCED THAN OUR OWN. AMERICAN MEN DREAD EMOTIONAL GOODBYES AND WILL WALK AWAY FROM A MARRIAGE AS IF GOING TO THE CORNER STORE FOR A PACK OF SMOKES. IN OTHER CULTURES, PEOPLE SAY GOODBYE BY SITTING DOWN AND ENJOYING A LAST POT OF TEA TOGETHER, RELISHING THEIR COMMON HISTORY, NOT AFRAID TO SHED TEARS, EMBRACING, FACING THE FUTURE BRAVELY.

The Hoover Institution was locked. He pushed the buzzer and a voice came over the intercom: "State your name, your business, and whom you wish to see."

"My name is Earl Grey, and I am here to be reunited with my father, Congressman Grey," said Earl, looking into the intercom speaker as if it had eyes he could appeal to.

"The congressman is gone," said the voice. Earl asked, "Where?" The voice said it did not know, nor did it know when he would return. Furthermore, it said, he had never mentioned a missing child.

Earl asked if he could leave a message for his dad. "Go ahead," said the voice.

"Tell him," said Earl, "to go and get stuffed."

When he found out once and for all that he was abandoned, Earl Grey was free to go and make his own life. And he did, with one stroke of good fortune after another. He met Malene Monroe, who was then singing with the Tommy D'Orsay Orchestra, and he made her a pot of Earl Grey tea that cured her croup and enabled her to go on and record "Tea for Two." His royalties from that paid for three years in Sumatra, where he perfected his tea blend. He set up shop in London, developed a nice accent, and when he arrived back in America in 1970, people assumed he was English nobility, and sales of his tea took off. He became a multi-millionaire.

But success didn't affect him. He knew that middleness is an inner quality and you carry it all your life, in all circumstances. A middle child can become a star, stand on a stage in a gold lamé suit with six spotlights trained on him, and people in the audience will be looking at the band, the third saxophonist from the right, and thinking, "He reminds me of somebody, but who? A guy who was at my wedding . . . But which marriage? The third, I think. Was he one of the caterers? Was he Barb's brother?" — meanwhile, the middle child has performed the Sextet from *Lucia,* all six parts, but his essential middleness deflects the crowd's attention to the decor, the candle in the lamp on the table, the waiter — doesn't he remind you of someone who was in a movie once?

Earl and his folks were almost reunited on a cable TV show called *Bringing It Home* many years later. His mom and dad were living in Miami and the cable network flew them first class to New York City, where Earl's headquarters were. Earl rode the subway to the studios, only to find out that his father had a headache and he and Mom were not feeling up to seeing Earl, and that rather than cancel the show, his parents would be portrayed by actors. The host of the show, a smiley man named Brant whose hair was as big as a breadbox, introduced the actors, who came out with tear-dimmed eyes and threw their arms around Earl, who hugged them back but only a little. He was forty-seven now and owned six homes and was in excellent health and his parents just didn't matter that much, and besides the actors were nothing like his mother and dad. They wore wigs and they spoke in very fakey Southern accents.

Brant grinned like a house afire. "Earl Grey," he cried, "today your tea business has made you a multimillionaire, your name known around the world. Wouldn't you have to agree that maybe, *just maybe,* your being left behind in North Dakota may have been the best thing that ever happened to you?"

"No," Earl said, "of course it wasn't. Don't be ridiculous. It is criminal for parents to abandon a child, and though I forgive them, I know that my parents deserve to be given long prison sentences."

The actor playing his dad said, "What kind of a nutcase are you to say that about your own parents?"

"Narcissists make lousy parents and mine were two of the worst. They had children for one reason, personal vanity, and they used us as props, and hadn't the faintest idea who we were."

Brant did not blink. He looked at "Mrs. Grey" and said, "He's quite a boy. You must be very proud of him."

"Yes," the actress said. "He has brought so much happiness into our lives." And Earl realized that his accusations would be edited out of the program and that in the final cut he would appear to be a loyal and grateful

366

son. He was a middle child, easily ignored, and there was nothing he could do about it.

2.
DON GIOVANNI

My bread and butter was the good people of Lake Wobegon, but writing about good people is an uphill climb. Their industriousness, their infernal humility, their schoolmarmish sincerity, their earnest interest in *you,* their clichés falling like clockwork — it can be tiring to be around them. One wants them for neighbors, of course. But a dinner party with the righteous can be a long three hours. And so a man who was well brought up is naturally attracted to people who sit slugging down whiskey, blowing clouds of smoke, reminiscing about misspent lives — and without contrition! Alcoholic adventures cheerfully recalled, lubricious nights, ingenious larceny and graft, laws scoffed at, justice avoided, authority bamboozled. Scripture tells us not to sit in the seat of the scornful, but I have enjoyed sitting *near* those seats, close enough to catch what they have to say and to admire their adventurous spirit.

Marriage is the deathbed of romance, says the old seducer through a cloud of cigarette smoke. *Figaro, my friend, a man owes it to himself to stop and consider the three advantages of the single life.*

One, if you're single, you can think. Two, you can act. Three, you can feel.

You put your money in the bank and you land great bargains from auctions. You come and go, you eat when you're hungry, you stay up late, you get drunk as it pleases you, and you have two or three terrific lovers who visit when you invite them and stay about the right length of time.

Enjoy yourself. That's what we're here for.

Some men should have two lovers, some three, it depends on the man, said the Don. *Never limit yourself to one: monogamy leads to matrimony, and marriage, my boy, is pure struggle. Of course the single life has problems — having two lovers is a scheduling problem, and three is a real test of a man's organizational ability, and yet those are the very problems a man hopes for, Figaro. Living alone in a cushy old apartment with your friendly housekeeper coming on Fridays to put a shine on things, the corner laundry delivering clean clothes on Wednesdays, and your girlfriends dropping in on various evenings, each of them crazy about you, eager to please — you know how accommodating young women can be when they want to be. Think of having three like that at once, their eyes alight at the sight of you, their lips moist, the flush of desire on their cheeks. Sound good? My, yes.* The Don smiled at the thought.

"No woman would accept such an arrangement. You would have to lie to her," said Figaro.

Yes, certainly, said the Don.

"To lie to three women at once? To keep inventing stories about where you went? Is that nice?"

The girls who share my bed want to share my life, said the Don, *and that would leave me no life at all.*

"But to be so selfish — what if everyone were? What if your parents had been?"

I am selfish, Figaro, because I have a larger capacity for pleasure than other people do. Pleasure is only a hobby to them and to me it is a true vocation: the joy of eating a sumptuous meal in the company of a sharp-tongued woman who secretly adores me — who argues with me and ridicules my politics and my ideas, the things I don't care about, and who, in a couple hours, will lie happily next to me, damp and drowsy, smiling — this is to me the beauty of the male existence. As for my parents, what they did wasn't my responsibility.

Figaro had dropped in to see his old friend at the Sportsman's Bar in Fargo, where the Don was engaged for three weeks to play the piano. Figaro had moved to Fargo with Susanna shortly after their marriage, and he had not laid eyes on the Don since the lothario had attempted to seduce Susanna on their wedding night — one of those cases of mistaken identity in dimly lit places, so Figaro bore no grudge.

The Sportsman was an old dive near the Great Northern yards where the switching crews liked to duck in for a bump of whiskey on their coffee breaks. It was not a place you would bring a woman, Figaro thought, and any woman you might find in there you wouldn't want to know better. The little marquee out front said, BBQ BEEF S'WICH $1.95 HAPPY HOUR 4–6 TWO DRINKS FOR PRICE OF ONE D G'VANNI IN HUNTERS LOUNGE NITELY.

When Figaro stepped into the gloom, through the cloud of beer and smoke and grease he heard someone playing "Glow Worm," and recognized the Don's florid glissandos, the tremors and trills, the quavers and dips, the big purple chords rising,

371

the mists, the Spanish moss, the grape arbor in the moonlight, the sighs, the throbbing of the thrush. The Don sat all big and glittery at the keyboard in the rear of the deserted room, in an iridescent silver jacket that picked up every speck of light from the 60-watt spotlight overhead. The silver threads went nicely with the Don's flowing bleached-blond hair and the gaudy rings on his fingers, chosen for maximum sparkle. Six rings and six chunks of diamond, a ruby-studded bolero tie, a silver satin shirt with pearl buttons, and silver-and-turquoise earrings.

He looked much the worse for wear, Figaro thought, as if he had been living in these clothes for a number of days, including some rainy ones, but he was full of beans, as always. He told Figaro he would soon be back in New York, where a big recording contract was in the offing, a major label, large sums of cash that he was not at liberty to disclose — he rubbed his fingers together to suggest the heavy dough involved — the people were secretive types, *you* understand, said the Don.

"And you? How are you? Have you found a wife yet?" asked Figaro.

The Don laughed. It was their old joke.

Marriage looks very appealing until you

are in the company of married people and then the horrors of the institution cry out to you, said the Don. Married guys can't go nowhere. There always has to be a plan, a list of errands, a system, a destination. Alone, your life is intuitive, like poetry. With a woman, it's a form of bookkeeping.

"So — how long are you in town?" asked Figaro, trying to change the subject, but the Don had more to say.

And a married guy is responsible for *everything,* no matter what. The guy alone is responsible for every day of marriage that is less than marvelous and meaningful. "Why don't we ever make love anymore?" That is the number 2 all-time woman's question in the world. Number 1 is "Why don't we ever talk to each other?" Now, there's a great conversational opener. You're ensconced on the couch, perusing the funny papers, sipping your hot toddy, feeling mellow and beloved, and she plops down full of anger. You take her hand.

"My love, light of my life, my interest in you is as vast as the Great Plains. Please. Share with me what is in your heart so that we may draw close in the great duet of matrimony."

But she doesn't want to converse, of course, she only means to strike a blow.

"Humph," she says, standing up. "I know you. You are only saying that."

That is marriage, Figaro. A boy's constant struggle to maintain his buoyancy.

"Some of what you say, I suppose, is true," said Figaro, "but a guy needs a wife, someone who cares if you've collapsed in the shower with your leg broken."

Well, your chances of collapsing in the shower are sharply improved by being married, the Don said. Marriage is a disaster for a man, it cuts him up and broils his spirit piece by piece, until there is nothing left of him but the hair and the harness.

An unhappy man with heavy eyelids appeared in the doorway to the Lounge, hands on hips, chewing a mouthful of peanuts. He appeared to be an owner or manager of some sort. "You on a break right now, Giovanni? Or is the piano busted?"

The Don turned with the greatest disdain and said, "Oh. Cy. I *thought* it was you."

"I hired you as a piano player, Giovanni, not a philosopher. I'd like to hear less thinking and more tinkling. A word to the wise." The man turned and disappeared.

The Don looked down at the keyboard, plunked a couple notes, got up from the bench, and motioned to a table in the corner. "We can sit there," he said.

"A life without a woman is the lonesomest life I can imagine," Figaro said with a sigh. "I would be miserable without Susanna."

Life *is* lonesome, said the Don, and lonesome isn't bad, compared to desperate. But of course a man should not live without women. Luckily, marriage is not a requirement. Nobody needs monogamy except the unenterprising. Hungry women are everywhere! Lonely housewives who advertise on recipe cards pinned to a bulletin board in the Piggly Wiggly — wistful ladies at the copier, putting flesh to glass, faxing themselves to far-off officedom — fervid women sending out e-mail invites — hearty gals working out on the weight machine who drop a note in your street shoes — cocktail joints along the freeway, wall-to-wall with women whose lights are on and motors are running! — Figaro, they're out there! Free. No legal contract required. What could be better?

Figaro shook his head. "The life of a libertine ends badly," he said. "You get old, your teeth turn yellow, you smell like a mutt, and you have to pay women to look at you. Much better to marry, to be faithful, to build a deeper partnership that will hold together through the terrible storms of old age."

My dear Figaro, seduction is an art, to be learned, practiced, adapted, and improvised according to the situation, and, like other arts, it will not desert you late in life.

"Seduction is a lie, and as we get older, we get tired of lies," said Figaro. "We know them all and they're not amusing anymore."

Seduction is a sweet story, and if the listener wants so much to hear it, then it is no lie. Seduction is a mutual endeavor in which I conspire with a woman to give her an opening to do what she wants to do without reminding her that this goes against her principles. A woman's principles and her desires are constantly at war, and if there were no one to seduce a woman, she would have to figure out how to do it herself. Her principles call for her to remain aloof and uninterested until she meets a man who makes her faint. Her desires are otherwise. She wants to say, "That man, there. Unwrap him and send him over here so he can love me." She cannot say this. So I try to help her. I say, *Zerlina, I would like to hold your hand for two minutes and then you can shoot me and I will die a happy man.*

She laughs, but she does not turn away. She rolls her eyes. She says, "Oh, phoo."

376

She gives me her hand.

I say: *The greatest tragedy is to be cut off from intimacy, from touch, which is the most human of languages, Zerlina, and the most honest. There is no lie in a touch, a caress, never. The language of the body is a language of the purest truth.*

She is amused. I put my other hand on her shoulder. She turns and leans against me. "You're something," she says.

Zerlina, I say, *there's a bottle of champagne waiting on ice at the Olympia Hotel, and a couple dozen oysters. When we get there, we'll order up a big salad in a wooden bowl, with basil and spinach and fennel and cilantro and radicchio, and we'll have it with olive oil and vinegar and pepper and garlic. Then a steak tartare, with chopped onions and an egg yolk. And then we'll undress quickly without shame, as adults, and jump into the big bed and amuse each other as only adults can do. And afterward, we'll eat an omelet. And then do it again.*

Her hand twitches in mine, and I guess that I have touched a chord — *This is the best time of year for oysters,* I say in a low voice, *and one should never eat them without erotic plans for later.*

She tells me to be real, but even so, she is

reaching for her purse, putting on her coat, checking her lipstick. "You're outrageous," she says, and now we are almost to the hotel, and then in the room, she says, "I can't believe I'm actually doing this." But she is. She is. A wonderful occasion, Figaro. The sort of evening that someday, as you lie dying, you will remember and it will bring a smile to your lips.

"You *slept* with her? Zerlina? But she is married to Maseppo," said Figaro. "I can't believe this!"

I may have slept with her, I may not have slept with her, I only mention her as an example. Zerlina, Marilyn, Marlene — what's the difference? A *woman.*

"Having an affair is not the same as marital happiness," said Figaro.

You are right. Marital happiness is briefer and it has a sword hanging over its head. The happiness in marriage is fitful, occasional. It is the pleasure one gets from the absence of the pain of not conforming exactly to the wishes of your wife. A married man walks into the room and his wife looks up and smiles — he is dressed and groomed exactly as she has trained him, his gait is perfect, his personality is champion quality, and he is prepared to converse on topics of her liking, a neat trick it took her years to teach him — and for the duration of her smile, he is happy. But her smile is brief. She spots the flaw: the spiritual emptiness in his eye. She has warned him against emptiness, but there it is. He must think of a way to fill up his spirit.

The man with the heavy eyelids reappeared in the door, an envelope in his hand. "Time to go, Giovanni," he said, setting his big hand on the table. "Yer outta here. You broke the deal. Yer history. The job's over. Move it."

The Don sneered. What a relief to get out of this mausoleum, he said. I am, he said, the greatest romantic pianist of all time. But a romantic pianist in Fargo is like an All-Star shortstop in Paris. Not a priority item.

"Go to hell," said the man, and he stamped his foot on the floor. Figaro looked down. The man had hooves instead of shoes.

The Don stood up. *Gladly,* he said, *it would be better than looking at your ugly face.*

The man strode to the back door by the piano and opened it, and Figaro saw the orange glow of flames in the basement, fingers of flame licking the doorsill.

"Stop!" he cried. "No! Giovanni! Repent!" He took the Don by the arm. "It's not too late. *Repent!*"

The Don put a hand on Figaro's shoulder.

Believe me, he said, it's easier simply to go. And compared to marriage, it isn't that bad. Farewell, *mon ami.* And he took off his great silver jacket and gave it to Figaro and walked to the stairs, put his hands on the door frame, and then, with a mighty cry, plunged down into the fiery abyss.

"Your hair smells of smoke," Susanna said to Figaro when he arrived home. "Where were you? In a bar? You stopped in a bar on your way home? I thought you had out-grown that, darling. And what are you go-ing to do with that hideous jacket? My gosh. You can put it in the garage. It reeks of shellfish. I don't want it in the house. Go on. Take it out of here."

So he did. He put the silver jacket on a hanger and hung it on a nail next to the rakes and shovels, and it stayed there for years. Twice she threw it in the trash and twice he retrieved it.

3.
Taking a Meeting
with Mr. Roast Beef

The discovery of Guy Noir, Private Eye, was a breakthrough on *A Prairie Home Companion,* the character done in a tough-guy voice. He is a heavy-set fellow in a rumpled blue suit and a porkpie hat, with a bottle of bourbon in the file drawer, electric fan whirring, and a theme song ("He's smooth and he's cool, he's good with a gun, a master in the boudoir. A man in a trench coat who gets the job done. . . . That's Guy — Guy Noir"). Tim Russell played Jimmy the bartender at the Five Spot, Lt. McCafferty of the St. Paul P.D., Rico, and various other heavies, and Sue Scott was the girlfriend Sugar and the landlady Doris and various bimbos and femme fatales, and Tom Keith did the ringing phone, the door knocks, the footsteps, the gunshots, the sirens, and also played Mr. Biggie. And I got to be Guy, who said things like *She was tall and beautiful. She gave me a look so sweet you could've poured it on your pancakes. She wore jeans so tight I could read the embroidery on her underwear. It said "Saturday." And she wore a Mount Rushmore T-shirt, and let me tell you, those guys never looked so good. Especially Lincoln and Jefferson.* He was perpetually broke and in love and ever astonished by the greed and cruelty and general cluelessness around him. This is the first chapter of the novella *Guy Noir and the Straight Skinny.*

Call me a cynic but there is nothing can clarify a man's thinking quite like looking down the barrel of a revolver in the hand of a man who is seriously irked with you and considering homicide as a solution to a problem. This has happened to me occasionally in my so-called career as a private eye in St. Paul, Minnesota, and each occurrence promoted clear thinking, inconvenient though it seemed at the time. Christians try to find clarity through prayer but you don't really know what prayer is until you meet someone who's eager to shoot you. I am referring to an afternoon last February when an eighty-two-year-old mobster named Joey Roast Beef sat in my office on the twelfth floor of the Acme Building with a cocked pistol aimed at my chest and ordered me to tell him something that I had no intention of telling him because it involved large sums of money that I would be reaping a percentage of. His hairy finger was coaxing the trigger and he yelled "Talk to me!" and suddenly everything got clearer.

Moments before, on this particular February day, I was in my twelfth-floor office, high above the poor souls on the street struggling through the snowbanks, and reading a trashy novel in which a twenty-three-year-old fashion model is attracted to a heavyset sixty-four-year-old guy in a wrinkled suit. I was thinking about ordering a hot pastrami from Danny's Deli and hoping Danny would add it to my tab though my tab was long, two or three hundred bucks, which is not good but business was slow and a guy's got to eat. Preferably pastrami on a kaiser, slice of onion, and a squort of hearty mustard to clear the sinuses. So I'm in a Cloudy State of Mind when I hear heavy thumping on the door and the thumper yells, "Hey, Noir, open up. I know you're in there, you snake in the grass." And it was him, the Senior Citizen of Organized Crime.

"The office is closed, Joey," I said calmly.

"Not to me it ain't." And he threw open the door and stomped in, all 340 pounds of him. "Forgot to lock your door, Noir. What a genius you are. It's amazing someone didn't rub you out a long time ago."

He was draped in a blue seersucker suit like a toad in gift wrap and a yellow shirt and pink tie, his thinning black hair slicked back, peering out through thick black horn-rims, and he looked like one of those fat guys with a chestful of medals who run South American republics. The jacket lapels had traces of smutz on them but his beetle brow was set for battle, his jaw jutting out, his dewlaps quivering. He was also wheezing — as you or I would if we were 5 feet 4 and weighed 340 pounds and carried an oxygen tank with a plastic tube stuck up our nose.

"No Good Morning?" I said. "No How Are You?"

"I know how you are. You are in big, big trouble, Smart Guy. I'm done with you. If you don't tell me what I need to know, you're going to be sleeping in the dirt and making friends with the maggots." He lowered himself gingerly into my old oak chair, which groaned under him, and pulled out his Colt .45 and aimed it at my sternum. It appeared to be loaded. With bullets.

"I'm expecting visitors, Joey," I said in the same quiet tone. "So I don't have time for an extended conversation."

It was a lie, of course, but when dealing

with an angry armed man you'd like him to think that witnesses could arrive at any moment.

"This won't take long. About two minutes. The word on the street, Noir, is that you are holding out on me on a very lucrative deal involving millions — and you made a big big mistake thinking I'm such a dope I wouldn't find out about it, which is an insult. I'm insulted. And I'm going to give you about two minutes to tell me what is going down exactly and what your take is gonna be and when you will split that with me," he said. "So out with it."

"Give me a hint," I said. "I got no idea what you're talking about. You want to know who to pick in the seventh at Belmont? You want the formula of the atomic bomb? What you want, Joey?"

"It involves you and that dancer at the Kit Kat Klub named Naomi Fallopian. The one who got her Ph.D. and now she's teaching women's rights or something at the U. So let's start with her." He shifted his enormity in the chair and it groaned, so I could imagine it collapsing and him sprawled on the floor and me leaping up and whacking him senseless with the desk lamp. I could also imagine the shock of the fall twitching his trigger finger and a poof of flame and the bullet hitting me in the frontal lobe and turning me into a cauliflower. The second possibility seemed just as likely.

He cleared his throat. "Don't make me repeat myself, Noir. You are walking around about to make a killing and retire to a penthouse somewhere with a revolving king-size bed under a ceiling mirror with you and her in a pink peignoir reflected in it and that's okay, I don't begrudge you the comforts of life, I'm only looking to collect my share, otherwise Miss Fallopian is going to be wearing a black suit and a hat with a veil and crying into a hanky as she gazes at the china vase containing your ashes." He set the pistol down on the desk and adjusted his air hose, which was taped to his upper lip.

I said, "Joey, I respect your perspicacity in most things, but as to this bum information somebody sold you about me and Miss Fallopian, Joey, you are woofing down the wrong rainbow, there is no pot of gold at the end, just an old private eye with lower-back pain and a pocketful of breath mints, namely me. There is no killing about to be made. Whoever whispered this in your ear is pulling your leg. I say this as an old and dear friend. This is delusional thinking, Joey. If you're not careful, you're going to wind up on the funny farm, talking to the window shades."

I was hoping to build doubt in the man's mind but his firm grip on the peashooter told me I was not succeeding. He was in no mood for storytelling.

"Tell me what's going on, Noir, or else you are going to get you a new buttonhole. Right in between those other buttonholes."

It occurred to me just then that Life Without Parole might not be a deterrent to one in such bad shape as Mr. Roast Beef. A hospital is a hospital, whether it's Mount Sinai or Sing Sing.

"If I were you, I would go home and ask the beautiful Adele to fix you a Reuben sandwich and then lie down and take a nice nap. You're obviously under a lot of stress right now so don't have a coronary."

"You're going to be under even more stress when this bullet hits your rib cage," he said. "The last man who double-crossed me is wearing the pine kimono, mister. He's taking the dirt nap. If you get my drift. Start talking or I'm going to roll the credits." And then he cocked the pistol.

That little metallic skritch and click clarified my thinking but good. *I am not going to beg for my life. Au contraire. I will try pushing Joey's buttons and rile him up so he can't think straight and maybe shoots himself in the foot.*

"Listen, Fat Man. You ever hang out up around One Hundred Second and Broadway?" I says. "That's where I grew up. Good old New York, New York, the city so nice they named it twice. We used to use guys like you for footrests. You're darned right I have hit pay dirt and it's mine, Lard Ass, no freeloading. Your mooching days are done. You can wave your little peashooter all you like, I am not going to allow a schtoonk with an air hose and piss on his pants to horn in on the deal. No freebies." I said it quiet but I said it straight.

He was mightily peeved. "Time is running out, buddy boy. You take this wiseacre attitude with me and I will mash you like a grasshopper." He stamped his foot so hard the tassel came off his shoe, and the exertion squeezed his hemorrhoids and he let out a yelp.

"You ought to see a proctologist," I said. "They can snip those hemmies off with a pair of pinking shears and cauterize them with a curling iron and you'll be pain-free for years to come and it'll probably add twenty points to your bowling score, too."

He shifted the pistol from his left hand to his right and suddenly his tone changed.

He was pleading. "You and me go way back, Guy. I have been like an uncle to you. So many times when Rico or Tony wanted to run you out of town on a marble slab, I told them, 'Hands off Noir, he's family.' I did that for you. More than once. Otherwise you would've been floating down the Mississippi in a barge full of soybeans and processed into tofu and eaten by skinny women in hundred-dollar jeans and evacuated into the sewers of San Francisco and out to sea. Is that what you want for yourself? To be sludge on the ocean floor?"

I suggested that I could take him into the deal as a consultant. He snorted. "I had a cat once and I had him neutered but he still went out at night and served as a consultant. Not me. Stop wasting my time."

I suggested that we go to Danny's and talk about it over a bowl of chicken noodle soup and a hot Reuben.

He thumped the pistol butt on the desk and wheezed from the effort. He whispered, "You got ten seconds to talk, Noir. You're trying to cut me out of the gravy train and I don't want to do it but I'm not going to take that laying down."

I corrected his grammar and pointed out gently that *laying* is a transitive verb, it takes an object — you lay down your head on a pillow, but you yourself lie down on a bed, so what he should've said was *lying down* — and Joey did not care for this. He shifted in his seat as if to get better aim at my aorta and he landed smack on those painful hemmorhoids and whimpered and I grabbed his right arm and twisted it and made him lay down his pistol on the table. And then I pinched his oxygen tube to make him lie down. Which he did. He laid his big noggin down on the desk and his body let out something long and hissy that smelled of fried automobile tires.

"Sweet dreams, pal." I crimped the tube for forty-five seconds, long enough to shift his synapses into neutral, and then released. He opened his eyes and blinked. "What you doing with my gun?" he croaked.

"Just borrowing it for a day or two," I said.

"Oh," he said. "Okay."

I helped him to his feet. "Lulu LaFollette called, Joey. She's upset that you forgot you said you'd meet her waiting for you at the Hotel Cranston. Room Seven Sixteen. She's got her green chiffon nightie on and she's all hot and sweaty thinking about getting her ashes hauled."

He grinned and heaved himself to his feet. "My memory isn't what it used to be," he whispered. "Thanks, Guy." And he lumbered off to perform amatory wonders on the buxom bombshell — who, for all I knew, was back home on her sheep ranch in Stanley, North Dakota.

A minute later, he was back.

"Lulu who?"

"LaFollette."

"The name is familiar."

"The singer, Joey."

"Oh yeah."

And I put a hand on his shoulder and sang —

Even those who write prose do it.
People wearing all their clothes do it.
Let's do it. Let's fall in love.
Some intertwined centipedes do it.
In winter, even Swedes do it.
Let's do it. Let's fall in love.
Gorillas deep in the mists do it,
Hanging by their palms.
True feminists do it,
Though they have qualms.
The lower halfs of giraffes do it,
Even managers of office staffs do it,
Let's do it. Let's fall in love.

And he headed for the Cranston, its lobby lined with grizzled old-timers in their undershirts hacking up loogies, and looked around for Lulu, a smiling hopeful man, not the homicidal bozo he was fifteen minutes previous. The prospect of Lulu has made him a much nicer human being, all in all. It should happen to more people than it does.

4.
YOUR BOOK SAVED
MY LIFE, MISTER

I love writing about the tribulations of author-
ship because there are none worth mention-
ing, nothing that compares to the troubles of
middle school teachers or waitresses in diners or ballet dancers. So here is the western
author Dusty Pages, who feels underappreci-
ated by his readers but then goes back and
peruses some of his work and is surprised by
its crappiness. This has happened to me more
than once and not all that long ago. I am
handed a book of mine, a historical novel set
in tsarist Russia, by a fan who wants me to
sign it "To Vern & Earlene, happy anniversary,"
and I inadvertently open it to page 17 instead
of the title page and there is a sentence —
"Lady Ouspenskaya swept down the black
marble staircase under the sunburst chande-
lier, gathering her blue silk gown about her,
and paused at the balustrade and took a deep
breath. Her nostrils flared. 'Is something
amiss, your ladyship?' whispered the foot-

page. 'I detect the unmistakable odor of a load of wet warsh,' she said." — and I see *warsh* and cringe. How did that boner get past me? I taught myself to say *wash* a long time ago. *Warsh* is a relic from my sharecropper childhood and Mama doing the family laundry at the Sudsarama in town. To my young self I would say: Writing gets easier and easier as you get older, along with most other things. So grow up.

All of my books, including *Wagons Westward!!! Hiiiii-YAW* and *Ck-ck Giddup, Beauty! C'mon, Big Girl, Awaaaaayy!* and *Pa! Look Out! It's — Aiiiiieee!* have been difficult for my readers, I guess, judging from their reactions when they see me shopping at Val-Mar or sitting in the Quad County Library & Media Center. After a rough morning at the keyboard, I sort of like to slip into my black leather vest, big white hat, and red kerchief, same as in the book-jacket photos, and saunter up and down the aisle by the fruit and other perishable items and let my fans have the thrill of running into me, and if nobody does I park myself at a table dead smack in front of the western-adventure shelf in Quad County's fiction department, lean back, plant my big boots on the table, and prepare to endure the terrible price of celebrity, but it's not uncommon for a reader to come by, glance down, and say, "Aren't you Dusty Pages, the author of *Ck-ck Giddup, Beauty! C'mon, Big Girl, Awaaaaayy!*" and when I look down and blush and say, "Well, yes, ma'am, I reckon I am him," she says, "I thought so. You look just like him." Then an awful silence while she studies the shelf and selects Ray A. James, Jr., or Chuck Young or another of my rivals. It's a painful moment for an author, the reader two feet away and moments passing during which she does not say, "Your books have meant so much to me," or "I can't tell you how much I admire your work." She just reaches past the author like he was a sack of potatoes and chooses a book by somebody else. Same thing happens with men. They say, "You're an author, aren'tcha? I read a book of yours once, what was the name of it?"

I try to be helpful.

"Could it have been *Wagons Westward!!! Hiiiii-YAW!?*"

"No, it had someone's name in the title."

"Well, I wrote a book entitled *Pa! Look Out! It's — Aiiiiieee!*"

"No, I think it had the name of a horse."

"Could it have been *Ck-ck Giddup, Beauty! C'mon, Big Girl, Awaaaaayy!?*"

395

"That's the one. Did you write that?"

"Yes, sir, I did."

"Huh. I thought so."

And right there you brace yourself for him to say, "Y'know, I never was one for books and then my brother gave me yours for Christmas and I said, 'Naw, I don't read books, Craig, you know that,' and he said, 'But this is different, Jim Earl, read this, this isn't the girls' literature they stuffed down our throats in high school, this is the real potatoes,' so I read it and by George I couldn't put the sucker down, I ran out and did the chores and tore out and back in the pickup to check on those dogies and I read for two days and two nights without a minute of shuteye. Your book changed my life, mister. I'm glad I got a chance to tell you that. You cleared up a bunch of stuff that has bothered me for years — you took something that had been inside me and you put it into words so I could feel, I donno, not so weird, feel sorta like *understood,* y'might say. That was me you put in that book of yours, mister. That was my life you wrote about there, and I want to say thanks. Just remember, anytime you're ever in Big Junction, Wyoming, you got a friend there name o' Jim Earl Wilcox" — but instead he says, "You wouldn't know where the little boys' room is, wouldja?" as if I were a library employee and not a book author. So it's clear to me that when people read my books they like me a little less at the end than at the beginning. My fourth book, *Company A, Chaaaaaaarge!*, is evidently the worst. Nobody bought it at all.

I know what it's like to be disappointed by a hero. You think I don't know? Believe me, I know. I met my idol, Smokey W. Kaiser, when I was twelve. I'd read every one of his books twice — the Curly Bob and Lefty Slim series, the Lazy A Gang series, the Powder River Hank series — and I had waited outside the YMCA in Des Moines for three hours while he regaled the Rotary with humorous anecdotes, and when he emerged at the side door, a fat man in tight green pants tucked into silver-studded boots, he looked down and growled, "I don't sign pieces of paper, kid. I sign books. No paper. You want my autograph, you can buy a book. That's a rule of mine. Don't waste my time and I won't waste yours."

Smokey's problem was that he was a jerk, but mine is that I get halfway through a story and everything goes to pieces. In *Wagons Westward!!! Hiiiii-YAW!* the pioneers reach Council Bluffs, having endured two hundred solid pages of Indian attacks, smallpox, cattle stampedes, thirst, terror, bitter backbiting, scattered atheism, and adulterous inclinations, and then they sit on the bluffs and have a meeting to decide whether they really want to forge onward to Oregon or whether maybe they should head east toward Oak Park or Evanston instead. Buck Bradley, the tall, taciturn, sandy-haired, God-fearing man who led them through the rough stuff, stands up and says, "Well, it's up to the rest of you. Makes no nevermind to yours truly, I could go either way and be happy — west, south, you name it. I don't *need* to go west or anything. You choose. I'll go along with whatever."

I don't know. I wrote that scene the way I heard it in my head but now I see it in print, it looks dumb. I can certainly see why it would throw a reader, same as in *Ck-ck Gid-dup, Beauty! C'mon, Big Girl, Awaaaaayy!* when Buck rides two thousand miles across blazing deserts searching for Julie Ann and finally, after killing twenty men and wearing out three mounts and surviving two avalanches, a prairie fire, a blizzard, and a passel of varmints, he finds her held captive by the bloodthirsty Arapaho. "So, how are you doing?" he asks her. "Oh, all right, I guess," she says, gazing up at him, wiping the sweat from her brow. "You want to come in for a cup of coffee?" "Naw, I just wanted to make sure you were okay. You *look* okay." "Yeah, I lost some weight, about twenty pounds." "Oh, really. How?" "Eating toads and grasshoppers." "Uh-huh. Well, now that I look at you, you *do* look lighter." "Sure you won't have coffee?" "Naw, I gotta ride. Be seein' ya, now." "Okay, bye!" To me it seemed more realistic that way, but maybe to the guy reader it sounded sort of unfocused or something. I don't know. Guys have always been a tough audience for me. The other day a guy grabbed my arm in the Quad County and said, "Hey, Dusty! Dusty Pages! That right? Am I right or am I right?"

"Both," I said.

"Mister," he said, "your book saved my life. My brother gave it to me and said, 'Buck, read this sometime when you're sober,' and I put it in my pocket and didn't think about it until, October, I was elk hunting up in the Big Coulee country, other side of the Little Crazy River, and suddenly *wham* it felt like somebody swung a bat and hit me in the left nipple. I fell over and lay there and, doggone it, I felt around and didn't find blood — I go 'Huh???????' Well, it was your book in my jacket pocket saved my life — bullet tore through the first half of it, stopping at page 143. So, by Jim, I thought, 'This is too crazy, I got to *read* this,' and I started to read and I couldn't believe it. That was me in the book — my life, my thoughts, it was weird. Names, dates, places — it was my life down to the last detail, except for the beer. I don't drink Coors. The rest you got right. Here." And he slipped an envelope into my hand. "This is for you," he said.

It was a subpoena to appear in U.S. District Court on November 27 to defend myself in a civil suit for wrongful misuse of the life of another for literary gain. I appeared and I tried to defend, but I lost. My attorney, a very, very nice man named Howard Furst, was simply outgunned by three tall ferret-faced bushwhackers in black pinstripes who flew in from Houston and tore him limb from limb in two and a half hours in that cold windy courtroom. They and their client, Buck Bradley, toted away three saddlebags full of my bank account, leaving me with nothing except this latest book. It's the first in a new series, the Lonesome Bud series, called *The Case of the Black Mesa,* and it begins with a snake biting Bud in the wrist as he hangs from a cliff while Navajo shoot flaming arrows at him from below and a torrent of sharp gravel showers down on his old bald head. From there to the end, it never lets up, except maybe in Chapter 4, where he and the boys shop for bunk beds. I don't know what I had in mind there at all.

5.
ZEUS THE LUTHERAN

I wrote this story after my wife Ulla and I had spent a month in a rented house in a little village alongside a monastery on the island of Patmos, where St. John is alleged to have dreamed his Book of Revelation. To this whitewashed stone house, with a little courtyard where we ate yogurt and oranges for breakfast, a deliveryman on a Vespa came to the door bearing an enormous box containing my very first laptop, a Toshiba, and when I'd finally figured out how to set it up and turn it on, I got into a fever of writing. I sat in a shady alcove and my wife, a Dane, lay naked in the sun, and that's where this story originated.

I. Hera, Fed Up with His Philandering, Hires a Lawyer

Zeus the Father of Heaven, the Father of the Seasons, the Fates, and the Muses, the father of Athena and Apollo and Artemis and Dionysus, plus the father of Hephaestus by Hera, his wife, and of Eros by his daughter Aphrodite, was a guy who didn't take no for an answer. Armed with his thunderbolts, he did exactly as he pleased and followed every amorous impulse of his heart, coupling with nymphs or gods or mortal women as he desired, sometimes changing himself into a swan or a horse or a snake or taking the form of a mortal so as to avoid detection. Once, he became a chicken to make it more of a challenge.

His wife, Hera, was furious and hired a lawyer, Alan, to talk some sense into him. The day before, she had heard that Zeus was involved with a minor deity named Janice, shacked up with her on the island of Patmos, riding around on a Vespa with her clinging to him like a monkey.

"Tail him," she said. "Track down the bastard and nail him to the wall and put the bimbo on a plane to Peru." Hera threw her great bulk into a chair and glared blackly out the temple window. "One of these days, I'll catch him when he has set his thunderbolts aside and I will *trap him*! And then —" She laughed, *ho ho ho ho ho.* "Then we will have the Mother of Heaven. The patriarchy will be put on the shelf once and for all. With Athena, the goddess of wisdom, on my right hand, and Artemis, the goddess of the moon, on my left, I will civilize this bloody hellhole that men have made of the world." Alan picked up his briefcase. "Whatever you say. You're the client," he said, and got on a boat to Patmos.

When Alan spotted Zeus, sitting at a table in an outdoor café by the harbor, there was no bimbo, only the ageless gentleman himself in a blue T-shirt and white shorts, fragrant with juniper, the Father of Heaven nursing a glass of nectar on the rocks and picking at a spinach salad. Alan introduced himself and sat down. He didn't ask, "How are you?" because he knew the answer: GREAT, ALL-POWERFUL.

"I realize you're omniscient, but let me come right to the point and say what's on my mind," he said. "Knock it off with the fornication, okay? What are you trying to prove? You're a god, for Pete's sake. Be a little divine for a change. Otherwise, Hera means business, and we're not talking divorce, mister. You should be so lucky. Hera intends to take over the world. She's serious."

"You like magic? You want to see a magic trick?" said Zeus. And right there at the table he turned the young lawyer into a pitcher of vinaigrette dressing and his briefcase into a pine nut and he poured him over the spinach salad and then Zeus waved the waiter over and said, "The spinach is wilted, pal. Take it away, and feed it to the pigs. And bring me a beautiful young woman."

Hera was swimming laps in the pool at her summerhouse when she got the tragic news from Victor, Alan's partner. "Alan is gone, eaten by pigs," said Victor. "We found his shoes. They were full of salad dressing." She was hardly surprised; Alan was her six hundredth lawyer in fourteen centuries. Zeus was rough on lawyers. She climbed out of the water and wrapped herself in a vast white towel. "Some god!" she said. "Omniscient except when it comes to himself."

She had always been puzzled by Zeus's lust for mortal women — what did he see in them? they were so shallow, weak, insipid, childish — and once she asked him straight out: *Why fool around with lightweights?* He told her, "The spirit of love is the cosmic teacher who brings gods and mortals together, lighting the path of beauty, which is both mortal and godly, from each generation to the next. One makes love as a gift and a sacrament so that people in years to come can enjoy music and poetry and feel passion at the sight of flowers."

She said, "You're not that drunk — don't be that stupid."

Now she vowed to redouble her efforts against him, put Victor on the case. But the next day she was in Thebes, being adored, which she loved, and what with all the flower-strewing and calf-roasting, Hera was out of the loop when a beautiful American woman, Diane, sailed into the harbor at Patmos aboard the S.S. *Bethel* with her husband, Pastor Wes.

II. Bored, He Falls for an American

Wes and Diane were on the second leg of a two-week cruise that the grateful congregation of Zion Lutheran Church in Odense, Pennsylvania, had given them in gratitude for Wes's ten years of ministry. Zeus, who was drinking coffee in the same sidewalk café with the passionate, compliant woman and was becoming bored with her, saw Diane standing at the rail high overhead as the *Bethel* tied up. The strawberry-blond hair and great tan against the blue Mediterranean sky, the healthy American good looks made his heart go boom and he felt the old, familiar itch — except sharper. He arose. She stood, leaning over the rail, wearing a bright red windbreaker and blue jeans that showed off her fabulous thighs, and she seemed to be furious at the chubby man in the yellow pants who was laying his big arm on her shoulder, her hubby of sixteen years. She turned, and the arm fell off her. "Please, Diane," he said, and she looked away, up the mountain toward the monastery and the village of white houses.

Zeus paid the check and headed for the gangplank.

The night before, over a standing rib roast and a 1949 Bordeaux that cost enough to feed fifty Ugandan children for a week, Wes and Diane had talked about their good life back in Odense, their four wonderful children, their luck, their kind fellow Lutherans, and had somehow got onto the subject of divine grace, which led into a discussion of pretentious Lutheran clergy Diane had known, and Wes had to sit and hear her ridicule close friends of his — make fun of their immense reserve, their dopey clothes, their tremendous lack of sex appeal — which led to a bitter argument about their marriage. They leaned across the baklava, quietly yelling things like "How can you say that?" and "I always knew you felt that way!" until diners nearby were studying the ceiling for hairline cracks. In the morning, Diane announced that she wanted a separation. Now Wes gestured at the blue sea, the fishing boats, the mountain, the handsome Greek man in white shorts below who was smiling up at them — "This is the dream trip of a lifetime," he said. "We came all this way to Greece to be miserable? We could have done that at home! This is nuts. To go on a vacation trip so you can break up? Give me a break. Why are you so hostile?"

And in that moment, as he stood, arms out, palms up, begging for an answer, the god entered his body.

III. In the Heat of Passion, He Converts to Lutheranism

It took three convulsive seconds for Zeus to become Wes, and to the fifty-year-old minister, it felt exactly like a fatal heart attack, the painful tightening in the chest — Oh, shit! he thought. Death. And he had quit smoking three years before! All that self-denial and for what? He was going to fall down dead anyway. Tears filled his eyes. Then Zeus took over, and the soul of Wes dropped into an old dog named Spiros, who lived on the docks and suffered from a bad hernia. *Arf,* said Wes, and felt a pain in his crotch. He groaned and leaned down and licked his balls, a strange sensation for a Lutheran.

The transformation shook Zeus up, too. He felt suddenly nauseous and clutched at the rail and nearly vomited; in the last hour, Wes had consumed a shovelful of bacon and fried eggs and many cups of dreadful coffee. The god was filled with disgust, but he touched the woman's porcelain wrist.

"What?" she said.

The god coughed. He tried to focus Wes's watery blue eyes; there was some sort of plastic disc in them. "O Lady whose beauty lights the darkening western skies, your white face flashes when I close my eyes," he said in a rumbly voice.

She stared at him. "*What* did you say?"

The god swallowed. He wanted to talk beautifully, but English sounded raspy and dull to him, an inferior language; it tasted like a cheap cigar.

"A face of such reflection as if carved in stone, and such beauty as only in great paintings shone. O Lady of light, fly no higher, but come into my bed and know eternal fire."

"Where'd you get that? Off a calendar? Is this supposed to be a joke or what?" she said. She told him to be real.

All in all, Zeus thought, *I would rather be a swan.* The dumb mustache, the poofy hair around the bald spot on top, the heavy brass medallion with a fish on it, the sunken chest and wobbly gut and big lunkers of blubber on his hips, the balloon butt, the weak arms and shaky legs, and the poor brain — corroded, stuffed with useless, sad, remorseful thoughts. It was hard for Zeus to keep his mind on love with the brain of Wes thinking of such dumb things to say to her — "I'm sorry you're angry. Let's try to have a nice day together and see the town and write some postcards. Buy some presents for the kids, take some pictures, have lunch, and forget about last night." Zeus didn't want to write postcards, he wanted to take her below and peel off her clothes and make love so that the *Bethel* rocked in her berth.

Just below, the dog sat on his haunches, a professional theologian covered with filthy, matted fur, and the remains of his breakfast lying before him, the chewed-up hindquarters of a rat, and the rest of the rat in his belly.

"Look. That sweet little dog on the dock," said Diane, who loved dogs.

Zeus cleared his throat. "When you open your thighs, the soft clanging of bells is heard across the valley, O daughter of Harrisburg. Come, glorious woman, and let us waken the day with the music of your clamorous thighs."

"Grow up," she said, and headed down the gangplank, smiling at the dog.

The god's innards rumbled, and a bubble of gas shifted in his belly, a fart as big as a child. He clamped his bowels around it and held it in; he followed her down to the dock, saying: "Dear, dear Lady, O Light of my soul — to you I offer an earnest heart longing for the paradise that awaits us in a bed not far away, I trust. Look at me, Lady, or else I turn to dust." His best effort so far. But the language was so flat, and the voice of Wes so pompous.

"I could swear this dog is human," she cried, taking its head in her hands, stroking under its chin, scratching its tattered ears.

"Thank you, Diane," said the dog. "I don't know how I became schizophrenic, but I do know I've never loved you more." This came from his mouth as a whine, and then he felt a terrible twinge in the hernia and moaned. The woman knelt and cradled his head in her arms. She crooned, "Oh, honey, precious, baby, sweetness, Mama gonna be so good to you, little darling." She had never said this to him before. He felt small and cozy in her arms.

IV. The Great Lover Tries and Falls Short

The dog, the woman, and the god rode a bus three miles over the mountain to the Sheraton St. John Hotel, the woman holding the dog's head on her lap. She was thinking about the future: she'd leave Wes, take the kids, move to Philadelphia, and go to Bryn Mawr College — the simple glories of the disciplined intellectual life! What a tonic after years of slouching around in a lousy marriage. The god vowed to go without food until she surrendered to him. The dog felt no pain, but he hoped to find a cigarette lying on the floor somewhere, even a cigarette butt, and figure out how to light it.

The hotel room had twin beds, hard as benches, and looked out on a village of white stucco houses with small gardens of tomato plants and beans, where chickens strolled among the vines. Brown goats roamed across the brown hills, their bells clanging softly. Diane undressed in the bathroom, and slid into bed sideways, and lay facing the wall. Zeus sat on the edge of her bed and lightly traced with his finger the neckline of her white negligee. She shrugged. The dog lay at her feet, listening. Zeus held her shoulder strap between his thumb and index finger. It was bewildering, trying to steer his passion through the narrow, twisting mind of Wes. All he wanted was to make love enthusiastically for hours, but dismal Lutheran thoughts sprang up: Go to sleep. Stop making a fool of yourself. You're a grown man. Settle down. Don't be ridiculous. Who do you think you are?

He wished he could change to somebody trim and taut, an athlete, but he could feel the cold, wiggly flesh glued on him and he knew that Hera had caught him in the naked moment of metamorphosis and with a well-aimed curse had locked him tight inside the flabby body, this clown sack. A god of grandeur and gallantry living in a dump, wearing a mask of pork. He could hear his fellow gods hooting and cackling up on Olympus. (The Father of Heaven! Turned Down, Given the Heave-Ho! By a Housewife!)

Zeus pulled in his gut and spoke. "Lady, your quiet demeanor mocks the turmoil in my chest. Surely you see this, Lady, unless you are the cruelest of your race. Surely you hear my heart pound with mounting waves upon your long, passive shore. Miles from your coast, you sit in a placid town, feeling faint reverberations from beneath the floor. It is your lover the sea, who can never rest until you come to him."

413

"I don't know who you're trying to impress, me or yourself," she said. Soon she was snoring.

V. The Husband (the Dog) Takes the Long View

"This is not such a bad deal," said the dog. "Becoming a dog would never have been my choice, but now that I am one, I can see that in the course of following my maleness, as my culture taught me to think of maleness, I got separated from my beingness, my creaturehood. It is so liberating to see things from down here at floor level. You learn a lot about man's relentlessness."

They spent two sunny days at the Sheraton, during which Zeus worked to seduce Diane and she treated him like a husband. She laughed at him, not at his witty stories but at his ardor. The lines that had worked for him in the past ("Sex is a token of a deeper friendship, an affirmation of mutual humanity, an extension of conversation") made her roll her eyes and snort. She lay on a blue wicker lounge beside the pool — her caramel skin set off by two red bands of bikini, her perfect breasts, her long, tan legs with a pale golden fuzz. Her slender hands held a book, *The Concrete Shoes of Motherhood,* and she read it as he spoke to her.

"Let's take a shower. They have a sauna. Let me give you a backrub. Let's lie down and take a nap," he said.

"Cheese it," she said. "I'm not interested. Beat it."

He lost eighteen pounds. He ran ten miles every morning and swam in the afternoon. He shaved off the mustache. She refused to look at him, but, being a god, he could read her thoughts. She was curious about this sea change in her husband, his new regimen, his amazing discipline. She hiked over the dry brown hills and he walked behind and sang songs to her:

Lady, your shining skin will slide on mine,
And rise to the temple of Aphrodite,
Where you will live forever, no more
Lutheran but venerated by mortals. This I
  pledge.

She pretended not to hear, sweeping the horizon with her binoculars, looking for rare seabirds. Zeus thought, *I should have been a swan. Definitely a swan.* The dog trotted along, his hernia cured by love. She had named him Sweetness. "You go ahead and use my body as long as you like," he said to Zeus. "You're doing wonders for it. I never

415

looked so good until you became me. No kidding. But when it comes to lyrics, you're no Cole Porter, pal."

VI. The Great Lover Tries Again

She wouldn't let him touch her until they got on the plane back to America and they had eaten the lasagna and watched the movie and were almost over Newfoundland. The FASTEN SEAT BELTS signs flashed on and the pilot announced that they would be passing through a turbulent period and suddenly the plane bucked and shuddered in the boiling clouds, and Diane reached over and grabbed him as the plane tipped and plunged and rattled, and people shrieked and children cried. "If this is our time to die, then I want you to know that they were good years, they really were," Diane said, kissing him. "I love you, Wes. I'm crazy about you." Her kisses were hot and excited, and soon she was grabbing him and groping under his sport coat, digging her sharp tongue into the corners of his mouth and writhing in his arms and groaning and saying his name, but Zeus was unable to respond somehow. He tried thinking of smokestacks, pistols, pedestals, pole vaults, peninsulas, but nothing worked. Her hands reached for his zipper but he fought her off.

"Not here, people are watching," he muttered, and then the plane hit the concrete at Kennedy and bounced and touched down and rolled to a stop, and Diane shuddered and said, "I can't wait to get you home, big boy."

In the terminal, Zeus felt so weak, he could not carry their bags through customs. They fetched the dog, who emerged from the baggage room dopey and confused and out of sorts. He bit Zeus on the hand. Zeus limped to the curb and collapsed into the backseat of a van driven by a burly man named Paul, who, Zeus gathered, was his brother. Paul and Diane sat in front, Zeus and the dog in back. "Wes is pretty jet-lagged," Diane said, but the man yammered on and on about some football team that Zeus gathered he was supposedly interested in. "Hope you had a great time," said Paul. Yes, they said, they had. "Always wanted to go over there myself," he said. "But things come up. You know." He talked for many miles about what he had done instead of going to Greece: re-sodding, finishing the attic, adding on a bedroom, taking the kids to Yellowstone.

Do we have kids? Zeus wondered. "Four," said the dog, beaming. "Great kids. I can't wait for you to meet them, mister." Then he dropped his chin on the seat and groaned. "The littlest guy is murder on animals. One look at me, he'll have me in a headlock until my eyeballs pop." He groaned again. "I forgot about Mojo. Our black Lab." His big brown eyes filled with tears. "I've come home in disgrace to die like a dog," he said. "I feed Mojo for ten years and now he's going to go for my throat. It's too hard." The god told him to buck up, but the dog was gloomy all the way home.

VII. The Husband Disappears

When Paul pulled up to the double garage behind the green frame house and Diane climbed out, the dog squeezed out the door behind her and tore off down the street and across a playground and disappeared. *"Sweetness!"* she screeched. Paul and Zeus cruised the streets for half an hour searching for the mutt, Zeus with gathering apprehension, even panic. Without Wes to resume being Wes, he now realized, he couldn't get out of Wes and back into Zeus. There was, however, no way to explain this to Paul.

"You seem a little — I don't know — distant," said Paul.

"Just tired," said Zeus.

They circled the blocks, peering into the

bushes, whistling for the dog, calling his name, and then Paul went home for a warm jacket (he said, but Zeus guessed he was tired and would find some reason not to come back). The god strode across yards, through hedges, crying, "Sweetness! Sweetness!" The yards were cluttered with machines, which he threw aside. Sweetness!

The dog was huddled by an incinerator behind the school. He had coached boys' hockey here for ten years. "I'm so ashamed," he wept.

The god held him tightly in his arms.

"To be a dog in a foreign place is one thing, but to come home and have to crawl around your own neighborhood —" He was a small dog, but he sobbed like a man — deep, convulsive sobs.

Zeus was about to say, "Oh, it's not all that bad," and then he felt a feathery hand on his shoulder. Actually, a wing. It was Victor, Hera's lawyer, in a blue pin-striped suit and two transparent wings like a locust's.

VIII. The Lover's Feet Held to the Fire

Zeus tried to turn him into a kumquat, but the lawyer only chuckled. "Heh, heh, heh. Don't waste my time. You wanna know how come you feel a little limp? Lemme tell ya.

Hera is extremely upset, Mr. Z. Frankly, I don't know if godhood is something you're ever going to experience again. It wouldn't surprise me that much if you spent the rest of recorded time as a frozen meatball."

"What does she want?"

"She wants what's right. Justice. She wants half your power. No more, no less."

"Divide power? Impossible. It wouldn't be power if I gave it up."

"Okay. Then see how you like these potatoes." And Victor snatched up the dog, and his wings buzzed as he zoomed up and over the pleasant rooftops of Odense.

"Wait!" the god cried. "Forty-five percent!" But his voice was thin and whispery. On the way home, he swayed, his knees caved in, he had to hang on to a mailbox.

IX. Trapped

For three days, Zeus was flat on his back, stunned by monogamy: what a cruel fate for a great man! The dog Mojo barked and barked at him, and Diane waited on him hand and foot, bringing him bad food and despicable wine; wretched little children hung around, onlookers at the site of a disaster, children who he had to pretend were his own. They clung to him on the couch, fighting over the choice locations, whining, weeping, pounding each other. They stank of sugar and yet he had to embrace them. He could not get their names straight. The god swung down his legs and sat up on the couch and raised his voice: "I am trapped here, a divine being fallen from a very high estate indeed — you have no idea — and what I see around me I do not want."

Everybody felt lousy, except Diane. "It's only jet lag!" she cried, bringing in a tray of cold, greasy, repulsive food, which he could see from her smile was considered a real treat here. He ate a nugget of cheese and gagged.

"You'll feel better tomorrow," she said.

From outside came a burst of fierce barks and a brief dogfight and then yelping, and Diane tore out the door and returned a moment later with her husband, wounded, weeping, in her arms. "Oh, Sweetness, Sweetness," she murmured, kissing him on the snout, "we'll make it up to you somehow."

Later, Penny, the youngest, asked Zeus if Greece was as dirty as they said. She asked if he and Mom had had a big fight. She asked why he felt trapped. She wanted to hear all the bad news.

"I felt crazy the moment we landed in

America. The air is full of piercing voices, thousands of perfectly normal, handsome, tall people talk-talk-talk-talk-talking away like chickadees, and I can hear each one of them all the time, and they make me insane. You're used to this, I'm not. What do you people have against silence? Your country is so beautiful, and it is in the grip of invincible stupidity. Your politicians are habitual liars and toadies, and the writers are arrogant hacks," he said. "The country is inflamed with debt and swollen with blight and trash and sworn to flaming idiocy, and there is no civility left except among drunks and cab-drivers."

"How can you say that, Dad?"

"Because I'm omniscient."

"You are?"

"I know everything. It's a fact." She looked at him with a level gaze, not smirking, not pouting, an intelligent child. The only one prepared to understand him.

"Do my homework," she whispered. So he did. He whipped off dozens of geometry exercises, algebra, trigonometry, in a flash. He identified the nations of Africa, the law of averages, the use of the dative. "You are so smart," she said.

X. The Wife Courts the Lover While the Husband Watches

Diane packed the kids off to bed. "Now," she said, "where's that guy I rode home with on the plane?"

How could she understand? Passion isn't an arrangement, it's an accident, and Zeus was worn out. Nonetheless, he allowed himself to be undressed and helped into bed, and then Diane slowly undressed, letting her white silk slip slide to the floor, unhooking her garter belt and stripping the nylons slowly from her magnificent golden legs, unsnapping the brassiere and tossing it over her right shoulder, and stepping out of her silver panties. Then, naked, she stood a moment for his admiration, and turned and went into the bathroom.

"Relax, she'll be in there fifteen minutes if I know Diane," said the dog, sitting in the doorway. "She likes to do her nails before making love, I don't know why. Anyway, let me give you a few pointers about making love to her. She comes out of the gate pretty fast and gets excited and you think you're onto the straightaway stretch, but you're not — she slows down at that point, and she doesn't mount you until you're practically clawing at the walls."

"She mounts *me*?" asked Zeus.

"Yes," the dog said. "She's always on top."

When Diane emerged from the bathroom, she found Zeus in the living room, fully dressed, trying to make a long-distance call to Greece. She wanted him to see a therapist, but Zeus knew he was going back to Olympus. He just had to talk Hera down a little.

XI. Last Chance

The next morning, Zeus drove to the church, with Penny snuggled at his side. The town lay in a river valley, the avenues of homes extending up and over the hills like branches laden with fruit. The church stood on a hill, a redbrick hangar with a weathervane for a steeple, a sanctuary done up with fake beams and mosaics, and a plump secretary named Tammy with piano legs. She cornered him, hugged him, and fawned like a house afire. "Oh, Pastor Wes, we missed you so much! I've been reading your sermons over and over — they're so spirit-filled! We've got to publish them in a book!" she squealed.

"Go home," said Zeus. "Put your head under cold water." He escaped from the sanctuary into the study and slammed the door. The dog sat in the big leather chair behind the long desk. He cleared his throat.

"I'd be glad to help with the sermon for tomorrow," he said. "I think your topic has got to be change — the life-affirming nature of change — how it teaches us not to confuse being with having . . . the Christian's willingness to accept and nurture change. . . . I'll work up an outline for you."

"That's a lot of balloon juice," said Zeus. "If I weren't going home tomorrow, I'd give a sermon and tell them to go home and hump like bunnies." He caught a look at himself in a long mirror: a powerful, handsome, tanned fellow in a white collar. Not bad.

"You sure you want to leave tomorrow?" asked the dog.

"That's the deal I made with Victor. Didn't he tell you?"

"You couldn't stay until Monday? This town needs shaking up. I always wanted to do it and didn't know how, and now you could preach on Sunday and it'd be a wonderful experience for all of us."

"You're a fool," Zeus said. "This is not a long-term problem, and the answer to it is not the willingness to accept change. You need heart, but you're Lutherans, and you go along with things. We know this from history. You're in danger and months will pass and it'll get worse, but you won't

425

change your minds. You'll sit and wait. Lutherans are fifteen percent faith and eighty-five percent loyalty. They are nobody to lead a revolt. Your country is coming apart."

The dog looked up at the god with tears in his brown eyes. "Please tell my people," he whispered.

"Tell them yourself."

"They won't believe me."

"Good for them. Neither do I."

"Love me," Diane told Zeus that night in bed. "Forget yourself. Forget that we're Lutheran. Hurl your body off the cliff into the dark abyss of wild, mindless, passionate love." But he was too tired. He couldn't find the cliff. He seemed to be on a prairie.

XII. The Lover Leaves, the Husband Returns

In the morning, he hauled himself out of bed and dressed in a brown suit and white shirt. He peered into the closet. "These your only ties?" he asked the dog. The dog nodded.

Zeus glanced out the bedroom window to the east, to a beech tree by the garage, where a figure with waxen wings was sitting on a low limb. He said, silently, "Be with you in one minute." He limped into the

426

kitchen and found Diane in the breakfast nook, eating bran flakes and reading an article in the Sunday paper about a couple who are able to spend four days a week in their country home now that they have a fax machine. He brushed her cheek with his lips and whispered, "O you woman, farewell, you sweet, sexy Lutheran love of my life," and jumped out of Wes and into the dog, loped out the back door, and climbed into Victor's car.

"She'll be glad to hear you're coming," said Victor. "She misses you. I'm sorry you'll have to make the return flight in a small cage, doped on a heavy depressant, and be quarantined for sixty days in Athens, both July and August, but after that, things should start to get better for you."

XIII. How the Husband Saw It

At eleven o'clock, having spent the previous two hours tangled in the sheets with his amazing wife, Wes stood in the pulpit and grinned. The church was almost half full, not bad for July, and the congregation seemed glad to see him. "First of all, Diane and I want to thank you for the magnificent gift of the trip to Greece, which will be a permanent memory, a token of your generosity and love," he said. "A tremendous thing happened on the trip that I want to share with you this morning. For the past week, I have lived in the body of a dog while an ancient god lived with Diane and tried to seduce her." He didn't expect the congregation to welcome this news, but he was unprepared for their stony looks: they glared at him as if he were a criminal. They cried out, "Get down out of that pulpit, you filth, you!"

"Why are you so hostile?" he said.

Why are you so hostile? The lamp swayed as the ship rolled, and Diane said, "Why so hostile? Why? You want to know why I'm hostile? Is that what you're asking? About hostility? My hostility to you? Okay. I'll answer your question. Why I'm hostile — right? Me. Hostile. I'll tell you why. Why are you smiling?"

He was smiling, of course, because it was a week ago — and they were still in Greece, the big fight was still on, and God had kindly allowed him one more try. He could remember exactly the horrible words he'd said the first time, and this time he did not have to say them and become a dog. He was able to swallow the 1949 wine, and think, and say, "The sight of you fills me with tender affection and a sweet longing to be flat on my back in a dark, locked room with you naked, lying on top, kissing me, and me naked, too."

So they did, and in the morning the boat docked at Patmos, and they went up to the monastery and walked through the narrow twisting streets of the village, looking for a restaurant someone had told them about that served great lamb.

XIV. What the Lover Learned

The lawyer and the dog rode to the airport in the limousine, and somewhere along the way Zeus signed a document that gave Hera half his power and promised absolute fidelity. "Absolute?" he woofed. "You mean 'total' in the sense of bottom line, right? A sort of basic faithfulness? Fidelity in principle? Isn't that what you mean here? The spirit of fidelity?"

"I mean pure," the lawyer said.

Zeus signed. The lawyer tossed him a small, dry biscuit. Zeus wolfed it down and barked. In the back of his mind, he thought maybe he'd find a brilliant lawyer to argue that the paw print wasn't a valid signature. He thought about a twenty-four-ounce T-bone steak, and he wasn't sure he'd get that either.

6.
AL DENNY

My Minnesota friends are stoics and skeptics, unlikely to attend megachurches to hear men with big hair and big teeth preach the gospel of prosperity or invest in a scheme to earn double-digit profits through tiny fluctuations in currency markets. They would not pay $500 to attend a one-day seminar, "Why Not Be Fabulous?" nor would they be persuaded to send away for a food additive guaranteed to make you lose 15 pounds a month, no exercise, no special diet. But of course I don't know this for a fact. They may harbor secret desires for transformation that I am unaware of. Meanwhile, I sympathize with the hustlers and ballyhoo artists who sell the self-help books and the inspirational seminars and the secret additives. It's no bed of roses, selling. All those naysayers looking at you, their gimlet eyes, their hard mouths.

So much dead wood and garbage in our

lives, phoniness, grandstanding, humbug-
gery: How to rid ourselves of it and move
on to richer, deeper things? How to shuck
these lures and snares and give the delicate
beauty within us space in which to grow
and bloom? How to be more the good
person we set out to be when we were
nineteen instead of this dull greedy old
weasel snarfing all the food on the plate who
we turned into instead?

These questions began to bear down on
me a few years ago, when I was in San
Francisco to participate in a conference on
Birthing Our Self-Affirmation of Wellness
and I enjoyed a beautiful massage from a
holist named Sha-tsi in a white caftan who
completely emptied my being of all having-
ness (just as she said she would) and afterward my billfold was gone. It wasn't in my
briefcase or in my overcoat or my pants.

And there was no name tag on my gar-
ment bag or my carry-on.

A great massage, but I could not recall my
home telephone number or even remember
where I lived.

Suddenly I recalled Thoreau's advice,
"Simplify, simplify." So I called my agent,
Larry. "Where am I from?" I asked. He
wasn't sure either. Ohio, he thought. I
looked at a map of Ohio. Nothing rang a

bell. I had been on the road for three years since I wrote *Being the Person You Are,* and gradually Mona and I had lost touch. "How many children do I have, Larry?" I asked. He thought three. Three sounded right. Mona had been the primary caregiver in the family, so I wasn't sure. Three daughters, he thought, but I thought I remembered a boy.

Arnie?

I never thought this would ever happen to me. *Being the Person You Are* was short, thirty thousand words, and nobody at Chester White Publishing thought the book would cut much lumber in the self-esteem field up against giants like Wayne Dyer and Leo Buscaglia, but it went out and it sold five million copies or so in more than eleven languages and seventeen dialects.

Not bad for a Methodist minister who, in fifteen years of Sunday sermons, never had anyone come up to him afterward and request a copy.

So many people have told me that *Being the Person You Are* completely changed their lives, and others said they have had their lives changed partially.

Well, it changed mine, too. The book was about taking charge of your life and tapping into your deep inner chakras and power sources, but the success of the book was like a flash flood, and I floated away like a loose canoe. I ballooned from 180 to 238 pounds and chewed my fingernails and my hair got thin and three months later there I was, a big, lumbering galoot with bleeding cuticles clambering in and out of limos and adjusting his toupee, and though I could afford a good one, made of Native American hair, not nylon, still I felt stressed, jumpy, owly, and the weight gain affected my balance so I was liable at any time to topple over into a heap.

I fell on a woman in the lobby of the Four Seasons Clift hotel in San Francisco. She was small and delicate, Japanese, visiting our country perhaps for the first time, garnering impressions, and suddenly a big load of blubber lands in her lap. I apologized profusely but she thought I was hitting on her, I think, and went away. I fell across the head table on the dais at the Bobist Institute in Santa Fe, tumbled into the tofu salad, arms and legs akimbo. People applauded, thinking that I had done it to illustrate a bold point that would be clearer to them later.

Doctors puzzled over my dizziness. An acupuncturist put needles in my knuckles, an herbalist made a saffron sachet to hang around my neck. One morning, I woke up in Dayton, Ohio, fully dressed, sprawled across a hotel bed, my pants moist from creamy desserts stuffed in my pockets. I was registered there under the name Dr. Santana Mens, and a pink name tag with the Mens name on it was gummed to my breast pocket. It was a name tag from a large bookstore in a nearby mall, and I assumed I was supposed to go and autograph books, but when I called, they said that I had been there a week ago.

Was Dayton, Ohio, my home? Had some homing instinct brought me there, some unconscious imprint of flight schedules? There was no Al Denny in the phone book. Had Mona gone back to being a Thompson?

"You've got to get your life on track, Al," I thought, and Larry had provided a week's break on the lecture tour, so I hunkered down in the Mayfair Hotel in Chicago and wrote *Rebirthing the Me You Used to Be,* and that sucker sold fourteen million copies — in fact, it's still selling — in thirty languages, including a New Guinea tribal dialect in which my book was the first written literature. Through an interpreter, the chief, a man named Wallace Boogada, invited me to come and be their deity. They had been

Christianized by Army chaplains during World War II, but God had disappointed them and they wanted to try me.

Evidently, *Rebirthing* rang the wind chimes of a lot of folks, and it certainly dinged my doorbell too. I thought, "Al, you have got to simplify your life now." One day, I met Larry for lunch and noticed his tie, deep blue with a majestic stag elk standing on high rocks as ducks wing across an autumn sky and an Indian paddles a canoe across a broad pine-rimmed lake — "Larry," I said, "I'm taking the loot and buying a mountain and building a log lodge on top of it and moving up there with nothing but dry clothes and a notepad and some coffee beans and warm bedding and a scout knife. Doggone it. And I want an elk. And a canoe."

"Great," he said. "I'll take care of that, while you finish up the lecture tour."

I told him I desperately needed to get out into nature and put my priorities in order, but he had put together a great package, "An Evening with Dr. Al Denny," thirty lectures in twelve cities, at $90,000 per crack, and it was too late to back out, so I went — BIG SUCCESS, standing room only, hockey arenas packed with quiet people in meaningful T-shirts, people with

435

interesting hair, there were press confer-
ences and blizzards of questions about
polarity and rebirthing and chrysalis awareness and re-aging and the ancient Inca
secrets channeled through a Cleveland man
now known as El Hugo, and three-hour au-
tographing sessions and people fawning over
my every word — I'd say, "Hi, how are
you?" and they would say, "Yes! Of course!
How are you! It's not the whereness or the
whyness or the whoness of the You, it's how!
How!"

A month later, the tour ended in Tallahas-
see, and Larry sent a Learjet to take me to
the mountain. Except it wasn't a mountain,
it was more like a plateau, and it was in
Iowa. A vast complex of buildings he had
bought from the Maharishi for $200 mil-
lion. He drove me around fast in the dark
on a golf cart, pointing out a dormitory here
and a dormitory there, a gymnasium that
would be our TV studio, a barn where the
llamas would be housed.

"Llamas?"

"A very peaceful creature. You'll love
them. They'll be in the petting park, with
the deer," he said. "People will come, live
here at the resort, go to the spa, take your
courses at the study center, be rebirthed,
pet the llamas, visit you in your home, and

have a tremendous two weeks. We have more than two thousand reservations for June already. You're hot, Al. People want to be near you."

All the buildings looked the same to me, three-story light brown brick things with narrow windows and flat roofs, like nursing homes or an office park. The gymnasium had a thirty-foot satellite dish in back of it.

"For your cable show," he explained, parking the cart, and we opened the big steel doors and there was the studio, three hundred feet long, bleachers for two thousand, six cameras on dollies, a set with a long white couch and fake windows and plants. "State of the art," he said, proudly.

So I had to write another book to pay the overhead.

Coexisting with Your Other Self did not do as well as *Rebirthing* but it sold five million and had a blue cover with primitive masks on it. It was about using your inner potential to create an outer protective self to guard the secret beautiful you.

Meanwhile, I moved into my home on the grounds of the Dr. Al Denny Study Center, fully furnished, toothpaste and night-light and wine carafe, throw rugs, accent pieces, all there and ready. Larry took care of it. I seldom left the home due to the disciples lurking in the trees and because I was a little down since losing track of Mona and the children. Mona and I had been married for twenty-four years, and I loved her, but I was never clear on exactly what she did — some sort of teaching, I believe, or investment services — so it was hard to trace her through professional associations. I believed she used to attend meetings now and then in Chicago, but forgot why. I laid low for a while. I watched old movies and slept, and every day Larry drove a van into the garage (attached) and closed the door, I climbed in and lay on the floor, he zoomed out past the disciples and took me to the studio.

On *The Circle of Life with Dr. Al Denny,* a half-hour program carried everywhere in America, I sat on the couch in front of the audience and chatted with persons of wisdom such as quilt-makers, for example, and woodcarvers and Southern people and farmers and old blues singers and old ballplayers and old shepherds and Iowans and people over eighty and country doctors and guys named Walt, people you seldom see on TV. Their simple philosophies were deeply moving to me though also confusing.

They all said that the best things in life are spiritual, and I myself was in a very acquisitive stage of life at that point.

I owned four Bentleys. I owned paintings. I owned two fine horses, who terrified me. I owned 164 cases of a 1952 Bordeaux that I loved to drink with a particular kind of lobster that was flown in live from the Mindanao archipelago. I kept buying sweaters and loafers and those baggy pants with the fronts that pooch out. I purchased expensive dogs, one after the other, because I kept losing track of them. I'd leave them in stores and places. One was a Dalmatian, and another was a Weimaraner, I think. Somebody said it was, and then it was gone too.

Once on my show there was a heavyset gal from Mobile named Vernelle Tomahasset who devoted her life to creating art from bread bags and said the most important thing in life is to keep busy — she gave me a little horse made out of nine hundred bread bags — and a one-armed accordion man said he felt lucky because he had his health, and the very same day I paid $7,000 for a German-made CD player. Only a hundred like it in the world, and I have one, and Prince Charles has another. It was like that a lot of the time.

A shepherd came on and said, "Waste not, want not, that's my motto. Also: There's such a thing as too much of a good thing." Meanwhile, I owned three separate houses

439

within ten miles of each other, two on the Study Center grounds, and one in Mason City that I never saw, the remodeling went on and on.

An old rug-hooker from Omaha said, "Dr. Al, you know it's true: There's no summer without winter."

I had just purchased a $3.5 million home on a private island off Antigua where I planned to spend December, January, February, March, and the first part of April.

But before I got to fly down there, a child Autoharp player named Little Ginny came onto the show. She was terminally ill, and Larry had read somewhere that dying children possess preternatural wisdom. She died a few days afterward of a mysterious raging fever. She was an assertive little tyke and she spoke right up in her sickly voice and told you what she thought. She wasn't whiny or grumpy. When I asked her what her name was, she said, "God gives us new names in heaven, and I want to be a Theresa but right now I'm Ginny."

I'll never forget the hush in the studio when that tiny pale child staggered to the couch in her pure-white dress, lugging the harp, and climbed up, and sat there with an oxygen tube in her nose, her chin on her chest, listing to one side, and strummed "O

Dem Golden Slippers" and faintly sang, "I'se goin up de ribbah wheah de golden rainbow shine," as her relatives collapsed sobbing in the wings. She was white and had learned the song from an old book of spirituals.

The audience clapped and clapped until our production people had to tell them to hush.

At this point, she was supposed to tell me a folktale about a mother hen and her chicks, but instead she climbed up on my lap and draped her skinny arm around my neck and put her little cheek next to mine.

My gosh, she was hot, burning up with fever, and sweat poured off her. An extremely hot damp child. A bead of her sweat fell on the back of my hand and — this sounds insensitive, I know, but nobody had informed me if her fatal illness was contagious or not — I thought to myself: "Al, you need a fatal disease right now like you need a hole in the head."

I tried to pry her loose but her bony fingers were clamped on to my wrist and my lapel, and when I tried to bend her fingers back, she flopped around like a dying fish and her eyes rolled back up in her head.

I tried to signal the staff with my eyebrows

to come and take this hot potato off my hands, but they were overcome with emotion, I guess. When I tried to stand up, she clung to me like a bat and tore the rug off my head, and then Little Ginny pressed her burning face to mine and whispered in her hoarse little voice, "God says to cut out this shit. He says, stop it and shape up."

I knew right then that my career had peaked and that the long grim slide had begun, but of course I couldn't know how far it was to the bottom. I smiled and said, "Friends and neighbors, I know this show is one I'll remember as long as I live. What do you say we invite Little Ginny to come back next week?" Everybody clapped again, but Little Ginny looked at me with pure disgust. She said, "Don't be stupid. You know I'll be in my grave next week."

And she turned to the camera and whispered, "Every word he says is a big fat lie."

She died a few days later.

I sat at home and thought, "What shit am I supposed to cut out?"

Am I supposed to give away money? Fine. But where do you draw the line? There's the heart fund and the bladder fund and the Save the Snakes foundation and the Center for the Dull and there's a cabdriver whose mom is waiting to come over from

Zagreb and a waitress with a slight limp and who do you say no to? Once you start giving away dough, if you say no they'll write long accusatory letters and lurk around your home and attack you with coat hangers. No, a rich man can't buy peace of mind.

I began to discuss these issues in *Empowering Others by Enabling Yourself,* and the next thing I knew, there was a knock on the door and it was the FBI. An unfriendly agent in a shiny gray suit talked to me for four hours. He asked me about some Life Savings Certificates that had been sold across the country by mail, certificates issued by the Al Denny Savings Institute — I hadn't heard about that at all!

Evidently, fifteen thousand people had mailed in $60,000 apiece on the promise that they could live at the Study Center through their declining years and be rebirthed.

Some of them now wished to obtain their money back.

"Talk to Larry," I told the FBI, but they said that Larry was gone. He had flown to the private island off Antigua, and he was not answering the phone.

The FBI drove me to Mason City and led me through a gauntlet of TV cameras and flashbulbs and put me in a small cinder-block cell.

Then they located Mona. She was in *Akron,* Ohio, not Dayton. Akron. And we had two daughters and a son named Aaron.

"Al, you big wombat, how the heck are you?" she cried, throwing her arms around me. "I always said you oughta be locked up. Gosh, I love you, you big lug." She wasn't a teacher or an investment person, it turned out — she was a *lawyer,* and a darned good one. She got me out of the clinker and back to Akron in a jiffy.

The kids all have her red hair and big beak and melting brown eyes. My son looked up as I walked in and said, "Did you remember the butter brickle?"

"No, I forgot," I said.

"Oh." He wasn't surprised. Evidently, forgetting had been a habit with me.

It's good to be a regular daddy again instead of a big cheese, and I have promised the kiddos not to write a book again. I started one called *Starting Over,* which was about men finding new roles as daddies and homemakers, but then I got too busy to write. You make breakfast for Mona, pack her a healthy bag lunch, send her off, wake up the kids, and shepherd them through the cleansing-dressing process, answer all their questions, feed them, get them out the door with their lunches and homework in hand, wash the breakfast dishes, and go from room to room with a vacuum and a feather duster, and change the beds and scrub the bathrooms, and after five hours your urge to sit and write and regale the reader with insights has mostly dissipated, you would rather go dig in the garden and put in the crocus bulbs. Life is good. More than good. You have a clean house and feel like a clean man! You have not told a single lie and it is almost lunchtime! Praise God for His goodness! Now you must plan the supper.

7.
Jimmy Seeks His
Fortune in Fairbanks

In 1998, when a professional wrestler named Jim Janos, a.k.a. Jesse (The Body) Ventura, was elected governor of Minnesota with 37 percent of the vote in a three-way race, I put away other diversions and sat down and wrote *Me: The Jimmy (Big Boy) Valente Story,* which came out three months after his election, which is rather sudden in the world of publishing. The book suffered from the sheer improbability of a wrestler who wore pink boas in the ring being elected governor of a righteous Midwestern state, but then so did Mr. Ventura, and he quietly left office after one term and went on cable TV and disappeared.

My tour of duty in Nam as a U.S. Navy Walrus ended on New Year's Day 1970. I was tempted to stay, but by then the war was lost, so I didn't bother to re-up.

One night when we pulled patrol duty along the Ho Chi Minh Trail, a Walrus named Walt Unruh told me all about his home along the Iditarod Trail in Alaska and how you could take off in your float plane from Anchorage and in twenty minutes land on a sky-blue wilderness lake with no living soul within thirty miles and toss your lure in the water and catch a king salmon.

"The north is man's country," he said. "Up there, you can urinate your name in the snow nine months out of the year. Nobody cares if you bathe or not or whether you eat with your fingers or lean to one side in your chair and let her rip. And cold weather, you know, is a proven aphrodisiac. Northern men can go all night where southern guys peter out in fifteen minutes."

Sitting in a tree in Vietnam, I thought Alaska sounded wonderful. After two years of jungle life, frozen tundras seemed like a piece of cake.

I flew Da Nang to Los Angeles first-class courtesy of the CO whose butt I'd saved from court-martial when I told the higher-ups that he was leading the unit in battle on a particular day he had chosen to spend at the beach at Qui Nhon with a honey named Dixie Dexter.

With about five grand in back pay and an airline pass to anywhere in the U.S., I landed in Fairbanks on January 5. Thirty-

447

seven below zero and the airport wind sock stuck straight out, pointing east. Snowbanks as big as New Hampshire. I rented a back room in a mobile home on the edge of town, an old trailer surrounded by junked cars and oil barrels, with a satellite dish out back and a BEWARE OF OWNER sign in front. He was a guy named White Blaze who resided in the front room and earned his living with a deck of cards. He had been a thoracic surgeon in Memphis and got addicted to muscle relaxants, which did him no good in surgery but helped his poker playing enormously. After he had perfected his game (losing a wife and two houses in the process), he emigrated north, to where money flowed freely, where the sun rose at eleven and set at one and there was little else to do with money except risk it in manly games of chance.

Everybody I met in Fairbanks was someone who'd screwed up big-time in the Lower Forty-eight. Gratuitous screwups. They'd fooled around with a sister-in-law or got hooked on cough medicines, maybe embezzled from the March of Dimes or swiped the Hopi tapestry from the Unitarian church (and then tried to sell it to the Methodists) or attempted to shoplift a garden tractor or phoned in bomb threats to group homes for paraplegics. Having thus hit bottom and become social pariahs, they hitch-hiked to Fairbanks to remake their lives as short-order cooks and reside in a trailer in a climate where, for half the year, you don't need a freezer.

My five grand leaked away in about a month, half of it spent on a used Rambler that wouldn't ramble, and I was forced to hike into town and find work. I went to the courthouse and took a civil service exam and got a job in the post office, sorting parcel post.

But Jimmy (Big Boy) Valente is not happy in a confined space performing tasks assigned to him by small-minded people. The art of clerical sorting does not engage my mind: the cogs simply do not mesh. I stuck to my post until lunch hour and then looked around at the cubicle, the helpful lists and charts taped to the wall, the pigeonholes, the tape and scissors and ruler and paper clips, and I said goodbye to it as a bear would say goodbye to a leg trap and went out to lunch and stayed there.

In Mom's Café I ordered a hamburger, very rare, with a raw onion, mustard, a glass of gin, and a raw egg yolk in a china cup. Next to me sat a hatchet-faced guy whose narrow head supported a toupee that looked like a raccoon crushed under a semi, all eighteen wheels. He had glazed it with gel and it glittered like cat turds in the moonlight. He wore a livid green plaid sportcoat made of petrochemicals and a yellowish shirt and blue-blob tie and brown slacks with a lived-in look. He was the unhealthiest-looking human being I had ever laid eyes on, very sallow and liverish, all splotches and rheum and exploded capillaries, a stub of a cigarette smoldering on his lower lip, a fresh one on its way. He lit it and cast his bulbous eyes on me and said, "The name's Felix. I.W.W. International World Wrestling. You look like a warrior to me. Glad to meetcha." Then he reached into his breast pocket and pulled out a roll of cash big enough to choke a caribou and peeled off fifteen hundreds and handed them over. "That's for fifteen minutes of your time."

So I sat and listened.

"It's a new pro wrestling circuit, the I.W.W. We've got a terrific show here. Eight guys. You fight the same guy every day, you get to know each other's moves, it's like ballet. Good money. Winter is great. No sun for three months, and the towns are full of construction guys and oil workers, their pockets full of dough, going stir crazy, desperate for entertainment, and these are not theatergoers here. The night shift gets off at seven in the morning and by seven forty-five they're pretty well oiled and that's when we put on our first show. We'll pack a hangar, a warehouse, with a thousand men, all of them betting like mad — I'll handle your side action for you — and when we've milked that cow, we go up the road to the next venue and do it again at four and come back to the first place for the midnight show. You go out and perform and I handle all the monkey business. How does four hundred a day sound?"

It sounded good to me. It sounded fantastic. I packed my stuff and Felix's bus picked me up at noon. An old Eskimo guy named Iron Eyes was at the wheel and Felix was camped in the seat behind him, wrapping bundles of tens and twenties and plopping them in an open suitcase. It was almost full. Behind him, sprawled across the seats, leaning every which way, buried under quilts and bear skins, were eight men fast asleep, mouths agape, each one snoring in a different tempo and key, each one quietly emitting his own brand of gas. One man, with a dirty blond beard, wore a horned helmet and a black mask. The floor was littered with pistachio shells and empty beer cans and pizza crusts. The aroma was pretty stiff and a guy would think twice about lighting a match: between the alcohol and the methane, the bus had enough fuel to achieve low orbit.

Felix nodded toward the helmeted man. "That's Svend. He's the foreman. Soon as he wakes up, he'll work you into the show."

I flopped down in back and a crusty old dude in the seat opposite opened one bloodshot eye and said, "You wouldn't be interested in purchasing a crossbow and a broadsword and a Satan cape, would you? Sell you the whole kit and caboodle and toss in my Mongolian goatskin boots free, all for five hundred bucks. What do you say?"

I said it sounded good but what would I use them for?

"I'll toss in a wooden altar, six candles, a hex medallion, and a vial of powdered elk antler," he said.

He reached over and shook my hand. "I'm the Duke of Dubuque and this sad sack next to me is the Dauphin Louie de Louie." He nodded toward a figure wrapped in a horse blanket, dead to the world, snoring like a Piper Cub on takeoff. The Duke leaned toward me, confidentially. "We are only temporarily in the wrestling line while we get our real-estate licenses. Came to Alaska last spring with a theater troupe. Did Beckett and Shepard and all the newer playwrights. Taught acting, stage movement, public speaking, deconstruction if there was a call for it. But alas, Alaska is no fit home for the artistic temperament. The conceptual way of thinking is not welcome in the North, my boy. These are engineers, not savants. And so we were forced to join this gang of cretins and thugs and common ruffians."

He lowered his voice. "I blush to say it, but the Dauphin and I wrestle in the altogether. Au naturel, in other words. It's been a big hit and a boon to our social lives, but it's time to move on."

He leaned closer. "I sense that you possess a noble spirit, sir, and that I can confide in you." He glanced at the Dauphin to make sure he was truly asleep. "I am the illegitimate son of Nelson D. Rockefeller," he whispered. "A love child by an actress who shall remain nameless. Shoveled into an orphanage and deprived of my heritage so as not to compromise my father's presidential hopes. A Rockefeller by birth, entitled to a country estate and a fourteen-room apartment on Sutton Place, but instead — this." And he gestured limply toward the detritus in the bus aisle and dabbed at his eyes. "A life of squalor in the frozen north among rug-chewing goons."

I said, "You seem a little old to be the son of Nelson Rockefeller." The moment I said it, I could see I had struck a nerve.

The Duke looked away, stung, and said quietly, "I knew I shouldn't have put my trust in you. You're like all the others. Forgive me for imparting that information. And now excuse me. I must rest."

I tried to apologize but he waved it off. "It's nothing. A man's story is his own and he should keep it to himself. Silly of me to forget. Have a good life, sir." And then the bus turned at the Fairbanks International Airport sign and stopped in front of the terminal and the Duke shook his partner's shoulder. "Daylight in the swamps, your highness. Up and at 'em," he growled, and he hauled down a duffel bag from the overhead and shouldered it and marched off the bus, the Dauphin slinking behind. Felix gave them each a manila envelope and shook hands and into the terminal they went. Felix patted the seat next to him. I sat down.

"Big Boy, I have come to a decision. The show needs a fairy, and, son, you're the one who can do it for us. Hear me out. Your name will be the Flower Child, and you'll come out and mince around with daffodils twined about your brow and a peace sign painted on your scalp and you'll blow kisses to the crowd and talk about the importance of preserving the environment and not doing anything to negatively impact the caribou herds."

"Please. No. I am a Navy veteran," I begged him. "People will shun me in the street, nobody will sit next to me in bars, even hookers will look at me with moral disfavor."

"Exactly. And we'll double the gate, kid. We need that extra attraction. We got all the heroes we can stand, what we need is somebody the crowd can hate. There's nothing that brings joy to so many people like giving them the chance to despise you."

"I'd rather kill myself with a dull knife."

"Please. For the guys' sake. For the sake of the pure art of wrestling."

"What would my Walrus buddies think if they saw me? You can't make me do it, Felix."

He sighed. "This is a privilege, kid, what I'm offering you. Any idiot can be a hero. It takes ability to play a heel. Did you ever hear of acting? You think actors would rather play George Washington or Count Dracula? How about I pay you four hundred a match plus a percentage of the gate to maintain your interest?"

He was a persuasive guy, Felix. He appealed to my vanity. He made me feel like Lon Chaney, Jr. And that night I walked into the Tanana High School gymnasium with daffodils on my head and wearing beads and sandals and an R. Crumb T-shirt as Felix screamed, "At two hundred and thirty-eight pounds, in the tie-dye trunks, a man who wishes to dedicate this next match to his friends Ralph Nader and Jane Fonda — from Berkeley, California, the Flower Child!" and a thousand oil workers booed from the depths of their beer-soaked hearts.

I danced up the steps to the ring and posed for the crowd and grabbed the microphone and asked everyone to join me in singing "Give Peace a Chance" and someone yelled, "Give me a chance to get a piece of you, fruitcake!" and I ranted about love and brotherhood and about how the exploitation of our precious oil resources was interfering with the breeding patterns of the great snowy owl and that for the sake of our children we should place a moratorium on drilling until we learned how to lessen its impact on these owls and also on the extremely rare snow spider and the Arctic moth — I yik-yakked until everyone was standing and screeching and shaking their fists at me and frothing at the mouth, and my gosh, what a thrill it was to have that audience in the palm of my hand — to stand in the ring and throw a pose and feel the anger flow my way — and then Yukon Bob came trotting down the aisle to thunderous acclaim, a figure of manly rectitude preceded by his booming belly, and he grinned a purposeful grin and heaved his great carcass into the ring and bared his chest and flexed his breasts and did a couple knee bends and we dove into a clinch and circled and I proceeded to whale away on him for a while, getting him in an illegal nostril hold, rubbing his eyes along the top rope, giving him an instep stomp, a nipple pinch, playing my dirty tricks as the referee, Iron Eyes, looked on solemnly, until Bob was dizzy with pain and then came the heinous Hangman maneuver — hurling him into the ropes so his head caught between them and he flipped over and hung by his neck and I kicked him a few times in the groin — Oh my! The pain! The exquisite suffering! — and then came the Backbreaker and then somehow Bob struggled free of my grasp. He shook his noble head. His nostrils flared. His outrage was awakened. He popped me one on the jaw and I fell and convulsed for a while and the crowd was in ecstasy. He whaled away on me and I popped my blood cartridges and the audience ate from our hands, it was exactly what a thousand sex-starved pipe fitters sky-high on boilermakers wanted to see at twilight on a Wednesday in January, blood smeared on the canvas, and the Flower Child in a dazed stupor, poleaxed by Yukon Bob's *Flying Augur,* and the victor modestly acknowledging the cheers and the vile environmentalist, bloody and dejected, hustled away by security guys warding off the drunks trying to kick me in the gonads, and then Bob and me had a beer, showered, climbed on the bus, and Felix said that the gate was twice what he'd estimated and Yukon and Mike and Dave and Felix continued their bridge game as we rolled on toward Koyukuk.

I had earned fifteen hundred bucks that first day, what with the percentage of the gate. I counted it six times. My gosh, it was like a license to steal. To ride around on a bus and sleep and three times a day go and work hard for fifteen minutes — who couldn't handle that?

The I.W.W. routine was a snap compared to Vietnam. We wrestled three bouts a day, six days a week, and ate four meals a day. The chow was good if you like meat. On Monday, our day off, we chowed down on unabridged T-bone steaks washed down with a snootful of hooch strong enough to take the chrome off a Cadillac. We continued drinking at a nightclub where ugly women dance on your table and you stuff twenties in their garter belts and they remove their underwear. We stayed until midnight and awoke at 5 a.m. with headaches you could split kindling with and crawled out of bed and resumed the suffering.

We wrestled in hangars, warehouses, the holds of ships, we wrestled in mud or coated with oil, and sometimes we wrestled in a ring with a few thousand live mackerel flopping around, just for the added interest. The alpha wrestler was Svend the Yellow-Toothed, a Nordic warrior with shoulder-length snowy blond hair and a caribou-skin cape with the head and teeth intact, and there was Ahmad Jihad in Bedouin robes, and Oberkapitan Werner Wehnnadd with his black boots and jodhpurs and gleaming monocle, and Ivan the Terrible in his fur cap and red sickle-and-hammer cape. There were various heroes, Yukon Bob and Matanuska Mike and Dawson Dave. And there was me, the Flower Child.

Svend had the best rant of anybody. He'd grab the microphone away from Felix, the ring announcer, and yell that he had never, never in his career, ever set foot in the ring with such heinous trash as this — pointing at his opponent, whoever it was — and he cried out, "I put it to you, the fans: What shall I do with this bucket of pus, this piss-pot, this maggot, this abomination?"

And the crowd roared, "KILL HIM!"

And then he asked the fans on the other side of the arena, and they felt that homicide was the only fair solution, too.

Svend climbed up onto the turnbuckle and screamed, "I will thrash him, lash him, paste him, waste him, batter and lambaste him, and force the contemptuous black-guard to crawl across the ring and lick the sweat off my socks!"

This suited the crowd just fine.

Sometimes his opponent was Ivan, the perfidious Russian, and sometimes it was Prince Harry Belial, and sometimes it was me.

"Behold this degenerate molester of women!" he screeched, pointing at me one night when I was taking a night off from the Flower Child and wrestling under the name Richard Speck. "Tonight, my friends, this putrid pervert gets the punishment he deserves!" And the crowd roared, like high surf hitting a cliff, and Svend hurled himself at me and we locked arms and he said, "Stomp and chin kick," and I stomped on his foot, and he fell down, writhing, and I took a run at him and kicked him about two inches east of his chin, and he clutched at his face and toppled over and lay, legs twitching, and I dove on him for the pin and he said, "Fourteen, double T, seventy-eight, sixteen," and I jumped up and climbed onto the turnbuckle and jumped, my feet landing a couple inches south of his testicles, and he flopped over and writhed around on his belly as if he'd been reamed with a hot poker, and I got him in a toe twist, and that caused him no end of agony — of course the audience by now was foaming and raging freely, standing on their chairs, trying to hurl beer at me — and then I smacked him in the small of his back, and he screamed and banged his forehead on the canvas and his legs twitched, and then I got him in the Stretcher hold, and he was in hellish agony, but not so much that he couldn't tell me what came next — "Forty-four, nineteen, thirty-six, ten, and down double," he said, and then he managed to wriggle out of the Stretcher, bonk me on the forehead, run and carom off the ropes

461

and do a flying mule and knock me down, do a pile driver, get me in a half nelson, and pin me, and leap up, arms raised, for the adulation of the mob, as I slithered under the ropes and into the protective custody of the ushers and limped back to the dressing room.

And afterward Svend and I would have a beer and he gave me pointers on how to improve my performance, how to roar better and harangue the crowd and work on my rant, using a thesaurus to piece together new expressions, like "malodorous moron" and "nefarious nincompoop" and "perfidious pipsqueak."

He explained how to receive his flying mule and flop throat-first against the top rope and hang there by my chin, tongue out, eyes crossed, to be hauled off and put in a toehold and pinned. He taught me to get the right kind of trunks, with strong elastic waistbands so they stretch tight over your butt and don't bunch up in your crack. And a nut cup that can stand up to a steel-toed boot or a folding chair. He taught me breathology and escapology and how, if you need to pee real bad during a bout, you have your opponent lift you up and do the Helicopter and the pee doesn't land in the ring.

I enjoyed being the Flower Child because I was good at it. I added a pink boa to the act and let my hair grow out long and dyed it blond and took to wearing long dangly earrings. The sight of earrings on a man in Alaska made a crowd go bananas. I loved being the bad boy.

One night as I slept, someone filled up my bed with butterscotch pudding. I said nothing. The next night someone took the lightbulb out of the socket in my bathroom and put Saran Wrap over the toilet so when I peed, it all ran down on my shoes. The next day there was a glass of fresh-squeezed orange juice by my bed when I awoke. My suspicions should have been aroused, but I am a Minnesotan, a trusting soul. The juice was doctored, as it turned out, with a mysterious homeopathic powder that gave me the worst case of hemorrhoids in the Arctic, a set of butt grapes that made bowel movements not the pure pleasure they should have been. It got so I couldn't sit down. I had a foam doughnut sewn into the seat of my trunks, which got me the nickname Balloon Butt. And one night someone spooned a soy supplement onto my corn flakes that resulted in a rock-hard stool. It was like passing an axe. I fainted in the can.

That was the night the Flower Child lost

it. I truly went ballistic.

I was the last event, fighting Yukon Bob, and I hurt like blazes. I grabbed the mike and I bent over and pointed to the relevant spot and told the crowd to pucker up. I was out of my mind with pain. I told the crowd to stick their hands in their pants and see if they could find their manhood. I said I was proud to be an atheist and Communist and that I could beat anybody in the place with one hand. And then Bob came waltzing in and I tore him apart — he kept yelling in my ear, "Cut it out, man! Slow down! What's got into you?" and I kept whopping him in the chops, and the crowd went berserk and stormed the ring, waving two-by-fours and ball-peen hammers. Iron Eyes tore off his referee shirt and dove for safety, and Yukon Bob followed him, and I was all alone, surrounded by six thousand berserk oil riggers who were feeling no pain whatsoever.

I climbed up on the turnbuckle and held my arms up for silence and said, "Whoever wants to die first, step forward. I'll kill ten of you before you so much as scratch me, and probably by that time the cops will be here. And when I'm on trial for mass murder, I am going to plead diminished mental capacity on account of hemorrhoids, and believe me, in my case it's the truth. I am no flower child. I am a mad dog veteran of the U.S. Navy Walruses, a walking time bomb, and I want to die and take you with me!"

And two guys stepped forward with pistols drawn and knives in their teeth. The crowd shrank back.

"Walrus," they said. "Bark."

I barked the Walrus code for "brother."

They said, "You were kidding about the Communist stuff, right?" I barked in the affirmative.

They barked back, "Three Walruses together can rule any mob."

And we moved toward the now-silent crowd and they melted away in front of us. We charged up the aisle and into the locker room and I pulled on my clothes while they guarded the bus against tire slashers and I ran to climb aboard and we three gave each other the Walrus neck lock and the secret woof and the snuffle of brotherhood. And then I walked to the back of the bus and addressed my colleagues.

"I have taken enough crap from you idiots," I said in a low cold voice. "It is enough to endure the bus rides, the darkness and cold, the drunken mobs, the lice-ridden hotels, the vile foods and condiments. I will not tolerate your perfidious schemes and evil powders. Whoever is responsible, prepare to die. I know six ways to kill a man with my bare hands and I am working on a seventh. Stand up like a man and take your punishment or else be exposed as the coward that you are."

Felix stood up and smiled. "You were beautiful tonight, babes. All you needed was a little motivation. We cleared almost a hundred grand. You earned fifty grand in side bets. It was worth the pain."

I pointed at him. "Et tu, Felix?"

He nodded.

"I will get you for this," I said but with less conviction. Fifty grand. I'd never earned that much in one night.

8.
AT *THE NEW YORKER:*
MY OWN MEMOIR

More memoirs have been written on the theme "Me and *The New Yorker*" than about the Spanish-American War or homesteading in Nebraska or train trips down South America way, which is a tribute to its legendary editors Harold Ross and William Shawn and also to the hot steamy self-consciousness of some of their writers. Mr. Shawn was followed by Bob Gottlieb, who could easily have become legendary but didn't stick around long enough, who was followed by Tina Brown, who was legendary in her own mind and didn't need to be remembered, and then David Remnick, a good guy who will surely inspire a memoir or two someday. But the magazine now is rather straight compared to the bundle of eccentricities I loved so much in my youth in Anoka, Minnesota — the absence of a masthead or Table of Contents, the unsigned Talk of the Town pieces with their brisk whimsical tone, the Letter from Paris signed simply "Genêt," the horse-racing column by "Audax Minor," squibs about Ivy League football, the Long-Winded Lady, "The Wayward Press," the great two-initial authors (E.B., J.D., A.J., S.J., J.F.), and enormous long pieces about exotic places winding their way through columns of ads for Baccarat and Jaguar and Chanel. It was another world from mine. I only knew Mr. Shawn from his neatly penciled comments signed W.S. in the margins of galley proofs and a couple of awkward lunches at the Algonquin, not enough material for a book-length memoir. So I invented some stuff about him and stuck it in the novel *Love Me.* And while I was at it, I murdered a publisher, which I'd always wanted to do.

William Shawn took a shine to me right off the bat when I arrived at the magazine back in the fall of 1969. "Glad you're not creepy and obsessive like some of these introspective sons of bitches around here," he said. "I've had a bellyful of neurotics. White and Thurber drove me nuts, and all those Harvard snots. You look like a Midwesterner. Me, too. Chicago. Call me Bill."

We liked to shoot pocket billiards at a little smoke-filled joint called Patsy's and we discovered we shared a fondness for old Chicago bands like the Jazz Equestrians and the Skippers of Rhythm and we both knew the rules for a poker variant called footsie. He was an excellent bowler and arm wrestler and could toss playing cards into a top hat with accuracy at up to thirty-five feet, farther if he was drunk. He could size a man up by studying the soles of his shoes and the back of his shirt collar. He could tell if you'd recently been to church or taken an unmarried woman to the movies. He knew every species of bird and he could open any lock with a paper clip and could disassemble a typewriter and put it back together in two minutes flat. One night over a pitcher of martinis he told me his life story: it just flowed out. His childhood in Chitown. His Irish dad, Sean Hanratty, a button man for the Bugs Moran gang, killed in the Arbor Day Massacre. Young William changed his name and hitchhiked to Vegas to deal blackjack for Bugsy Siegel and then a man named Crossandotti sent him to New York as Harold Ross's stickman, back when the magazine was a hotbed of steady tipplers and wisecracking women with hinges on their heels.

"The Mafia owned it, you know," he told me.

"They owned *The New Yorker*?"

"What we talking about? Silk undies? Yes.

The New Yorker. Still do."

"The Mafia owns the magazine?"

He was lining up a very tricky bank shot, a Lucky Strike in the corner of his mouth, smoke curling up under his fedora — "What does it matter? Owners are owners. Thank God it's not the Newhouses, I say. At least the Crossandottis *know* they don't know anything. All the Newhouses want is to stick their noses up the butts of the rich and famous." And then he banked the eight ball into the side pocket off the fourteen and picked up the money off the bar and stuffed it in his breast pocket. "Want to go again? For double?" he muttered.

"You're so different from the William Shawn I always imagined," I said. "James Thurber portrayed you as a flustered guy who spoke in a whisper and obsessed over commas and ate dry cornflakes for lunch and dreaded elevators and other motor vehicles."

He chuckled. "Thurber was blind, you know. The phone rang and he'd pick up the steam iron. He needed a lot of supervision. Him and White both. White struggled to operate an ordinary stapler. A coffeemaker was beyond him. His ambition was to raise chickens. And *The Years with Ross* was about as true to life as *Rebecca of Sunny-*

brook Farm.

"Sometimes I feign fluster — it's a useful stratagem with women," he said.

He gave me the nickname Prairie Dog and he'd ring me up around 5:30 on a Friday afternoon and holler into the phone, "Come on, Skip, let's go get our pantlegs wet," and off we'd go to the Seventy-ninth Street Boat Basin with a sack of grub and a bottle of bourbon and board the *Shawnee* and cast off the lines and motor down the Hudson. "Ain't this the life!" he said. "To hell with Harvard and fuck the fact-checkers, let's have a party!" He got out of his suit and into shorts and a black muscle shirt as midtown Manhattan slid past on the port side, the cross streets like corn rows, and when Forty-third passed, we yelled, "Boogers!" and hooked little fingers. Around Canal Street I hoisted the mainsail and we caught fresh wind at the Battery and flew around Governors Island and out under the Verrazano Bridge to sea and he sang out, "The sun's over the yardarm, Prairie Dog!" and I broke out the bourbon and poured two china cups full and he drew a chestful of salt air and started talking.

"I'm a hunted man. Crazy magazine's got me jumping like a poisoned rat in a coffee can. Some fool stuck his head in my office

471

today and asked what's the difference between a solecism and a solipsism. Go spend a week with a dictionary, I told him. A writer is supposed to know the English language, dang it."

I asked him about the perils of success and how fame and fortune seem to dig a deeper hole for a guy. I was thinking of J. D. Salinger and J. F. Powers, two heavy hitters who hadn't been heard from for a long long time.

"They're swinging too hard. Trying to aim the ball." He hawked and spat. "Listen, kid. Every writer I know is on a winding mountain road in the fog, headlights on high beam, worried about plunging over the cliff. That's what it means to be in the business. Some of these bozos get confused about their capabilities, like a sumo wrestler trying to run the four-forty low hurdles. Or they wind up as preachers pandering to high-minded dipshits. The Betterment of Man is the worst motive for writing. Better to write out of sheer cussedness and fling a cherry bomb into the ladies' latrine and make them all jump out of their camisoles than climb into the pulpit and pontificate about the sun and moon and the Milky Way and the meaning of it all.

"John O'Hara had it about right. The purest motivation for a writer is to earn a pile of money. Which of course makes you the target of envy and you wind up with gobs of spit on your shoes and you don't win the Pulitzer and critics spitball you for the rest of your life. But what the hell. You can cry on your way to the bank." Mr. Shawn walked to the rail and looked at the houses of Brooklyn as they slipped past in the twilight. "That's Bay Ridge," he said, pointing to a low rise. "I was in love with a lady who lived there. Bright red nail polish and curlicue hair and some of the nicest epidermis you ever saw. Met her at a party at Norman Mailer's. What an arrogant blowhole he was before I slapped him around a little. He was coming on to the Brooklyn girl at that party and I had to take him outside and give him a nosebleed. Now the guy can almost write sometimes. My gosh, she was an angel. I'd be sailing along and she'd come swimming out from Coney Island with her clothes tied on top of her head. Not that the woman needed clothes. My gosh.

"Andy White used to come sailing with me sometimes and then I caught him belowdecks writing a Talk of the Town piece about the sea and the skyline and whatnot and I threw him over the side. The guy was

473

what you might call oversensitive. Wrote that crazy *Elements of Style* that screwed up millions of college kids. *Cleanliness, accuracy, brevity* — my aunt Sally. Somebody told him he was a great prose stylist and it went to his head and he devoted his life to painting Easter eggs. Him and Strunk have screwed up more writers than gin and scotch combined. You take that *Elements of Style* too seriously and you'll get so you spend three days trying to write a simple thank-you note.

"If I were teaching college composition, my first assignment would be: Write something that would horrify E. B. White. Write a scene in which a man backs his pickup to the edge of Yosemite and dumps a load of empties into a stand of Ansel Adams birch trees. Make it gutsy and wild and to hell with brevity. *A sentence should contain no unnecessary words* — what a prissy idea of literature! Tell it to Tolstoy! Damn it, am I drunk or what? Pour me another." I refilled his cup.

"You're the greatest editor of the twentieth century," I said with a degree of sincerity. "You're my main man, Mr. Shawn. If nobody else does it, I will *write* your autobiography myself."

"I never wanted to edit," he said. "All I

ever wanted was to go out on a boat with a bottle of bourbon and fish."

We got through the Narrows and tossed out a line and he pulled in a fine sea bass ("Chilean," he said, removing the hook from its lip) and he told me how he'd fished with Hemingway in the Keys and had to show him how to jig for grouper, and meanwhile I cleaned the fish and grilled it on a hibachi in the cockpit as Mr. Shawn played Gershwin and Kern and Porter on his concertina and then I hollered, "Eats is ready, Mr. Shawn, baby!" and he and I sat on the deck and ate the fish with raw onions doused in gin between slices of pumpernickel and got good and tight.

Mr. Shawn took me golfing at the Westchester Country Club. He had a beautiful swing. To correct for some bursitis in his left shoulder, he adjusted his stance about 18 degrees clockwise and turned his right foot in and pinned a lead sinker to the bill of his cap, which hung down like a plumb bob, helping him to keep his shoulders level.

"Some people only know me from people's memoirs of life at *The New Yorker,* and in the office I try to impersonate a spooky little recluse who obsesses over commas and semicolons," he said, "but my big loves are fishing and women and golf and what I obsess over is my swing."

It took him a minute to set himself up for the shot. He picked up some grass and tossed it to test the wind, got his feet dug in, adjusted the plumb bob, and waggled the club a few times. "I whipped Updike's ass but good. Many times. He's a yakker, you know. Likes to stand behind you on the tee and just as you get your feet planted, he'll say something like 'That sand trap sure reminds me of the crotch of a woman I knew once' and try to throw you mentally off your game, but here's what you do to shut a guy up —" And Mr. Shawn hit a beautiful drive that flew straight and long and dropped and rolled and rolled, a dream shot, and he marched down the fairway and hit a five-iron to the green, and then a long putt that curved and caught the corner of the cup and fell in for a birdie, meanwhile I had topped my tee shot and sent it dribbling twenty yards and then laced it into the neighboring fairway and wound up with an 8.

He turned to me as he shoved the putter in his bag. "Writers like to think that writing is like Arctic exploration or flying the Atlantic solo but actually it's more like golf. You've got to go out and do it every day and live by the results. You can brood over it but in the end you've got to take the club out of the bag and take your swing. You hit the ball to where it wants to go, a series of eighteen small steel cups recessed in turf, on a course that others have traversed before you. You are not the first. You accomplish this by making big mistakes and turning them into advantages and overcoming your damn self-consciousness."

He teed up and tied the lead weight to his cap and turned 18 degrees and set the back foot and waggled the club and hit a 200-yard beauty straight down the fairway.

"I can tell that you're of the self-consciousness school," he said.

"Oh?" I replied.

"Guys who spend a lifetime lining up a four-foot putt, reading the bent of the grass, the wind, the planets, checking out the geologic formations below, and then they tap the ball and it rolls eighteen feet into a mud puddle."

I wasn't sure what he meant, I said.

"Talking about your writing, Mr. Keillor. You've got the problem so many English majors have. You're all fluttery inside. You suffer from a girlish sensibility. Your writing is all mannered and fussy and —"

"Girlish?" I was shocked.

■ ■ ■ ■

Three weeks after Mr. Shawn said my writing was girlish, he told me to go to Alaska and write about it. "Get out there in the Alaska wilderness and climb those mountains and cross those vast frozen wastes and camp with the migrating caribou and meet the aboriginal peoples and go north until you can go no farther and pitch your tent and look at death and spit in its eye. Don't you come back here and write some fitful fifteen-hundred-word showpiece of puissant sensibility and irony and ambiguity, some half-assed feuilleton about Canada. Sit your butt down in the tent with a paper and pencil and a bottle of rock 'n' rye and write your damn heart out and come back here with a hundred thousand words and none of them modifiers and I'll print the whole damn thing, and if the boys at the Century Club don't like it, let them shake their wattles all they like. You understand me, boy?"

So I flew to Seattle and sat in the airport and a girl sat down next to me. Her name was Alana, her high cheekbones were flush with vitality and her lips were broad and full. I didn't want her to be attracted to me but she was. She sat next to me on the plane to Juneau. "I can't talk to you," I said. "I'm writing for *The New Yorker,* I have to focus on my experiences so I can write."

"I'd love to be an experience someone writes about in *The New Yorker,*" she remarked. I said that I was already in a relationship, one that begins with the letter *M,* and had no interest in fooling around. "Life doesn't always turn out according to plan," she said.

It was a rough ride. Juneau was socked in by clouds and the plane hurtled down through 10,000 feet of murk into a narrow mountain pass, jagged ridges visible at three o'clock and nine — the wheels lowered, the ground still not visible, and then the plane began to shake violently. I caught a glimpse of a pale flight attendant weeping and holding a rosary to her lips. The cockpit door flew open and the co-pilot stuck his head into the lavatory and cast up his lunch just as a serving cart tore loose from its moorings and careered down the aisle, scattering ice and hot coffee. The plane rolled over to one side, then the other. Amid the wailing and gnashing, Alana took my hand and told me she loved me, that she felt we must affirm life in the face of death — she unbuttoned her blouse. As the plane pitched and bucked, we groped and kissed passionately and her blouse was off and my face was crimson with lipstick when finally the plane bounced twice on the tarmac. I staggered into the terminal full of profound feelings. We took a courtesy van to a place called Dave's Wilderness Lodge and tumbled into bed for more turbulence and slept for twelve hours and did it all over again.

"It was a good experience for you, wasn't it?" she said. "I certainly felt it had literary qualities."

"Well, I don't know. It strikes me as unreal."

"I want to be as meaningful for you as any other wilderness experience," she said. Two weeks, day after day, night after night, Alana and I shacked up at the Wilderness Lodge. I walked up and down the trail a little but I have never been good at the identification of birds or trees, and after two weeks, the Alaska piece seemed to be mostly about me and Alana. It began:

"What the heck are you doing in Alaska?" the old-timer said to us at the urinal in the Malamute Saloon one Sunday night not long ago after we had come down from two weeks on the Chilkoot Trail and found the bar made famous by the late Robert W. Service in his poem "The Shooting of Dan McGrew," once a

staple of amateur recitations, at least in this Midwesterner's boyhood, and ordered a pint of beer.

There was quite a bit about the Lodge and saunas and sleeping naked and "taking Mr. Scroggins to town in the pink convertible."

Mr. Shawn called me the next morning. "What does 'getting the pole in the tent flap' mean?" he asked. "And how about 'parallel parking'?"

"I can tell that you don't like it," I said.

He said, "Don't give it a thought. It was a warm-up piece. Alaska got your juices going. You'll come back to New York and find something you really care about and everything will be jim-dandy."

That was Mr. Shawn for you. The guy was a font of hope. He had unlimited faith in writers and their ability to work things out eventually, or if not unlimited, then darned near unlimited, certainly more than 65 percent.

I tiptoed out of the Pinecone Room while Alana was asleep and flew back to New York and took a taxi to *The New Yorker* to find the staff in ferment, people huddled in the hallway on the seventeenth floor whispering, office doors closed, secretaries weeping, urgent memos circulating and a petition to the publisher, Mr. Tony

Crossandotti, pleading with him not to fire Mr. Shawn. And a note from Mr. Updike: "Keillor — Call me. John." It thrilled me. A note from my hero, signed by his first name.

Mr. Shawn was in his office, his head out the window, elbows on the sill, watching a fire blazing out of control a few blocks away. Two hook-and-ladders were in the street, apparatus raised, pouring water on the blaze. Billows of smoke drifted westward.

"*Vanity Fair,*" he said. "One of those dang celebrity rags. Somebody must've left a curling iron on and set fire to the glossies. Used to date a woman who worked there. A nice person but naïve. You worried about her having to cross busy streets. And of course the magazine is a piece of shit. Celebrity profiles, edited by the subject's publicist."

"Why were you fired, Mr. Shawn?"

"I wasn't," he said.

He reached down behind the galley proofs, the *Webster's Second Unabridged,* and a photo of Dietrich, and took out a bottle of Jim Beam and a couple Dixie cups and poured us drinks.

"I fell in love," he said. "I'm going to L.A. to marry her. Ever hear of a songwriter named Joni Mitchell?" And he sang to me —

Pickle jars and foreign cars
The sun is setting here on Mars.
The saffron in the consommé
God, I love a rainy day
It's raining on the jungle gyms
The tile roofs and spreading limbs
What can I say?
Just one more lonely lady in L.A.

"How can you leave us in the hands of Tony Crossandotti?" I said. "The man is a beast. He doesn't understand writers."

"Neither do I," said Mr. Shawn. "You, for example. You don't learn from experience, Keillor. You're a guy who's capable of singing his song and doing his dance but you go crashing around trying to be all things to all people — and then suddenly you can't write anymore. Big surprise.

"Anyway, I'm done with it. Meeting Joni changed everything. Life is too short to spend it trying to protect the inept from the insensitive. She and I are going to make a beautiful life in Topanga Canyon and enjoy the dappled foliage and the flickering shadows and water running over rocks, and you knuckleheads can edit yourselves." He drained his cup of whiskey and grinned and shook my hand. "Go home, Keillor. New York is too rough for you. Go back to Minnesota. And learn how to fish."

Updike's office was packed with staff members when I got there and I had to squeeze in between Trillin and Salinger, who were perched on the windowsill.

"Here's the situation," said a lady with long braids who I think was Penelope Gilliatt or else it was Veronica Geng. "Crossandotti told Shawn that there were too many short stories in the magazine in which people take trains. Or they come back from Ireland and sit and recall a conversation they had with somebody in County Sligo. Somebody on a train. 'Train travel is dead in this country,' he tells Shawn. 'And what's the big deal about Ireland? You need more stories in which people fish and hunt and get laid.' So Crossandotti is replacing Shawn with a guy from *Field and Stream.*"

"How can he do this?" said Trillin. "Even for a publisher, this is insane."

The lady laughed. "Publishers care about writing the way bears care about butterflies."

"What in God's name can we do?" said Powers. "We're screwed. Might as well move to Ireland."

Pauline Kael looked slowly around the room. "Imagine this as a movie," she said.

"You've got yourself a peaceful little town and this gangster moves in and pushes people around to see how far he can go. And then somebody comes in and sizes up the situation and walks across Forty-fourth Street and faces the bully down. And somebody in this room is that person." She looked at me. So did Updike.

"Well, shoot," I said. "It sure seems to me that we can't sit by and let this fella wreck a great American magazine like *The New Yorker.*"

Updike said, "We've taken a vote, Mr. Keillor, and decided you're the shooter. The rest of us have books coming out, lecture tours, awards to receive — you seem to be going through a dry spell. Maybe homicide can help. There's a pistol in your desk. Head over to the Algonquin and when he's not looking, perforate him two or three times. Being a tall person, you can get a good angle. Aim for vital organs. If you're caught, the rest of us will testify that you were under horrible stress and that you simply snapped. You'll spend a year or two in a mental hospital and be released and you'll have material for a best-seller."

How could I say no?

When I got to my office to pick up the gun, there was a note on my door:

Keillor: Understand you drew the assignment to shoot yrs truly. Well, I'm waiting, Mr. Numb Nuts. So write out your Last Will and Testament and leave it on your chair where the mourners can find it and don't worry about putting on clean underwear. It ain't going to be clean for long. Tony

Updike stuck his head in my door to see how I was and I said I was fine. I was filling my mind with murderous thoughts and preparing to do the deed.

"Don't screw this up. It's extremely important. Everybody at *The New Yorker* is counting on you. American literature is counting on you. J. D. McClatchy at the Academy of Arts and Letters called to wish you well. Philip Roth wants you to whack this bastard and so does Edward Hoagland. And Michiko Kakutani from the *Times.*"

"Miss Kakutani called? About *me*?"

"Yes."

"Consider the trigger pulled," I said.

"We don't want to open up *The New Yorker* someday and find a photograph of two guys in a boat on Lake Mille Lacs holding up a stringer of walleyes, do we?"

"No, sir."

"The magazine that was home to Edmund Wilson and Richard Rovere, telling people

486

what kind of bait to use for rock bass?"

I promised to do what I said I'd do. I said, "After I kill him, could I possibly call you John? If the answer is no, I would certainly understand, but I'd love to be able to do that."

"Yes," he said. "Certainly."

And so I stood up, cheeks burning, and crossed Forty-fourth Street and walked into the Algonquin, where the lobby was empty except for Tony Crossandotti sitting in a wingback chair near the door to the Oak Room surrounded by six empty beer bottles and a pile of pistachio shells on the floor. He had just sprayed himself with cologne and slicked back his hair. He stood up. "Mr. Keillor," he said.

It was right then, facing him ten feet away, I realized I'd forgotten my pistol in my desk drawer.

"I was afraid you had gotten engrossed in a long book," he said. He looked me over. "You have broccoli on your lapel," he said. He brushed it away with a pinkie. "How long you been going around with broccoli on your lapel? I would think someone would point this out."

"You just did," I said, "and I'm grateful. I wouldn't expect an asshole like you to take an interest in my personal grooming."

"I don't think I heard you clearly." His breath was very rank. It reeked of beer and pistachios and something else — actually, it smelled of blood.

"Assholes like you, Mr. Crossandotti. People who take a good magazine and beat the shit out of it."

"Let me give you a word of advice," he said. "You maybe shouldn't have come here, seeing as you're so upset. You maybe should've headed over to France on a Guggenheim for a couple years. You could easily get yourself shot in the ear hole for saying things like that. Not by me. I'm a pussycat. But maybe some person loyal to me might hear about what you just said and come after you and blow a hole in your skull." There was an odd vibrato in his voice, a sort of throbbing in the pineal gland.

"What I'm going to do for you," he said, tapping me on the chest, "is teach you about gun safety."

I said, "Mr. Crossandotti, what you're going to do is leave *The New Yorker* alone. It's a great American institution. So tell your *Field and Stream* guy to go sit on his thumb and find somebody smart to edit the magazine."

"Hey. Thanks for the opinion. But I'm concerned about *you*. Let me demonstrate the workings of a pistol and give you a tip or two about firearm safety. Let us step into the Oak Room so as not to alarm the tourists."

The lobby was deserted except for a man and a woman, English majors by the looks of them, stealing a few coasters for souvenirs.

"Fuck off!" Tony yelled. "Or I'll rip the lungs out of your chests. Hers first." They flapped away like startled pigeons.

I said, "Right after you teach me about gun safety, I'll call up the *Times* and inform them that you are taking a well-deserved sabbatical in Weehawken and that you've agreed to let the staff of *The New Yorker* elect a new editor."

"Hey. I appreciate your interest, Keillor. All that you know about publishing would about fit in a cockroach's left nostril, but never mind. Come this way and let me show you how to wrest a forty-five revolver away from a crazed attacker."

He grabbed my sleeve and started to pull me toward the Oak Room. He was pretty riled and that was my plan, insofar as I had one, to infuriate him until he was frothing at the mouth and pissing his pants and then — do something sudden and violent and unexpected like shoving my forefinger in his eye socket. Or tripping him. Or maybe a sharp blow to the nose with the heel of the hand, driving the nasal bone into the frontal lobe and causing extreme disorientation and then death. I had a number of possibilities in mind.

He towed me into the Oak Room and pulled out his pistol and aimed it at the ceiling and said, "The first lesson in how to deal with a guy who is stronger than you and smarter than you and who is just about to blow a big hole in your ear is not to let yourself be drawn into the type of situation where it's you and him alone in a room with no other people, okay? That's the thing you want to avoid."

"Got it," I said.

"Number two: Don't attempt to distract him with a sudden move or coughing fit or that old trick of looking over his shoulder and saying, 'Hi, Jim!' — that works in cartoons, it doesn't work in real life.

"Number three: Don't have illusions about your own strength. Some guys, from having watched Alan Ladd movies, get the idea that they could hurl themselves at somebody and knock him to the floor. In your case, this just fucking ain't gonna happen. It would be like a parakeet hurling itself at a late-model Chevrolet. Strictly unproductive in the larger scheme of things."

He was about to get to number four when a man walks in with a big Leica around his neck and says, "Is this the room where Dorothy Parker and Benchley and Woollcott and George Kaufman and Marc Connelly and Harpo Marx and Edna Ferber and their friends used to gather for the famous Algonquin Round Table? Which table was that, exactly? I've read so much about them and their witty *bon mots* and how much Harold Ross admired them but it was he, the roughneck from Colorado, who started *The New Yorker* and those great wits are largely forgotten today."

And Tony yells, "Who gives a fuck! Get your ass out of here or I'll blow it off you one cheek at a time."

The guy says, "I'm sorry, but are you talking to me?"

"Get your ass out of here, I said."

"We came all the way from Minnesota to see the Round Table. Is that a problem? Is now not a good time?"

Tony yells, "Get the hell out!"

"I'm sorry," the guy says. "I didn't mean to upset you. I just came in to take a picture.

We're *New Yorker* readers, going back years and years. My gosh, I grew up with the magazine. A big fan of A. J. Liebling and Wolcott Gibbs and Frank Sullivan. And I loved Benchley. And all of them." And then he recognized me. "Aren't you an author yourself?" he said.

"Yes, I'm Garrison Keillor," I said. "I'm from Minnesota as well."

"Right," he said. "You used to do that radio show. What was it called? We used to listen to it sometimes." He turned to ask his wife, but she was gone.

Tony held up the gun so the guy could see it. "This ain't some book club or discussion group you walked into, this is a gangland-style execution. This is something you definitely don't want to be a witness to because if you are, I would need to blow you away, too. You hear me?"

"I loved when you used to tell stories about that little town, Lake Wabasso or whatever it was," the guy said. "I grew up on a farm near Morris. You ever get out that way?"

"Not as often as I'd like. I wish I were there right now."

Tony is miffed. He stamps his foot.

"Hey," he says. "You ever hear of the fucking Mafia?"

The guy said he had seen *The Godfather,* the first one, but thought the book was better.

"Brando was good and Duvall, but the rest of it was a piece of crap," says Tony. "Only guy who can write about that stuff is Elmore Leonard."

"Is he an actor?"

"Elmore Leonard?" Tony looks at me. "I cannot believe this yahoo never heard of Elmore Leonard."

"Does he write for *The New Yorker?*" the guy said.

"You never heard of Elmore Leonard? You're bullshitting me."

Tony was saying something in Italian that sounded like a curse for when somebody spits in your mother's tomato sauce. Either that, or a recipe for ground glass. And he was poking the gun in the guy's ribs.

"Hey," the guy said. "I can take a hint. Don't get all hot and bothered. I can come back another time. We're here for the whole week. I apologize for the trouble. Have a nice day, okay?"

And that was when I killed Tony, when the man said, "Have a nice day, okay?" Tony sort of lost control of himself at that point. He threw his head back and snarled and his arm twitched, and I grabbed the wrist of his gun hand and he yanked with all his strength and in the process pulled the gun down and shot himself in the forehead. The room goes *boom* and Tony falls down like a load of fresh sod and the guy says, "What happened to him?"

I said, "He tripped on a wrinkle in the carpet. It happens all the time."

"Is he all right?"

"He's better than he's been in a long time. He's resting now. Let's tip-toe out and leave him to his thoughts."

And Tony opens one red eye and says, "You'll never write for my magazine again, Mr. Keillor."

I tried to think of a witty retort — *Oh? Really? Who died and made you editor?* — and his head rolled to one side and he was out of here, he'd left the building. A powerful publishing tycoon murdered by a second-rate writer. Accidental, in a way, but in another way, quite deliberate. I certainly had homicide in mind when I entered the Algonquin, but the manner in which it happened was unintended so probably it'd be second- or third-degree manslaughter. My defense lawyer would argue that Tony, in resisting my attempt to disarm him, had caused his own demise, and the jury would deliberate for ten minutes and I'd go scot-free and soon thereafter would be waylaid by a van full of shooters and my bullet-riddled body lie on Ninetieth Street, with punctured containers of chicken salad and tabouli strewn from hell to breakfast.

"Should we call an ambulance?" the guy says.

"The hotel will take care of it."

I leaned down and opened Tony's jacket and got a roll of bills out of his breast pocket. No sense leaving it for the cops. "Just making sure he's got cab money," I say to the guy. I'd never seen ten-thousand-dollar bills before. I didn't know Reagan's picture was on them. "I sure never expected something like this," the guy says to his wife, and then remembered she wasn't there, so he went to look for her.

The money came to $128,656. I stuck it in my pocket and thought to myself, This whole thing would make a good story, except I'd change it and make the murder more deliberate. I'd have the writer struggle with the tycoon and trip him and the tycoon's noggin would bonk the leg of the sideboard and the tycoon's eyes glaze and the writer snatch up the pistol and kill him. Or hold him until the cops arrive. Or maybe kill him, but with a fork. And I wouldn't have me be a writer. Maybe a choreographer or composer. A more lethal line of work.

I walked out through the lobby. A bellman had locked the front door and pulled the drapes, and waiters had put up partitions to shield the brunch crowd in the Rose Room. A man in a black suit got off the elevator pushing a wheelbarrow. He went in and got Tony and covered him with a tablecloth and wheeled him out to the curb and laid him in the backseat of a taxi and gave the cabbie some bills and away he went. The janitor tore up the carpet Tony died on and laid a black rug there and set a table on the rug. The place was back in business in ten minutes. That's New York for you. When we die, we leave a hole behind that it takes them less than half an hour to fill. I turned left on Forty-fourth Street past the man with the sign FORMER *NEW YORKER* WRITER DOWN ON LUCK and I dropped forty dollars in his lap.

I felt good. While I as a Christian am opposed to homicide, nonetheless the death of Tony Crossandotti was for the good of journalism. *The New Yorker* would live on, thanks to me. But I would have to leave New York. Publishing tycoons would be gunning for me after I offed one of their own and I'd be safer in St. Paul because New Yorkers are not sure exactly where it is. They keep getting it mixed up with Omaha.

So R.I.P. Tony Crossandotti. Goodbye to Manhattan and 25 West Forty-third. Goodbye, Rainbow Room and Tower Records and H&H Bagels and Scribner's beautiful bookstore on Fifth Avenue with the wrought-iron railing around the balcony. Goodbye to all that. I return to Minnesota, home of humorous, charitable, modest, soft-spoken people. A state on the same latitude as Italy, with the same slant of light that moved Raphael and Michelangelo illuminating our trees in the afternoon. A state of passionate hockey teams and world-class choirs where, God willing, I shall gain some clarity and lead a happy, productive life.

9.
SNOWMAN

I used to live across the street from a triangular park in St. Paul which featured a statue of Nathan Hale, his hands tied behind his back, about to be hung by the British for spying on assignment from General Washington. Every winter, the Parks Department hung strings of hundreds of white Christmas lights from tree to tree, and flooded the park to make a skating rink, and Mr. Hale appeared to be not a martyr for the Revolution, but the Spirit of Christmas Present. Our neighbors made a snowman on a snowbank facing our house and I looked at him as he looked at us and I put him into a story before he got diminished by mild weather.

Once there was a snowman who stood in a park in St. Paul in front of a statue of Nathan Hale. The park was on a quiet street where the streetlights lit up soon after five and Christmas lights flickered in the front windows of the big brick houses. He was tall and had nice strong shoulders. He worried that his head might fall off. It felt unsteady sometimes. And then one day a boy accidentally skied into him and knocked his head off and set it back on his shoulders but at a different angle so instead of looking across the street he was looking at the trunk of a tree and the front yard of a green stucco house where a person who seemed to be made of snow stood perfectly still in the yard. She said good morning. "I was waiting for you to look at me," she said.

She was beautiful, shining, shimmering.

He was already familiar with the tree, a black walnut named Joanne, who had been nattering at him for months, criticizing his posture, laughing when dogs peed on him. She told him that the end was imminent, that soon he would melt and become part of her and she would grow longer limbs so as to caress Ingvar, the Norway pine who stood next to her. "You are precipitation, baby. The purpose of your life is to give me a big drink of water," she said. "You're not the bluebird of happiness, you're not the spirit of Christmas past, so don't give yourself airs. You're nothing but snow. So get over yourself."

The snowman thought there should be

more to life than simply melting. He had plenty of time to think and now, thanks to the boy, he had a fresh perspective. Until now, he'd been looking at the row of lighted houses and thinking how cheerful it would be to live inside a house until Joanne informed him that the houses were heated and he would die in there and so would she — "They chop trees into little pieces to fit them into a house. My daddy went like that. Oh, it looks very pleasant from a distance. But it would kill you. Remember that." But now he looked at the Snow Queen, who stood fifteen feet away, only a sidewalk between them. It was she who, after Joanne said he was "nothing but snow" — she, the Queen, who whispered, Look up in the sky, that's where we come from, we're made of stardust. And when our life on earth is over, we'll rise up into the sky and become clouds and be even more beautiful than you are now.

"O goddess of East Thirty-eighth Street light, glimmering with evanescent desire and invisible emanations of licorice and languish and cinnamon and sycamore," he said to the Queen. (His thoughts had been a little disconnected since his head got knocked off.) "O you and thou and we and thee! O there is so much more to this world

500

than we will ever ever know."

Joanne chortled in her low woody voice. "You just wait."

Water dripped from the trees sometimes. He noticed kids walking around in shirts and jeans, no jackets. A man walked by who was all excited about a trip to Phoenix to visit his girlfriend LaVonne and yet the snowman could see that in another two days the man would walk into the Phoenix terminal and collapse onto the marble floor and die of a cerebral hemorrhage without ever feeling the warmth of the desert. He told the Snow Queen and she said, "You and I are made of millions of unique crystals and we pick up what's in the air around us — we can feel what people are thinking sometimes as they walk by."

"Why did the creator give a brain to someone who can't walk or even move his head and look around and see the world?"

Joanne said, "Here she comes. Ask her."

A girl in a pink parka and furry cap came into view and stood at the curb by Nathan Hale, apparently waiting for a ride.

"She and her dad made you a few days before Christmas," said Joanne.

The snowman didn't know what a dad was, nor Christmas, for that matter, but he said nothing, not wanting to display his ignorance.

"They made you in their own image," said the Queen. "Winter is lonely for them and it gives them pleasure to see you here."

"But I have a brain and the power of speech!" cried the snowman. "What is speech for if not to discuss things and make rational choices?"

Joanne laughed. "You ever hear them talk?? It's nothing but noise. The rustling of my leaves makes more sense than all their talk. What matters is the sun, and rain, and Ingvar. When he touches the tips of my leaves, he thrills me with happiness."

Cars passed, their tires whispering on the snowy street, and the girl in the pink parka stood at the curb, texting on her cell phone. When she pressed SEND, it gave the snowman tremors and he could feel her message pass through him.

WHERE R U?????

And then: R U MAD AT ME??

He could feel what she felt, her being alone on a cold day and expecting someone to come who did not come and did not come, and then her fear that she had offended the Great U and was unworthy and would now be punished by abandonment.

R U THERE?

"What can we do?" he cried, and the Queen said, "We can only be here for her and feel what she feels."

The girl was crying. He could almost taste the salt of her tears.

I LOVE U. PLEASE TEXT ME.

She turned toward the snowman and her face was red and rubbery and tears ran down her cheeks. And then he felt tears on his own face. Sharp rays of sunshine through the branches of Joanne. He was starting to melt.

The girl in pink walked away. She looked at the snowman but said nothing. He heard a door slam. A car rolled up a few minutes later. A boy looked out the window. A girl drove the car and three girls sat in the back, all of them laughing and singing. He turned to the driver and said, "Oh well, never mind," and the car drove away.

The next day the snowman felt smaller. Small and wet. People walked by whistling and commenting on the nice weather. They were all happy and the snowman felt nauseous.

"You doing okay?" said the Snow Queen.

"My head feels like it's just about to slide off my shoulders."

"You look good. And I have a feeling we're

going to get a cold snap."

"I don't think so."

"You have to have faith," said the Queen.

It was a miserable day. Snow was melting in the street and cars went by and splashed sheets of water onto the snowman and he got smaller and smaller and grayer and sadder.

Joanne was singing.

"Snow's gotta melt,
Water will flow.
I feel my branches
Starting to grow."

And then his head slid off his shoulders. He could feel it going and there was nothing he could do. It fell on the ground and there he was looking up at the sky. He watched it get dark and he watched the stars come out. A red light crossed the sky and the stars got brighter and brighter. All he could see was the stars and that was his last look and in the morning he was not there, just a park and green grass, and the girl, who had changed from a pink parka to a blue jacket with a big *S*, walked by in a hurry to get somewhere.

The author looking authorly in 1990, wearing a three-piece suit and big horn-rims, flashing a warm authorial smile, which now looks faintly smug to me. He was earning good money at the time and felt that he had it all figured out, and if the guy on page 340 had run into this fellow, he would've sneered at him as a sell-out. I contain both of these men and have to endure their bickering on a daily basis.

IV.
LIFE'S LITTLE DAY

Comedy is a fundamental part of ordinary civility and an antidote to anger, the screaming meemies on the radio, the furious motorists on the freeway, the drunks in the bar railing against the TV screen. A man like me who has escaped disaster by the skin of his teeth on a few occasions comes away with a finer appreciation of the ordinary pleasures, of steam rooms, steak cooked rare, rhubarb pie, a cappella gospel singing by bluegrass bands like Del McCoury's or Doyle Lawson's, lying in a lower berth on a night train clipping along through little towns, talking to tall women, watching baseball in June, jumping into a cold swimming pool, St. Paul the morning after a snowstorm, standing in the middle of a frozen lake late at night, napping in a hammock between two trees, telling jokes. In Lake Wobegon on a cold rainy day, you'll find farmers, carpenters, painters, roofers, and backhoe operators in the Sidetrack Tap, enjoying lunch and a beer, telling jokes. *Ole on his deathbed says to Lena, "Forty-eight years we've been married. You've stuck with me through it all. The tornado that blew the house down, the lousy crops, the year all the pigs died, my bankruptcy, my heart attack, the night the lightning struck and burned down the house, and now liver cancer. And you know what? I'm starting to think that you're bad luck."* If you were new in town, this is where you might come to get a little acceptance. If you sat on the periphery of a circle of people telling jokes and you listened appreciatively and laughed appropriately and didn't thrust yourself into the group but waited for a lull and then offered your joke *(So — Ole is on his deathbed and he whispers to Lena, "Lena, is everyone here?" Lena says, "Yes, Ole, we're all here, Ole Jr. and Christina, Svend, Solveig, your brother Karl, your sister Lottie, your cousin Hjalmar, we're all here, Ole." Ole said, "If you're all here, why are the lights on in the living room?")* and if it is at least somewhat fresh and if you tell it well and don't flounder around in the setup and if you drop the punch line gracefully, you'll be welcomed here. It is a skill, like hammering a nail. If you teach your children to tell jokes, you've given them a skill that'll be useful in all sorts of situations. You can go your whole life and never need mathematics for a minute. *So — Ole lay dying and he smelled Lena's rhubarb pie and it was so good, he crawled down the stairs to the kitchen and reached up on the counter to get a bite, and she slapped his hand, and she said, "That's for the funeral, leave it alone."*

1.
RULES OF ORCHESTRA

I used to do concerts with orchestras, New York, Chicago, L.A., San Francisco, St. Louis, Seattle, Minnesota, and it always was scary, making my entrance up a narrow path between the first and second violins, and nodding to Maestro Philip Brunelle, and picking up my note from the cello as I sang the *Habanera* — "I always wanted to sing in the opera, / To sing with passion, to sing with rage / And fall in love with inappropriate women, / Fight senseless duels, and die on stage." Then I did a concert with the Boston Symphony at Symphony Hall and thought, *It will never get better than this,* and sensibly retired from the field. Orchestras exist on a higher plane than the one I inhabit and consist of a secretive tribe of chummy perfectionists, one of whom I am married to.

My wife is a violinist and violist, a freelancer, a foot soldier in God's floating orchestra who goes off to play a wedding one night, an opera the next, and comes back to tell me stories about the squeaky soprano with the big diva attitude, the timid oboist, the blatty trombone, the conductor whose hand movements are a mystery to everyone so thank goodness for the concertmaster's bow. Her work demands great skill for which she is paid a pittance, but she is glad for the work and proud to be among the rank and file.

When she was fourteen, she went off to music school, then landed in New York City, still a teenager, and worked there for twenty years, bopping around from opera tour to regional symphony to pop show to Broadway pit to church gig and off to Japan with a pick-up band to do Bach and Vivaldi. She has played for Leonard Bernstein and also for the Lippizaner horses. She is a pro. And she is not tolerant of unprofessional behavior. A big star who is haughty toward the commoners backstage — that's unprofessional. A conductor who glares at someone who just played a bad note — unprofessional. Worse than the bad note.

You won't find this list posted backstage, but that's because everybody knows this stuff right out of music school.

1. You are, of course, on time. Always. It's amateurish to come an hour early, but never come late. Never. So orchestra players are students of public transportation and, if they drive, adept at finding parking places, legal or illegal. Everyone has a strategy for Getting to the Gig, and a back-up strategy, in case the area is cordoned off for a presidential motorcade or a gas leak or some other civil disorder.
2. Don't show off warming up backstage. Don't do the Brahms Concerto. Don't whip through the Paganini you did for your last audition. Warm up and be cool about it.
3. Backstage you hang out with your own kind. String players with other string players, not brass or percussion. You don't get into a big conversation with the tuba player, lest you be lulled into relaxation. He is not playing the Brandenburg No. 3 that opens the show; you are. Stick with your own kind so you can start to get nervous when you should.
4. You never chum around with the conductor too much. Likewise the contractor who hired you; you can

be nice but not fawning, subservient. If either one of them is perched in the musicians' commons backstage, don't gravitate there. Don't orbit.

5. You never look askance at someone who's made a mistake. Never. If the clarinet squeaks, if the oboe honks, if a cello lumbers in two bars early like lost livestock, you keep your eyes where your eyes should be. You're a musician, not a critic. String players never disparage their stand partners to others. Stand partnership is an intimate relationship, and there is a zone of safety here. Actually, you shouldn't disparage any musician in the orchestra to anybody unless to your husband, or very good friends. But you never say anything bad about your stand partner.

6. If the conductor is a jerk, don't react to him whatsoever. Ignore the shows of temper, the hissy snits, the nasty looks. Turn a stone face toward him. If he makes a sarcastic joke at the expense of a musician, do not laugh, not even a slight wheeze or titter.

7. Try to do the conductor's bidding, no matter how ridiculous. If he says, "Play this very dry but with plenty of vibrato," go ahead and do it, though it's impossible. If he says, "This should be very quick but sustained," then go ahead and sustain the quick, or levitate, or walk across the ceiling, or whatever he wants. He's the boss.

8. Don't bend and sway as you play. Stay in your space. You're not a soloist, don't move like one. No big sweeps of the bow. And absolutely never never ever tap your foot to the music.

9. Go through channels. If you, a fifth-stand violin, are unsure if that note in bar 134 should be C-natural as shown or B-flat, don't raise your hand and ask the maestro, ask your section head, and let her ask Mr. Big.

10. You do not accept violations of work rules passively. When it's time to go, it's time to go. If it's Bruno Walter and the Mahler Fourth and you're in seventh heaven, then of course you ignore the clock, but if it's some ordinary yahoo flapping

514

around at the podium, you put your instrument in the case when the rehearsal is supposed to end. It was his arrogant pedantry that chewed up the first hour of rehearsal, and now time is up and he's only half-way through *The Planets* and is in a panic. If he wants to pay overtime, fine. Otherwise, let him hang, it's his rope. At the performance, you can show him what terrific sight readers you all are.

It's all about manners and maintaining a sense of integrity in a selfless situation and surviving in a body of neurotic perfection-ists. And it's about holding up your head, even as orchestras in America languish and die out, victims of their own rigidity and stuffiness and of a sea change in American culture. Perhaps in a hundred years orches-tras will be as obsolete as the six-day bicycle race. But in America's Last Surviving Orchestra, the players will arrive on time and take their places and not look askance at malefactors and play drily but with vibrato and not tap their feet. And one violinist will come home and have a glass of wine and say to her husband, "Why can't they find a decent trombonist?"

2.
FIVE COLUMNS

I started out writing sports for the Anoka *Herald,* a weekly paper in my hometown, and forty years later returned to newsprint with a weekly syndicated column that appeared in little papers and some big ones. The pay was measly and the pleasure was enormous, like reuniting with the first girl you had a crush on and resuming your crush. Every Monday morning I sat down and wrote 750 words about whatever I wanted to write about, and the next morning it was in print and being read by bus passengers, patrons of barbershops, hospital patients, diners in cafés, and homeless people hanging out in public libraries. By that time, the American newspaper, like the Broadway theater or organized labor or the American short story, had been reported as near death and the desirable readership had abandoned print and was getting their news via blips of text on mobile devices. Still, a man loves what he loves. If you grow up on the grand hymns of Wesley and Watts and Fanny Crosby, you cannot bear to stand in church and sing choruses that sound like Coke jingles; if you grow up on newspapers, then electronic publishing is a hollow pleasure. I had an editor in Chicago who I enjoyed tormenting with very very long sentences, which he, a newspaper guy, was not well disposed to. I wrote:

I sit in wonderment at the story of W. Lance Anderson the president of NovaStar Financial in Kansas City who while handing out subprime mortgages to any applicant wearing shoes and a shirt managed to sink the company's stock from $40 in June to $1.72, meanwhile earning $1.7 million in salary and bonuses, plus $711,386 in deferred compensation, plus more dough in various arrangements that dopes like me can't quite grasp, and he goes sailing on to his next venture, which may be making purses from dog poop; meanwhile I wonder who would invest in a loan company headed by a man named W. Lance (and does the *W* stand for Whoopee or Weasel?) — whoever they are, they are cutting back on Christmas gifts and canceling their winter vacations in Daytona Beach in favor of a Holiday Inn in Minot.

He wrote back: "Couldn't we break this up?"

And he and I had the great pleasure of arguing about it. In electronic publishing, they're are no editors and if their are there not very good.

Newspapers

It seems to me, observing the young in coffee shops, that something is missing from their lives, the fine art of holding a newspaper. They sit staring at computer screens, sometimes with wires coming out of their ears, life passing them by as they drift through MySpace, that encyclopedia of the pathetic, and check out a video of a dog dancing the Macarena — it is so lumpen, so sad that nobody has shown them that opening up a newspaper is the key to looking classy and smart. Never mind the bronze-plated stuff about the role of the press in a democracy — a newspaper, kiddo, is about Style.

Whether you're sitting or standing, indoors or out, leaning against a hitching post or with your brogans on a desk, a newspaper gives you a whole rich vocabulary of gesture. You open it with a flourish and a ripple of newsprint, your buoyant self-confidence evident in the way you turn the pages with a snap of the wrist, taking in the gray matter swiftly, your eyes dancing over the world's sorrows and moving on, crinkling the page, snapping it, rolling it, folding the paper in halves and quarters, tucking it under the arm or tapping it against the palm. Cary Grant, Spencer Tracy, Jimmy Stewart, all the greats used the newspaper to demonstrate cool. Sitting and staring at the profile of Kerri ("Dreamer of dreams") Jodhpur, 18, of Muncie, Indiana, and her cat Snowball is not cool.

A man at a laptop is a man at a desk, a stiff, a drone. Where is the nobility here? He hunches forward, his eyes glaze, and beads of saliva glitter in the corners of his mouth and make their way down his chin as he becomes engrossed in the video of the fisherman falling out of the boat. A newspaper reader, by comparison, is a swordsman, a wrangler, a private eye. Holding a newspaper frees you up to express yourself, sort of like holding a sax did for Coltrane. Just observe a few simple rules:

1. If you want to make a serious impression, don't buy one paper, buy three or four. A person walking into Starbucks with four papers folded under his wing is immediately taken for a mogul. If he's young, he's a software mogul. If he is unshaven

and wearing pajamas under his raincoat, he is an eccentric mogul, perhaps a Mafia kingpin.

2. Take your sweet time opening the paper. You already know what's in it, boss man, you only read it so you'll know how much other people know, so there's no big rush.

3. Once you open it, never look up unless someone speaks your name. Don't be distracted just because a leggy blonde has crossed the room, leaving a trail of cigarette smoke and Chanel No. 5. You're the actor so let others be the audience, you be the scene.

4. Scan the front page, check out the headlines, but don't pore, don't be a drudge. Be cool. Jump to the sports page, then the comics, then the society page, then editorials. That's the beauty of the inverted pyramid news story. A glance is usually good enough.

5. Always rip out a story or two and tuck it in your pocket. Not casually, like it was a recipe for meatballs, but with urgency and purpose. This creates an indelible aura of mystery.

6. When you're done with a paper,

clap it shut and toss it aside. (You can't do that with a laptop.) A gesture of dismissal that says, "Feh! Enough of this pettiness! Onward! To the barricades!"

All of this should take no more than twenty minutes.

I know a man who is almost my age and so he grew up with ink on his fingers and then, for reasons he couldn't explain, he switched over to reading online publications and checking out the *Times* and the *Washington Post* and *Slate* and then found Dom .com with streaming video in which a mature Austrian woman with braids tells you what to do. He sits, his eyes locked to hers, as she says, "You vill eat, mein little schweinhund," and upbraids him for imaginary transgressions. If he reaches for the OFF switch, she screeches at him and a Rottweiler growls low in its throat and so he is a prisoner of his laptop, his days shot. This sort of thing happens all the time. The Internet will eat you alive. With newspapers, you're in and out, twenty minutes. It's your life, you choose.

Health

I caught part of a radio call-in show the other day on which a vet was fielding questions about Addison's disease among basset hounds and a cocker spaniel's hypothyroid problem and what can be done about a bulldog who snores (he needs to lose weight). It was interesting to discover the excellent medical care that dogs have come to expect these days. The vet was herself a dog parent, as she put it, and there was genuine feeling in her voice when she discussed the bassets' hormonal problems, something I haven't heard in the debate over health care for humans this summer.

I have not been a pet parent for twenty years, so perhaps I'm not up to speed here, but back in the day, dogs slept in the garage or on the porch so they could defend the home against socialism, and if they snored, it definitely was their problem and not ours. Ditto hypothyroidism. There was a death panel for that, chaired by Dad.

Dad grew up on a farm and was not overly sentimental about animals. He did not purchase jewelry for them or talk to them in a high-pitched voice. He would have blanched at the thought that the average cost of a visit to the vet with your cat is now $172. The chance of Dad paying that much to care for Snowball was about the same as Snowball's chances in hell. But that has all changed, and now the American people shell out upward of $10 billion a year for health care for pets.

Fine. Not an issue. Nobody called in to the show to suggest that the knee operation on the fourteen-year-old golden retriever (a recent cancer survivor) shows a level of caring far beyond what we extend to three-fourths of the world's human population. I could have but I don't care to upset the golden retriever community. Live and let live is my motto, dear reader. If your gerbil Mitzi needs a new heart valve and you've got the fifteen grand to spend on it, I am not here to stand in your way. Period.

And so the summer fades into September. Here on the upper Mississippi we've already felt an autumnal chill. I have gone to the State Fair and fed my child her allotment of corn dogs and deep-fried cheese curds and led her through the poultry barn so she knows where the omelet comes from and now it's time for her to resume science and mathematics and learn the subjunctive mood.

Here is an example of the subjunctive: Had we known that Americans were so paranoid about public health, we would have packaged health care reform differently and come up with better slogans.

Perhaps there should be a public pet option.

There was real sympathy for the parent of the bassets with the adrenal deficiency, whereas our 48 million uninsured citizens (of whom two-thirds come from a family with at least one full-time worker) are merely a big fat statistic, thus far lacking in a poster child. We can sort of imagine the misery of walking into an emergency room with no money, no plastic, no Blue Cross card, and trying to obtain treatment for some ailment that doesn't involve bone fragments protruding from the skin, but it doesn't speak to the heart the way an injured dog does.

Animals love us unconditionally and we love them back, maybe more than we love our neighbors, and that's just the truth, Ruth. People can be irksome, petty, especially raggedy ones — poverty does not always bring out the best in folks — and that's why it's difficult to get people to care about the uninsured.

If you put a pet option in the health care reform scheme, Americans would be in a bind. It's one thing to oppose big government taking over from those little mom-

and-pop insurance companies, but do you favor throwing Mr. Mittens out the car window when he gets old and feeble and needs an IV because he can't chew his kibble? You'd have weepy pet parents at town hall meetings waving photographs of kitty cats in need of new kidneys, and finally you'd start to see some empathy. People love their animals, and if we could just agree that everybody in America should receive the same level of care enjoyed by an elderly golden retriever, we could be done with this debate and get ready for the World Series.

George

A month has passed since my friend George Plimpton died, and I am still thinking about him. He was seventy-six, fifteen years older, a vulnerable age, but as Roy Blount said, "I was astonished that George died. It was so unlike him." And it was deeply confusing, a few weeks after his death, to attend the fiftieth anniversary party in New York for *The Paris Review,* which George had edited since its founding in Paris in 1953. It was George's party and he had arranged for the can-can dancers and the fireworks, and then there I was emceeing it. Billy Collins was there, and Alec Baldwin read Jack Kerouac, and Kurt Vonnegut made a toast, and at the end of it, the young *Paris Review* staff came to the stage for a standing O, and hundreds of George's pals were there, famous authors, movie stars, living legends, and Peter Duchin's orchestra, but the host himself was missing and that left a hole in the middle of the proceedings.

I am not like George Plimpton. I have the social skills of a marmot. He was Exeter, Harvard, Cambridge, and the Upper East Side, and I'm not, so we weren't born to be friends, and he had that odd fruity accent that sounded like he had a bandage around his tongue, but he was a man with beautiful manners and that goes a long way to smooth over life's little irregularities. Even if you weren't close to George, he made you think you were. He beamed at you from his great height under his thatch of white hair as if he were resuming a delightful conversation that had been interrupted six months ago and now here you were rejoined, thank God. He crashed a party at my apartment once and sat at the dining room table deep into the night jiggling a glass of scotch and holding court and at first it irritated me to hear him rambling on about Hemingway at the bar at the Ritz and then, like everyone else, I got pulled into the story. George relished being an Old Guy of Letters who had known Hemingway and E. M. Forster and Ezra Pound and Frost and the other statuettes on the shelf and he was glad to reminisce about them and their lady friends and revels, and thus, subtly, he included you in the great club of writers that extends back across the centuries. He was a grand story-teller, East Side accent and all, and I remember thinking that night, "Nobody does this much anymore. There ought to be less lit. crit. in college and more of this, what Hemingway smelled like and how he liked his eggs in the morning and what his conver-sation was about." I saw George last sum-mer when he and John Updike and I did the Charlie Rose show, and afterward he walked me down Park Avenue and insisted on taking me up to the New York Racquet Club and showing me a tennis court there modeled after the one Henry VIII played on, with walls and a roof to play the ball off. He explained the arcane rules of court tennis to me, and then took me down to the library, where he told about the book he'd found in which an Old Member had hidden his correspondence with his mistress. George relished the notion of passion among the staid and stately, an old financier describing a woman's breasts as "gleaming rosy-tipped orbs." He offered me a drink.

"Okay," I said. Sitting there in the den of privilege, leather chairs and hushed footsteps and all, I felt as if I could see George at last despite all my midwestern biases.

He went to Paris in 1953, a sunny time when America was admired as the savior of Europe and the exchange rate was good and you could rent a room for fifteen dollars a month and dine well for a dollar. And the authorities were tolerant of the extravagant gestures of the young. He and his friends Peter Matthiessen and Donald Hall and Robert Silvers were all there, hanging out in the Café de Tournon, writing, drinking *vin ordinaire,* looking for Hemingway, living proudly in tiny, cold fifth-floor walk-ups, being artists. They were thousands of miles away from anyone they might meet on the street who would ask, "What are you doing these days?" like dogs sniffing your résumé, expecting you to say, "I'm here for a few days and starting medical school in the fall," expecting you to have a reasonable plan for your life.

I came away from the party thinking about what terrific parents the guy must have had. In Paris in 1953, George visited the Hotel Plaza Athénée from time to time to write letters on hotel stationery and assure the folks that he was fine, just fine, and then returned to the toolshed where he lived, sleeping on an army cot among a platoon of alley cats. The elder Plimptons smiled on his adventure and didn't bully him into taking up his cross and going down to Wall Street. And now his life was over, and here was a party with eight hundred people in attendance, most of whom felt really close to him, in addition to his readers, who may have felt even closer. His books *Paper Lion* and *Out of My League* are part of the permanent literature of sports. George was twenty-six years old right up into his seventies. You can't really mourn a man who got a life as good as that.

Fame

Let us speak of the sorrows of fame. You are a hot young thing on a promotional tour for your book or movie or perfume and the limo brings you to the small luxury hotel and the celebrity suite where you step into the toilet and notice a wad of snot protruding from your left nostril. It is the size of the Hope diamond. How long has this been hanging there? You've spent all day mingling with people ecstatic at the sight of you you you, and yet not one of them dared mention this crusty green mucus ballooning from your nasal cavity. Nor did your publicist, Stephanie, nor the reporters at the press opportunity. Have you been walking around all day with this excrescence sticking out of your nose?

You lie awake, hot tears on your cheek. You are friendless in this world. People fawn over you but they don't like you enough to even lean over and say, "Hey, pal, you need a hanky." The next day, en route to the airport, you notice an item in the paper:

People are talking about a certain large enchilada who stood around with a noseful of blechhh the other day as he chatted cluelessly with members of the media. They say that heavy use of cocaine can desensitize the tissues. Anyway, check it out on YouTube.

You fire Stephanie. But the video of you makes its way around the Internet, you smiling, emoting charm, and a big green thing like an emerald in your nose. And everywhere you go, little knots of hecklers are waiting for you, pointing to their left nostrils.

You issue a statement through your new publicist, Jessica, announcing that you have a rare disease that is seldom fatal but that produces mucus unexpectedly. You caught it in Africa while trying to adopt an orphan and it was exacerbated by overwork, stress, and alcohol abuse. You are checking yourself into rehab at a clinic. So far, so good.

Ninety days later, you emerge into the bright sunlight, smiling, focused, and in a totally different place from where you were three months ago, and happy to talk about your journey, and the press is not waiting for you. No cameras, no microphones, just a velvet rope with nobody behind it. What gives?

Your cell phone rings and it's Jessica. She's weeping. She did her best to try to draw a crowd for your press conference to discuss your spiritual journey but today was not your day, other larger elephants were active in the bush, sweetheart, and so the press swarmed them and not you. You are in a totally different place in your life now and nobody gives a rip. Nobody.

Right here is where you have a chance to learn what a great thing it is to have real work to do. When you fall off the A list, you simply return to your work, whatever it may be, and that rescues you from insanity. Even if you have the misfortune to be born rich and not too bright, you could still be taught a useful skill. In the end, this would do you more good than cosmetic surgery.

People decry Lindsay Lohan but she serves a purpose. We're a big country and we have so little in common anymore.

Television and pop music have splintered into hundreds of niches. There are no singers like Satchmo or Sinatra or Elvis whose voices everyone knows. The audience for even the most successful TV show is a small minority. Most famous persons in America are persons most Americans have never heard of.

But if we don't admire the same people, at least we can find people to scorn and feel sorry for. That is the role of ditzy pop stars and rich bimbos and the old tycoon with the comb-over and the home-run kings on steroids — they are the village lunatics in our ongoing national fairy tale. We check on their comings and goings and then we turn to our jobs with fresh appreciation. Maybe our feuds aren't widely reported and maybe people aren't looking for pictures of us without underwear, but we have steady work and that's a consolation, just being good at accomplishing useful things.

I, for example, am good at washing dishes. I used to do it professionally and it's still satisfying. You clear away the wreckage and run a sink full of soapy water and make everything sparkly clean again and you look around the kitchen and get a feeling that money and fame can't buy.

Power

It dawned on me slowly, after a man in a tuxedo brought me breakfast on a tray, quail eggs, boiled, perfect, on toast points, and my wife curtsied and kissed my hand, and I noticed the armed guards on the lawn, that I had become Ruler of the World. It was nothing I ever wanted for myself and perhaps that's why it was given to me.

So I tested my powers with a few little righteous deeds. I repaired the Arctic ice cap and shut down the Internet on Saturdays and Sundays. I made Mitt Romney a doorman at a Manhattan apartment building and he fit right in, suave, good-humored, helpful with packages and calling taxis. I gave his vast fortune to struggling orchestras. I gave the Nobel Prize for literature to John Updike, posthumously, and then I tried to raise him from the dead. That was when God called. "Don't go there," he said. "Jesus did it a few times and it just raised havoc." We talked about a lot of things. He told me I needn't capitalize his pronouns anymore, that we should be on a first-name basis. "Call me Fred," he said. He asked me not to be harsh with the pope. He reminded me of his great fondness for the Jews. I asked him if Jesus ever got married and he said, "Not that I know of."

World domination is nothing I ever wanted for myself. I am a Midwesterner, a Minnesota boy, brought up to be sheepish and deferential. My mother never told me to follow my dream; she told me to "be appropriate." So ruling the world has not been a source of great pleasure for me. Extracting the Royal Family from their various palaces and placing them in public housing next to the railway tracks in Croydon was no fun, nor was the extermination of a number of pesky little dialects in favor of plain ordinary English, nor was the elimination of hip-hop music, but it had to be done.

I cut oil consumption in the U.S. by almost half, switching trucks to natural gas, distributing bicycles to the able, creating public transportation where there hadn't been any, such as Los Angeles, Texas, the South. I brought the world's bankers into one large arena and I showed them what I could do with locusts, frogs, blood, lice, hail, and pestilence. Then I brought in the Israelis and Iranians and Hezbollah and Hamas and showed them the same tricks. A veiled woman in a chador ran in with a backpack and cried out praise to Allah and pulled a string and the backpack fell open and fifty pounds of jelly beans fell out. So I'm hopeful about the Middle East.

It's been interesting, I'll say that. The load of daily mail is staggering – truckloads — people wanting favors — and I can no longer go out in public. If I have dinner with friends, people keep sticking notes under my plate — "Get Freddie into Harvard," "Get Lyle out of prison," "Our dog has liver cancer. Please do something." It wears a person out. And my wife is after me continually: "Why don't we spend time together, just the two of us? Why don't we make love the way we used to?"

I wasn't going to bring that up but there it is. The ruler of the world has become a nonperformer in the sack. I take hot showers, I look at pictures of naked girls, I read hot novels, I take the little blue pill: nothing. World dominance does not lead to self-confidence. Adolf Hitler had the same problem, so did Josef Stalin, Alexander the Great, Julius Caesar, the list goes on. It is an odd feeling — to be able to banish the word *relationship* and forbid PowerPoint presentations and eliminate PIN numbers and yet be unable to make a woman happy. "Just relax," she says. Easy for someone who isn't ruling the world to say.

And what about retirement, I wonder. How do I turn the job over to someone else and move to Antigua? I made myself a fabulous villa there, swimming pool, cabanas, guest house, orchard, long white-sand beach — when do I get to take life easy? I asked Fred and he said, "I've been struggling with that for millions of years. Welcome to the club." The people who are waiting to rule the world when I'm done are people who couldn't organize a three-car parade. So onward we go, exhausted, unappreciated, and impotent where it really matters. So how are you doing? Everything okay in your sector?

3.

A SPEECH TO THE WHITE HOUSE CORRESPONDENTS' ASSOCIATION DINNER,

WASHINGTON HILTON, MARCH 18, 1999

A person should never turn down an invitation to speak to a group of journalists — how else to set them straight? — and in the spring of 1999, there was plenty to talk about. The impeachment of President Clinton had died a natural death a month before when he was acquitted by the Senate, Mrs. Clinton was said to be interested in running for the Senate from New York, and Jesse (The Body) Ventura had been elected governor of Minnesota. An embarrassment of riches.

Mr. President, Mrs. Clinton, Members of the White House Radio-TV Correspondents Association, Distinguished Guests, Ordinary Average Guests:

It's a pleasure to be here in Washington. I was here for your winter, which was on Tuesday, and it's good to be back for spring. And to come and speak at an occasion whose purpose is civility, where people who distrust each other, and for good reason, will nevertheless sit down and break bread together. Of course, the same happens at any Republican prayer breakfast.

I have always been in favor of civility — kindness to people who you have reason to dislike. Americans believe in the power of friendship to overcome all barriers of race and gender and religion. We believe that the really bitter animosities are between women who are related to each other.

We are in need of civility, especially this year, with people suffering the premillennial jitters. What's going to happen on New Year's Eve? People are already in a dither over it. Of course it was worse two thousand years ago for the Romans — every year, the date got smaller — it was 20 B.C. and then suddenly it was 1 B.C. and what would happen next? Would you go to zero? Start counting up? Switch to the Jewish calendar? Nobody knew.

My hero when it comes to civility was Justice Harry A. Blackmun, a great Minnesotan, who died two weeks ago at the age of ninety, who served twenty-four years on the Supreme Court, starting at the age of sixty-one, and distinguished himself as the shy person's justice. Somehow he found a right to privacy in the Constitution, and based on that, he wrote the majority opinion in *Roe v. Wade*, a decision that got him more hate mail than you or I could ever imagine. He read a good deal of it himself, and the violence of it didn't affect him except to make him compassionate for the writers. He didn't feel anger toward them. What got Justice Blackmun riled was that the company that sold him his homeowners' insurance, after a sniper fired a bullet through the window of his living room and into the back of a wingback chair, would only pay to re-cover that chair and not the matching one, though after the first chair had been recovered, they didn't match anymore because the covering was so old. He was a true Minnesotan.

Civility is the acknowledgment of our own humanity. And it's practical. It is based on the fact that, loathsome as those sons of bitches are, you may someday need to borrow money from them. Don't lord it over people: the podium will not be yours indefinitely. Nor the limo. So you should keep a decent tongue and if you are a journalist, you should strive to be fair. It will diminish the impact of your work, but do it anyway.

I am pleased that the president has joined

us tonight. He is at the point in his presidency where ordinarily a man enjoys foreign travel and being driven through throngs of people waving tiny flags, who are delighted to see you, a wonderful prospect compared to eating chicken at the Washington Hilton with a roomful of people who would regard your downfall as a professional opportunity.

This is a durable president. He has already gone four hundred days beyond when he was expected to resign. F. Scott Fitzgerald said, "There are no second acts in American lives," but he didn't know Mr. Clinton. He's had two already, and in a couple of years, he may have yet another as a candidate's spouse. It's interesting to imagine Mr. Clinton sitting on a platform and looking pleasant and engaged through the candidate's speech, smiling at the happy parts and grimacing at the serious parts. And then come back to Washington as a member of a group of older women married to senators, who gather for tea and to hear about literacy programs.

I'm not sure the First Lady is getting good advice on this idea of running for the Senate from New York. The numbers look good — in this morning's *Times,* she's leading Mayor Giuliani 48 to 39 percent.

But running for office in New York is

about two-thirds ritual and one-third fund-raising. As a candidate for the Senate, you're expected to pay ceremonial visits to a long series of grand poobahs and there is ring-kissing to be done, and you've got to march in ethnic parades and be photographed eating ethnic food such as knishes — I'm not sure if you've ever eaten a knish, Mrs. Clinton. A knish is a potato sandwich. You bite one end, it oozes at the other. People take a bite of a knish and they look around to see if there's a dog in the vicinity.

Mrs. Clinton, there is a Republican seat coming up in Minnesota next year and I think you ought to consider it. Minnesota is a state of polite and modest people. They'd be happy to see you. The fact that you had passed up New York to run in Minnesota would be enough to elect you going away. And you would provide employment for many of these fine journalists in the audience, who are in need of new material, now that the impeachment is over.

The impeachment created a news industry with tremendous production capacity, but now raw materials have dwindled. For two years, White House correspondents have stood on the White House lawn every day and said to a camera that it isn't clear what

will happen next but that something probably will, but now it hasn't, and in recent
weeks, we've seen famous news anchors
reading stories about the salmon shortage
and the dangers of halogen lamps and new
varieties of streptococcus — this is not why
you went to J-school, to talk about streptococcus — there even was a story on the
evening news recently, "Are you getting
enough sleep?" If you watch the news, you
are.

But there is hope on the horizon and it's in
Minnesota. There's a new survey that says
that one-third of the American people
would consider voting for Jesse (The Body)
Ventura for president of the United States.

Of course, it's hard to say what "consider
voting for" means exactly. It's sort of like
asking, "Have you ever considered eating
squirrel?" — yes, considered it, and decided
against it both times.

If he should run, however, it's going to be
a big boost for the news business.

Jesse (The Body) Ventura is a new venture,
combining entertainment and politics in
one package, who sneers and swaggers better than almost anyone. He is a man of fixed
opinions who doesn't look or sound like
anybody else, the first governor who used to

earn his living throwing large men out of the ring and then hitting them with folding chairs, which has given him a limited view of the world. He got elected saying that he could only promise to do his best and I would have to say that he's kept his word. He also said that he was no politician and I think he was right about that, too. A couple of weeks ago, he came out and accused Minnesotans of having no sense of humor, which is an odd thing to say about the people who elected him.

On a slow news day, Governor Ventura is a gift, and these are slow news days. The other day, there was a story about agriculture on the front page of *The New York Times.* I remember it because it identified the Secretary of Agriculture as a man named Dan Glickman. After the past year, I'd forgotten there was a secretary of agriculture.

Washington is a city of ten thousand journalists, all of whom are terrified that they may be assigned to cover the farm crisis. A Washington journalist would rather go to Afghanistan and sleep on the ground and get fleas and eat rancid yogurt than have to go to Kansas or North Dakota to interview large taciturn people, and stay in cinder-block motels, the kind that put the shampoo in little plastic packs, not bottles, and it's not the shampoo with aloe in it, it's got bad chemicals in it that do weird things to your hair and also cause depression. A Washington journalist's fear is that he might file a story about the farm crisis that sounds intelligent and gets him reassigned to the Chicago bureau. And then you go to work for Iowa Power and Light, writing press releases about conserving electricity.

I love *CBS Sunday Morning,* which epitomizes civility in journalism. It has never said anything nasty about anybody. It's Mr. Rogers without puppets. They do about five different stories and keep doing them over and over — the Indomitable Geezer story, and the Man on a Quest to Revive a Long-Lost Art story, and the Community-Pitching-in-to-Help-a-Stranger story, and the Joys-of-Living-in-a-Backwater story, and the Great-Artist-as-a-Regular-Person-Just-Like-You-and-Me-Not-Weird-Whatsoever story, and at the end, as the credits roll, there is a long sequence of a quiet pond and geese landing on it — *CBS Sunday Morning* is like going to church.

The journalist in our family was my aunt Flo, who went to the Bon Marche Beauty Salon every Saturday morning and came up

544

to visit us afterward. It was for news that she went there, it certainly was not for beauty. They did only one style at the Bon Marche, and that was helmet hair, a combination of styling and engineering that keeps a woman looking fifty-three years old from the age of twenty-one until the day you die and then Luanne comes up to the funeral home and gives you your eternal permanent.

Aunt Flo would sit down by my mother and she'd give us the dirt that the local paper couldn't report. We enjoyed hearing these things. We were good Christian people and we believed in forgiveness but meanwhile we liked to know exactly what it was we were forgiving them for.

When you grow up listening to gossip, you develop an ear for it and you can hear that faint tone of pleasure that this story wasn't about us or anyone related to us but about a family we disliked — the sense of pride that we, our people, are not capable of this sort of behavior. But this pride gets in your way. You can't tell a story decently unless you can imagine yourself in the place of the main characters, and this is true whether it's news or fiction. This is the standard of civility in journalism.

And one summer night she came over and told us about the tornado that struck north of us and hit our cousin Joe's house. *A quiet summer day, and then the sky turned black, and a cloud like a snake came slithering across the countryside and tore the roof off his house and left his neighbor's house untouched, his neighbor who was a drunk and beat his wife. The tornado tore off Joe's roof and destroyed furniture and impaled blades of grass in a bedroom vanity mirror and carried some dishes into the neighbor's pasture and set them down undamaged and drove seed corn into Joe's linoleum floor and for years afterward every spring they had to sponge-mop with a herbicide, but they made it into the basement just as the roof went.* And right then my aunt Flo started to cry. She'd told the story so well that she scared herself to death and she could imagine it happening to her.

That's what I call real reporting.

4.
CHET

Leona Atkins asked me to give the eulogy at the funeral for her husband, Chester, in Nashville in May 2001, and I didn't want to do it but I couldn't say no to Leona and so flew down to Nashville the night before and sat in a hotel room on Broadway and wrote my eulogy. I loved Chet. He was fifty-eight when we met and I was forty. He played the show a dozen times or so and he and I did some touring together. I didn't know what friendship was until I met Chet — he really bestowed himself on people he liked. You sat in his office in Nashville and time stopped. He sat noodling on a guitar and telling stories about the stars and people he knew in radio in the Forties and pretty young women he'd met along the way. He never talked business, it was mostly about his scuffling early years, working with the Delmores and Maybelle Carter and Red Foley, and it was all for pleasure, there was no meanness in it, though he did particularly

547

like to talk about sanctimonious gospel singers who enjoyed liquor and lasciviousness on
the side. He did a good impression of the TV
faith healer Ernest Ainsley, who would press
his palm against the afflicted area and cry out,
Heal!! A woman came to the reverend who
said she had a tumor in her breast and he
cried, *I will not touch you there. But heal!!!*
Chet was not a religious man, certainly not a
Christian — "But it's a beautiful story," he said
— and he didn't change his mind even when
he hit a bad streak, cancer, a brain tumor, a
stroke, in his early seventies. I visited him a
couple times and it was hard for him to be
seen like that, using a walker, unable to play
the guitar like Chet Atkins, just sort of strum.
The last time he played on the show, we
turned his microphone way down, and Pat
Donohue, sitting behind him, played his part,
and that, I believe, was his last performance.
He died at home, tended by Leona and his
daughter Merle. The funeral service was held
in the Ryman Auditorium, the longtime home
of the *Grand Ole Opry,* and I stood on the
stage, the coffin down on the floor, and tried
to give a good account of the man, but it was
a heavy occasion, no pleasure in it, and I was
glad to get in a cab and head for the airport.

"I went up home to east Tennessee the

other day. I was invited, went and saw a dozen folks that I hadn't seen in forty-five or fifty years. Every damn one of them said, 'I'll bet you don't know who I am,' et cetera. I admitted I didn't and they seemed disappointed. I left there when I had just turned eleven. I received an award for just growing up there, I suppose, and I couldn't think of one nice thing to say. Those were some of the worst years of the old man's life, don't you know. But even the bad ones are good now that I think about it."

— Chet Atkins

It was a Saturday night in the summer of 1946, Red Foley came on the *Grand Ole Opry* at the Ryman Auditorium in Nashville and sang "Old Shep" and then, before the commercial break for Prince Albert tobacco, nodded to his guitarist and said, "Ladies and gentlemen, Mr. Chester Atkins will now play 'Maggie' on the acoustic guitar," and Mr. Atkins did, and afterward Minnie Pearl came up and kissed him and said, "You're a wonderful musician, you're just what we've been needing around here."

He played guitar in a style that hadn't been seen before, with a thumb pick for the bass note and two fingers to play the contra-puntal melody, and at a time when guitarists were expected to be flashy and play "Under the Double Eagle" with the guitar up behind their head, this one hunched down over the guitar and made it sing, made a melody line that was beautiful and legato. A woman wrote, who saw him play in a roadhouse in Cincinnati in 1946, "He sat hunched in the spotlight and played and the whole room suddenly got quiet. It was a drinking and dancing crowd, but there was something about Chet Atkins that could take your breath away."

Chester Burton Atkins was born June 20, 1924, the son of Ida Sharp and James Arley Atkins, a music teacher and piano tuner and singer, near Luttrell, Tennessee, on the farm of his grandfather who fought on the Union side in the Civil War.

Chet was born into a mess of trouble: his people were poor, his folks split up when he was six, he suffered from asthma, he grew up lonely and scared, tongue-tied and shy. His older brothers played music and he listened, and when he was six, he got a ukulele. When he broke a string, he pulled a wire off the screen door and tuned it up. He took up the guitar when he was nine, a Sears Silvertone with the action about a half-inch high at the twelfth fret, torture to play. He'd tune it up to a major chord and play it with a kitchen knife for a slide, Hawaiian style, "Steel Guitar Rag." When he was eleven, he went to live with his daddy in Columbus, Georgia, where on a summer day you could see the snake tracks in the dust on a dirt road, but at night the radio brought in Cincinnati and Atlanta and Knoxville and even New York City.

That was the music that spoke to his heart.

Chet got a lot of music from his dad, who was a trained singer in the old hymns and sentimental ballads, which Chet remembered all his life — he could sing you several verses of "In the Gloaming" or "Seeing Nellie Home," whether you asked for them or not. He knew the fiddle tunes and mountain music that he picked up trying to play the fiddle. But it was on the radio that he heard music that really entranced him, that was freer and looser and more jangly and elegant and brazen. His brother Jim played rhythm guitar with Les Paul when Les was with Fred Waring and His Pennsylvanians, and Chet paid close attention to that, and to George Barnes and the Sons of the Pioneers and the Hoosier Hot Shots, and Merle Travis, whom he heard on a crystal set from WLW in Cincinnati. Chet tried to get the Merle Travis sound, and in the process, he came up with his own and then he discovered Django Reinhardt and that set something loose in him.

You might be shy and homely and puny and from the sticks and feel looked down upon, but if you could play the guitar like that, you would be aristocracy and never have to point it out, anybody with sense would know it and the others don't matter anyway.

He met Django backstage once in Chicago when Django was touring with Duke Ellington and got his autograph. Chet said, "I wanted to play for him but I didn't get the chance." But in Knoxville, doing the *Midday Merry Go Round,* he met Homer and Jethro, Henry Haynes and Kenneth Burns, who were hip to Django too and on Chet's wavelength, and in 1949 they made an instrumental album called *Galloping Guitar* — sort of the Hot Club of Nashville. It got some airplay and that was his first big success and he was on his way.

Chet had dropped out of high school to go into radio and the music business — first with Jumping Bill Carlisle and Archie Campbell in Knoxville, and Johnnie and Jack in Raleigh, then Red Foley in Chicago and Springfield, Missouri, and Mother Maybelle and the Carter Sisters. In Cincinnati, he met Leona Johnson, who was singing on WLW with her twin sister, Lois, and after a year of courtship they married in 1946. He wrote in 1984: "Our percolator went out the other day and we counted up . . . she has stayed with me through four of them. If I were her, I wouldn't have stayed around through the first one, which was a non-electric. After drinking coffee, there would be a residue on the cup and folks would read it and tell your fortune. Anyway, she is mine and she is a winner."

Chet got himself fired numerous times along the way, a badge of honor for a musician with a mind of his own, and he kept getting fired in an upward direction and wound up coming to Nashville and WSM and the *Opry* and RCA, under the patronage of Fred Rose and Steve Sholes. He got to see the end of the era of the medicine show and the hillbilly band with the comedian with the blacked-out teeth and the beginnings of rock 'n' roll — Chet had a front-row seat, as the guitarist, and he remembered everything he saw and he knew so many giants.

This man was a giant himself. He was the guitar player of the twentieth century. He was the model of who you should be and what you should look like. You could tell it whenever he picked up a guitar, the way it fit him. His upper body was shaped to it, from a lifetime of playing: his back was slightly hunched, his shoulders rounded, and the guitar was the missing piece. He was an artist and there was no pretense in him; he never waved the flag or held up the cross or traded on his own sorrows. He was the guitarist. His humor was self-deprecating; he was his own best critic. He inspired all sorts of players who never played anything like him. He was generous and admired other players' work and he told them so. He had a natural reserve to him, but when he admired people, he went all out to tell them about it. And because there was no deception in him, his praise meant more than just about anything else. If Chet was a fan of yours, you never needed another one.

When he was almost fifty, he had a stroke of good luck, when he got colon cancer and thought he was going to die, and when he didn't die, he found a whole new love of life. He walked away from the corporate music world and fell in love with the guitar again and went all over performing with Paul Yandell, playing with all the great orchestras, notably the Boston Pops, and started living by his own clock, so he had time to sit and talk with people and pick music with them and enjoy the social side of music and have more fun. He had a gift for friendship. He was so generous with stories, and if you drove around Nashville with him, he remembered one after another, it was a documentary movie about country music. Chet loved so many people. He especially loved the ones who seemed a little wild to him and who made him laugh. Dolly Parton always made him laugh, the way she flirted with him. She came to see him as he lay dying, and she made him laugh for about an hour. He loved Waylon Jennings. He loved Lenny Breaux. Jerry Reed. Ray Stevens. Vince Gill. Steve Wariner. And Brother Dave Gardner, the hipster revivalist comedian whom Chet discovered doing stand-up in a Nashville club between sets as a drummer and who said, "Dear hearts, gathered here to rejoice in the glorious Southland. Joy to the world! The South has always been the South. And I believe the only reason that folks live in the North is because they have jobs up there."

He loved doing shows. He never had a bad night. He played some notes he didn't mean to play but they never were bad notes. They simply were other notes. He liked to be alone backstage. He liked it quiet and calm. I remember him backstage, alone, walking around in the cavernous dark of some opera house out west, holding the guitar, playing, singing to himself; he needed to be alone with himself and get squared away, because the Chet people saw on stage was the same Chet you hung around with in his office, joking with Paul about having a swimming pool shaped like a guitar amp, the joke about "By the time I learned I couldn't tune very well, I was too rich to care," and singing "Would Jesus Wear a Rolex" and "I Just Can't Say Goodbye," and ending the show with his ravishing, beautiful solo, "Vincent," the audience sitting in rapt silence. It was all the same Chet who sat at home with Leona, watching a golf tournament with the sound off, and playing his guitar, a long stream-of-consciousness medley in which twenty or thirty tunes came together perfectly, as in a dream, his daddy's songs and "The Banks of the Ohio" and "Recuerdos de la Alhambra" and "Smile" and Stephen Foster and Boudleaux Bryant and the Beatles and "Freight Train," one long sparkling stream of music, as men in plaid pants hit their long high approach shots in a green paradise.

He said: "I enjoy the fruits of my efforts but I have never felt comfortable promoting myself. The condition is worsening now that

I am on the back nine. My passion for the guitar and for fame is slowly dying and it makes me sad. I never thought my love for the guitar would fade. There are a lot of reasons, as we get older the high frequencies go, music doesn't sound so good. And for some damn reason after hearing so many great players, I lose the competitive desire. Here I am baring my soul. That's good though, isn't it. I'm not a Catholic but I love that facet of their religion."

Chet was curious and thoughtful about religion, though he was dubious about shysters and TV evangelists. He said, "I am seventy and still don't know anything about life, what universal entity designed the body I live in or what will come after I am gone. I figure there will be eternity and nothing much else. Like pulling a finger out of water. If it's as the Baptists claim, I think I would tire of streets of gold and would want to see brick houses. I believe that when I die I'll probably go to Minnesota. The last time I was up there, it was freezing and I remember smiling and my upper lip went up and didn't come back down."

5.
MARK

The New York Times asked me to review Mark Twain's autobiography — actually, the first volume of a new unabridged multivolume scholarly edition of everything autobiographical he ever wrote — because I'm an admirer of Twain and when I plunged into it I felt obliged to defend the Master against his collectors. Too much Twain. A lesson to all of us: Even when you're in fine form and the audience is happy, there is a time for the curtain to be pulled and it's sooner than you think. And a corollary: A great master can be as tedious as anybody else, maybe more so. The Mark Twain we know and love is the product of editing; the gentleman himself could be a major blowhard. A person almost always improves his reputation by shutting up.

Autobiography of Mark Twain, *Volume 1, edited by Harriet Elinor Smith (Berkeley, CA: University of California Press, 2010).*

Samuel L. Clemens was a cheerful promoter of himself, and even after he'd retired from the lecture circuit, the old man liked to dress up as Mark Twain in a fresh white suit and take a Sunday morning stroll up Fifth Avenue just as churches were letting out and see the heads turn and hear his name murmured, the crowds of Presbyterians and Episcopalians standing awestruck as the most beloved mustache in America passed by, tipping his silk hat to the ladies. Mr. Twain's autobiography was meant to be a last stroll around the block, and to build up suspense and improve sales, Sam told everybody that he was writing one and that it contained material so explosive that it would need to be embargoed for a hundred years (though he allowed his official biographer to excavate all the interesting material) — well, that century has passed now and here it is, Volume 1 of *THE COMPLETE AUTHENTIC UNEXPURGATED EDITION, NOTHING HAS BEEN OMITTED, NOT EVEN SCANDALOUS PASSAGES LIKELY TO CAUSE GROWN MEN TO GASP AND WOMEN TO COLLAPSE IN TEARS — NO CHILDREN UNDER 7 ALLOWED TO READ THIS BOOK UNDER ANY CIRCUMSTANCES,* which made Sam front-page news when the book was announced last spring, which turns out to be a wonderful fraud on the order of the

Duke and the Dauphin in their Shakespearean romp, and bravo to Samuel Clemens, still able to catch the public's attention a century after he expired.

He speaks from the grave, he writes, so that he can speak freely — "as frank and free and unembarrassed as a love letter" — but there's precious little frankness and freedom here and plenty of proof that Mark Twain, in the hands of academics, can be just as tedious as anybody else when he is under the burden of his own reputation. Here, sandwiched between a 58-page barrage of an introduction and 250 pages of footnotes, is a ragbag of scraps, some of interest, most of them not: travel notes, the dictated reminiscences of an old man in a dithery voice ("Shortly after my marriage, in 1870, I received a letter from a young man in St. Louis who was possibly a distant relative of mine — I don't remember now about that" begins one story that goes nowhere), various false starts, anecdotes that must have been amusing at one time, a rough essay (with the author's revisions carefully delineated) on Joan of Arc, a critique of the lecture performance of Petroleum V. Nasby, a recap of the voyage of the ill-fated clipper ship *Hornet* to Hawaii in 1866, a piece about German compound words, an account of medicine on the frontier, well-worn passages from lectures, a fair amount of self-congratulation ("I expected the speech to go off well — and it did"), a detailed report on the testimony of Henry H. Rogers in a lawsuit in Boston, newspaper clippings, generous quotations from his daughter Susy's writing about her father ("He always walks up and down the room while thinking and between each course at meals"), ruminations on his methodology of autobiographicizing ("I shall talk about the matter which for the moment interests me, and cast it aside and talk about something else the moment its interest for me is exhausted . . . a complete and purposed jumble"), recollections of Reuel Gridley and other Hannibal classmates. There is precious little that could be considered scandalous — maybe a rant against James W. Paige, the inventor of the typesetting machine that Mark lost $170,000 on ("If I had his nuts in a steel trap I would shut out all human succor and watch that trap till he died") — but you have to wade through eighteen pages of mind-numbing inventory of the Countess Massiglia's Villa di Quarto that he leased in Florence ("I shall go into the details of this house, not because I imagine it differs much from any other old-time palace or new-time palace on the continent of Europe, but because every one of its crazy details interests me, and therefore may be expected to interest others of the human race, particularly women"), the only point of which is that the man can afford to rent a palace that is fancier than anything you'd find in Missouri. His wife is dying and he compiles an inventory of furniture.

Here is a powerful argument for writers burning their papers — you'd like to be remembered for *Innocents Abroad* and *Life on the Mississippi* and the first two-thirds of *The Adventures of Huckleberry Finn* and not for excruciating passages of hero worship of General Grant and his son Fred and accounts of your proximity to the general and your business dealings as the publisher of his memoirs, which only reminds the reader that the general wrote a classic autobiography, and you tried to and could not.

Think twice about donating your papers to an institution of higher learning, Famous Writer: someday they may be used against you.

Olivia Clemens's nickname for her husband was Youth and she knew him up close. Boyish hijinks are his strong suit, and energetic high spirits and sly irreverence. Here is Sam Clemens at fourteen dancing naked in a room, unaware that girls were watching from behind a screen — well, he said he was unaware anyway and why not take his word for it? — and the story of Jim Wolfe climbing naked up the roof to silence the cats, and Sam tricking his mother into putting her hand in his jacket pocket, where he had stuffed a dead bat. Even in his maturity, he could take an appreciative boy's view of his neighbor, the author of *Uncle Tom's Cabin:*

Harriet Beecher Stowe . . . was a near neighbor of ours in Hartford, with no fences between. . . . Her mind had decayed, and she was a pathetic figure. She wandered about all the day long in the care of a muscular Irish woman. Among the colonists of our neighborhood the doors always stood open in pleasant weather. Mrs. Stowe entered them at her own free will and as she was always softly slippered and full of animal spirits, she was able to deal in surprises and she liked to do it. She would slip up behind a person who was deep in dreams and musings and fetch a war whoop that would jump that person out of his clothes.

Mark Twain sprang to life at a young age. His voice is clear when Samuel Clemens was seventeen and got to New York and wrote to his mother, August 24, 1853: "My dear Mother: you will doubtless be a little surprised, and somewhat angry when you receive this, and find me so far from home; but you must bear a little with me, for you know I was always the best boy you had, and perhaps you remember that people used to say to their children — 'Now don't do like Orion and Henry Clemens but take Sam for your guide!' " He took lodging on Duane Street near Broadway and got a job setting type in a large printing shop near the East River. He stuck around the city for a couple months and wrote home about the fruit market, the Wild Men of Borneo displayed in P. T. Barnum's museum on Broadway, the Crystal Palace on Forty-second Street, and, knowing the letters would appear in his brother Orion's Hanni-bal *Journal,* the boy struck up a style that we recognize as Twain ("I have taken a lik-ing to the abominable place, and every time I get ready to leave, I put it off a day or two, from some unaccountable cause. It is just as hard on my conscience to leave New York as it was easy to leave Hannibal. I think I shall get off Tuesday, though"), a style that makes him seem fresh and friendly a century later. This is the Mark Twain people love to quote — "Clothes make the man. Naked people have little or no influence in society," "A man who carries a cat by the tail learns something he can learn in no other way." And whenever he hits his stride in the autobiography, you feel happy for him — e.g., writing about Virginia City, Nevada, in 1863:

I secured a place in a near-by quartz mill to screen sand with a long-handled shovel. I hate a long-handled shovel. I never could learn to swing it properly. As often as any other way the sand didn't reach the screen at all, but went over my head and down my back, inside of my clothes. It was the most detestable work I have ever engaged in, but it paid ten dollars a week and board — and the board was worth while, because it consisted not only of bacon, beans, coffee, bread and molasses, but we had stewed dried apples every day in the week just the same as if it were Sunday. But this palatial life, this gross and luxurious life, had to come to an end, and there were two sufficient reasons for it. On my side, I could not endure the heavy labor; and on the Company's side, they did not feel justified in paying me to shovel sand down my back; so I was discharged just at the moment that I was going to resign.

The reader hikes across the hard dusty ground of a famous man's reminiscences and is delighted to come across the occasional waterhole. The famous man is in Berlin, hobnobbing with aristocracy at dinner at the ambassador's, and meets a count — "This nobleman was of long and illustrious descent. Of course I wanted to let out the fact that I had some ancestors, too; but I did not want to pull them out of their graves by the ears, and never could seem to get a chance to work them in in a way that would look sufficiently casual." And this leads to a story about a Clemens ancestor running for office in Virginia whose opponent sent six young men with drums to stand in front of Mr. Clemens's platform and drum during his speech. Mr. Clemens stood up and took out a revolver and spoke, softly: "I do not wish to hurt anybody, and shall try not to; but I have got just a bullet apiece for those six drums, and if you should want to play on them, don't stand behind them."

He takes a good swing at John D. Rockefeller, that monster of greed and ambition who liked to give little talks to his Baptist church about the beauty of holiness and following in the footsteps of the Master Who alone can satisfy our hearts ("Satan, twaddling sentimental sillinesses to a Sunday-school, could be no burlesque upon John D. Rockefeller. . . . he can't be burlesqued — he is himself a burlesque"). And he preaches well against imperialism, but then you must hear about Robert Louis Stevenson ("His splendid eyes . . . burned with a smouldering rich fire under the pent-house of his brows, and they made him beautiful") and the meeting with Helen Keller, who laughed at Sam's jokes, and the meeting with Lewis Carroll ("He was the stillest and shyest full-grown man I ever met except 'Uncle Remus' "), and then you start turning the pages two and three at a time.

Sam intended to give us an unblushing autobiography on the order of Casanova's or Rousseau's *Confessions* or Samuel Pepys's diary, which Sam heartily admired, with its matter-of-fact inventories of parties attended and meals enjoyed and the skirts of chambermaids raised, but Sam knew that frankness comes with a price. "None of us likes to be hated, none of us likes to be shunned," he said. "The man has yet to be born who could write the truth about himself." And when he described his brother Orion as having "an intense lust for approval" he is surely describing himself: "He was so eager to be approved, so girlishly anxious to be approved by anybody and everybody, without discrimination, that he was commonly ready to forsake his . . . convictions at a moment's notice. . . . He never acquired a conviction that could survive a disapproving remark from a cat." The younger brother sees the older with a clear satirical eye, and what he sees is himself.

Orion was foolish about money and so was Sam, a spendthrift to the end. Their father, Judge Clemens, before the boys were born, bought 75,000 acres of land in Tennessee that contained coal, copper, iron, timber, oil, and produced wild grapes — "There's millions in it!" said a cousin, James Lampton — and "it influenced our life," writes Sam, "it cheered us up and said, 'Do not be afraid — trust in me — wait.' . . . It kept us hoping and hoping, during forty years, and forsook us at last. It put our energies to sleep and made visionaries of us — dreamers, and indolent. . . . We were always going to be rich next year." When the father died, "we began to manage it ourselves . . . managed it all away except 10,000 acres," which Orion traded for a house and a lot worth $250. The only one to turn a profit was Mark Twain, who turned Mr. Lampton ("the happy light in his eye, the abounding hope in his heart, the persuasive tongue, the miracle-breeding imagination") into Colonel Sellers in *The Gilded Age*.

It is the sad fate of an icon to be mummified alive, pickled by his own reputation, and midway through this dreary meander of a memoir, Sam throws up his hands in despair: "What a wee little part of a person's life are his acts and his words! His real life is led in his head, and is known to none but himself. . . . His *acts* and his *words* are merely the visible thin crust of his world . . . and they are so trifling a part of his bulk! a mere skin enveloping it. The mass of him is hidden — it and its volcanic fires that toss and boil, and never rest, night nor day. *These are his life,* and they are not written, and cannot be written. . . . Biographies are but the clothes and buttons of the man — the biography of the man himself cannot be written." There is very little real feeling here and no volcanic fires until you come upon the account of the death of his daughter Susy, twenty-four, in Hartford, of meningitis, August 18, 1896.

It is agony to read. Susy took ill and was

taken to the house in Hartford, the home of her childhood, where she once wrote, "We are a very happy family. We consist of Papa, Mamma, Jean, Clara, and me." Her mother and Clara set sail from England to be with her. Her sister Jean and an aunt and uncle and some servants and the minister Joseph Twichell were at the bedside. Meningitis set in on the fifteenth. She ate her last supper that evening. The next morning, a high fever and delirium. She mistook a gown hanging in the closet for her mother and clutched it, kissed it, and wept. She went blind. She stroked the face of Katy Leary, the house-maid, and said her last word, "Mamma."

The father writes: "How gracious it was that in that forlorn hour of wreck and ruin, with the night of death closing around her, she should have been granted that beautiful illusion . . . and the latest emotion she should know in life the joy and peace of that dear imagined presence." Susy was unconscious for two days and died on a Tuesday at 7 p.m. — "she that had been our wonder and our worship." Sam was in England when he got the cablegram August 18 that said: "Susy was peacefully released today." ("It is one of the mysteries of our nature that a man, all unprepared, can receive a thunderstroke like that and live. . . . The intellect is stunned by the shock and but gropingly gathers the meaning of the words. . . . It will be years before . . . he truly knows the magnitude of his disaster.")

Of all the cruel deaths in the book (the death of Sam's father just at the time when prosperity seemed to be in his grasp; the death of his younger brother Henry when a boiler burst on a steamboat in 1858 — Henry, who had taken a job on the boat at Sam's urging; the death of the infant son Langdon Clemens, for which Sam felt responsible), the death of the beloved daughter far beyond her father's love and care is a tragedy from which there is no recovery. Boyishness cannot prevail, nor irreverence. The story can't be written. The man buttons up his clothes and resigns himself to the inexpressible.

6.
WHAT A LUXURY

A poem rejected by every serious journal I submitted it to, from *The New Yorker* on down, and yet it has given pleasure to thousands of people who heard me recite it, including women who don't want to be seen taking an interest in a poem about urination. Of course they don't. Nobody does. And so Allen Ginsberg didn't go there in his poem about the best minds of his generation destroyed by madness. People don't mind hearing about heroin addiction, but pissing is beneath them. T. S. Eliot did not have Prufrock pee, though it certainly would've added some life to the poem. I do wonder if Frost's man who stopped by the woods on that snowy evening wasn't relieving himself. Anyway, this verse of mine, which was scorned by the Bigs, has made a lot of people laugh hard, which is more than you can say for "The Waste Land," and it's the image of men standing in the dark and peeing at the stars that convulses them.

Humor is singular and pathos is generic.

O what a luxury it be
What pleasure O what perfect bliss
So ordinary and yet chic
To pee to piss to take a leak

To feel your bladder just go free
And open like the Mighty Miss
And all your cares go down the creek
To pee to piss to take a leak

For gentlemen of great physique
Who can hold water for one week
For ladies who one quarter-cup
Of tea can fill completely up
For folks in urinalysis
For little kids just learning this
For Viennese or Swiss or Greek
For everyone it's pretty great
To urinate.

Women are quite circumspect
But men can piss with great effect
With terrible hydraulic force
Can make a stream or change its course
Can put out fires or cigarettes
And sometimes, laying down our bets,
Late at night outside the bars
We like to aim up at the stars.

O yes for men it's much more grand
Women sit or squat
We stand
And hold the fellow in our hand
And proudly watch the golden arc
Adjust the range and make our mark
On stones and posts for rival men
To smell and not come back again.

7.
MY LIFE IN PRISON

After a broadcast of *A Prairie Home Companion,* middle-aged men and women come around backstage and say, "I've listened to your stories since I was a child and my favorite one of all is your Tomato Butt story." This is a humbling moment since Tomato Butt is far from my best story, but what can I say? *Never insult someone who has just complimented you.* My sister who appears in the story says that it didn't happen the way I tell it and she is right. Here is the correct version.

It was an enormous tomato, as big as a grapefruit, and it was in October and the tomato had been hit by a hard frost and turned brownish and was liquidy. It was resting on the ground just south of our pumpkin patch, where my sister was searching for a perfect pumpkin for her Halloween party. I slipped my hand under the tomato and scooped it up and observed little white life-forms swimming around very rapidly in figure eights, and I sensed an urgent desire to survive though they did know they were going to die. This is knowledge that even primitive life-forms carry in their cells, but who are we to call them primitive? We who wage war on others who've done us no harm. You and I possess the foreknowledge of doom in our brain stems and so do the paramecium and bacillus. I put my cheek against the tomato to offer them warmth and could feel them pushing against the wall, the inmates of the tomato, occupants of the tomato planet, meanwhile my sister was busy preparing for the Halloween party, which she would attend dressed as a queen and I as a bum. I did not mind. When I put on tattered clothes and blacked my face with burnt cork, I felt fulfilled in a way.

So there I was with the tomato nation against my cheek, its citizens silently crying out against the apocalypse, and I thought, How do we know they don't possess a language, a culture, literature, a religion of their own? And if they do have a religion, then I must be their god. I hummed to the tomato. I thought the vibration might be something they could relate to. My sister turned around and yelled at me to put it down. She was practicing to be somebody's mother, I suppose. I held the tomato close to me. I was the last comfort to a culture that was coming to an end and they were racing around, putting their affairs in order, knowing the end was near — it was so sad. I sang to them,

Abide with me, fast falls the eventide.
This world is rotten, Lord with me abide.

She stood, hands on her hips, and said, "Put the tomato down. Do you hear me?" I gave her a look that I knew really really irritated her, my patented moronic stare, eyes blank, mouth open, a thin trickle of drool running out of the corner. It drove her nuts. She told me I was disgusting. Well, I knew that. That was the point, wasn't it. I was an idiot singing a hymn to a rotten tomato. It doesn't get better than that. She said, "You make me so mad, I could cry," and she cried and she bent over to pick up a perfect pumpkin and there was her big butt in front of me and I threw the tomato at her. It felt like it was meant to be, that the larvae not suffer but go out with a splash. The reddish brown planet flew through the air, rotating slowly clockwise, and I took off running as fast as I could go — I heard the splat, and the screech — and I ducked under the clothesline with her in hot pursuit yelling, "I am going to wring your neck" — which is not a Christian thing to say — and I dashed through a pile of dead leaves and she caught up with me there and latched on to my shoulder, like a lioness bringing down an eland in a *National Geographic* special, and I fell and as I did my mother cried out my sister's name. My sister took her hand off me, but slowly. And she leaned down and said I would be very sorry for what I had done. She said I would go to prison for the rest of my life.

I thought no more of it until thirty years later, after I'd become a big success, I read an interview in *Inside Radio*.

"He is not the easygoing laidback character he is on the radio," said a woman who is close to Keillor. "He has been known to throw things. People are afraid to talk, otherwise there'd be a lot more that'd come out that you wouldn't believe."

I read that story and realized why PR people send out gallons of Johnnie Walker at Christmas and serve prime-rib sandwiches in hospitality suites and walk up to the sleaziest writer in the room and lay an arm across his shoulders and murmur, "You remind me of that line from William Butler Yeats, 'Nor law, nor duty bade me fight, /

Nor public men, nor cheering crowds, A lonely impulse of delight / Drove to this tumult in the clouds.' Can I get you a scotch?"

The reporter, a man with watery eyes and forty pounds of old cheeseburgers around his waist, blushes and stares down at his Hush Puppies, and for the next twenty years you will have no problem with him at all. He will go chase the university president (TAX MONEY LAVISHED ON EXECUTIVE SUITE WHILE THE DYING LIE IN DIM ALCOVES AT U HOSPITAL) or snipe at the archbishop (PRELATE FAILS TO ATTEND CRIPPLES' DINNER FOR THIRD YEAR IN ROW) or haul off and slug the mayor (POLITICIAN DENIES PERSISTENT RUMORS OF PET MOLESTING), and he will write lovely stuff about you:

> Everyone in this town knows Garrison Keillor as a wonderful entertainer and devoted father, but I wonder how many of us are aware of those dozens of little unsung deeds he does for the poor and unfortunate every week.

I don't have a PR guy, but once I did hire someone named Milo to attend rehearsals and yell "All *right*!" at the end of every song

I sang. I was sensitive about my voice and needed affirmation in order to do my best. He yelled, "All *right*! Far out! *Whooo!* You sang that one, all right!"

One thing a PR guy can't do is resolve your own guilt, and there I was, riding around in limos and residing in a mansion and brooding about that big tomato and the damage it did to my sister, who could never eat tomatoes after that or tomato sauce or even V-8 juice, and thinking about the curse she had put on me. Prison. Steel doors clanging shut. The squeaking of rats and water dripping in the dank sewers below. Prison. Well deserved in my case. My sister has never eaten pizza, never had a BLT.

You would think the Statute of Limitations would have run out on the tomato assault, a juvenile crime, but what they came up with was Conspiracy to Evade Detection. After a show once, a man walked up to me and said, "Is that tomato butt story on the level?" and I, not knowing he was an undercover police officer, said yes. This was in New York. I guess it was a slow day for the NYPD. It was at Carnegie Hall, where I'd done a benefit concert for an audience of elderly nuns who were enjoying the show as they wove simple cotton garments for the poor on tiny hand looms, and the cops hauled me off to the precinct station. "Tell us about the tomato," they said. "How big was it? Why did you throw it at your sister?"

If only I had told the truth. But I lied over and over. I denied that it had hit her. I said that it slipped out of my hand. I said it was small.

"Deny everything and make them prove it," said the lawyer my family hired, a skinny guy with dandruff whose degree is from Texas A&M and who mainly does real estate law. So I did. I told 512 separate and distinct lies and the judge gave me a year in the pen for each one. My lawyer said to give up my right to a jury trial. "You look guilty as can be. Furtive. Sweaty." So I threw myself on the mercy of the court and got 512 years in prison.

They drive me to LaGuardia for a flight to Minneapolis. I preboard on a conveyor belt that carries me into a special section for miscreants in the rear, where trusties prod us with sharp sticks to make us squeeze in tight on the steel floor of the aircraft. There are a dozen of us, and one guy builds a campfire on the floor and we cook chunks of chicken on clothes hangers, hunkered around the fire, smoking, not talking. What's

581

there to say? We're going to prison and we know it. The plane bucks and the fire flickers. Through the tiny window appear the lights of Minneapolis, a big city where I attended church regularly and tried to be a good citizen, but it's too late to think about that now, or about the neat book reports that received gold stars, the bowline hitch I tied that was shown to other Scouts as a model of how that knot looks when it is perfect — they are immaterial evidence now that I am prison-bound.

The press waits at the gate, a blaze of lights, a thicket of microphones, and my sister — they are interviewing her. She says that she feels no bitterness at all. Her husband, Buck, is smiling. He always thought I thought I had a superior attitude, so this is a sweet moment and he has brought his video camera. "We'll always love you," my sister says. "We'll do everything we can." One thing she did the day after the big tomato was bang me on the head with a cast-iron skillet as I knelt pouring water into the cat's dish. I could see the Milky Way shining between the bright blue veins in my eyeballs. She yelled, "It was an accident — it slipped when I was putting it away!" and my mother accepted that story even though the skillets were kept in a drawer under the stove, which was in the other direction.

And then we get into buses for the long ride to Sandstone Prison. The walls of my cell are beige with green trim, similar to my old high school, and it smells of the same disinfectant. The bed is not unlike what we had at YMCA camp, where I hid in the woods to avoid swim class. The army blankets are like old friends, my dad having bought all our bedding from surplus stores. The food is the same as what I ate for years, fish sticks and string beans and Jell-O, and every morning the guard, Rich, who was in Sunday school class with me, stops at my door and says, "So how's everything this morning, then?" "Oh, about the same, then," I say. "They treatin' you okay, then?" They're treating me fair and square. I was the guy who threw the tomato. I am only sorry that kids who heard me tell that story on the radio may be tempted to make the same mistake I did and wind up in the slammer. Though it's not so bad. That's the honest truth. My sister came to visit the other day and asked how I am doing and I could see she was devastated when I told her, "I'm doing great. I'm a lucky guy. Some of us are happier incarcerated than we would be if loose and free. I had my good times, sang my song, did my dance, and now it's like

I'm thirteen again and back home." She was hoping I'd burst into tears and apologize for that tomato, but that is one thing I am not going to do, believe me. I have no regrets.

8.
DROWNING 1954

The death of my cousin Roger was a dark episode in my childhood and not because I knew him so well but because I heard such horrible grief in my mother's voice when she took the call. She was standing in the upstairs hall of our house and picked up the phone on the second ring and a half-minute later said, "Oh no," in a tone I'd never heard before. Roger was Aunt Margaret's youngest, seventeen years old, and it had been only fifteen years since Margaret's husband had run off and never come back, leaving her to a straitened life, and then came this even harder blow. Roger was a sweet-tempered kid, something of a comic, and was graduating from high school when he went out on Lake Minnetonka with his girlfriend. I met the girlfriend on a flight to New York fifty-some years later and wanted to ask her about Roger and she didn't want to talk about him. "Drowning 1954" is all true but it would be even truer if she could be here in it somehow.

When I was twelve, my cousin Roger drowned in Lake Independence, and my mother enrolled me in a swimming class at the YMCA on La Salle Avenue in downtown Minneapolis. Twice a week for most of June and July, I got on the West River Road bus near our home in Brooklyn Park Township, a truck-farming community north of Minneapolis, and rode into the stink and heat of the city. When we rounded the corner of Ninth Street and La Salle and smelled the chlorine air that the building breathed out, I started to feel afraid. After a week, I couldn't bear to go to swimming class anymore.

Never before had I stood naked among strangers (the rule in the class was no swimming trunks), and it was loathsome to undress and then walk quickly through the cold showers to the pool and sit shivering with my feet dangling in the water (Absolute Silence, No Splashing) and wait for the dread moment. The instructor — a man in his early twenties, who was tanned and had the smooth muscles of a swimmer (he wore trunks) — had us plunge into the pool one at a time, so that he could give us his personal attention. He strode up and down

586

the side of the pool yelling at those of us who couldn't swim, while we thrashed hopelessly beneath him and tried to *look* like swimmers. "You're walking on the bottom!" he would shout. "Get your legs up! What's the matter, you afraid to get your face wet? What's *wrong* with you?" The truth was that my cousin's death had instilled in me a terrible fear, and when I tried to swim and started to sink it felt not so much as if I was sinking but as if something were pulling me down. I panicked, every time. It was just like the dreams of drowning that came to me right after Roger died, in which I was dragged deeper and deeper, with my body bursting and my arms and legs flailing against nothing, down and down, until I shot back to the surface and lay in my dark bedroom exhausted, trying to make myself stay awake.

I tried to quit the swimming class, but my mother wouldn't hear of it, so I continued to board the bus every swimming morning, and then, ashamed of myself and knowing God would punish me for my cowardice and deceit, I hurried across La Salle and past the Y and walked along Hennepin Avenue, past the pinball parlors and bars and shoeshine stands to the old public library, where I viewed the Egyptian mummy and the fossils and a facsimile of the Declaration of Independence. I stayed there until 11:30, when I headed straight for the WCCO radio studio to watch *Good Neighbor Time.*

We listened regularly to this show at home — Bob DeHaven, with Wally Olson and His Band, and Ernie Garvin and Burt Hanson and Jeanne Arland — and then to the noontime news, with Cedric Adams, the most famous man in the upper Midwest. It amazed me to sit in the studio audience and watch the little band crowded around the back wall, the engineers in the darkened booth, and the show people gliding up to a microphone for a song, a few words, or an Oxydol commercial. I loved everything except the part of the show in which Bob DeHaven interviewed people in the audience. I was afraid he might pick me, and then my mother, and probably half of Minnesota, would find out that I was scared of water and a liar to boot. The radio stars dazzled me. One day, I squeezed into the WCCO elevator with Cedric Adams and five or six other people. I stood next to him, and a sweet smell of greatness and wealth drifted off him. I later imagined Cedric Adams swimming in Lake Minnetonka — a powerful whale of happiness and purpose

— and I wished that I were like him and the others, but as the weeks wore on I began to see clearly that I was more closely related to the bums and winos and old men who sat around in the library and wandered up and down Hennepin Avenue. I tried to look away and not see them, but they were all around me there, and almost every day some poor ragged creature, filthy drunk at noon, would stagger at me wildly out of a doorway, with his arms stretched out toward me, and I saw a look of fellowship in his eyes: *You are one of us.*

I ran from them, but clearly I was well on my way. Drinking and all the rest of the bum's life would come with time, inevitably. My life was set on its tragic course by a sinful error in youth. This was the dark theme of the fundamentalist Christian tracts in our home: one misstep would lead you down into the life of the infidel.

One misstep! A lie, perhaps, or disobedience to your mother. There were countless young men in those tracts who stumbled and fell from the path — *one misstep!* — and were dragged down like drowning men into debauchery, unbelief, and utter damnation. I felt sure that my lie, which was repeated twice a week and whenever my mother asked about my swimming, was sufficient for my downfall. Even as I worked at the deception, I marveled that my fear of water should be greater than my fear of Hell.

I still remember the sadness of wandering in downtown Minneapolis in 1954, wasting my life and losing my soul, and my great relief when the class term ended and I became a kid again around the big white house and garden, the green lawns and cool shady ravine of our lovely suburb. A week-end came when we went to a lake for a family picnic, and my mother, sitting on the beach, asked me to swim for her, but I was able to fool her, even at that little distance, by walking on the bottom and making arm strokes.

When I went to a lake with my friends that summer, or to the Mississippi River a block away, I tried to get the knack of swimming, and one afternoon the next summer I did get it — the crawl and the backstroke and the sidestroke, all in just a couple of weeks. I dived from a dock and opened my eyes underwater and everything. The sad part was that my mother and father couldn't appreciate this wonderful success; to them, I had been a swimmer all along. I felt restored — grateful that I would not be a bum all my life, grateful to God for letting me learn to swim. It was so quick and so simple that I can't remember it today. Probably I just stood in the water and took a little plunge; my feet left the bottom, and that was it.

When my boy was seven, he showed some timidity around water. Every time I saw him standing in the shallows, working up nerve to put his head under, I loved him more. His eyes are closed tight, and his pale slender body is tense as a drawn bow, ready to spring up instantly should he start to drown. Then I feel it all over again, the way I used to feel. I also feel it when I see people like the imperial swimming instructor at the YMCA — powerful people who delight in towering over some little twerp who is struggling and scared, and casting the terrible shadow of their just and perfect selves. The Big Snapper knows who you are, you bastards, and in a little while he is going to come after you with a fury you will not believe and grab you in his giant mouth and pull you under until your brain turns to jelly and your heart almost bursts. You will never recover from this terror. You will relive it every day, as you lose your fine job and your home and the respect of your friends and family. You will remember it every night in your little room at the Mission, and you will need a quart of Petri muscatel to put you to sleep, and when you awake between your yellow-stained sheets your hands will start to shake all over again.

You have fifteen minutes. Get changed.

9.

COLLEGE DAYS

The night before classes started in September 1960, my freshman year at the U of M, I took a Greyhound bus up to Isle, Minnesota, to pick up a car at my uncle's Ford agency, and as I rode along, reading a book, there was a burst of light up front and a big jolt that threw me to my feet and then the bus careened into the ditch and onto an open field and stopped. Some of us passengers herded up the aisle — the driver sat, in shock, but opened the door — and we walked out into a cool fall night, stars overhead, and on the highway, a long line of headlights stopped. A station wagon full of people had collided head-on with the bus and as we walked along the shoulder of the road we saw three bodies sprawled on the pavement and one in the wreck. I made it back to campus for my Latin class at 8:00 a.m. and then political science and composition and walked around all day with the burden of that experience that I wanted to tell somebody but couldn't. It felt like the beginning of real adult life.

College is a time when you can be gloriously ridiculously full of yourself and get away with it, a luxury once reserved for the aristocracy but, in America, extended to the child of a carpenter and postal worker, namely me. I was a middle-class kid from the West River Road, where late at night fireflies sparkled in the field behind the dark houses and I sat on our rich green lawn and stared at the blinking red light on a distant water tower and tried to imagine a larger life though it seemed presumptuous, and that fall I found it, ten miles south of us, at the University of Minnesota. I had been a B student at Anoka High School but I was encouraged by some tireless encouragers, my teachers Helen Story, Lois Melby, Helen Fleischman, Katherine Hattendorf, children of the Depression who grew up in farm families and for them teaching was a shining ideal and also the path out of a hard life they knew too well, the life of serfs. Miss Hattendorf grew up on a farm in Iowa; her German parents sent her and her sisters to board with a family in town so they could attend high school. When she was about to leave for the University of Chicago and it came time to say goodbye and get in the car and go to the train, she looked at her mother standing at the kitchen sink — "I wanted to hug her, but I couldn't do it. She was a stranger to me. They wanted me and my sisters to get a good education and they made big sacrifices and that was one of them: they didn't know us anymore and we didn't know them." She was sure I could be a writer, and to show her faith in me, she paid me $20 to write her obituary, though she was in pretty good health.

I secretly imagined getting published in *The New Yorker,* though of course I couldn't tell anybody that. I had imagined it since junior high school. I still have the first copy I bought, 35 cents, with E. B. White in it, John Cheever, and A. J. Liebling, my hero. A. J. Liebling knocked me out, and he still does. He used to sit up in his office at the magazine and look down Forty-third and see the Hotel Dixie and the Paramount Building, home of the Paramount Theater. To the Paramount, he had gone as a young reporter to interview the Hollywood femme fatale Pola Negri, with whom he had fallen in love when he saw her in a German silent film, *Passion,* in Hanover, New Hampshire, when he was about to be kicked out of Dartmouth for cutting chapel. Liebling interviewed her as she lay in a white peignoir on a white chaise longue like a crumpled gardenia petal and said, of Rudolph Valentino, "He was the only man I evair luffed. But I am fated always to be unhappy in luff. Because I expect so mawch." And the Hotel Dixie was the home of Liebling's friend Colonel John R. Stingo, the horse-racing columnist for the *National Enquirer.* Colonel Stingo said, "I sit up there in my room at the Dixie, working away on my column. I finish, and it is perhaps one o'clock. Up there in my retreat, I feel the city calling to me. It winks at me with its myriad eyes, and I go out and get stiff as a board. I seek out companionship, and if I do not find friends, I make them. A wonderful, grand old Babylon."

That summer after high school, I worked as a dishwasher at the Evangeline Hotel for Women in downtown Minneapolis, a skinny kid with glasses in a white apron, lugging the racks of steaming hot plates off the conveyer, chipping the black crusts of food off the bottoms of the cooking pots. Dishwashing can bring out the romantic in a man. On a hot summer day, you come out of the steam and heat of the scullery and the beauty of the world overwhelms you and you feel cool and comfortable for the rest of the day. I walked onto campus for the first day of classes and strolled up the mall to Northrop Auditorium and gazed up at its great pillars and the Jeffersonian inscription on the facade above, *founded in the faith that men are ennobled by understanding, dedicated to the advancement of learning and the search for truth, devoted to the instruction of youth and the welfare of the state.* Along the mall, a stately parade of utilitarian brick buildings with pillars pasted to their fronts overlooked a river of youth flowing under the canopy of majestic elms. Lost freshmen lolled on the steps studying campus maps and planning their route from one class to the next. Africans with skin blacker than I'd ever seen before were speaking with British accents like John Gielgud's; others, beautiful French (I turned and followed them, eavesdropping, so astonishing this was to hear). Bearded Sikhs in turbans, women in saris with red dots painted on their foreheads, Korean War vets in fatigues and GI sunglasses, old bearded lefties in turtlenecks clutching their *I. F. Stone's Weekly* and *The Realist,* cigarette-smoking women playing the role of beat princess or troubled intellect or Audrey Hepburn heroine, cool people who might possibly have been poets, anxious bookish people en route to serious encounters with history and literature — ambition was everywhere you looked, electrical currents jazzing the air.

I walked over to Dinkytown to buy my books at Perrine's, down the street from Al's Breakfast Nook, near Vescio's Italian restaurant and a rats' nest of a bookstore called Heddon's whose snowy-haired proprietor, after pondering a moment, could reach into the third orange crate from the bottom and pull out the very book you asked for, and Virg 'n' Don's Grocery and a coin laundry called the Tub, and McCosh's Bookstore with the sweet-faced bearded anarchist and bibliomaniac McCosh, Gray's Drugstore lunch counter (a grilled cheese sandwich, chili, and a vanilla shake, please) and a fine little coffeehouse called the Ten O'Clock Scholar, where a beaky kid with brushy hair played a battered guitar and sang "O Fair and Tender Ladies" and *It's dark as a dungeon and damp as the dew, / Where the dangers are many and the pleasures are few.* The stage was in front, before the big double plateglass window, and sometimes a passerby stopped on the sidewalk, peered in the window, into the dark room, and then realized he was part of a show and fled.

I walked over to Folwell Hall, home of the English Department and the divine Miss

Sarah Youngblood and craggy old Huntington Brown and Samuel Monk, the eighteenth-century man. To be here with Toni McNaron, who propounded Milton, and Archibald Leyasmeyer, the Chaucerian, and other noble and learned friends of literature made me feel grateful that this institution had opened its doors to a dreamer like me who had no clear vocation whatsoever. I was operating on a wistful urge to sit in libraries and be a writer and that was all.

I paid $71 for a quarter's tuition and another $10 or so for my books: a political science text, a volume of Horace and a Latin dictionary, and Strunk and White's *Elements of Style* for my composition course, and notebooks with the university seal on the cover (*Omnibus Artibus, Commune Vinculum*). Then I took a seat in the long reading room in Walter Library among men and women bent to the hard work of scholarship, folks for whom attending college was not an assumed privilege. The vets on the GI Bill and the African and Asian exchange students and the ones who were the first in their family to attend college, whose parents' own hopes had been deferred by the Depression and the War — these students approached the U with a great chins-up pencils-sharpened sense of purpose. They sat at the long oak library tables, heads bowed, rows and rows of them, reading, reading, reading — sons of garage mechanics on their way to medical school, daughters of dairy farmers who would march on to distinction developing polymers — a great American migration as inspiring as anything that took place on the Oregon Trail. These pioneers craved a life in which beauty and delight and intellectual challenge are staples; they wanted to travel to far-flung places, read novels, go to the theater, be smart about the world and not reflexively pessimistic like their parents. The craving for experience was powerful. Love and adventure and interesting work — a great many of us, fearing the regimentation of corporate life, would head for the burgeoning nonprofit world. Such a purposeful bunch — who looked like me, were dressed like me, and like me had very little money — who plowed through the texts and took notes and shushed up the goofballs in their midst. Boys and girls who came to the library to sit and giggle were glared at and told to be still — this never happened in high school! These were people with a sense of vocation. It was a Thomas Hart Benton mural come to life — *The Children of the*

Great Plains Claiming Their Birthright at Last.
Their once-in-a-lifetime chance to realize
their God-given talent, as scholars of medi-
eval painting or operas or the breeding ritu-
als of the Arctic ptarmigan. No guarantee
of success, or even of gainful employment.
Pure free enterprise.

The University was a monument to the Jeffersonian faith in the power of learning and
in the ability of all people to recognize and
embrace excellence, a grand old American
notion. To offer Jussi Bjoerling and Arthur
Rubinstein to eighteen-year-old kids at
prices they can afford is an astonishment.
Utterly. To witness such grandeur can
change a person's life. But that was the
spirit of the Morrill Act of 1862 that granted
to the states a tract of land in proportion to
their population for the endowment of a
state university to teach the classic cur-
riculum as well as courses relating to agriculture and industry, open to qualified
students regardless of financial means.
   My Latin teacher, Margaret Forbes, was
an auntly woman, cheery and kind, who ran
us through daily translations and sniped at
us with questions about the anticipatory
subjunctive, *Expectabum dum frater redirect*
(I was waiting for my brother to return),

and we responded to her *aequo animo* —
without anxiety — as she lay open the
folded language — *patefacio, patefacere,
patefeci, patefactum, O pace in perpetuum,
Margareta, felicitas aeternas!* Richard Cody
taught composition, a slender Englishman
sitting at a table on a raised platform, lectur-
ing drily on the art of the essay, which he
described as a 440-yard dash through
natural obstacles, over rough terrain, an
intellectual exercise also meant to be estheti-
cally elegant. We were Minnesota kids striv-
ing to imitate William Hazlitt, Joseph Addison, George Orwell, E. B. White, and
Norman Mailer. Once Mr. Cody called on
me to come forward and read the first page
of my essay on manure spreading, one of
my jobs on Uncle Jim's farm — a humorous essay, supposedly — and I jumped up
to do it and fainted dead away across a row
of empty chairs and crashed to the floor.
"Are you all right?" a girl asked under her
breath. I got up and Mr. Cody called on
someone else. Asher Christiansen taught
American government, an elegant little man
in dark slacks and a gray blazer, bushy
eyebrows, mustache, smoking his pipe —
half the class smoked too, and I came to as-
sociate intellectual seriousness with bad air
— propounding his grand theme, that the

Constitution was a natural force for civilization, its checks and balances serving to dampen the fires of inner-directed ideologues and bring them into a respectful relationship to their antagonists and attend to the serious business of government. After class, some students formed another, smaller class that followed Professor Christiansen out the door and stood in the alley behind Nicholson Hall for a few minutes, a gaggle of fifteen or twenty that dwindled as he headed down the Mall to his office in Ford Hall, arriving there with four or five of us still hanging on. I was a student in the last class he taught. In January I saw the front-page story in the *Daily:* Professor Christiansen had felt ill during lunch at the faculty club and went to a quiet room to lie down and died there of a heart attack. The story said he grew up in Little Falls, graduated from the U, where he taught from 1936 on, with guest stints in Wales, Germany, and Argentina, where he lectured in Spanish. He was fifty-seven years old, married, no children. Just us students.

Dad had made it clear that he couldn't contribute to pay for my education, which I hadn't asked him to, and I was relieved not to have to consider an offer. A nice clean

603

break. I got a job working the 6:00 to 10:00 a.m. shift in the big parking lot on the river flats for $1.48 an hour. Nine hundred cars, and it filled up by 7:30, so there you were with a couple hours of paid study time. You learned to ignore your fellow attendant who liked to tell about students he had seen having sex in parked cars and you applied yourself to the U.S. Constitution and the separation of powers.

I got a job at the student radio station, WMMR, in October and a tall good-looking guy named Barry Halper taught me how to piece together a newscast from the Associated Press teletype. They needed someone to do the 12:15. "Today?" I said. "Today," he said. He showed me how to switch on the microphone, read the VU meter, adjust the headphone volume, flip the cough switch, and an hour later I sat down in a tiny room with green acoustic-tile walls at a table covered with green felt and switched on the mike and a red bulb lit up and I read the news under a gooseneck lamp, one eye on the big clock on the wall in front of my face. I was nervous, of course, but it was a delicious nervousness. It felt safe being sequestered in the studio, a little fortress. I did the newscast and said, "That's the news, reported by Garrison Keillor. This is

604

WMMR, from studios in Coffman Memorial Union, broadcasting at 730 kilocycles," then pressed a PLAY button and the tape deck clunked and a recorded voice talked about Campus Pizza. I got up and the next announcer slipped in and played something by Johnny Mathis and I walked out to the hall and Barry Halper nodded at me. "That was not bad," he said.

An egalitarian spirit prevailed at the U that truly was noble. There was no rank, no hazing, no freshman beanies, we were all in the same boat. You were Mr. Keillor to your professor and he was Mr. Brown to you. You looked him in the eye. You said, "I don't get this," and he explained it to you. That was his job. Yours was to pay attention. Money was no social asset whatsoever and if you went around in expensive clothes you were regarded with pity or scorn. A few goofball freshmen showed up in brand-new suits for fall classes and they stood out in the crowd as if they wore red rubber noses and fright wigs. Everybody from the president to the deans and the faculty had their home addresses and phone numbers listed in the University directory, and if you were brave enough, you could ring up Dean McDiarmid or Vice President Willey and tell him your troubles. I did not but the phone numbers were there and I suppose somebody did. On my slender parking lot wages I was able to buy a season ticket to the concerts in Northrup and I saw Isaac Stern, Arthur Rubinstein, Andrés Segovia, the Royal Danish Ballet doing a Balanchine program, the great Swedish tenor Jussi Bjoerling, the Cleveland Orchestra, Glenn Gould — you could get a balcony seat for $1.50, about an hour's wage. I couldn't afford to see the Metropolitan Opera on their annual tour but one evening I did look up at a window on the side of Northrup and see a tall slender dark-haired woman standing naked in front of a full-length mirror for a whole minute, studying herself. A wardrobe lady sat nearby, smoking, reading a newspaper. The dark-haired woman turned, facing me, her hands on hips, one leg extended, looking over her shoulder at her rump, her delicate bush and maroon nipples, like a painting.

Robert Frost came to campus soon after Kennedy's speech and drew a capacity crowd, the great stooped white-maned old bear reciting by heart "Stopping by Woods on a Snowy Evening" and the crowd hushed in the cathedral of poetry — "For Once, Then, Something" and "The Oven Bird" and "Fire and Ice" and the one about the lover's quarrel with the world — that soft cranky-uncle voice beloved since junior high, a godlike presence in our midst, and afterward a hundred of us gathered at the back door to view the great man up close. He eased his old body down the stairs, our grand paterfamilias, and mingled with us, chatted, answered a few questions and then he climbed into a black Chrysler and was taken off to lunch with the faculty. But we students were as important as anybody else and weren't held behind ropes or shushed. That was how it was at the U. The field was wide open. At the Minnesota *Daily* and its literary arm, *The Ivory Tower,* you submitted your stuff and back came a polite note, "Sorry," and that week they printed George Amabile's poems instead of yours, but you sent more and of that second batch the editor accepted two and the next month they appeared, big glutinous symbolist things about owls on moonless nights flying to Arabia, all in lowercase, and you snatched ten copies out of a paper box and took them home to save to show your grandchildren you once were a writer. The publications weren't in the grip of a gang, they were open to walk-ons.

I hung around the *Daily* offices, free of the

607

petty miseries of high school, that small fixed universe. The University was freedom. A friend of mine dropped out sophomore year and married his girlfriend and they bought a little yellow rambler in Coon Rapids, the down payment a gift from her parents. He was a warehouse clerk and his wife got pregnant and woke up in a foul mood every morning and he went off to eight hours of an automaton job. I longed for my flesh to touch someone else's flesh but I remained chaste. Women, I knew, would put their arms around you and cry that they loved you and wanted to make you happy and bwanngggg a trapdoor would pop open and you'd drop down the chute into a job you despised and a frazzled marriage in a crackerjack house with a mortgage as big as Montana — I intended to escape that. I sat in clouds of cigarette smoke in a classroom smelling of linseed-oiled floors and listened to James Wright lecture on Dickens and gazed at the lovely girls in horn-rim glasses. I liked strolling around campus at night with Gail, who wrote for the paper, or my classmate Mary. With my arm around her waist and my little finger hooked in her belt loop and she with her arm around the back of me, we talked about Chaucer, Shakespeare, Eliot, arms riding across each other's butts, our hips moving in meter, which, we two being different heights, came out in 9/7 time, like an old Swedish step dance, and I would maybe recite Housman's poem about being twenty — "And take from seventy springs a score, / It only leaves me fifty more. / And since to look at things in bloom / Fifty springs are little room, / About the woodlands I will go / To see the cherry hung with snow" — and wind up back at Murphy Hall and the *Daily* office.

For winter quarter, I got the 5:00 a.m. shift at a ten-acre gravel parking lot on the West Bank, overlooking the Mississippi. I was turning into a night owl, always up past midnight, and the alarm clock went off at 4:00 and I lay in the warm trench of my bed, reviewing my options, preferring sleep, longed for it, nodded off, which shocked me into wakefulness and I rolled out and drove to town through the snowy world and parked beside the parking lot shack and hiked to the far end of the lot, flashlight in hand, like a sheep shearer waiting for the herd to come piling through the gate. The lot sloped down to the edge of the bluff and I looked down on Bohemian Flats, a ragtag village on the riverbank. In their frame houses that got flooded out every spring, old Swedes and Bohunks lived a subsistence life in the middle of the Twin Cities. Smoke rose from their chimneys. One of the other parking attendants said there was a whorehouse down there. "Ten bucks a shot," he said. "Indian women." The cars came in a rush, starting at 6:30. Three ticket sellers stood in the street, and the flagman stood at the top of the lot and directed the flow to where I was conducting them into their spots, straight lines, double rows. No painted lines on the gravel, I did it all by eye.

The Leonard Bernstein of the automobile, I directed each car with strong hand signals into its correct space and discouraged the tendency to freelance and veer off toward a more convenient place. Every morning there were three or four pioneers who wanted to start their own rows. You had to yell to the flagman to hold the traffic and then you ran over toward the miscreant's car and yelled, "Your car will be towed in ten minutes." The mention of towing got their attention, but you had to make it sound real. "That's a twenty-five-dollar fine." Usually that was enough to get them to move the car. If they hesitated, I said, "Plus twenty-five for the impound lot. It's up to you." I had no idea

610

who to call to come tow a car or what they would say — I just did what other attendants said to do, and it worked. Creative parking couldn't be allowed, chaos would result, cars skewed everywhere, blocking other cars, holding up traffic, people late, angry, honking — it was my responsibility to make the grid system work. For the common good. To be direct. Exercise authority. *No, sir. Not there. Over here. Right here. Yes. Here.* Your individualists and comedians would test the limits and if you gave them an inch, anarchy would ensue, cars going every which way like confused buffalo. Be firm. Make that bozo back up six inches. Straighten that line. Thank you. If you accept that variance, the line will buckle. If you do your job right, the lot fills to capacity in half an hour, you put up the full sign and huddle in the shack, the electric heater blazing away, and you take up with Natasha and Prince Andrei for Mr. Milgrom's humanities class until 9:00 a.m., when the shift ends and you leg it over the Washington Avenue bridge to the East Bank. A cup of vending machine coffee and a cheese danish and off to class.

In the winter, we packed into Williams Arena to cheer the hockey team against our deadly rival, the Fighting Sioux of North

Dakota. Blood lust in the air. Our Gophers were all Minnesota boys and the Sioux were all Canucks, paid thugs, big bruisers, mercenaries, and when a Sioux got ridden into the boards, we cheered from the bottom of our hearts. I dated a quiet girl, a church organist, and at hockey games she screeched and booed like a true peasant. I wrote a poem about hockey and took it to a writers' club meeting at Professor Hage's house and the poet James Wright said something encouraging about it and my face burned with pleasure. I can still picture it in my mind, where I was sitting, where he sat, and I still feel my face getting warm.

That spring the Mississippi River rose and there were urgent flood warnings on the radio. One afternoon I put on warm clothes and took the bus to St. Paul and crossed the Wabasha Bridge to the West Side, where people were at work filling sandbags to bolster the dikes to save the low-lying houses. It was foggy, and then it began to rain. An army of hundreds of volunteers hard at work, men and women, drawn up in assembly lines, holding the sacks and filling them and passing them in a chain to the dike. It got dark. Nobody left. The Red Cross brought around sandwiches and coffee. We rested and went back to work. Trucks brought in more sand and bags. A couple of front loaders worked at anchoring the dikes with earthen banks. I worked until after midnight and lay down in the back of a truck under a tarp and slept until daybreak and got up stiff and cold and they brought us more sandwiches and coffee and I got back in the gang and worked until noon. I stayed because everyone else stayed. I sort of collapsed in the afternoon and was going to go home but slept a couple hours on a tarp in somebody's front yard, and when I woke up, there was water in the street, people wading through it, some men with muddy overalls, pitched emotion in the air, though nobody said much. We had put so much into beating back the flood, and we kept working — shovel, fill, tie, and pass, shovel, fill, tie, and pass — and felt privileged to be there doing it. I could hear the river boiling by and slabs of ice heaved up on the dike and National Guardsmen patrolling, and when people couldn't stand up any longer, they sat down and ate baloney sandwiches and drank coffee. And got back up.

I went home in the morning. I sat on the bed and cried. For the relief of getting out of those mud-crusted clothes and standing under a hot shower, but also for what I'd seen, the spirit of all those workers caught up in the job of saving their neighbors' houses. Forget all the jabber and gossip, all the theoretical balderdash and horsefeathers, here is reality: the river rises up in its power and majesty, and the people rise up in theirs, and while one can do only so much, you must do that much, and we did. We saved several blocks of homes. Nobody thanked us. It didn't matter. It was an experience.

I stuck around at WMMR and did the noon newscast for six months, five days a week, and then in May was told that the station had been off the air for at least that long. Doggone it. Our engineer, a brilliant young man, had been busy building a state-of-the-art control room and hadn't had time to do maintenance on the transmitter and it had burned out. I was in some anguish over having spent six months editing a newscast so I could sit in a room and read it to myself, but as Barry Halper said, "It was good experience." Had I ever, in those six months, thought about the listeners and wondered why the cards and letters weren't pouring in, or trickling in, or even dripping in? No. I was having too much fun. "You sound terrific," said Barry. "You could get a job on any station in town." He was a pal and a real positive guy. He was twenty, he drove a big white convertible, he was Jewish and smart, he'd been to L.A. and Las Vegas and met Jack Benny and Shelley Berman. If he'd asked me to, I would've shined his shoes.

I was a serious young man and did not go to parties at the U except one in the spring of my sophomore year at somebody's parents' house in Kenwood, a tony neighborhood in Minneapolis, where a mob of students was drinking something called Purple Death out of a washtub in the kitchen. Fortified with this, people started spouting off their big opinions about Kennedy and Hemingway and Ornette Coleman and some of us got into a contest to see who knew more dirty limericks. The base of Purple Death was grape Kool-Aid, plus whatever the guests had brought. It was a potluck cocktail: Old Buzzard Breath bourbon, crème de banana, licorice schnapps, vodka, anything would do, and after drinking for a while and telling dirty jokes, some of us headed over to Cedar Lake to go skinny-dipping, and we stripped off our clothes, but it wasn't the erotic thrill it should've been, not for me anyway: I could feel the hangover mounting up behind my forehead, a truly monumental one, with shades of surrealism — I remember naked women and I also remember throwing up — and in the morning I awoke with a taste of what mental illness might be like, a sort of vacancy with dark shadows. I was glad to be alone.

As U of M students we walked around with a fine chip on our shoulder toward eastern finishing schools like Yale and Harvard where children of privilege slept until noon after a night of inebriation, were brought cucumber sandwiches by a porter, sashayed off to their 3:00 p.m. music appreciation class, and then played squash until dinner. Oxford and Cambridge were held in even greater contempt: dandruffy men quivering with borrowed sensibility drinking sherry and propounding fabulous foolishness with great certainty. You walk around with a brown bag lunch and a few bucks in your pocket, trying to scrape together next quarter's tuition, and a little class resentment is good for you, a balm and a prod both. I envied cool people, good tennis players, opera singers, sandy-haired rich guys who looked princely even in ratty old clothes, all Frenchmen, men with lovely girlfriends, guitarists, but the U was the antidote to envy. So many cool people seem on closer examination to be trapped in a set of mannerisms that are not so interesting and lead nowhere, whereas the U appealed to your curiosity and drew you into scholarship, which took you through doors you hadn't known existed. In one smoky classroom after another, sitting elbow to elbow at little arm desks, you felt illuminated; there was a quickening almost like drunkenness, a feeling that you and the professor were conspiring in a noble enterprise that would last you to the end of your days. I learned how to plant myself in a library chair and open the books and take notes on a yellow legal pad. Having a good ear for multiple-choice tests had gotten me through high school (the correct answer, two-thirds of the time, was C) but now I needed to actually do the work. I soldiered through and learned how to write profoundly at great speed late at night about books I barely understood.

American universities have seen plenty of radicals and revolutionaries come and go over the years, and all of them put together were not nearly so revolutionary as a land-grant university itself on an ordinary weekday. To give people with little money a chance to get the best education there is —

that is true revolution. When I graduated from Anoka High School, I believed that my chances would be as good as anybody else's, and the good people of Minnesota did not let me down. I got my chance and right there is where a Democrat is made — a kid from Anoka sits in a parking lot shack on Fourth Street SE where, earning $1.48 an hour, he translates Horace for Mrs. Forbes — whose standards are high — as birds sit scritching on the telephone wire and a fly buzzes at the window. A bright fall day and he has no money to speak of and no clear plan for the future but he has teachers who engage him with gravity and fervor and that's enough. That was the true spirit of the University, the spirit of professors who loved their work. That was the heart and soul of the place, not the athletic teams, not the architecture. The University was Mary Malcolm, a native of Worthington, who studied in Paris with Nadia Boulanger and came back to teach music theory for forty-three years. She had perfect pitch and could write down on paper anything you could hum or plunk on the piano. It was Izaak M. Kolthoff, a Dutch chemist who guided Jewish scientists out of Germany in the thirties and worked on the crucial war project of creating synthetic rubber and became a peacenik in the fifties. It was Marcia Edwards, a chain-smoking authority on adolescent psychology and a fanatical Gopher sports fan who went to angelic lengths to help her students, even lending them money, and who turned down the offer to become dean of the College of Education because she didn't want the hassle, especially the foofaraw of being the first woman dean. It was Bill Marchand, who taught Shakespeare to kids majoring in animal husbandry and horticulture. It was Nils Hasselmo, who came from Sweden to study the Swedish emigrants and got his doctorate and became chair of the Scandinavian Languages Department and eventually president of the U. And it was Margaret Forbes, who could make you feel that a few lines of Horace held the key to everything noble. If you start to feel ennobled, you lose interest in how you are perceived by other people. You walk into the library and that Niagara of scholarship holds you in its sway, the deluge and glory of learning, and you begin to see where work and play become one. And imagine working at something you love. That was how the University of Minnesota gave me my life.

10.
MY STROKE (I'M OVER IT)

My neurologist showed me a map of my brain last year, taken by magnetic resonance imaging, and pointed to a dark spot: "That's where your stroke hit." And pointed a couple millimeters away: "And if it had hit there, you would've had significant motor and speech losses." A matter of fact. The blood clot that got fired from the atrium could have landed here or it could've landed there. It landed there, and so you can walk and talk. You may believe it was the Lord's Will, or blind fortune, or the result of regular strenuous exercise, but Dr. Science only says what he knows: had it landed in this busy neural metropolis here, you would be in a wheelchair, a gimp, a feeb, a crip, a wacko with big Xs for eyeballs trying to say *She sells seashells by the seashore* slowly and distinctly but it comes out *q&w$e#r%t!y$u&i*o%p,* but instead it landed in a "silent area," as he put it, sort of the Wyoming of the brain, where not all that much is going on so if a meteorite drops from the sky, no big deal, life goes on as before, except with a little wisdom that you got practically for free.

It happened on Labor Day, in Minneapolis at a spa with Peruvian flute music playing, aromatic candles, jasmine in the air. A powerful Jamaican masseuse named Angelica was working on my neck and shoulders and telling me how good her life had been since she turned it over to the Lord Jesus Christ and let Him make all the decisions. "Including what to eat for lunch?" I said. Yes, she said. I started to say something witty about honey and locusts and in that instant my brain fogged up, my mouth felt numb, I slurred the word *locusts*. I heisted up on my elbows. I took a deep breath. She said, "Are you okay?" and I said, of course, "I am just fine. But I have to leave now. I forgot something." I managed to pull my jeans on and T-shirt. I paid her. I stepped into my shoes. My head felt as if a balloon were expanding inside it. A mystical experience, one a person would rather not have. I careened out the door, listing slightly to the left. I climbed into my old Volvo. Call me a fool but I don't believe in calling 911 anytime you feel woozy. So I drove twelve miles *very* carefully to United Hospital in St. Paul and on my way from the parking ramp to Emergency bumped into a man I hadn't seen in years and couldn't remember his name.

"Are you okay?" he said.

"I'm about to find out."

"You look okay."

"Good to know."

Not many people in the waiting room. I took a number and when I was called to the desk, I said in a clear voice, "I believe I am having a stroke." An orderly brought a wheelchair and took me down a series of halls to a curtained alcove and I stripped down to my shorts and put on a hospital gown and lay on the examining table. It was a flowery gown and I lay with hands clasped over my abdomen, and imagined my funeral, my family walking past the coffin, dabbing at their eyes, as a soupy organ plays "Beautiful Isle of Somewhere," looking down at my inert form, saying, "What is he doing in that little gown?" and someone says, "Because he's going to be cremated and they didn't want to waste a good suit."

The nurse announced my numbers — Blood pressure: 139/72. Pulse: 59. Not bad for a stricken man.

■ ■ ■ ■

The young Chinese lady neurologist told
me, as she tapped me with her little silver
hammer and scratched the sole of my foot
and moved her index finger back and forth
and up and down for me to follow with my
eyes, that she used to listen to my show
when she was in medical school. The words
used to gonged in my head. *How had I disappointed her?* It made me sad, lying on the
gurney in my burial gown. I watched her
write on a form in her clipboard, "Very
pleasant 67 y.o. male, tall, well-developed,
well-nourished, flat affect, awake, alert and
appropriate." I've had a flat affect since I
was a kid, I'm from Minnesota, I thought it
was the appropriate way to be. I make it a
point to be appropriate. I am perfectly
comfortable with appropriateness.

She shipped me off to the MRI Space-
Time Cyclotron, where they laid me on a
narrow platform and ran it up a rail and
into the maw of the beast for fifty minutes
of banging and whanging, buzzing and
dinging, and I lay with my eyes shut, to
avoid claustrophobia, and imagined myself
on the beach in Denmark, the day I swam
in the cold cold sea with my friend Euan,

who said, "You don't have to do this, you know," which truly obligated me to do it, so I stripped and ran into the water through a wall of pain and dove for total immersion and trotted back on shore. Euan suffered a major stroke in Paris a year before mine and was still in rehab, a healthier man than I, a Scot for heaven's sake. Lying there, I recited to myself, "When, in disgrace with fortune and men's eyes, I all alone beweep my outcast state" and "You shake my nerves and you rattle my brain, too much love drives a man insane" and "Minnesota, hats off to thee, to our colors true we shall ever be. Firm and strong, united are we," all the words present and accounted for.

I got transferred to Mayo and St. Mary's Hospital in Rochester because that's where I go for stuff. They know me there. I was wheeled into Intensive Care and a set of electrodes was taped to my chest to broadcast my vital signs to a monitor at the nursing desk. A plastic sack of blood thinner dripped into me through an IV. I fell asleep in the faint glow and hum and then a nurse asked me to say my name and birth date and was I experiencing any pain or dizziness. A few hours later, my internist Dr. Rodysill came in and asked for the story, so I told him, as I'd told the Chinese neurologist, a cardiologist, and a nurse the night before. A technician came in to make sure I could swallow and another arrived with an ultrasound wand to check out the veins in my neck. A neurologist arrived — an important one, judging by the retinue of disciples in his wake — who had me stand on one foot, arms extended, in my little gown. He and his entourage gathered at the bedside, eight men and women in long white coats, folks who'd aced the math and science courses I'd skipped in favor of Chaucer and Shakespeare and the Transcendentalists, and a couple of the disciples tapped me and peered into my eyes, and the troupe exited. Enter a speech pathologist and a physical therapist, and I told my story again. I wished I could add a speeding car to it, a shady man with a bulge under his tux jacket, a Great Dane who leaped out from the bushes. I felt inappropriate lying there, a man with excellent blood pressure, but at the same time comforted, to be in the care of extremely capable people. My dad distrusted doctors, having a dim view of higher education in general. I, who loved college dearly, am fond of smart people who put their smarts at the service of another, who study the data and explain it so an English major can understand. *You suffered a cere-*

bral event that could've been catastrophic. We don't yet know why. We shall endeavor to find out. Meanwhile, we will do what we can to protect you against a recurrence.

I was transferred to the stroke ward in the morning and took a long solo walk down the hall and back, in pajamas and bathrobe, towing my IV apparatus on wheels, and felt okay. Legs worked fine, balance good. Passed a thirtyish woman, slender, wistful, with a pronounced limp, slim, scared, sliding her slippers along, gripping a walker, her mother at her side. The daughter looked like somebody's beloved third-grade teacher. Heartbreaking, but the mother had a brisk, let's-get-it-done air about her, and what else can one do? Take the blow and go to rehab. Walking down the hall, you tell yourself over and over not to glance in through open doorways, which seems rude and crude, and then you do it anyway. I mean, the doors were open after all. And these are my brethren, the Order of the Stricken, fellow petitioners at the Throne of Mercy. *Dear Lord, thank you for my life and please may it continue.* In the rooms I saw elderly persons, some my age, who had been smacked hard and now lay speechless in bed, or moved slowly around the room like a lobster trying to claw its way out of the tank at the restaurant, or slumped in a chair, awake but not alert. ("Hello, I'm not here right now. Sorry. Tell someone else.") And here I was waltzing along, lightly grazed by the bullet, the sinner who escapes scot-free while the righteous languish. Now that I was up, I didn't think morbid thoughts anymore. The one thought that can bring me to tears is the thought of my little daughter losing me, living without her daddy's love and protection, but weeping is not appropriate now, and I put the thought away.

So I had a thromboembolic stroke likely due to atrial fibrillation. A bomb lands in Wyoming; a few Herefords are startled; a twelve-foot crater in the scrub brush. The prognosis: Who knows? What you want to know — When will I die? — the doctors can't tell you, which is okay because you don't really want to know. In the afternoon, a lady called from the paper to update my obituary. She was very very nice. "We just want to update our information," she said. "You're on your third marriage — is that correct?" *Yes, ma'am.* "Anything big coming up in the fall?" (LOCAL AUTHOR, 67, SUCCUMBS ON EVE OF GREAT SUCCESS.) *No, ma'am.* "How are you feeling, if you don't mind my asking?" *I don't mind. I feel fine.*

And then the next day and the next. Lying around, reading *The New York Times,* working on my laptop, drinking coffee, normal life except in a hospital with electrodes stuck to me. Rochester is fifty miles from the Cities, which discourages casual visits by friends and relatives, which is all right by me: they mean well, surely, and it is a good deed and all, but I am okay, thank you very much. Quite happy to be here, in fact. I got plenty of social interaction from nurses, brisk, cheerful Lutheran women, small-town girls, who strode into my room, took the blood pressure, noted the urine flow chart, asked the questions, prepped me on upcoming events. "How are we doing today?" the nurses asked, and I said, "Doing great. Never felt better." The appropriate thing to say, unless you're paralyzed and your eyeballs have popped out of your head. The neurologist and his entourage arrived with more questions about my brain, and I began to feel solicitous for this beloved organ. The heart is only a muscle, and my lungs, scarred by twenty years of smoke, are doing the best they can, but my brain is where I live. Maybe more meteoroids were on their way — *blammo* — *boomboomboom* — *ker-blam* — the frontal lobe, the parietal

628

lobe, the sensual lobe, the Bobo the Clown lobe, all damaged, and there I am, slumped in a chair at a table with large wooden blocks as a therapist named Meghan leads me through the unit on shapes, just like in kindergarten, and her voice makes me tingle, except I can't come up with the word *tingle.*

O my brain, beloved brain, beautiful lumpy gelatinous organ ambitious to do great things still, O do not abandon me now. I would rather be homeless, on social security, living in a series of shelters in church basements, subject to the brutal charity of the righteous, but with my marbles intact, my memories of autumn in New York and Trondhjemsgade in Copenhagen and the beaches of Patmos and the north shore of Lake Superior — O sweet Sarah Bellum, don't leave me to rattle around in a panic of fog and rumbles, only knowing a vast dimness where the city of memory used to be — I would rather die, Sarah. And you know it's true because, *Duh,* you're my brain.

Being in the stroke ward surrounded by the stricken, it seemed like a good idea to think about a funeral and spare the family the guesswork, so I scribbled a few notes (*Epis-*

copal low mass, no eulogies, none — hire a choir — "Abide with Me" and "O Love That Will Not Let Me Go" and Mozart's Ave Verum *and "The Blind Man Stood in the Road and Cried"*) and that made me think about sex — any monastic situation would, I suppose — and brought to mind that first-floor apartment on Jagtvej in Copenhagen in October 1985, and the time in waist-deep water off Oahu and once at the Ritz in Boston. The screened porch in the log cabin in Wisconsin, the bed suspended from the beams on chains. The fifty-seventh floor of the hotel in New York. Recollecting the quality of light, the presence of music or sound of insects, the feel of skin, the urgency, the taste of sweetness, I left behind the fluorescent bulbs, the tile floor, the dangling tube connecting the bag of blood thinner to the needle in my forearm.

I revisited Anoka, Minnesota, in 1954, the swanky window of Colburn-Hilliard men's clothiers and their wool sportcoats, the soda fountain at Shadick's, the front window of the Anoka *Herald,* where I typed my sports stories, the ice cream shop across the street. I remembered how it felt to ride a bike no-handed. I remembered Mrs. Moehlenbrock, who gave my fourth-grade class the essay topic "What would you do if you had one day left to live?" We had just read an inspiring story about the rich, full life Helen Keller led despite being blind, deaf, speechless, and rather homely, and Mrs. Moehlenbrock suggested we write something inspiring about appreciating the ordinary things of life but I wrote that I wanted to get on a plane and fly to Paris. I had never flown anywhere in my life and Paris seemed like a cool place to go. Mrs. Moehlenbrock pointed out that it would take a day just to get to Paris. I thought that I could live with that. Maybe I could get a good tailwind and glimpse it for an hour before I died. Maybe the prospect of seeing Paris would cure my fatal illness.

They kept me in the hospital for five days of observation, and I tried to be as normal as I knew how to be. "Fine," I kept telling them when they asked. "Great. Wonderful." Mr. Neurologist put me on the blood thinner Coumadin, and sent me home, and here I am. Every other week I prick my finger and squeeze a drop of blood onto a metal strip in a wallet-sized device that measures blood thickness. Thin blood makes sense if you've been struck (stroked, stricken) by a blood clot, and I wondered if I needed to cut back on caffeine — change my life entirely, become slender, virtuous, nimble, dutiful, pure of heart and deed? They shrugged. They were MDs, not doctors of divinity: the stroke was an accident, like a drive-by shooting, and maybe you increase your risk somewhat by living in a bad neighborhood and sitting out on the stoop at 2 a.m. as the bars are closing, but that isn't what pulled the trigger, and meanwhile, be glad the bullet hit your left buttock and not your heart.

I came home to St. Paul and went back to work. Unfortunately a story appeared in the paper saying I'd had a stroke, and that was the day all sorts of people started treating me with great deference. I walked into the corner coffee shop and kids with spiky hair and fishhooks in their eyebrows looked at me with sympathy and nodded as I passed. There was admiration in their bloodshot eyes, as if I were a wounded vet, returned from the front; two people jumped up and offered me their table. I sat with my coffee and newspaper and felt people looking my way. *Stroke survivor. Stroke* is a powerful word, especially to people in their twenties. It means you were on Death Row, the Raven perched on your mantel, you heard the gentle voices calling "Old Black Joe." But I don't feel that way myself. I don't think much about death because I thought about it all the time when I was young. I wore it out.

The only reason I'd want to know my departure date is so I can savor those Last Months, throw away stuff, give away the books and clothes, burn the letters, resume the bad habits, and wind up at that Last Day I first wrote about for Mrs. Moehlenbrock's class. We'd skip the luncheon and weepy speeches and the proclamation from the governor, skip the fond farewells, and simply get on the plane to Paris, my sweetie and me, and I'd order a martini over Wisconsin and the steak entrée with a glass of Barolo and a snifter of Armagnac over Newfoundland and into the darkness we'd fly and land at Charles DeGaulle at 8 a.m. and pass swiftly through Customs, no baggage (who needs clean underwear when you're close to death?), and tell the taxi driver to step on it, and there's the Louvre and the Tuileries and take me to the Ritz, please, a big opulent suite with gilded armoire and 15-foot ceilings, hang the expense, let the heirs get by on leftovers, and call room service, darling, order a bottle of Champagne and a dozen oysters, make that two dozen, and I will lie down and nap for a moment, just hold my hand, don't pull the shades, I want to look at you, just as I did in the beginning.

11.
HOME

National Geographic was the magazine of choice in our home, a gift subscription from Uncle Lew, a monthly compendium of exotic sights we did not expect ever to see in real life — New Guinea, Antarctica, the Serengeti, Calcutta, a woman with bare breasts — and I was honored when they asked me to write about Minneapolis and St. Paul, my home-towns. Uncle Lew was long gone from the world, but I still wanted to impress him even posthumously, I could imagine how pleased he'd be, he'd read it slowly beginning to end, and say, "That's not bad. Not a single word misspelled." The *Geographic* photographer Erika Larsen came and lived with my family for weeks while she shot the pictures around town — she'd just finished a book of stunning photos of the Sami people of northern Sweden and had just returned from Peru but seemed enthused to be in Minnesota and in fact made elegant pictures that to me looked like Provence or the Lake Country or the steppes of Russia except it was Anoka and Lake Calhoun and the prairie west of Minneapolis, shooting on a big old 4×5 view camera not so different from what Mathew Brady used at Antietam.

Flying in to Minneapolis–St. Paul Airport from the east, the plane descends over the green fields of Wisconsin and the St. Croix River downstream from the sandbars where gangs of youths including me played volleyball in the shallows, into Minnesota just above the farm in Denmark township where my teenaged mother and her sisters spent summer days on her sister Margaret's farm — Grace and Elsie and Ina in white summer dresses, squinting in the bright 1934 sunlight — and passes south of downtown St. Paul and the gleam of steel rails that carried Dad in the mail car of the *Empire Builder* departing Union Depot for Seattle, a .38 snub-nosed revolver on his hip, and past the cathedral near where I live and the hospital where I walked in one day and said, "I think I'm having a stroke" (and I was), and we bank over Mendota, where back in my drinking days I heard New Orleans jazz luminaries like Billie and DeDe Pierce and Willie and Percy Humphrey, and we come in low over the Minnesota River where I learned to hate canoeing thanks to an OCD scoutmaster who wanted the canoes of Troop 252 to be evenly spaced and in a straight line, and as the plane touches down on the runway, I can see the hill where I used to park in a car with a girl and watch planes land and also make out back in the days of the bench seat where two people could get involved with each other in thrilling ways. A one-minute aerial tour of my life. Once I was on a plane that aborted the landing and ascended northward over downtown and the University and up the Mississippi and over my hometown of Anoka and I saw forty years of my life go by.

There's a newer north–south runway, and on that approach I don't recognize a thing. It's all road tangle and strip malls, and we descend below 5,000 feet, and still I can't get my bearings — it could be the outskirts of Dallas or Atlanta — and I start to feel I've lost my place in the world. I was born here. I'm seventy-one years old. I've lived most of my life here. I refuse to use a GPS here. And it is distressing to come home and not know where I am. A sort of dementia, the strangeness of the beloved familiar. But driving east from the airport, we cross the Mississippi, and I am reoriented.

My grandma Dora Keillor was riding in my dad's car one winter day in 1957 when the car spun out of control on an icy highway and did a doughnut or two and stopped, still on the road. Grandma didn't cry out; she looked straight ahead out the windshield and said, "John, which way is north?" I share that need for clarity. When a man has lived in one place for a long time, he has his landmarks. The Stone Arch bridge and the old flour mills. Seven Corners. The basilica of St. Mary. Porky's drive-in. The white tower of the Horticulture building at the State Fairgrounds and the grandstand and the remains of the racetrack where auto thrill show drivers drove late-model Fords off ramps to leap through flaming hoops. When Northwestern Bank was sold to a banking conglomerate and their brass decided to dismantle the beloved Weatherball on the bank roof ("When the Weatherball is white, colder weather is in sight"), it was like a death in the family. It was like the German commandant in Paris, 1940, had decreed that the Eiffel Tower come down.

The geography of MSP is simple: two interlocked cities, Minneapolis (382,578) and St. Paul (285,068) in a sprawling metro area (3.5 million) — the Great River with its rhythmic spelling M-i-ss-i-ss-i-pp-i flowing in from the north, through Anoka and over St. Anthony Falls, past the glass towers of downtown Minneapolis packed tightly around the Foshay Tower, the little skyscraper of my childhood, and the University campus with its long leafy mall and stone columns and the inscription about men being ennobled by understanding. Steep riverbanks, buoys to guide barge traffic toward the downtown locks, river roads lined with mansions, Fort Snelling on a bluff above the Minnesota River where it flows into the Mississippi, which then does a sideways *S* through St. Paul, its railyards, University Avenue with its entrepreneurial churn of storefront start-ups, Asian restaurants, muffler shops, across town to the great dome of the Capitol with the team of golden horses on the roof, past downtown, where the river bends south toward Red Wing, Winona, Dubuque, down to Prof. Harold Hill and Huck Finn territory. The cities are dotted with lakes — Como and Phalen in St. Paul; in Minneapolis, Nokomis, Hiawatha, Harriet, Calhoun, Cedar, and Lake of the Isles, pools of ease and elegance on the asphalt grid — and Lake Minnetonka, the prairie Riviera, to the southwest.

This geography was imprinted in my brain in the Forties, back when I learned my alphabet from the avenues of Minneapolis (Aldrich, Brya, Dupont, Emerson, Fremont, Girard, Humboldt, Irving, James, Knox, through Xerxes, York, and Zenith). Superimposed over that geography is the geography of a man's life, the defeats and pleasures of various locales, the landmarks of experience — the ball field at Diamond Lake where I dropped an easy fly to deep right and let three runs score, the stone rowhouse where I cheerfully committed adultery on February 14, 1976, and ended a ten-year marriage, the street where my car got buried by the snowplow and a woman driving by gave me a ride to my 6 a.m. radio shift, the street where my Danish lover and I walked through waist-deep snow to look at a house and bought it on the spot, Loring Park, where I liked to sit and smoke after a ten-hour day in the hotel scullery where I washed pots and pans after high school. After a day in the steam of the dishwasher, a summer evening was blessedly cool, and the smoke was ecstasy. Girls walked by in loose white blouses and wraparound skirts, and a few stopped and asked for a light and leaned down, holding their hair back, and the lit match illuminated their faces like

Renaissance saints, a procession of Botticellis and Michelangelos. In that park I am always sort of eighteen, but driving east on Franklin I get an ache in my gut seeing the building where I helped clean the small dim apartment of my first wife after she died, the souvenirs of our old marriage scattered around, the loneliness of the furniture, the unspeakable sadness of the cupboards full of health foods. I drove to the river and sat by the bridge and wept ten years' worth of tears.

My Minneapolis is the South Side, blocks of little Spanish stucco bungalows under majestic archways of elms, small well-kept yards, the birdbath, the coiled green rubber hose, grape arbor, steel barrel incinerator, and skinny frame garage on the alley, the part of town where my mother grew up around Thirty-eighth and Longfellow with her twelve siblings, most of whom settled in the neighborhood as people tended to do then: you wanted family nearby, should assistance be needed. And if I walk those blocks today, I feel the claustrophobia of Sunday afternoon after dinner, the overpowering fastidiousness (no reading comics on the Lord's Day, no ball tossing, no worldly music, just sit still and have uplifting conversations), the smell of furniture polish, the radio on the walnut highboy tuned to the Christian station and George Beverly Shea singing "How Great Thou Art," the good china in the glass cabinets, Grandpa and Grandma sitting contented, nibbling on butterscotch caramel candy. We attended church at the Grace & Truth Gospel Hall on Fourteenth Avenue South, where a preacher spoke with utter certainty on the Chart on the Course of Time from Eternity to Eternity, and I grew up one of the Chosen to whom God had vouchsafed the Knowledge of All Things that was denied to the great and mighty. The Second Coming was imminent, hours away. We walked around Minneapolis carefully, wary of television, dance music, tobacco, baubles, bangles, flashy cars, liquor, the theater, the modern novel — all of them tempting us away from the singular life that Jesus commanded us to lead.

In 1947 Dad got a GI loan and built us a little white house on an acre of cornfield north of the city, a stone's throw from the Mississippi, so he could have a garden, farm boy that he was. He loved fresh vegetables, sweet corn and tomatoes especially, and he felt that work was a privilege, and he wanted his children to grow up privileged. Brooklyn Park township was a boys' paradise. We made our own ball field in January in a vacant lot with a chickenwire backstop and shot baskets, sliding around on frozen gravel driveways wearing cotton gloves with the fingertips cut off. Beyond the backyard gardens lay a twisting ravine, site of Civil War and Three Musketeers reenactments (*sacre bleu, mon Dieu,* unhand that rapier!), that led to a stretch of sandy riverbank under the cottonwoods. Grown-ups seldom ventured there. We got to run naked through tall corn and skate on the river ice, but we were only five miles from the big city, which after the war was still a streetcar city — at the end of the line, the city stopped short; the country began. From the thirty-first-floor observation deck of the Foshay Tower downtown, you saw farmland and silos to the north and west.

When I was twelve, I rode my bike alone into the city, past the lumber mills, foundries, machine shops, barrel factory, and printing plants, along Washington Avenue and past a meatpacking plant where bare-chested men wrestled whole beef carcasses hung on hooks on little overhead trolleys along a rail and into the waiting trucks. I pedaled up Hennepin Avenue, past dirty-book stores, penny arcades, walk-up hotels, Augie's Theatre Lounge and the Gay 90s, men slumped in doorways clutching empty bottles, to the magnificent old public library on Tenth across from White Castle, home of the 10-cent hamburger ("Buy Em By The Sack"), and climbed up to the reading room, skipping the swimming lesson at the Y Mother had paid for so I'd learn to swim after cousin Roger drowned in Lake Minnetonka; but the Y conducted swim class in the nude and I was shy, so I went to the library instead and met the book that changed my life — transformed, diversified, turned it upsy-daisy, too — *Roget's International Thesaurus,* supplier of idiom, lingo, jargon, argot, blather, and phraseology that transformed me from nerd and nobody to visionary, sporting man, roughneck, and raconteur.

Growing up in the Brethren neighborhood, a boy was ever aware of worldly temptation, and from that comes a keener interest in the world. A school field trip to the Milwaukee depot where the *Hiawatha* stood throbbing, waiting to depart for Chicago, steam hissing from the locomotive, the luxurious club car blue with cigar smoke from slick gents in three-piece suits — for the Brethren boy, an electric vision of worldly success and glamour. When I was fourteen, I got a tour of the Moderne headquarters of the *Minneapolis Star & Tribune:* upstairs, pencil-neck geeks like me, and down below, the giant presses roaring, miles of newsprint flying out, chopped and folded into the afternoon *Star,* bundles of papers conveyed onto trucks and rushed to the readers, and the thought rang like a bell: I could be one of those guys upstairs. There were the neon lights of Hennepin Avenue and the promise of naked girls at the Alvin Theater, which our family passed on Sunday morning on our way to church. This last attraction was lost on me, a boy for whom dating girls was like exploring the Amazon — interesting idea, but how to get there? Writing for print, on the other hand — why not? And then came the beautiful connection: You write for print, it impresses girls, they want to drive around in a car with you.

A boy named Frankie drowned in the river one spring at the sandy bank where we boys hung out. I was eating supper when the fire truck went by, and I wanted to go see, but Mother said, "There's no point in a bunch of rubberneckers standing around gawking." She said it was unseemly to look upon the sufferings of others if you were powerless to help. Years later, a photographer at the *St. Paul Pioneer Press,* where I worked on the copy desk, writing obits, showed me his collection of pictures of dead people, drowned or shot or crushed in cars, but I did not look at them long. (I wanted to, but I didn't want him to think I was the sort of person who did.)

For days after Frankie drowned, I visited the death scene, trying to imagine what had happened. He was paddling a canoe with two other boys and fell in, and the current swept him away. I imagined myself saving him, imagined his mother's gratitude as the lifesaving medal was pinned on my chest. I don't recall discussing this with the others. We were more interested in what lay ahead in seventh grade, where (we had heard) you had to take showers after gym. Naked. As in with no clothes on. And it turned out to be true. Junior high was up the West River Road in Anoka, the town where I was born, 1942, in a house on Ferry Street, delivered by Dr. Mork. After seventh grade I was suddenly too old for the ravine and the riverbank. The next summer I worked on nearby truck farms, hoeing corn, picking potatoes. Other boys inherited the riverbank. I worked. At eighteen I proceeded directly to the University of Minnesota downriver and the smoke-filled classrooms of Folwell Hall and football Saturdays and the glorious blare of the Rouser and old alums in their forties lumbering lead-footed toward Memorial Stadium. I spent six years sorting through various personas (Boy Scholar, Embittered Poet, Dangerous Radical, Wry Humorist) and wound up with the one that paid a salary: Friendly Announcer. I did all of this a couple miles from the Brethren, which made for interesting collisions. Standing outside the 400 Bar, smoking a Pall Mall, and a car honks, and it's Aunt Jean and Uncle Les. Drop the smoke, walk to the car, say hi, smile, try not to exhale. And now devout Muslims from Somalia live in the old Brethren neighborhood; robed women and somber elders watch teenage Somali girls go by in short shorts and daring tank tops and product in their hair. Same play, new actors.

From the U, I traipsed down the long winding trail of adulthood, walk-up apartments, dingy offices, cheap cafés, public library, softball diamonds, beer joints, and Grand Avenue, the street I drove down to work at 4 a.m. to do the morning shift on KSJN in a storefront studio on Sixth Street, then the dramatic climb to home ownership on Goodrich, then Portland, then Summit Avenues, all on Cathedral Hill in St. Paul where I've lived most of the last twenty years, where you drive up from I-94 past

Masqueray's magnificent cathedral whose great dome and towers and arches give you a momentary vision of Europe and up Summit and the mansions of nineteenth-century grandees and poobahs in a ward that votes about 85 percent Democratic today. You look out the kitchen window at McKinley's America, and then three slender young women go running by, ponytails bouncing, wires coming out of their ears. In all, I count twenty-six places I've lived in the Twin Cities, about half on the west side of the river, half on the east, all within a few miles of each other: a restless fugitive for so many years, mostly within Hennepin and Ramsey counties, now in a neighborhood where Mother, at seventeen, sold peanut-butter cookies door-to-door during the Depression on a ridge above the river I loved as a boy.

The Old Resident mourns for the Old City, though he understands that his classmates and cousins wanted to raise their kids in rambling houses with big leafy yards like the one he grew up in, not dinky apartments, and so the cornfields were given over to settlements of ramblers on curvy streets with romantic names like Yosemite Avenue, Emerald Trail, Everest Path, and Evening Star Way, and the earthmovers gouged out the Interstates, the east–west 94, the north–

south 35, and the downtowns dwindled and urban renewal wiped out whole blocks of Victorian stone edifices, old picture palaces, department stores. And the planners created an infernal system of "skyways" — glass bridges connecting buildings at the second story — in effect turning buildings inside out, wiping out streets of little shops and show windows and the jingle of the opening door in favor of implacable corporations with brutal blank exteriors (he mourns this but learns not to see it). Instead, look up at the First National Bank building in St. Paul, the enormous numeral 1 on the roof outlined in flashing red neon — as a child, I thought it designated St. Paul as the number 1 city in America, a dazzling discovery for a child who was brought up modest. Pride goeth before a fall, so deprecate yourself lest others have to do the job for you. On the fourth-grade class trip to the Capitol, we all stood on the roof of the bank, and I explained the significance of the 1 as a yellow streetcar rolled past a grassy square with a fountain in the middle, old men lounging on park benches, smoking, looking into the distance. I wondered then what they were thinking, and now I am old enough to know.

When a man has lived in one place for

sixty years, he walks around hip-deep in history. He sees that life is not so brief; it is vast and contains multitudes. I drive down Seventh Street to a Twins game and pass the old Dayton's Department Store (Macy's now but still Dayton's to me), where in my poverty days I shoplifted an unabridged dictionary the size of a suitcase, and fifty years later I still feel the terror of walking out the door with it under my jacket, and I imagine the cops arresting my twenty-year-old self and what thirty days in the slammer might've done for me. From my seat above first base, I see the meatpacking plant where those men wrestled beef carcasses into trucks and the old Munsingwear factory with the low rumble and whine of machines, and I feel the fear of spending my days at a power loom making men's underwear. I think about this along about the eighth inning if the Twins are down by a few runs.

When we graduated from Anoka High, my classmate Corinne Guntzel drove her dad's white Cadillac Eldorado convertible with rocket tailfins at high speed down the West River Road and into the city on a street just beyond right centerfield, and I stood in the front seat and sang, "That'll be the day when you say goodbye, Oh that'll be the day when you make me cry," and now she and her parents, Hilmer and Helen, lie in Crystal Lake Cemetery on the North Side beyond left field; thoughts of them click into place whenever I pass the Dowling Avenue exit on 94. Corinne was a suicide twenty-five years ago, a professor of economics who hit a rough patch and paddled her canoe out on a lake and drowned with rocks in her pockets, and I still love her and am not over her death nor do I expect ever to be. If I drove a visitor past the Dowling Avenue sign, I wouldn't say a word about this.

I drive my little girl to school, a lovely ritual, and the route takes me through my Dangerous Radical years and past the place where my virginity went up in a burst of flames — the house replaced by an on-ramp to I-35W — and past a steep slope below Ridgewood Avenue and the house where Mary and I decided not to be married anymore, only to find out that she was pregnant, so we decided not to not be married. A bell tolls as I pass. My daughter says, "Tell me a story," so I tell her about riding the school bus in seventh grade, my gravel road the last stop, the bus packed with smelly children bundled in heavy mackinaws, no empty seats, nobody moving over, the whiskey-soaked bus driver yelling at me to sit down, dammit, which is maybe why I have such a poor self-image even today and flinch when people look at me and which naturally drove me into radio broadcasting instead of something more distinguished.

She says, "Tell me a funny story" — my daughter who never had to fight for a seat. I say, "So . . . there were these two penguins standing on an ice floe," and she says, "Tell the truth," so I say, "I like your ponytail. You know, years ago I wore my hair in a ponytail. Not a big ponytail. A little one. I had a beard, too." And she looks at me. "A ponytail? Are you joking?" No, I did. It was only for a year or two, around 1972. And she realizes I am telling the truth. And she laughs and laughs. My father never drove me to school. It was unheard of back then, so he never got to know me that well, just as he never wore his hair in a ponytail. Back in his day men who wore their hair in a ponytail were given electroshock therapy, which made them forget what day of the week it was. Today is Monday, and I am driving my daughter past Lake Calhoun, where, back in the ponytail era, I went skinny-dipping with a woman who now is a distinguished surgeon in town. I doubt that she remembers, but I do.

The great American myth is the hero who

652

leaves home to remake himself in another place: James Gatz leaves North Dakota to become Jay Gatsby of West Egg, Long Island; Robert Jordan leaves his teaching job in Montana to fight in the Spanish Civil War; Huck Finn took a raft, Dorothy flew off in a tornado, Sister Carrie rode the train, Jack Kerouac hitched rides — and so forth — but in my experience the Cities have been quite roomy enough for a restless, impulsive person. I never felt stranded here. Sometimes I felt the pull of the roads going west, Highway 7 out of Excelsior and Clara City toward South Dakota, and Highway 212 through Chaska and Granite Falls, and Highway 12 through Litchfield and Willmar and Benson and Ortonville. And now and then, just for a glimpse of freedom, I'd drive out west late at night through the little towns and stop around 2 or 3 a.m. at a crossroads and get out of the car and walk around in the dark for a while and then head back to do my 6 a.m. radio shift. After the University I spent part of a summer in New York City, thinking that a young writer ought to live there, but Minnesota was a better place to be poor. You can go to your mother's for a huge supper, and she'll send you home with a big bag of vegetables from her garden.

■ ■ ■ ■

When my mother was nearing the end of her ninety-seven years, what was most vivid to her was her youth, and she ventured into the shadows to commune with her dead, which was a comfort to her. At seventy I sometimes forget last week, but I clearly remember the big house on Dupont Avenue North where Corinne lived one summer when we were nineteen, and I blew smoke on her African violets to kill aphids. She and I had this idea to form a commune of writers all working away in their rooms, doors open, and when we wrote something good, we could walk into someone's room and tell them about it. A sort of ten-year sleepover. It was a perfect idea, and we didn't torture it with details such as Who and Where and How Much, and because it never became a reality, it never died. It still exists in my mind. If I reach ninety-seven, I may finally go live there.

My parents were very clear that they wished to die in their old house and not in a hospital. They wanted family to be with them at the end, holding their hands and singing, "And we shall be where we should be, and we will be what we would be," as they passed to their heavenly home. The bedroom looks out on the driveway where Dad's Ford station wagon used to be parked, ready to leave early the next morning to drive to Idaho to visit relatives. My mother stayed up late, washing, ironing, packing, in an ecstasy of anxiety. My father changed the oil, checked tire pressures, adjusted the timing. We stood on the front lawn in the sunrise, watching him pack the car. They made a good team. He was laconic and undaunted, she was prone to excitation. We headed west on Highway 12, the rising sun to our backs, as she deliberated the perpetual question: Had she turned the oven off? And decided she had — and out onto the open prairie we went, with me sitting behind Mother, narrating the trip from the old federal writers' guide. Now they're buried in a little country cemetery full of aunts and uncles, grandparents, great-grandparents, and someday, I presume, cousins and siblings.

"So how was it to grow up there, then?" they say. "Oh, you know. It could've been worse," I reply. If you want to know the truth, I feel understood there. I sit down to lunch with Bill and Bob and my sister and brother whom I've known almost forever, and it's a conversation you can't have with people you just met last week. You can flash back to 1958 and the island in the river where we used to mess around, and they are right there with you. I come home among classmates and cousins and feel understood. I was not a good person. I have yelled at my children. I neglected my parents and was disloyal to loved ones. I have offended righteous people. People around here know all this about me, and yet they still smile and say hello, and so every day I feel forgiven. Ask me if it's a good place to live, and I don't know — that's real estate talk — but forgiveness and understanding are a beautiful combination.

12.

ANGLICANS

I was invited to sit in on a teen Bible study class at an Episcopal church and perched in the corner and paid attention to everything and was surprised at how much Bible study had changed since my Sanctified Brethren days. The Bible was hardly mentioned in an hour of free-form discussion of the young folks' feelings about sex, school, relationships, parents, sex, social responsibility, and sex. Their teacher, who made a point of not teaching, had told them they were free to say anything they wanted and so they said anything. The Bible has so much in it that is more interesting than our feelings about relationships, etc., and I was sorry that the teacher was not pointing this out. It seemed rather smug to me, and I know firsthand about smugness, I am an expert. I told the teacher afterward that I had seen an interesting statistic, that the proportion of agnostics, 60 percent, is the same in the church as outside the church. I made that number up but he accepted it as the truth, and it gave him something to think about.

The Christian faith is on a bumpy road these days, as you find out if you stand up in front of an audience and make comic reference to the Parable of the Prodigal Son. Depending on where in America you are, you sense confusion out there in the house, some people trying to remember the parable, others as uneasy about laughing at Christians as they would be if you had made a joke about morons or amputees. We one-legged morons laugh at each other all the time, but unbelievers are squeamish about it. In another twenty years, you won't be able to tell stories about Lutherans — nobody will know what you're talking about, it'll be like reminiscing about the Huguenots or the Hottentots. But that is none of my business, the decline of the mainstream church, the dwindling of true fundamentalism, the rise of the theology-free Happy Gospel churches with the PowerPoint hymns about Jesus the Good Boyfriend — I go to church on Sunday because I want to be there. It's very cheerful to be with the others who want to be there and hear the Scriptures and chant the psalm

together and listen to the sermon or not —
sometimes the minister tries too hard to be
profound and loses us in the first two
minutes and we turn our attention to the
hairstyles of the people in front of us —
then rise and go sailing through the Nicene
Creed and go forward for communion, singing *Laudate omnes gentes,* and then a big
closing hymn, and the pastor stands in back
and tells us to go forth into the world where
there are things to be done that won't be
done unless we do them, and out we go into
Sunday morning, feeling mightily blessed
and looking for those things.

I started out Sanctified Brethren, then
joined the Church of the Sunday Brunch,
and when I moved to Copenhagen became
an Anglican for the pleasure of hearing
English. Most of the folks at St. Alban's
were Brits, big tweedy people who strode
into the sanctuary like they'd been on a
good foxhunt that morning and knelt down,
addressed the Lord, got the thing done and
taken care of, and got up and went home to
dine on a side of beef. I liked them. I just
plain liked them a lot.

The theology's easy, the liturgy too.
Just stand up and kneel down and say

what the others do.
Episcopalian, saving my love for you.

Back in New York, I joined Holy Apostles, which had a powerful black lady preacher and an ambitious daily soup kitchen, and when I moved back to Minnesota, I shopped around among the Episcopalians. Crossed off the ones whose rector thought a service was a show and he was the happy emcee, and ones whose organist played too loud, and found the church I go to now, where there is a good deal of silence. "Be still and know that I am God," it says in Scripture, and we do. In the stillness, one can escape from self-righteousness, pomposity, and sentimentality. When we speak, we use the ancient prayers and texts, not our own words, and so resist the temptation to impress the others with our wit and original-ity and fervor. Left to our own devices, we would emphasize the happy aspects of the faith but God has said many things that are not comforting and those of us who have sinned know this. We sincerely confess to ourselves our sorry state and acknowledge that we are not in charge of our lives and then we find comfort in the four-part harmony of an old hymn that our aunts and uncles sang when they were alive and we shake hands with the people around us and walk home.

Once in downtown Baltimore, the morning after *A Prairie Home Companion,* feeling remorse as I always do after a show (for what I did and what I left undone), I found an old brownstone Anglican temple of 1852, wooden box pews, stained glass on all sides, stone floor, and sat through high Mass. The troops processed up the aisle behind an altar boy bearing a big brass cross and two candle bearers and a black man swinging the incense pot and producing billows of smoke, choristers in white marching through the fog and bearded priests in gaudy vestments, precision bowing and genuflecting, all rather exotic for an old fundamentalist like me but moving nonetheless, the formality of it. The priests were all about the ceremony, there was none of that grinning and tap-dancing *Hi-and-how-are-we-all-doing-this-morning* clubbiness and the homily only summarized the Scripture text about healing, it didn't turn into an essay on health care. Ten voices strong and true in the choir and positioned as they were under the great arch of the chancel, their tender polyphonic *Kyrie* and *Gloria* was O my God just heartbreakingly good. There were fewer than thirty of us in the pews, fewer than the names on the prayer list, and to hear "Behold, how good and joyful it is; brethren, to dwell together in unity" sung so eloquently as the priests swung to their tasks was to be present in a moment of grace that does not depend on numbers or any other measure of success for its meaning, just as the Grand Canyon does not depend on busloads of tourists to be magnificent. Most of our brethren, bless them, are off enjoying brunch or reading the funnies or lifting weights at the gym, and God bless them all. Our attendance at Mass does not make us better people — we simply happened to walk by and see this vast Canyon of God's Love and stand looking into it.

And being there made me think of my dad, it being his birthday, October 12, he having died a few years before, my dad who was faithful all his life to the Brethren, who were the anti-Anglicans. This formal high Mass was what J. N. Darby and the early Brethren revolted against in 1831, for its worldly pomp and show, its lack of prophetic fervor for the Second Coming of Christ, its unholy union with the state, and when they became the Brethren, they took nothing Anglican with them. They left behind the Gothic architecture, the chanting and choral music, the liturgy, the ecclesiastical order, the high altar, the clerical garments, incense, candles, statuary, the kneeling and blessing, the bowing and genuflecting, and every other scrap of papist paraphernalia. At Grace & Truth Gospel Hall, on Fourteenth Avenue South in Minneapolis, where I attended every Sunday for twenty years, the walls were white and bare, the seats plain, facing a small table in the middle with bread and wine on it. The Sunday morning meeting could last up to two hours, and the mood of it was solemn, plain, with long silences. No processions — we just clomped in and sat down, and no incense in the air, just Old Spice cologne, and no statuary (though some members were less lively than others). A boy who grew up in Sunday morning austerity is deeply impressed by this dim and mysterious church and ancient chanting, the beady gowns, the smoke, and next thing you know he is joining right in.

I bless myself with a flick of the wrist.
You'd never know I was raised
    fundamentalist.
Episcopalian, saving my love for you.
There's white folks and black, gay and
    morose,
Some white Anglo-Saxons but we watch

them pretty close.
Episcopalian, saving my love for you.

Faithfulness was a guiding principle in Dad's life. He was the fifth of eight children of a farmer and a schoolteacher on a little farm on Trott Brook in rural Anoka County. Dad worked with his hands, tending his garden, fixing his cars, cutting and joining wood. He was faithful to his family, to Ford automobiles, and also to his separatist theology — that if you are true to Christ and separate yourself from this world, you will be raised to glory in paradise. My father was faithful to this, even as his little band of believers dwindled, diminished by schism and by escaping children, and I was unfaithful.

I separated myself from the separatists with my eyes open. I wanted to live a big complicated life and not sit in a closet. I do not repent of that, though I have plenty else to repent of and am sorry that it came between Dad and me. There have been dozens of people who happened to sit next to me on airplanes over the years who knew more about me than my dad did. No more his fault than mine.

Now I'm an old tired Democrat, sick of the

infernal wars, sick of politics today, the klutziness of Democrats and the soulless-ness of the Republicans' "I got mine and to hell with the rest of you" — but here in an old brownstone church at an ancient cer-emony, there is a moment of separation from all the griefs of this world. We kneel for prayers, bringing to mind the poverty and the goodness of our lives, the lives of others, the life to come, we *pray for the Church . . . for peace and justice in the world . . . for all those in need or trouble . . . for all who seek God . . . for those who have died . . . and offer our thanks.* Ten men and women are singing a cappella, "Bless the Lord, O my soul, and all that is within me bless his holy name," and their voices drench us fugitive worshippers kneeling, naked, trembling, needy, in the knowledge of grace, and when we arise and go out into Baltimore, the blessing follows us. It fol-lowed me as I ate a dozen oysters that afternoon and hung around the library and paid homage to H. L. Mencken's house on Union Square, that hearty old sinner who said, "Church is where men who have never been to heaven brag about it to men who will never get there." Thank you for your service to our language, Henry. Thank you for your life, Dad. And now onward to

November and the first good snowfall, fire in the fireplace, the feel of wool, a pile of good books, the first day of ice-skating.

13.
THE OWL AND THE PUSSYCAT

My first stories were about animals who talked. My aunt Eleanor had a cat named Mrs. Gray, a sweet old dowager, and I wrote several stories in which Mrs. Gray described outlandish things that happened in that house when everyone was asleep. On the radio I like the occasional singing dolphin or the faithful mutt who unburdens himself ("The tail-wagging meant nothing, it was always about the food") or the cow who is ruminating on the meaning of life. Anthropomorphism: a grand old literary tradition. When I am older and beyond caring what people think, I might write a whole novel from the point of view of a red squirrel.

The Owl and the Pussycat fell in love
Though their families told them no
They rendezvoused in a tender mood
In a grove where the green grass grows.
The Owl looked up to the stars above

And sang to a blues guitar,
"O lovely Kathy, O Kathy my love,
If only we had a car.
A car.
A car.
If only we had a car."

Pussy said to the Owl, "Your tender avowal
Of love delights my heart.
Let us get carried away and be married,
I'm lonely when we're apart."
Said the Owl, "Let's join our hands in Des
    Moines
Or Omaha or Butte."
Said the elegant kitty, "How about a city
More romantic, like Duluth."
Duluth.
Duluth.
More romantic like Duluth.

They left at once and it took them two
    months
For their car did not run well,
But they headed for the great North Shore
And found a nice hotel.
And there in the lobby was a Pig named
    Bobby,
A very intelligent creature,
Full of knowledge, he knew theology
And was a Baptist preacher.

A preacher.
A preacher.
He was a Baptist preacher.

Dear Pig, is it possible to put down the
    gospel
And marry a Cat and a Bird?
Said the Pig, "For a dollar I'll put on a collar
And read you from God's Holy Word."
Down by the lake 'round a big wedding
    cake
They had them a ceremony.
And recited a verse and for better or worse
They entered matrimony.
They did.
They do.
They entered matrimony.

They looked at Two Harbors but there were
    no barbers
Who could style feathers and fur.
They looked at Chisholm where Catholicism
Was strong and that's not what they were.
They thought about Ely but found it really
Too wild and somewhat uncouth.
And Grand Marais was too far away
So they settled in Duluth.
Duluth.
Duluth.
So they settled in Duluth.

669

They promised of course to share
    household chores
And their names they would hyphenate.
They'd live happily and if children there be
They'd be raised in the Lutheran faith.

They feel elite on Superior Street,
Where they live in a telephone booth.
They are odd, I suppose, but no more than
    most
Who live here in Duluth.
Duluth.
Duluth.
Who live here in Duluth.

14.
CHEERFULNESS

There is a picture of my mother, Grace, in a white summer dress, standing astride her bicycle on a sidewalk near Lake Nokomis in south Minneapolis, with her sister Elsie and their friends the Haverberg sisters, in the summer of 1933, when my mother was eighteen. She is smiling shyly, the third youngest of twelve children of William and Marian Denham, who had emigrated from Glasgow in 1905. Marian died when Mother was seven and she went through life with no memory of her mother, not a scrap, which troubled her. A few years before she died, at age ninety-seven, still living at home, she said, "There is so much I'd still like to know and there's nobody left to ask." All of her peers were gone, swept away, mourned, buried, and mostly forgotten, their laughter, their smell, the twang of their voices — you die and the ones who remembered you die and your story vanishes, all its little twists and turns, your jokes, your songs, all gone. I said to my mother, "It goes to show you the importance of writers." She laughed. Mother was not one to write about herself — much much too forward — though she loved reminiscing and gossiping and laughing about oddball neighbors and childish hijinks and all. She loved jokes and the screwball comedy of Lucille Ball and Jonathan Winters. She was a good cook within her repertoire. She loved Christmas and made it beautiful every year, against the resistance of my dad, who considered it pagan excess and highly unscriptural. She once strode next door and lectured our tall truck-driver neighbor and told him to stop beating his wife and he did, at least for a while, so far as we could tell. She was a fearless traveler, and in her early nineties she flew off to London and Scotland for a two-week train odyssey with family, a very alert and cheerful grande dame in a wheelchair, chin up, smiling at the gate agent, game for whatever came next. She had to endure the death of her oldest son, Philip, and attend his funeral in Madison, Wisconsin, and sat stunned and weeping, watching his coffin lowered into the ground. Toward the end, she sat at her kitchen table and took my hand and murmured and kept murmuring things I couldn't understand, but I knew from the cadence of it that she was praying for me. My sisters and I kept watch the last night of Mother's life, taking shifts, holding her hand and singing to her and squirting morphine into her mouth to relieve the misery. She was conscious in the afternoon and knew who we were, and when we put her to bed, she fell asleep and didn't wake up. On my shifts, I sang "Abide with Me" and "O Love That Will Not Let Me Go" and after my sisters went to bed I sang "Minnesota, hail to thee, hail to thee our state so dear" and "What'll I do when you are far away" and "Let the Rest of the World Go By." In high school, I'd smoked forbidden cigarettes in that room, exhaling out the screened window, reading Hemingway's *The Sun Also Rises,* thinking long thoughts about the future, and now I thought about the volumes of history fading with her, about that young couple in rented rooms on Jefferson Street in Anoka, and then she was gone. A couple weeks after she died, I turned seventy and I sat down and wrote an essay about cheerfulness, which she possessed, and so did my dad, and all the more as they got old. It was a new topic for me.

Cheerfulness is a choice, like choosing what color socks to wear, the black or the red. Happiness is something that occurs, or it doesn't, and don't hold your breath. Joy is a theological idea, pretty rare among us mortals and what many people refer to as *joy* is what I would call *bragging.* Bliss is brief, about five seconds for the male, fifteen for the female. Contentment is something that belongs to older cultures: Americans are a hungry, restless people, ever in search of the rainbow, the true source, the big secret. Euphoria is a drug.

I found euphoria when I had a wisdom tooth extracted — three words, *wisdom tooth extracted,* that sound like pure agony to those of us who grew up in the Age of Pain when the dentist was a cranky bug-eyed guy with sour breath who climbed up on your lap with a pair of pliers and rassled you for the tooth, but now you go to an oral surgeon who asks if you'd like a sedative and you say, *Why not?* and they pop a needle in the crook of your elbow and usher you into a dreamy phase and five minutes later you wake up and a nurse says, *Are you okay?* Oh, my gosh, you have not been this okay for a long time. You are in a creamy dreamy state of happy buoyancy wafting high above this world of squalor and misery. There is no hangover, none. This is what my hippie pals were looking for back in the Sixties, sitting in candlelight smoking reefer that smelled like burning asphalt, that was no more effective than smoked trout. It's what I was aiming for when I used to make a martini. Alas, there was a second martini that made me stupid, which is not the same as ecstasy. In any case I was not brought up to expect ecstasy. Our God was a sober and practical God who appreciated cleanliness and good work habits more than outbursts of overenthusiasm. Suffering was an important part of the big picture — suffering drew us closer to Him — one more reason to feel good about living in Minnesota. So here is a drug to smooth out the rough places on the highway of life. I can hear my ancestors crying, *No no no no. That is a coward's way of thinking. An intelligent person craves reality over illusion. And the dosages are hard to control. A life of euphoria can easily slide into the life of hibernation.*

Cheerfulness, on the other hand, is a habit you assume in the morning and hang on to as best you can for the rest of the day. It fails at times and then it recovers. It's a job. The sour narcissism of others can dent your cheerfulness, or heartbreaking news on the radio — the college boy who left the party drunk and passed out in a snowbank and died, nineteen, a nice kid who did one dumb thing and *ffffft* he's gone — but the cheerful man retains his vim and verve, rises to the occasion, makes people laugh. You can cheerfully endure the deaths of loved ones, a gloomy marriage, a dopey job — you can drive away from a bad-luck town and make a fresh start on a new frontier — it's all possible if you maintain your good humor.

Cheerfulness is a great American virtue, found in Emerson, Whitman, Emily Dickinson, even in Mark Twain: Don't be held hostage by the past, the bonehead mistakes, the staggering losses, the betrayals of trust. Look ahead. Improve the day. Grow flowers. Walk in the woods. Be resilient. Clear away the wreckage and make spaghetti sauce. Power and influence are shadows, illusions. As Solomon said, the race is not to the big shots nor the battle to the tall nor success to a guy with connections.

I am a cheerful man though I don't look it. I walk down the street and see a gloomy man in a shop window and it's my reflection. People often ask if I am ill.

The long face I got from hearing serious gospel preaching in my youth, all about man's wretchedness and the Last Judgment when we shall stand before God and all shall be revealed, every slimy thing I ever did, and my aunt Eleanor and aunt Elsie will be there to hear it, not a smiley feel-good message. It also comes from listening to radio shows in which voracious beings from other galaxies came up the gravel path to the little cabin where Buddy and Sis lay whimpering under the bed. I got scared and turned off the radio and never heard the happy ending, so the horror lingers still, unresolved. And then there was a mean boy in the fourth grade who told me my teeth were rotten and green and said it with such authority that I believed him. I didn't smile so much after that.

It was a happy childhood as childhoods go. My parents were tender with each other and there was no yelling in our house, no alcohol, no looniness, some worries about money but nothing like poverty, always plenty to eat, so we were sheltered from the dark side of life. The Sanctified Brethren were strict: *Separate yourself from the things of this world — only what's done for the Lord has meaning and merit.* We Brethren had been entrusted with the true Word and we must avoid any association with false doctrine, including the very nice Lutherans. (Like most separatists, the Brethren rotted from the inside out rather than outside in, dissolved into schisms, prompted by feuds between alpha males equipped with the 18-point antlers of righteous dogma. But anyway.) Theater, fiction, dance music, comedy, spectator sports, partisan politics, wining and dining with unbelievers — none of it glorified the Lord and so had no worth. Worldly entertainment was shallow, empty, without real pleasure. Nonetheless we cheerfully tiptoed around these barricades — I read the books I wanted to read and had unsanctified friends and was not reproved; my favorite uncle kept a TV in the closet and rolled it out when the coast was clear to watch NFL football on Sundays, a sin for sure; and my mother slipped across the yard to the neighbors on Monday night about the time *I Love Lucy* was coming on and also Saturday night for *The Honeymooners.* These little inconsistencies were a revelation: we respected dogma but were not ruled by it and my parents did not share the harsh black-and-white dogmatism of some of our relatives. Perhaps this was due to the scandal of their love affair: she was pregnant by Dad when they eloped back in 1936 and their families were furious with them. My mother carried the shame all her days; their wedding anniversary went uncelebrated, and when, after fifty years, she consented to a dinner in their honor, it was on one condition: immediate family only, no aunts or uncles. The scandal was a blessing: it made them kinder people, and our lives were easier for it. I was not a good boy. My mother had to call my name many times over and over before I got up from the couch, put down the book, and went to pick beans. As a small boy in Minneapolis, I once fingered a dollar from the porcelain dish where Mother kept her cash and hoofed it down the alley to a little café on East Thirty-eighth Street and ordered a hamburger. Before it arrived, my father walked in and took me into custody. Mother told him to paddle me and gave him a yardstick for the job but he couldn't bring himself to do it. We stood in the garage, he and I, and he told me he was terribly disappointed in me, which was worse than being hit. I went through childhood without a hand being laid on me in anger nor even the threat of it. My mother simply said, quietly, "You are driving me to a nervous breakdown." And let it go at that. We grew up snug and well-loved (though parents back then did not actually *declare* their love), and all of us kids did well in school. We were expected to and we did.

My parents were cheerful folks. They came of age during the Great Depression, when everyone they knew was hard-pressed and scraping to get by, when frugality was the rule, and you did not complain about your misfortunes because, hey, everyone else was in the same boat. Dad graduated from Anoka High School in 1931 and went to work for his uncle Allie, a stonemason and carpenter, then at Uncle Lew's Pure Oil station in town. Nepotism in action. My mother sold peanut-butter cookies door-to-door in St. Paul. Money was not discussed in front of us kids. I worried that we were poor, I was ashamed of frugality, and they were not. They raised vegetables and canned the excess in glass jars. Mother darned socks and mended and patched. They bought day-old bread as a matter of course and watched the *Star* for department store sales and shopped around for the cheapest gasoline and slaughtered their own chickens. Dad cut our hair. Once in a while he would cry out against waste, against a thermostat turned up too high or a door left ajar, lights left on in an empty room (*How can anyone walk out of a room and not turn the light off?? You kids must think I am John D. Rockefeller! You must think we are Hollywood stars! Well, we are not*). But in general they kept their troubles to themselves — backaches, headaches, jittery stomachs, marital spats, ungrateful children, scarce money, disappointing vacations: Why dwell on it? Be of good courage. Into each life some rain must fall. And so what? Sew buttons on your underwear.

I was five when we drove north from our little apartment in south Minneapolis to the cornfield where Dad was building our house. There was only a basement at first, a low rectangular concrete bunker, where we lived while he framed up the walls above our heads. September 1947, just in time for school, which was a short walk away on the West River Road, the Mississippi a stone's throw east. The fear of drowning was on Mother's mind from the moment we arrived. Fear of sirens, people yelling, confusion, panic, and then a fireman carrying a small body (me) wrapped in a sheet. So she commanded me to never go near the river alone. But the riverbank was the Boys' Mecca, our sacred ground. Adults did not congregate there: our stretch of river was a series of rapids, nobody kept boats there, it belonged to boys, and to stay away would've marked me as a feeb, a gimp, a spaz, a shrinking violet, so from the age of five I practiced disobedience. I learned evasiveness at an early age. I snuck down to the river and lied about it afterward so as not to disturb Mother's peace of mind. Let her be cheerful and imagine that I was practicing the bowline hitch for a Boy Scout merit badge in knot-tying.

Across the road from Benson School, a little shack of a grocery store sold candy, soda pop, and sundries. Through an open door, you could see into the owner's living room, and once, shopping for Tootsie Rolls, I heard his wife harangue him about the bleakness of their life. She said, "When are we going to get out of this dump? I can't live like this. One of these days you're going to wake up and find me long gone, mister." Her bitterness was a tone I never heard at home. My parents savored their lives. We had a big social circle, all relatives — I had fifteen uncles and seventeen aunts — and we saw them regularly. Big Sunday dinners, especially in the warmer months, cousins sitting in the backyard, plates of chicken and potatoes and gravy on their laps, glasses of grape Kool-Aid. My mother's family and my father's were on opposite sides of a bitter schism that split the Brethren — the Boothites versus the Amesians — over a personal rivalry between preachers that was cloaked in doctrinal niceties, and yet we mingled and enjoyed each other and the grown-ups kept their bad feelings to themselves.

Mother was shy outside of her own family but Dad liked to make small talk with clerks, salespeople, waitresses: *How're you doing today? Good. Coffee? Thank you. I believe I will. Black. No sugar. I'm sweet enough as it is. Looks like we're finally getting spring. We can use the rain, that's for sure. Boy, that apple pie looks good. You wouldn't happen to have some cheese with that, would you? Apple pie without the cheese is like a hug without the squeeze.* As a little kid, I could see how the old waitress chippered up at his cheery greeting, and how small talk made life more graceful, all the little chirps and sighs and murmurs and birdsong that are the roots of language and that when you learn a new language, this is what they can't teach you: What do you say to the guy at the newsstand in Copenhagen, other than "I would like a copy of *Politiken*"? And American small talk is, almost inevitably, cheery.

I think about the glum poetry I wrote in teenage years ("My life is an owl with a broken wing / flying through pitch-black night / toward a spruce tree he remembers / that was chopped down last week") at a time when fortune was smiling at me and I was looking down at my shoes. The goodness of a neighbor lady, Helen, my confidante. The editor who let me write sports. Mother's Christmas that got more and more glimmery. My dad, who cut my hair in the basement, on a stool, bedsheet pinned around my neck, snip-snip-snipping, shaving, trimming, one hand holding my head still, his fingers in my hair: Why did I find this embarrassing — evidence of poverty — and not see it as the loving office that it was?

I got kicked out of ninth-grade shop class for talking after flunking the unit on sheet metal — just as I had flunked ball-peen hammer, flunked Skilsaw, even flunked plywood. Mr. Buehler was irked at me for talking and also for violating his oft-repeated rule *Never sit down on a workbench,* which I did and got acid on my pants that ate big holes in them over the course of the afternoon so you could see my underwear. He said, "As long as you talk all the time, we're going to move you to Miss Person's speech class," so I was kicked up to speech. In shop, I was a loser, and in speech, Miss LaVona Person beamed at me from the back of the room when I stood up to speak and so I kept my eyes on her, ignoring the smirking and eye-rolling of classmates in front of me, and I spoke with pleasure. To get kicked out of sheet metal and be punished by exposure to Miss Person's beneficent smile was staggering good luck.

I left Anoka High and trotted off to the University of Minnesota, ten miles south of my house as the crow flies, and landed in three excellent classes: Maggie Forbes's Latin Reading: Intermediate, Richard Cody's English Composition: The Essay, and Asher Christiansen's American Government. Three teachers who each seemed fully engaged and not merely passing the time. That fall I strolled into the student union and got a job as a newscaster on WMMR, just by asking for it. No experience, just bald-faced confidence.

I did a daily fifteen-minute noontime newscast, edited with great care from the AP teletype, yellow paper marked up with ballpoint, paragraphs snipped, rearranged, taped together, delivered in an authoritative Edward R. Murrow voice, and in the spring the WMMR engineer made a startling discovery. The transmitter had been out of commission all along — I had been reading the news to myself and the studio walls and nobody else. Somehow this did not discourage me. I was eighteen, invincible, working my way through college, and that spring the campus literary magazine published a poem of mine, and I was hired by a YMCA camp north of Duluth, a sweet summer of tennis doubles and singing "Kumbaya" around a bonfire and canoe trips down the St. Louis River. The key to cheerfulness, I discovered that summer, was forward movement. For me, the calm contemplative life equals melancholy. Keep knocking. If the door doesn't open, move on. Somewhere there's a place for you and you will know it when you get there.

And now, all these years later, here I am, in a house on a hill overlooking the Mississippi, feeling cheerful even though there is ice on the bathroom window and the floor is freezing cold thanks to Nanook of the North, who is offended by the waste of precious natural resources. I crank up the thermostat to a temperature that will support human life and head for the shower. Down the hill, the double row of lights on the High Bridge — a popular spot for suicides if you mean to get the job done. But this morning there are no flashing blue lights; today the desperate have decided to wait and see what develops. It's Sunday. On Friday I was at the Mayo Clinic, checking out the short list of boring ailments (glaucoma, enlarged prostate, atrial fibrillation, and risk of stroke), and came away with good grades. I feel good, thinking maybe I have a few years before the light dims or the heart blows up, time enough to do something noteworthy.

Madame appears in her thermalwear and says, "The thermostat was set at eighty-five. Do we have elderly people coming for breakfast?" I explain that I had found the thermostat set at 62 — "Is this Poland, 1938? Will we start busting up the furniture for fuel?" She says that a house need not replicate the uterus, I say that a room that is toasty warm helps to ward off depression that could cripple a writer for weeks so that he can no longer provide for his family. So we compromise at 65. I am pleased that she looked at my naked body with some interest and clicked her tongue, which is code for you-know-what.

I step into the shower, gingerly, recalling men my age who slipped on wet tile and jarred a vertebra and snapped a muscle into spasm and began a long journey through chiropractic and holistic herbs and acupuncture and then orthopedic surgery and the Vicodin Highway. I ease myself under the warm cascade, into the sacred sweat lodge of my Anglo people. We have a shower gizmo that lets you regulate water temperature precisely, not like our old shower knob, which, in one sixteenth-inch turn, went directly from arctic waterfall to fiery brimstone. With this one, you set the control to, say, 101.5 degrees, and water of that precise temperature shoots on you, the spray adjusted to Needle Sharp or Scattered Showers or Wistful Mist. It is such an improvement over the old days. (And so much of my cheerfulness is due to technological progress and the magical gifts created by methodical people — the marvelous iPhone, GPS, Wikipedia, Google, Facebook, heated car seats.) I love to stand and let the flow of hot water on the shoulders and backside relax the muscles and also the sphincter that has been trained since childhood — *Don't pee in the bathtub* — and it opens and there is the pure animal pleasure of urinating in a waterfall. Madame is disgusted by the thought of this. She says, "You don't do that, do you?" I say, "No, of course not." And of course I do. What sort of a man steps out of the shower to take a leak?

I dry off and put on manly deodorant and black underwear and a white shirt and a suit and come downstairs and look out at the snowy backyard and the Mississippi valley beyond.

I loved winter as a boy because parents didn't come looking for us when it was very cold; you put on a jacket and slipped out the door and there was a moment of danger when someone might say "Where do you think you are going?" and when nobody did, you were free and clear. No phone in your pocket, no pager, no chains around your ankles. You headed for the river, laced up your skates, opened your jacket and caught the wind and let it blow you south at high speed. Only kids were around; grown-ups stayed in. Nobody told you it wasn't a good idea to do what you were doing. With spring came more surveillance, but from December to April, a kid was free as could be.

Winter is a chastening time in the north. It scours the soul. Your natural meanness, the urge to bash your enemies and steal their meat, dissipates. I pour honey on my pancakes, the sweetness of life. I write a check to Episcopal Relief, not even knowing what relief Episcopalians need (laxatives? bicarbonate of soda?) and I e-mail a stranger that, yes, I will write a limerick for his pastor's birthday (*A Boston pastor named Manke / Avoided the hanky and panky / But during full moons / She sang ribald tunes / And cheered for the New York Yankees*). I pour a cup of coffee, open the paper. While

I slept, men and women compiled some of what is known about yesterday, and today there is nothing important. That's the beauty of the newspaper. Radio and TV are so ponderous, they make the weather forecast sound like the Magna Carta. The Internet can suck you in and you wind up watching YouTube videos of cats sitting on toilets. But with a newspaper one glance tells you: nothing new — negotiations continue, experts disagree, prospects remain uncertain, the rich get richer — so file yesterday away and let's deal with today. The coffee is dark and suggestive, my skin is clean, the obituary page is about other people.

In good spirits, I go to church to hear the Scripture, chant the psalm, join the prayers, and recite the creed whether today I believe most of it or only some. I arrive late, just in time for the prayer of contrition, and there's not room in the pew for a tall man to kneel comfortably. I have to twist into position, which reminds me of trying to make love in the backseat of an old VW. Her name was Sarah; she was tall too. She wore black leggings and fell over trying to remove them, bonked her head, had a laughing fit, which let the air out of the moment. "It's all right," she said, apropos of I didn't know what. We sat and kissed and made out and a car pulled up next to us, the radio playing a call-in show, people moaning about taxes, and that pretty much killed the moment. The homily this morning is on the Prodigal Son, his callow faithlessness, the joyful love of his father, the bitterness of the righteous brother. Like the P.S., I've wasted my inheritance in far countries, tried to buy friendship, been disloyal as most of us narcissists tend to be, but have not been reduced to eating pig food. Not yet, thank you. Nor have I bilked elderly widows of their life savings. Nor have I asked a lover to help me kill a spouse, as Clytemnestra did when her husband, Agamemnon, returned from the Trojan War, Perfectly nice people are capable of heinous deeds. That's what so much of great literature is about. Innocence is not what God expects of us. I used to think He expects us to find a way to self-mortification, perhaps martyrdom. Now I think He wants us to be grateful: in other words, cheerful. Lighten up.

After church, I come home and look through pictures. Mother spent years sorting through her boxes of pictures and somehow the collection got larger and larger, and now I've inherited my share of her archive. A picture of Grandpa Denham hoeing strawberry beds in a large garden, looking up at the camera and grinning. I remember him as a fretful old man, fussing, looking pained, but here he is grinning, and why? Because this is Annabel Wright's garden in Denmark township, near Hastings. Grandpa, a widower for three years, is courting this tall cheery woman and on weekends he takes a Soo Line train out to Hastings and she picks him up in her electric and he hoes her garden, grinning at the lady holding the camera, the lady he aims to marry. That is romance on Grandpa's face. He needs someone to hold hands with. He is anxious to climb into bed with the photographer. The look on his face says, *You will not regret this, I can assure you of that.* A man who fathers twelve children is a man of enthusiasm. The picture is a revelation.

There is a photograph of my grandpa James Keillor standing by his team of horses beside the house where his sisters Becky and Mary lived, north of Anoka, a handsome fellow, forty. He had been a carpenter in the shipyards of New Brunswick and came to Minnesota in 1880 to help out his sister Mary, whose husband, Mr. Hunt, was terribly sick, and soon after James arrived, the husband died of tuberculosis, leaving Mary with three small children and a 160-

acre homestead. So James stayed on. One spring day, two years from now, he will walk across the road to speak to the school-teacher, Dora Powell, twenty years younger than he, a lovely slip of a girl. She saw him cross the road, a handsome man with a full mustache, and he walked into her school-room and she saw that he had combed his hair and put on a cologne. He stood by her desk and talked about the building and what repairs it needs and she sensed that he had more on his mind. She said, "I'm glad you came over because I've been meaning to say goodbye. When the school term ends, I plan to go back to Iowa. And I want to bake you a pie to thank you for those times you came over here and lit a fire in the stove and warmed up the place before I got here, and I need to know what kind of pie you prefer, apple or blueberry." That was as far as she could go, and then it was his turn. He said he wished she would not leave, that he would miss her, that he has taken a shine to her, that he has wanted to kiss her for several months now. She did not blink. They gazed on each other, not smiling, and then he took two steps toward her and bent and kissed her. And kissed her again. A couple weeks later, they drove to St. Francis to be married by a judge and when they arrived home, James was so enthused, he forgot to unhitch the horses and they stood all night in the farmyard, the reins hanging down to the ground. He took Dora in his arms and carried her upstairs, a ritual he continued until he got old and feeble. He had a strong tenor voice and knew many songs by heart and he always had a book with him. People sometimes saw him sitting on a mower, cutting hay, reins in one hand and book in the other, and later, driving his Model T down the road, steering with his knees, reading. We have letters he wrote to Dora while traveling, addressed "Dear girl" and signed "Jimmy K" and letters to his children signed "Daddy J." He adored his children and paid close attention to them. He died in 1933, before I was born. My father believed that he would meet his parents in heaven and recognize them, but Scripture doesn't really promise that. I met my grandfather in my imagination, as a legendary figure, from stories told me by my aunts and my great-uncle Lew and Dad's cousin Dorothy. The poems he knew by heart. The love of Milton and Shakespeare by one whose life was marked by unrelenting hard labor, those big calloused fingers turning the tissue pages. His favorite hymns, such as "O Thou in Whose Presence My Soul Takes Delight."

Grandpa waking his children in the middle of the night to bundle up and follow him out through the woods to see a silver wolf on a snowbank in the moonlight, howling. The house burning down from a chimney fire and Grandpa raking the ashes, mourning the loss of photographs and books. The grief at his wayward daughter Ruth. His service on the town board. His purchase of a Model T when it first came out and driving it home from Anoka and driving it into the ditch while hollering, "Whoa! Whoa!" The story of his complaining that his mattress was too firm, that he "couldn't get a good purchase with his knees," which my aunts laughed and laughed about, which I didn't understand until much later. And the story of his funeral, at which some people were offended because the preacher took "For all have sinned and come short of the glory of God" as his text and that verse did not, in their opinion, apply to Jamie Keillor. And there he is in the picture, handsome, beside his horses, having served his sister and raised her children, now waiting for his own life to begin.

My father seemed to close the door on the past and that disappointed me deeply. If you asked him about his boyhood on the farm, he said, "That was a long time ago,"

and claimed not to remember. But my aunts Elizabeth and Eleanor and Ruth adored their father and in my mind he took on mythic proportion, the Good Brother who sacrificed for family, the man absorbed in Longfellow as the mower went clacketing along, the great brutes leaning into the harness, the reins in the man's lap. And the man who carried the schoolteacher in his arms upstairs to the soft mattress.

There were giants in my ancestry: Elder John Crandall of Rhode Island, who in early colonial days took a true Christian view of Indians and strove to learn the local languages; Prudence Crandall of Canterbury, Connecticut, who admitted young colored women to her school and was driven out of town for it; David Powell, a farmer who lived through most of the nineteenth century and spent it migrating westward, from Pennsylvania to Ohio, then Illinois, then Iowa, Missouri, a big jump out to Colorado where he served in the territorial legislature, and then the Oklahoma land rush, and then died, having left a string of Powell progeny in his wake. But James Keillor was the mighty oak whose branches overspread us and I sat in his shade. I spent a couple boyhood summers in his house, where Grandma and Uncle Jim lived, pumped his pump organ, read from his Bible, ate corn flakes at his breakfast table and johnnycake baked on his old woodstove, washed my face in cold water from his hand pump in the lean-to behind the house, played in his haymow, drew cream from the milk can sitting in the cold cistern in the milk house, rode on Grandpa's old hayrack and on the backs of Uncle Jim's big draft horses, who were descendants of Grandpa's horses, a little boy hanging on to the harness as the mane bounced and enormous shoulders swayed under me and chains jingled as we came galumping up the dirt road and into the pasture. Grandma was a dear and a good heart but she could also be peevish. The saintly dead grandfather was the colossus who stood invisibly over us, the seed from whom we sprang, and through the tumult of adolescence and beyond and all my troubles, Lord, I felt his light shine on me.

When I was a boy, attending parades around town, I often saw, riding in the back-seat of a convertible, slumped down, wearing a blue campaign hat, Albert Woolson of Duluth, the last living veteran of the Civil War, who rode in many parades until he died, age 109, in 1956. He was a few years older than Grandpa and had been a drummer boy in the 1st Minnesota Regiment and now he was a gaunt relic, our last live connection to Lincoln, horse-drawn caissons, ladies in crinoline gowns and tender songs about sad farewells in the moonlight, and he made me wish Grandpa were alive.

When a man dwells on the past as I did, and still do, you lead a double life. You're in L.A. working on a screenplay and sitting through production meetings attended by men in short-sleeved white shirts discussing the Narrative Arc and the Hero's Quest and what is the Gift that he brings back from his Journey, and none of it is real, what is real is the memory of driving last night in a convertible along Sunset Boulevard, traffic juking and bopping around you, through a canyon of glittering lights and billboards, and all you can think of is your dad, who is dead, and how much he loved driving around and the years he spent in the swaying mail car on the *Empire Builder* hurtling through the night, a .38 snub-nosed revolver on his belt, and the movie you're trying to write is a thin tissue of falsehoods — there is no memory in it whatsoever — and when the studio fires the executive producer and cancels the production, you are secretly relieved. The work did not stand up to the memory of the man in the mail car or the man on the mower reading Longfellow to the clip-clop of horse hooves. It was only blind ambition, no more.

In 1987, I quit *A Prairie Home Companion* and went off to Copenhagen thinking I had spent long enough being silly in public and it was time to become a novelist. I sat in a back bedroom at No. 3 Trondhjemsgade, at the keyboard of a word processor the size of a suitcase, working at a novel about a man in his late forties trying to find himself in a foreign city. It was a dramatic time in Europe and from my window I could see the front gate of the Soviet embassy as the Soviet Union was falling apart and hear a crowd of Danish demonstrators across the street. I walked around the corner and here, behind police barriers, were several hundred old Danish Communists protesting the liberal reforms of Gorbachev, protesting the imposition of democracy and freedom of speech. They had grown up on Marxist-Leninist dogma and enjoyed being radicals in a comfortable bourgeois country and they were angry that so many Russians wanted to be more like Denmark. The lunacy of this made me think of the Brethren, enjoying the benefits of a liberal society while maintaining a righteous contempt for it, which was also pleasurable. And it made me think of myself, who had abandoned what was good in my life to pursue an illusion. Writing a novel is like setting out to hike across Texas and somewhere around Dallas you discover that you don't really *like* Texas and you still have five hundred miles of Texas to go. Doing a weekly radio show is like walking into town to have lunch with your friends. So I thought about getting back to radio.

We were young people devoted to old-time music; that's where *A Prairie Home Companion* comes from, people who'd sit and play old 78s over and over, trying to decipher what the Possum Creek Boys were singing there — was it "hittin Pascagoula again" or was it "git yer mule a pint o' gin"? Our high school classmates were rising through the ranks of corporate life and living in the Seventies and we went around in home-steader clothes and sat on broken-down sofas on ramshackle porches singing "Angel Band" and "I'll Fly Away" and "Amazing grace, how sweet the sound that saved a wretch like me," singing grandpa songs, singing old blues as if all the good times were past and gone and the water tasted like turpentine and we were heading for California where they sleep out every night. Bill Hinkley was a regular from the beginning and years later when he lay dying at the V.A. hospital, miserable, legs not work-ing, fingers clumsy on the mandolin, he asked if I knew "Abide with Me," and we sang it together, about the Lord's unchang-ing love as life ebbs away and earth's joys grow dim, Help of the helpless, O abide with me. There was nothing you could do for him except be there.

How does one maintain a cheerful heart in the face of failure and loss, marching toward the cliff that lies ahead in the fog? I feel boyish most days and sort of jazzy and imagine I could still hit a hard cross-court backhand and ride a bike no-handed but then I cross a street and see oncoming traffic and I break into a gallop and there is no gallop, I run like a frightened duck. I no longer go down stairs two at a time; I reach for the railing. In junior high, my friends and I did imitations of elderly dither, the quavery voice, the trembling hand, the mental lapses on the verge of lunacy, and now we old satirists are becoming our victims.

When I turned seventy aboard the *Queen Mary 2* in the middle of the Atlantic with three women — fifty-five, twenty-five, fourteen — we didn't talk about aging, we lay out on deck, the three of them in sunshine, me in shadow, and breathed salt air and then got dressed up and went to the dining room for a hearty meal, oysters and steak and chocolate cake. But I thought about my aunts and uncles who toppled over in their seventies. The young women in their summer dresses, the young man in the Pure Oil uniform standing by the gas pumps in Anoka, the burly young farmer on the hayrack holding the horses' reins, the aunt who could swing a bat and run the bases, the aunts who baked bread, the uncle with the billiards table in the basement — they all lie under their self-effacing tombstones, the memory of them fading, as my words will fade, as even the great ones fade. I spent two nights at Sun Valley Lodge, room 206, where Hemingway liked to stay with his mistresses before they became his third and fourth wives and where, I'm sure, they washed each other's bodies tenderly and made love and he thought, *At last! Someone who really gets me.* The lodge is a stone's throw from the cemetery where his body lies. Several empty wine bottles lay on his tombstone, from people drinking to his health, I suppose. I think of him as an old old man with a gray beard — I was nineteen when he put the shotgun to his forehead and blew his head off — but he was not quite sixty-two.

A man starts to feel vulnerable when he turns seventy. We are programmed to degenerate. Nature only wanted us to find a willing female, impregnate her, raise the offspring until they could fend for themselves, and then get out of the way. Nature is not interested in our twilight years. Erectile dysfunction is common among older males: nature's way of saying, *Enough out of you. Time is up. Go sit in the corner.* So why go on? What, besides inertia and vanity, is the point? Your curiosity wanes, your ideas are old and stiff, you've said all you have to say

— haven't you? Most writers have shot their wad long before this age; maybe I have, too. I go to a convention of radio programmers and it's all foreign to me. I am a relic of the analog in a world of ones and zeros. I grew up in the stereo hi-fi era when people were thrilled by audio texture and clarity and now our ears are trained to accept tinniness, flatness, audio cardboard. The programmers are very welcoming, as you would be to a dotty old uncle, but I don't understand a word they say, not even the prepositions. They don't do radio "shows" anymore, they create content which is distributed on various platforms, and as each speaker murmurs on and the laser pointer waves at the bullet points on the PowerPoint I come to the point of mindless stupor and visualize large rooms with many small beige cubicles in which silent drones sit at desktops and spin audio tissue, each unit three minutes in length, the duration determined by neuropsychologists to be sufficient to impersonate intelligence with the least risk of boring the indifferent listener, and these tissues are randomly assembled into a patchwork format that is broadcast, podcast, upcast, downcast, recast as Web copy, which somehow satisfies the demographic much as white noise might, a choir of low-impact spoken content that creates the illusion of social engagement for the lonely motorist or the runner on the tread-mill, and the beauty of the whole enterprise is that *no individual in the entire organization feels keen personal responsibility for the out-come,* no more than the average bumblebee. Everyone, from those in the smallest cubicle on up to the largest enchilada, has the luxury of a faint cool disdain for the corpo-ration and for their own work. It's a no-fault deal. In my radio world there is real suffering. I've done *A Prairie Home Compan-ion* for forty years and never used my own name — the writing credit goes to Sarah Bellum — but I suffer for my screw-ups and the monologue that wanders off into the ditch and collapses, the laborious song, the wimpy sketch, the guest out in left field: I go home and hang my head and relive the low points over and over and wish I could anesthetize myself with a good stiff drink. I do know how to suffer. I learned some from the Brethren and some from other writers. I do a good job of it.

Suffering is the ground from which cheer-fulness springs.

I wrote that sentence to see how it looks and then I didn't delete it, so there it is.

■ ■ ■ ■

I watched my mother in her old age, for
clues about my own future, and watched as
her life got smaller and smaller. She stopped
traveling; it was no longer fun. She came
with me to Florida for a couple weeks and
we sat in a large soulless house day after
day in the rain looking out at the gray Gulf
and she was delighted to get back to snowy
Minnesota and the house where she had
raised her children. She picked up her
walker and did her daily dozen circuits of
living room, sun porch, dining room, hallway, and she perused the paper, read my
column when I was writing one, read her
Bible, prayed, welcomed visitors; the care-
givers came in shifts and made her lunch
and she sat at a table with empty chairs
around it and enjoyed her macaroni and
cheese, followed by butter brickle ice cream
and weak coffee. She missed John but did
not talk about it unless asked. (*You must
miss your husband, don't you?* Yes, of
course.) On warm sunny days she motored
out on the deck and sat under a broad-
brimmed hat and looked at the former
garden where bushels of tomatoes once
grew and were brought to the kitchen,

peeled, boiled, in an orgy of canning, but no more. It had become lawn. Tiny evergreens Dad had planted in pioneer days had become towering pines. In the yard stood the old square pipe frames between which clotheslines once stretched, the verticals anchored in concrete, and nobody felt it necessary to root them out, artifacts of the old life, monuments to years of labor at the wringer washing machine and hanging wet sheets and jeans on the lines. A couple dogs are buried under the apple tree. I can see where the incinerator was where I blew up aerosol cans and the path from the raspberries down to the ravine where I trotted off when I needed to disappear for a while. The old ball field is just north of here, the one that a gang of us boys created in a vacant field with a deep weedy ditch just behind second base where grounders sometimes turned into home runs.

In her late years it seemed to me that Mother found that spiritual awareness that Buddhism holds up as enlightenment, in which one does not covet more than one's small lot, one is free of animosity, and one lives in the immediate present, day by day, without dread of what might befall. You call it *satipatthana,* I call it cheerfulness. When I visited her, she never said, "Why so long since I've seen you?" She said, "You work too hard." I brought her a block of her favorite English cheese, Cheshire or Gloucester, and she savored a bite and had a sip of port. She didn't talk about her ailments unless asked. She did not reminisce unless you led her there. She wore her faith lightly and did not witness to you unless prompted. She wanted to hear your news, the comings and goings of grandchildren: family was preeminent and presidents and potentates and winners of Academy Awards were merely names. She had nothing bad to say about anybody. She spoke on the phone regularly to her sister Joan, who was an accomplished complainer, and Mother heard her out, no comment. In her last years, Mother drifted now and then into what you might call dementia, after her cohorts died and she became the last rose of summer. She alone was left to remember the yellow trolley clanging along East Thirty-eighth Street and the iceman in his horse-drawn wagon and be able to identify the old Brethren gents in dark suits and Brethren women in shapeless dresses standing under the trees in the panoramic photo of the 1927 Minneapolis Bible Conference. She and Dorothy Bacon had been high school classmates and when they got together, Mother was all delight, life came alive, but then Dorothy faded away, and Mother started talking to her dead sisters Elsie and Ina and brother George, as if they were present. She carried on extensive conversations, sometimes laughing at some remark we couldn't hear. Call it dementia but it struck me as strategic, Mother living in her imagination, creating a novel before our eyes, a very perfect invisible novel in which she was young, in the arms of family, surrounded by lively talk and maybe looking forward to riding the interurban trolley up to Anoka and catching a glimpse of Johnny. A very old lady with snow-white hair, almost blind, her skin papery, reaching out to put her old hand on the table toward the late Elsie, who is telling her something very amusing, and Mother laughs. It is not so different from what I do on the radio. All those Lake Wobegon people are dead now and I keep them alive: the children age but the grown-ups stay the same. She is talking cheerfully to Elsie and someone else and I can tell from the cadence that she is telling a story and that Elsie is laughing. Nothing she says makes literal sense at all, it is like birdsong and it's a story with wonderful things in it. She is enjoying telling it. I sit and watch, an alien but not for long. My time will come in due course and when it does, however it does, whether in a house in St. Paul or an apartment in New York or a room at the Good Shepherd, I am prepared to welcome it with a good heart. To do my part, pull my weight, don't be a crybaby, hold my horses, and get the job done, just as I was told long long ago to do.

ACKNOWLEDGMENTS

"Growing Up with the Flambeaus" and "The Death of Byron" appeared in *Wobegon Boy* by Garrison Keillor (Viking, 1997).

"My Sister Kate" appeared in *Lake Wobegon Summer 1956* by Garrison Keillor (Viking, 2001).

"Pontoon Boat" appeared in *Pontoon: A Novel of Lake Wobegon* by Garrison Keillor (Viking, 2007).

"Chickens" (as "Chicken") and "Truckstop" appeared in *Leaving Home* by Garrison Keillor (Viking, 1987). ("Chicken" was first published in *The Atlantic*).

"Henry" (as "Drop Dead, Lewis Carroll: History's Rejection Slips") appeared in *The New York Times*.

"Lonesome Shorty," "Casey at the Bat" (as

"Casey at the Bat (Road Game)"), "Marooned," "Earl Grey," "Don Giovanni," "Zeus the Lutheran," and "Al Denny" appeared in *The Book of Guys* by Garrison Keillor (Viking, 1993). ("Lonesome Shorty," "Zeus the Lutheran," and "Al Denny" were first published in *The New Yorker*.)

"The Babe," "Your Book Saved My Life, Mister," "My Life in Prison," and "Anglicans" (as "Episcopal") appeared in *We Are Still Married* by Garrison Keillor (Viking, 1989). ("The Babe" was first published in *Sports Illustrated;* "My Life in Prison" in *The Atlantic*.)

"Mother's Day" (as "Drama for Mama") and "Health" (as "Vetting the Health Care Issue") appeared in "The Old Scout" column, A Prairie Home Companion website.

"Taking a Meeting with Mr. Roast Beef" appeared in *Guy Noir and the Straight Skinny* by Garrison Keillor (Penguin, 2012).

"Jimmy Seeks His Fortune in Fairbanks" appeared in *Me: The Jimmy (Big Boy) Valente Story* by Garrison Keillor (Viking, 1999).

"At *The New Yorker:* My Own Memoir" appeared in *Love Me* by Garrison Keillor (Viking, 2003).

"Rules of Orchestra" (as "A Foot Soldier in God's Floating Orchestra") appeared in *BBC Magazine.*

"Newspapers" (as "Elements of Style in the 21st Century") appeared in *The Baltimore Sun.*

"George" (as "Remembering Plimpton") appeared on the A Prairie Home Companion website.

"Fame" (as "The Sorrows of Fame") appeared on *Salon.com.*

"Power" (as "If I Ruled the World") appeared in *Prospect Magazine.*

"Chet" appeared in *Tales from Country Music* by Gerry Wood (Sports Publishing, 2003).

"College Days" appeared in *Homegrown Democrat* by Garrison Keillor (Viking, 2004).

"My Stroke (I'm Over It)" (as "My Above-Average Stroke") appeared in *Men's Health.*

Illustration Credits